The French Revolution
1770–1814

𝔅

A History of France will, in five volumes, provide an account of 1,000 years of French history. The authors are among the most distinguished French historians, and the reception given to the first three volumes when they appeared in France in 1987 and 1988 suggests that this will be the standard history of France for many years to come.

Already published

France in the Middle Ages 987–1460
Georges Duby

The Royal French State 1460–1610
Emmanuel Le Roy Ladurie

Revolutionary France 1770–1880
The French Revolution 1770–1814
François Furet

The French Republic 1879–1992
Maurice Agulhon

Forthcoming

The Ancien Régime 1610–1774
Emmanuel Le Roy Ladurie

The French Revolution
1770–1814

FRANÇOIS FURET

Translated by
Antonia Nevill

Copyright © Hachette, 1988
English translation copyright © Blackwell Publishers Ltd, 1992, 1996

The right of François Furet to be identified as author of this work has been
asserted in accordance with the Copyright, Designs and Patents Act 1988.

First published 1988
English translation first published 1992
This edition first published 1996

Blackwell Publishers Ltd
108 Cowley Road, Oxford OX4 1JF, UK

Blackwell Publishers Inc.
238 Main Street, Cambridge, Massachusetts 02142, USA

All rights reserved. Except for the quotation of short passages for the purposes
of criticism and review, no part of this publication may be reproduced, stored
in a retrieval system, or transmitted, in any form or by any means, electronic,
mechanical, photocopying, recording or otherwise, without the prior permission
of the publisher.

Except in the United States of America, this book is sold subject to the condition
that it shall not, by way of trade or otherwise, be lent, re-sold, hired out, or
otherwise circulated without the publisher's prior consent in any form of binding
or cover other than that in which it is published and without a similar condition
including this condition being imposed on the subsequent purchaser.

British Library Cataloguing in Publication Data
A CIP catalogue record for this book is available from the British Library

Library of Congress Cataloging in Publication Data
Furet, François, 1927–
[Révolution. English. Selections]
The French Revolution, 1770–1814/François Furet :
translated by Antonia Nevill.
p. cm. — (History of France)
This edition comprised part 1 of Revolutionary France, 1770–1880.
Includes bibliographical references and index.
ISBN 0–631–20299–4
1. France—History—Revolution, 1789–1799.
2. Napoleon I, Emperor of the French, 1769–1821—Influence
3. France—History—Consulate and First Empire, 1799—1815.
I. Title. II. Series.
DC148.F87213   1996   96–24632
944.04—dc20   CIP

Typeset in 10.5 on 12pt Plantin by Best-set Typesetter Ltd, Hong Kong
Printed and bound in Great Britain by T. J. Press Ltd, Padstow, Cornwall

This book is printed on acid-free paper

Contents

List of Illustrations

The translator gratefully acknowledges the expert guidance on historical terminology and the invaluable textual clarifications given by Professor Norman Hampson.

The French Revolution is such an extraordinary event that it must serve as the starting-point for any systematic consideration of the affairs of our own times. Everything of importance which takes place in France is a direct consequence of this fundamental event, which has profoundly altered the conditions of life in our country.

Ernest Renan, 'Constitutional Monarchy in France', *Revue des Deux Mondes*, 1 November 1869.

I

The *Ancien Régime*

The French revolutionaries gave a name to what they had abolished. They christened it the *ancien régime*. In doing so they were defining not so much what they had suppressed, but more what they wanted to create – a complete break with the past, which was to be cast into the shadows of barbarism. Of the past itself, its nature and its history, the revolutionaries said scarcely more than the imprecatory phrase they used to decribe it, a phrase which was coined very early, at the end of the summer of 1789: the Abbé Sieyès, in his noted January pamphlet of the same year, had already made a sweeping condemnation of that 'night', as opposed to the day which was just dawning.

The notion of a past entirely corrupted by usurpation and irrationality was surely one of the paths by which his pamphlet, *Qu'est-ce que le Tiers Etat?* (What is the Third Estate?) penetrated public opinion so rapidly and so deeply. So the historian studying the history of France in the second half of the eighteenth century, some decades before the Revolution, can find a way in by means of this question about the term *ancien régime*: what did the men of 1789 understand by it? What sort of past did they have in mind, to damn it so utterly? That regime which they believed they were extirpating – how long had it lasted and who had begun it? The enigmatic strangeness of the French *tabula rasa*, which so disconcerted and angered the British whig parliamentarian, Edmund Burke, in 1790, can still serve as an introduction to the later years of eighteenth-century France.

As of old, the king of France was an absolute monarch. The adjective means that he enjoyed the *summa potestas* defined by Jean Bodin: he was not subject to the laws, since he was their originator. Supreme power, which may be exercised by the people (democracy), or by the few (aristocracy), in France had found its supreme upholder in the monarchy since the very dawn of the nation. The king was the fountainhead of all public authority, all magistracy, all legislation. His *dignitas* that is to say, both his office and his function, was immortal, received on the death of his predecessor and transmitted to his successor, transcending the mortal nature of his private person. For that lifelong possession of the highest authority in the land he was accountable to God alone, the true source of all human law. Thus behind the power of kings, however absolute, lay the essential constraint of an even greater power – infinitely great – beside which even monarchs were as nothing. This of itself entailed the obligation to behave as a Christian sovereign.

The respect for divine law, however, was not the only law to which the king of France had to submit, for all that he was absolute monarch and not bound by any human law. Over the centuries something had developed which it is perhaps too much to call a constitution, or even a body of doctrine, yet which appears in retrospect as a set of custom-based principles, untouchable and inalienable: primogeniture, the Catholic faith of the sovereign, respect for the liberty and property of his subjects, the integrity of the royal domain. Above the law, yet subject to law, the king of France was no tyrant: the French monarchy, a state based on law, must not be confused with despotism, which is the unfettered power of a master. Nevertheless, despotism was monarchy's temptation, as Montesquieu explained; to degenerate, it needed only to ignore the established body of laws.

Did this traditional concept change in the eighteenth century, at the zenith of state power? Not basically. Under Louis XIV it had noticeably shifted towards deification of the king himself. Starting from the idea of the divine origin of his power, the *Grand Roi* had instigated, or allowed to be formed about his person, a cult which was at the heart of court civilization at Versailles. Many other elements entered into it, besides the old monarchic doctrine, and the attribution of divinity to the king soon became a factor in the enfeeblement of royalty, as would be seen in his successors; unlike their illustrious ancestor, neither Louis XV nor Louis XVI was able to bear the weight of a burden which had become inseparable from their private persons.

From being the means of ceremonial acclamation, the court under their reigns became a battlefield for malicious cliques, spurred on by the atmosphere of the times. However, the idea of a king as the sole repository of sovereignty, in keeping with ancient tradition, and the concept of a monarchy both absolute and enshrined in custom, in the view of the king and his lawyers had undeniably survived absolutist exaggeration.

Evidence of this lies in Louis XV's famous text, declaimed in 1766 before the parlement of Paris, condemning the aspirations of the kingdom's judicial high courts to monitor or even have a share in royal authority:

To attempt to establish such pernicious innovations as principles is to affront the magistrature, to betray its interests and to ignore the true, fundamental laws of the state, as if it were permissible to disregard the fact that in my person alone lies that sovereign power whose very nature is the spirit of counsel, justice and reason. From me alone the courts receive their existence and authority. The fullness of this

Hyacinthe Rigaud Louis XV in coronation robes, *Musée Versailles, Paris.*
(Photo: Lauros-Giraudon)

authority, which they exercise in my name only, remains permanently vested in me, and its use can never be turned against me. Legislative power is mine alone, without subordination or division. It is by my sole authority that the officers of my courts effect, not the creation of the law, but its registration, promulgation and execution, and that they have the right of remonstrance, as is the duty of good and faithful counsellors. Public order in its entirety emanates from me. I am its supreme guardian. My people are one with me, and the rights and interests of the nation – which some dare to make into a body separate from the monarch – are of necessity united with my own and rest entirely in my hands.

This speech was composed by the king's counsellors to be read out solemnly at that famous session known as the 'Flagellation', but who among Louis XV's predecessors would not have claimed it for his own?

However, the nature of royalty changed more rapidly than its image. Dominated by wars, always short of money, the monarchy, while taking care to keep a tight hold on the reins, continued to spread an administrative network throughout the country in order to mobilize men and wealth more effectively. Gradually it placed alongside the pyramid of feudal vassalages from which it had derived its first principle the authority of a sovereign set at the heart of a more or less centralized administration capped by a council of ministers. The core of this system, progressively built up from the end of the fifteenth century, was constituted by levying direct taxation, organized by the Controller-General of Finance with the help of administrators appointed for the task, each within his own *généralité* – the *intendants*. Originally vested with a sort of judicial high office, the king had become the head of a government; lord of lords, he was also chief of a burgeoning bureaucracy.

The two roles, far from being incompatible, were superimposed; but the second was characteristic of absolutism and gained its classic image in the seventeenth century: Colbert, Louis XIV's Controller-General, is its most illustrious symbol. The leading specialist on this subject, Michel Antoine,[1] places the transition from the judicial state to the financial state in 1661, at the beginning of the personal reign of Louis XIV. At the precise moment when the king formed the focal point of his vast personal theatre, known as the court, he simultaneously became the most elevated person in the huge, abstract machinery of administration. He still reigned over his kingdom as possessor of the immortal *dignitas* which had surrounded his ancestors, but now as head of the state as well. The second part of his office overlapped the first the more easily because absolutism, in making a cult of royalty, tended to weaken its traditional image, while it firmly established the institution in the fulfilment of its modern functions.

However, the chief innovation of this development lay in its effects on society. On the one hand, it certainly tended towards the levelling off of an aristocratic world inherited from feudal times. For the top civil servants of the monarchy, symbolized by Colbert, had been constantly irritated by the

---

[1] M. Antoine, *Le Conseil du roi sous le règne de Louis XIV*.

obstacles raised against royal administration by privileges on all sides; the reasoning behind their action aimed at uniting the nation into so many individuals all bound by the same laws, the same regulations and the same taxes.

It was not enough that the monarchy had gradually deprived the aristocracy of its political rights, nibbled away at its judicial powers, rendered useless that protective function which had characterized the feudal period; it was not enough that it had reduced the greatest families in the kingdom to begging for a glance from the king at Versailles: it had to exercise over all the bodies and orders in the realm, starting with the nobility, a standardizing process which in this case was inseparable from the formation of the nation. On the other hand, at the very time when it was seeking uniformity, the administrative monarchy multiplied the obstacles to it; here lay what is without doubt its chief contradiction.

In fact, the kings of France did not build and extend their power over a passive society; on the contrary, they had to negotiate each increase in it – for example, the famous 'extraordinary' taxes, so called because they were new – with a social world organized on the aristocratic principle, in orders and bodies arranged in hierarchies. Holding entirely new offices, assuming an unprecedented role, the king also remained the highest lord on the feudal pyramid, in accordance with tradition.

His need for money was immense. To obtain the means of carrying on the interminable war for supremacy waged against the Habsburgs, the Bourbons – and before them the Valois – had raised money from all possible sources. They had gradually set up a centralized administration to levy the *taille* (a direct tax on commoners), and soon afterwards a poll tax, to try to increase the kingdom's wealth; they had leased out to the Farmers General a host of indirect taxes. But taxation was not enough to meet requirement. The monarchy also made money from the privileges and 'liberties' (the two words have the same sense) of various social bodies.

Privilege consisted of the particular rights of certain bodies in relation to society as a whole; tax exemption for the bourgeois of a town, rules of co-optation of a guild, exemptions from common law conferred by tenure of an office, advantages attached to noble rank – the sources were numerous. If some were lost in the mists of antiquity, the majority were not so old; the monarchic state had generally renegotiated the form of ancient privileges, or invented and constantly remodelled the terms of recent 'liberties'.

The mechanism was simple. Driven by the pressing need for money, the monarchy raised loans through one or more of the bodies in the realm: the order of clergy, the city government of Paris or the Company of the King's Secretaries. If the body in question did not have all the necessary money available, it had to raise it by pledging its assets, which consisted chiefly of the market value of the exclusive advantages which it enjoyed, defined by the office held by each of its members. In return, the king again guaranteed those privileges, if need be extending them, even if, ten or twenty years later, the principle was once more threatened so that the king could procure a fresh supply of money through a renegotiation of the advantages granted. The whole of the society of orders (which could also be termed aristocratic society) thus played the role of a vast bank for the government, in the absence of a state bank (only the English had had one since the beginning of the eighteenth century); but because of this it underwent a profound transformation.

The monarchy had thus sold off a portion of public power, included in a good number of those offices – for example, those involving the exercise of justice. The institution itself was old, but hereditary ownership of public offices dated only from the seventeenth century, and from then on the sales of those posts had proliferated, in step with the king's need for money, starting from the Thirty Years War. The most elevated, and therefore the most expensive, of them gave access to the nobility within one or two generations, on terms which varied according to the price.

Thus, alongside the *intendant*, an appointed and dismissible functionary, the kings had built up a body of state servants who owned their own offices. This was a double-edged sword, for though the massive sale of offices allowed the acquisition of the beneficiaries' cash – chiefly that of wealthy commoners – and simultaneously bound to the destiny of the state a new and powerful group of office-holders, dominated by the parlements, it also presented a twofold disadvantage.

First, all these officials enjoyed the independence conferred by ownership, even if from time to time they had to renegotiate the price with the king; since they were not dismissible, they could, should the day come, resist the king – mainly with the help of the right of remonstrance used by the parlements when required to register a royal edict which did not meet with their approval. Second, and more important, on another plane, ennoblement for money introduced into aristocratic society a principle which was as foreign to it as the admission into the nobility, at the will of the king, of senior civil servants of the administrative state: if nobility depended on the hazards of fortune or the will of the King, what was it and what would become of it?

There is no better record of that question bedevilling the inner core of the second order of the kingdom than the memoirs of the Duc de Saint-Simon. French nobility had ceased to be a sort of English-style gentry, with access from below for newcomers by custom, provided they had acquired a seigniory. On the one hand, its members had to cross a legal frontier, held by the administrative monarchy, if they were to be accepted. On the other, they were thereafter subject to the rule of *dérogeance* (losing rank and title), which excluded them from the majority of professions. In short, the nobility was a body defined by the state, which kept a register of its members, and by a set of privileges, both honorific and actual – of which the former were no less coveted, since they conferred the right of entry to the theatre of social distinctions.

The administrative monarchy was therefore an unstable compromise between the construction of a modern state and an aristocratic society remodelled by that state. On the one hand, it continued slyly to subvert the traditional social fabric by levelling its ranks under general submission to a sole authority, and breaking up the hierarchies of birth and tradition, which were by then reduced to the mere enjoyment of exemptions or honours. On the other hand, it separated the orders of society into castes by converting them into cash, weighing each privilege at its highest price, and creating out of an *esprit de corps* a passion for separateness.

At the summit of the edifice, the monarchy alone decreed who was noble and who was not: every candidate had to forget his origins, abandon all commercial or industrial activity, in order to be simply a privileged person – designated as such on the separate registers of fiscal administration – before he could hope one day to gain for his family the attention of the king's genealogists.

This evolution was probably essential in the formation of what could be termed 'national spirit': even after the Revolution and equality, Bonaparte would use as one of the mainsprings of his dominance what he, anticipating Stendhal, would call the 'vanity' of the French. The example had come from the *ancien régime* nobility, who were defined by what separated them from the body of society, taking as their very essence what 1789 would turn into the principle of their exclusion. To understand how the French monarchy had uprooted the nation's nobility before the Revolution drove them out, one should read the admirable ninth chapter of Book II of de Tocqueville's *L'Ancien Régime*, which is perhaps the most profound chapter in that profound book: it contains virtually everything.

The eighteenth century had aggravated the tensions of this mixed system of absolute monarchy and aristocratic society. The death of Louis XIV in 1715, after an interminable reign, had restored independence to society. The Regent had encouraged the movement. None of the Great King's successors was in a position to control even the court, let alone Paris. Everything conspired to enfeeble them: intellectual activity, the growth of wealth, the emergence of public opinion. However, the old French monarchy, simultaneously very ancient and very new, that of the Valois and that of the Bourbons, remained for a long time the centre of a matchless civilization.

It was no longer what it had been in the preceding century, the precarious means of mobilizing national resources to wage an almost permanent war against the Habsburgs; it inherited the progress accomplished under Louis XIV, not the constraints which the latter had demanded or accepted. Its offices were run by a small army of civil servants and technicians, often trained, from the start of the second half of the century, in special schools created for the purpose – for example, the schools of civil and mining engineering.

At the same time, specific sets of administrative regulations had been developed, through the concept of privilege applied to the state and its servants – a significant reversal which extended the particular scope of

individual rights to the whole of the machinery of state, emancipating
the king's officials in the name of public interest. Administrative affairs
received their own rules, sanctioned by their own jurisdictions, crowned by
the king's Council. The modern state was being formed.

With the spirit of the century assisting, it could devote more care and
money to the great tasks of the new age – town building, public health,
agricultural and commercial development, market unification, education.
Henceforth, the *intendant* was well and truly in command, outranking the
traditional authorities and with a finger in every pie. He was at the centre
of a vast effort for knowledge and administrative reform, proliferating
economic and demographic enquiries, rationalizing his actions with the
help of the first social statistics on a national scale in French history.
He wrested from the clergy and the nobility almost all their remaining
functions in local supervision; even elementary education, that old private
hunting-ground of the Church, came increasingly under his thumb, and
threatened to develop in a way which disturbed many of the *philosophes*,
who were concerned at the thought of seeing rural labours abandoned by
all these future educated Frenchmen. Far from being reactionary, or
imprisoned by self-interest, the monarchic state in the eighteenth century
was one of the foremost agents of change and progress – a permanent
building-ground for 'enlightened' reform.

THE NOBILITY

At the same time, however, the state remained bound to the social
compromise carefully developed over the preceding centuries, and was
rendered the more powerless to affect the society of orders because by its
actions it was completely destroying the spirit of that society. The latter
was falling apart under the joint pressure of economic improvement, the
increasing number of individual initiatives and aspirations and the spread
of culture. Money and merit were coming up against 'birth'; in their path
they found the state, guaranteeing privileges.

By ennoblement, by selling off the most coveted positions, that state
continued to integrate into the second order of the realm the commoners
who had served it best – above all, those who had made the most money,
often in its service (for example in financial posts) – but by doing so it
dangerously exposed its authority. In fact, the 'old' nobility (not only that
of the Middle Ages, which was relatively rare, but also that dating from the
sixteenth and seventeenth centuries), often less wealthy than the recently
ennobled, felt a great sense of resentment and insisted on elevating true
distinction to the celebrated four quarterings (that is, four generations of
nobility), which would define true 'blue blood'.

As for the new nobles, they behaved like all newcomers in this kind of
system: hardly had they squeezed through the narrow gate when their
first thought was to close it behind them, since a proliferation of bene-

ficiaries would devalue what they had just acquired. Thence sprang that French mania for rank, which resounded from top to bottom of society and doubtless gave rise, by reaction, to the surge of revolutionary egalitarianism. Under the *ancien régime*, the state became inseparable from this nexus of passions and personal interests, since it was the power which distributed rank and title, and far too parsimoniously, for an expanding society. All it succeeded in doing was to alienate 'its' nobility, without ever having the means to organize a ruling class in the English manner.

Everything points to this crisis in the eighteenth-century French nobility, though not in the sense in which it is usually understood. For the nobles were not a group – or a class – in decline. Nobility had never been so brilliant; never had civilization been so 'aristocratic' as in the time of the Enlightenment, and specially marked at this point by the adaptation of fine court manners to the conversation of the salons. Established on vast land ownership (though infinitely less extensive than that of the English gentry), often associated with huge trading concerns and owning interests in the management of the king's finances, the rich nobility embodied the prosperity of the era.

But the nobility as an order of society never managed to adjust its relations with the state. With the wane of its traditional powers, it had lost the essence of its *raison d'être*, and never succeeded in redefining its political vocation within the framework of the administrative monarchy. At the death of Louis XIV, three potential destinies lay before it: to become a 'Polish' nobility, hostile to the state, nostalgic for its old rights of jurisdiction, ready for the reconquest of a golden age; a 'Prussian' nobility, associated with an enlightened despotism, a class of dedicated administrative or military service linked to immense land ownership, the backbone of the national state; or, finally, an 'English' nobility, controlling the House of Lords, but together with the Commons making a constitutional monarchy – a parliamentary aristocracy of a much wider political class to which money provided open access.

However, French nobles had espoused none of those alternatives; the state had not offered them the opportunity. The first was hopeless, a backward-looking dream of a lost identity; in France it had nurtured a certain nobiliary anarchism, never a policy. The second was scarcely compatible with a rich and developed civil society, a nobility owning only a quarter of the land and made up of officials who owned their own offices. It is significant that this course had often been advocated by poor minor nobles – the very ones in whose favour the monarchy had designed preferential treatment in the army, with the opening of special military schools (1776).

One has only to look at the outcry raised in 1781 by the Marquis de Ségur's ordinance reserving officer grade in certain regiments for young nobles with four quarterings to realize the unsuitability of a 'Prussian' solution to the French situation. As for the 'English' answer, it was quite simply incompatible with the very principle of absolute monarchy, since it

Joseph Siffrein Duplessis Jacques Necker, *1791, Musée Versailles, Paris.*
(Photo: Lauros-Giraudon)

presupposed a sharing of sovereignty. Moreover, in the parlements for example, where the idea was to some extent developed, there existed also an ardent defence of French-style aristocratic society, based on privilege. An English kind of nobility supposed at least the end of tax exemptions; that was a minimum requirement for the constitution of a dominant class based on wealth, and the condition for that landowners' monarchy which was desired in such different quarters – two very different financial administrators, Turgot and Necker, for once in accord.

There lay the origins of the social and political crisis of eighteenth-century France, giving rise to a part of the French Revolution and its prolongation into the nineteenth century. Neither the French king nor the nobility put forward a policy which might unite state and ruling society around a minimum consensus: because of that, royal action oscillated between despotism and capitulation. Chiefly on the crucial question of taxation, which aroused the interests and passions of all: each man's place in society, and each man's conception of that place were simultaneously at stake. But if the state was unable to point the way, because of the host of ties by which it had bound itself to corporate society, the nobles were equally impotent, since they had lost their identity together with their social autonomy. They had but one principle left to reunify them: to defend their privileges in the name of a collective personality whose secret they had lost and whose memory or legend they had no other way of reviving.

Thus Louis XIV had been able to control the process of promotion and unification of elites within a society divided into orders, and had turned it into one of the foundations for building the state. Louis XV had no longer managed to do so, and Louis XVI even less. They were constantly torn between the demands of the administrative state and their solidarity with aristocratic society. Not only did they carry that loyalty in their blood, as descendants of the most illustrious family in French nobility, which had reigned over the kingdom for so many centuries; they had also mingled it with something more modern, related to both sentiment and necessity – for aristocratic society, since the end of the sixteenth century, had largely been the work of the Bourbons. It was they who had built the modern state on the sale of offices, privileges, status and rank; how could their descendants go back on the word of their predecessors? In any case, how could they materially do without privileges, which formed the resources of their kingdom? That was what Chancellor Maupeou had gambled on in his attempted reform in 1771, in the last years of Louis XV: could the King, in the name of the state's authority, go back on what he had guaranteed?

Thus the kings of France passed their time in yielding now to some, now to others, wavering between the clans and cliques of the court, the *philosophes* and the *dévots*, the Jansenists and the Jesuits, the physiocrats and the mercantilists. They tried successive policies, but never followed them through; they upheld Machault, then Choiseul, Maupeou then Turgot. Each time, the action of the state aroused hostility from one or other part of the ruling groups, without ever welding them together, either in favour of an enlightened despotism *à la* Maupeou, or of a liberal reformism *à la* Turgot. These eighteenth-century elites were at the same time close to the government, yet in revolt against it. In reality, they settled their internal differences to the detriment of absolutism.

Even the crisis of 1789 would be powerless to rebuild their unity, save in the imagination of Third Estate ideologists: neither the outbreak of the Revolution, through what historians call the 'aristocratic revolt', nor the revolutionary behaviour of several noble members of the Constituent Assembly, nor the work itself of the Assembly is intelligible without reference to the crisis between the monarchy and the nobility in the eighteenth century. If the French Revolution – like all revolutions – met with such poorly co-ordinated resistance at its start, it was because the political *ancien régime* had died before it was struck down. It had died of isolation and because it could no longer find any political support within 'its' nobility, although the latter was more than ever at the centre of its vision of society.

THE ENLIGHTENMENT

If that is how things were in the government of the kingdom, what can be said of the intellectual sphere? The society which the monarchy had fragmented was united by the culture of the century: public opinion was burgeoning in the twilight of the court and in the birth of a formidable power – which would last until universal suffrage was achieved – the omnipotence of Paris. The nobles of both Versailles and the capital read the same books as the cultured bourgeoisie, discussed Descartes and Newton, wept over the misfortunes of Prévost's Manon Lescaut, enjoyed Voltaires *Lettres philosophiques*, d'Alembert's *Encyclopédie* or Rousseau's *Nouvelle Héloïse*.

The monarchy, the orders, the guilds, had separated the elites by isolating them in rival strongholds. In contrast, ideas gave them a meeting-point, with special privileged place: the salons, academies, Freemasons' lodges, societies, cafés and theatres had woven an enlightened community which combined breeding, wealth and talent, and whose kings were the writers. An unstable and seductive combination of intelligence and rank, wit and snobbery, this world was capable of criticizing everything, including and not least itself; it was unwittingly presiding over a tremendous reshaping of ideas and values.

As if by chance, the ennobled nobility, in the legal profession and particularly in finance, played a vital part. They threw a bridge between the world from which they had come and the one in which they had arrived; an additional testimony to the strategic importance of that grave-yard area of society, groping – with that slightly masochistic irony born of a dual awareness of its strangeness and its success – for something which resembled neither of those worlds.

The new intellectual realm was the workshop where the notion of *ancien régime* would be forged, although it did not employ that term before the Revolution. What characterized it in the political field, quite apart from its philosophical and literary brilliance, was in fact the scale and the forceful-ness of the condemnation it brought to bear on contemporary life – including the Church and religion. There was a violently anticlerical and anti-Catholic side to the philosophy of the French Enlightenment which had no equivalent in European thought.

Take, for example, Voltaire and Hume: of the two, Voltaire was probably not the more irreligious, as he was a deist and at least regarded
religion as indispensable to the social order. But though Hume discredited
rational proofs of God's existence, including that of First Cause, so dear to
Voltaire, there was in his philosophical discourse none of the antireligious
aggressiveness to be found in the sage of Ferney. Hume lived at peace with
the diversity of Protestant churches, whereas the Frenchman made war on
the Catholic Church.

France had had her religious wars, but no victorious Reformation. On
the contrary, absolutism had extirpated Calvinism by brute force: the Edict
of Nantes had given toleration to Protestants for nearly a century; its
revocation in 1685 consecrated the king in his role of protector of the
Catholic Church, and the Church as indissolubly bound to the king. The
French movement of the Enlightenment has been little studied in the light
of its debt to that very recent past. Nevertheless, in a France brought back
to Catholicism by religious intolerance and royal power, the Church and
the absolute monarchy together had formed an almost natural target for the
attacks of a 'philosophy' which was all the more radical for not being built,
as in England, on the foundation of a previous religious revolution.

Moreover, that independent religious revolution had still sought an
identity, within Catholicism this time, in the form of Jansenism: a new
emphasis on the miracle of divine Grace in a world given over to sin. But
the Jansenism of solitary recluses engaged in meditation on Grace had
probably contributed to the isolation of the Church in old French society;
it had been too insistent on the difficulty of the asceticism which was
indispensable to the sinner wishing to receive the sacraments, and too
sharply condemned so many ministers of religion, Jesuits first and foremost. Also, the Jansenist movement itself in the eighteenth century had
been taken up and made subordinate to politics. It had become Gallican
and *parlementaire*, the banner which united lowly folk and great judges
against the Church, and often against the king, in the name of the rights of
the nation.

The transformation of this French-style belated Protestantism into a
movement for national liberties says a great deal about the secularization of
the public mentality. In the sixteenth century, politics had been completely
enveloped in religion; in the eighteenth, even currents of opinion with a
religious origin were absorbed by the debate on the state, in opposition to
the absolutism of the king and his ally, the Church. It is certainly true that
the Revolution, at the end of the century, did not deliberately seek conflict
with the Catholic Church; but many elements of the century's culture had
borne it in that direction, and it had taken that path as if naturally,
without, however, having decided to do so or weighed the consequences.

Together with the Church, the other great culprit was the absolute
monarchy, which was incapable of appearing before the court of reason.
Not the monarchy per se, because nobody could imagine a republic in a
large country, but that particular monarchy, encumbered with 'gothic'

prejudices, the distributor of arbitrary privileges, reigning over a kingdom filled with vestiges of feudalism. It mattered little that France was in reality the least feudal country in Europe, as a result of the very activities of the administrative state, and that it was also the country where criticism of the state by reason was the most systematic: suddenly the remains of feudalism – for example, seigniorial rights, or the last serfs in the kingdom – were perceived as all the more oppressive precisely because they were residual.

Features which came after feudalism – privileges bestowed by the king in return for the loan of money, the corporate structure of society, a nobility largely uprooted from the land and defined by the state, for instance – were included in the overall condemnation of that historical monster; not only a 'feudal monarchy' (already it was difficult to think of these two aspects in conjunction), but on top of that an 'administrative despotism'. The incoherent character of the definition at least has the merit of highlighting the nature of the accusation.

Royalty, which was too modern for what it had preserved and refashioned of the traditional, and too traditional for what it already had in the way of modern administration, tended to turn itself into the scapegoat for an increasingly independent society, which was nevertheless still bound hand and foot to the government, deprived of political rights and representation, trying to work out its autonomy in terms of government by reason.

That royalty reaffirmed its familiar image, or its mystery – the incarnation of the nation by the king. In 1766, for example, in the famous 'Flagellation' sitting cited earlier, Louis XV had appeared before the parlement in order to bring discredit on what was already being termed 'opinion': he let it be understood that public discussion had no place except within the body of the monarchy, which he represented in his person, alone having the power to create unity from the patchwork of private privileges.

In actual fact, the monarchy had lost its authority over opinion: it no longer obtained consent for its actions, or imposed its arbitration on the burning questions of the hour – the struggle of Jansenists and parlements with the Church, fiscal reform, and disputes about the grain trade. Paris, especially, produced an ever-increasing number of pamphlets and debates, dominated by the writers, orchestrated by the salons and cafés. The centralization effected by the royal administration had its bureaucratic heart at Versailles, near to the king, but had also turned Paris into the only arena of public discussion.

For want of a representational system implanted in the provinces, opposition to the Versailles bureaucracy became centralized in nearby Paris; by not associating the elites of the city with the government of the kingdom, it transformed the literary life of the capital into a forum for the reform of the state. Moreover, the Crown followed the trend; it too bought defenders, paid writers, financed pamphlets and argued its cause before the new tribunal.

From the middle of the century, and even more so in the last years of Louis XV's reign, the most important term was 'opinion'. The semantic derivation of this word is significant. Starting from the classic definition given in the *Encyclopédie* (Latin *opinio* (Greek *doxa*) as opposed to true knowledge), ten or twenty years later the noun came to designate something very different: a counterbalance to despotism, developed by men of letters. 'Opinion' was more generally produced by the activity of society, its development, its growing wealth, its *lumières* – a constant theme in *fin-de-siècle* France, to be systematically developed on the other side of the Channel by Scottish economists and philosophers.

It constituted a public tribunal, in contrast with the secrecy of the king; it was universal, in contrast with the particularism of 'feudal' laws; and objective, in contrast with monarchic arbitrariness: in short, a court of appeal of reason, judging all matters of state, in the name of public interest alone. It was a means of getting away from a society of orders and guilds without falling into the disarray of private interests and factions. Well before the Revolution, this idea transferred the features of royal sovereignty to a new authority, also unique, which was an exact copy of the monarchic idea: on the ruins of feudal monarchy, it had only to build a monarchy of reason. It was in this transfer that a revolution took place.

PROJECTS FOR REFORM

Nevertheless, in the last four years of his life, between 1770 and 1774, Louis XV, at the age of sixty, engaged in the decisive battle of his reign, and probably of the last monarchic century. He wanted to crush the parlements, regain the initiative and his authority, and rebuild the unity of the nation around the throne. The campaign began in January 1771, through Maupeou – a theorist of royal authority. The son of a chancellor who had presided over the Parlement of Paris, president himself until 1768, the new chancellor had the clear-sightedness and relentless determination of all who have changed sides. This learned and hard-working little man's office became his driving passion. In order to crush attempts by the parlements to monitor royal power on the pretext of the right of remonstrance, Maupeou forbade them to have any contact with one another, or to go on strike. The result was a refusal to register new laws, *lits de justice*, fresh remonstrances.

In January 1771 came a trial of strength: 130 Parisian representatives were exiled, and the entire legal profession went on strike. Maupeou retaliated in February with a general reorganization of the judiciary system: five upper councils were thenceforth given the task of dealing with all civil and criminal matters in the immense jurisdiction of the parlement of Paris, the parlement being confined to its right of registration and remonstrance. Above all – and these were major innovations – the sale of official and judicial posts was abolished. New magistrates, appointed for life by the king, would be paid by the Crown. Not without some difficulty, Maupeou found and installed his new judges and his new chambers.

It was more than a reform. It was a social revolution: it involved the expropriation of an order of society which for some centuries had been accustomed to passing on the family office from father to son. In this sense, the entire nobility was attacked, and with it the whole of corporate society.

It retaliated not only in support of its own interests and in selfish isolation. On the contrary, it enveloped the defence of its possessions in the defence of the liberties of the realm. On 18 February the Cour des Aides expressed this perfectly in the remonstrances drawn up by its first president, Malesherbes:

Our silence would make the whole nation accuse us of betrayal and cowardice. All we are asking for today is the rights of that nation . . . At present, the courts are the sole protectors of the weak and unfortunate; the Estates-General, and in the greater part of the country the Provincial Estates, have long since ceased to exist; all bodies except the courts are reduced to dumb and passive obedience. No private person in the provinces would dare to lay himself open to the vengeance of a commandant, of a ministerial agent, and even less, of one of your Majesty's ministers.

And the final touch: 'Sire, interrogate the nation itself, since it is the only thing that may gain your Majesty's ear.'

This fine speech was historic. The demands of the parlements widened into a national appeal. Of course, resort to the Estates-General was still a resort to tradition. But tradition here included the future in the past, the reformism of the *philosophes* in the society of intermediary bodies: a man like Malesherbes saw no contradiction in that, because restoration of the past was seen as a necessary condition for the future. This profound product of the collective consciousness explains, just as much as royal irregularities, the popularity of parlements. Despite Voltaire, who continued his lampoon war against them – and in company with the *parti dévot*! – public opinion saw the recent conquerors of the Jesuits as its indispensable defenders. Petty officials united behind important office-holders, the *basoche* (petty officers of the court) behind the magistrates, all the corps of local and provincial autonomous groups behind the most solidly entrenched privileges. Against the arbitrary rule of one person alone, democracy was mobilized behind oligarchy, the people behind the nobility: this was the century's tradition and political dynamic.

The king had only one way (ever the same) of dispersing this increasingly powerful trend: to take the initiative in reform, especially of financial and tax administration. This he could do the more easily since, in the years 1770–4, the Crown had liberated itself from the lawcourts by breaking up the parlements, and theoretically had a free hand.

The Controller of Finance was a former clerical counsellor to the parlement, the Abbé Terray. Without any particular doctrine, but quick and intelligent, he belonged to that breed of empirical financiers who mistrusted abstract innovation and took refuge in budgetary balance. His management was both effective and unpopular, financially sound and politically deplorable. On taking office in 1769, he found a budgetary deficit of 100 million, a debt due for payment of over 400 million livres, and all the 1770 revenues earmarked in advance, without a sou in the coffers. When he left office in 1774, the budgetary deficit had dropped from 100 to thirty million, and the state's debts were reduced to twenty million. But these are the historian's figures and not those of his contemporaries.

For Terray's creation of supplementary revenues had borrowed from the most classic methods: on the one hand, fleecing the state's creditors; on the other, increased taxation, chiefly indirect. He cut down pensions, reduced State annuities, suspended certain payments such as the *billets des fermes* owed to the Crown's creditors. There were also new consumer taxes. A further move was the extension of the second *vingtième*, a 5 per cent tax on income, justified by this clear comment: 'We do not doubt that our subjects . . . will bear these charges with the zeal which they have shown on so many occasions, and we count on it all the more since the price of goods – one of the causes of the increase in our expenditure – has at the same time improved returns on land to a proportion in excess of the increase in taxation.'

The undeniable technical success of Terray's management – which was measurable by the growing success of royal borrowing – certainly helped the monarchy to gain time. But in the longer term it was accompanied by a double political failure. Firstly, it aroused against the king and his minister not only the world of capitalist speculators, but also all the *rentiers* (people who lived on annuities). Most of all, and more profoundly, it revealed the narrow confines of monarchic reformism; Terray was looking for better productivity from taxation, but without being able to proceed to a general review of fiscal assessment, an idea which had occurred to him as it had to others.

In short, the traditional character of the financial recovery effected in 1771–4 enables one to make a precise analysis of the last and greatest of Louis XV's ministries: the regime created no reformist counterbalance, launched no fiscal counteroffensive such as might split up the anti-absolutist coalition which the war against the parlements had established. In the terminology of the time, it was less a matter of an attempt at enlightened despotism, than despotism plain and simple. The ageing Louis XV had not turned into Voltaire's king; he tried in vain to resuscitate Louis XIV.

In his last years, that meant solitude. When he died on 10 May 1774, he was so damned in public opinion that he had to be buried at night as if in great haste. Paris had not prayed for the king's salvation. It is at this moment that Jules Michelet fixes the death of the monarchy in France.

Son of the Dauphin who had died in 1765, himself born in 1754, Louis XVI was not yet twenty when he inherited the awesome succession of his

Joseph Siffrein Duplessis Louis XVI in coronation robes, *Musée Carnavalet, Paris.*
(Photo: Lauros-Giraudon)

grandfather. He could not talk with the ministers who had seen Louis XV during his last illness and might therefore contaminate him. He had to make a very quick decision between the two clans of the court. On the one side, the *parti dévot*, who wanted to pursue Maupeou's policies, the definitive crushing of the parlements, Jansenism and the *philosophes*. Mesdames, Louis XV's daughters and the King's aunts, felt strengthened by the precipitate departure of his mistress, Madame du Barry, and the Church took advantage of a rediscovered morality. But against them was the entire *parti Choiseuliste*: Louis XV's former minister, disgraced in 1770, had been restlessly waiting at his estate at Chanteloup for over four years, backed by a network of noble and *parlementaire* friends, his popularity still intact, and finally with the reliable support of the new queen of France, whose marriage Choiseul had arranged.

Nevertheless, the queen remained cautious, and the king had chosen not to make a choice. Louis XVI recalled a former Secretary of State for the Navy, who had been out of favour for a quarter of a century and was thus a stranger to recent struggles: the Comte de Maurepas, who took the title of Minister of State. He would become much more. For in this old man of seventy-three, who had waited so long in exile, there was much suppressed ambition, a great deal of *savoir-faire* and intellect, and that sensual love of power which was the crowning point of his existence so late in life. Installed in lodgings close to the king, Maurepas governed the first years of the reign.

The Duc d'Aiguillon was the first of the old ministers to go, irredeemably compromised by Madame du Barry's friendship: the Comte de Vergennes, who owed everything to Maurepas, succeeded him in Foreign Affairs. The following month, there was a secondary rearrangement: Turgot, *intendant* of the Limousin, was well recommended to Maurepas and appointed to the Navy. But the great problem was that of the parlements and the management of finances, the areas of Maupeou and Terray. It was settled on 24 August by the departure of the two ministers. Louis XVI gave the Seals to Miromesnil, and transferred Turgot to the post of Controller-General.

It is the second name which has made the first ministry of Louis XVI's reign famous. That is only fair, for one can say with Edgar Faure that 'the general control of finance was Monsieur Turgot's final cause.'[2] The son of a dynasty of office-holders, at first destined for the Church, he was almost obsessed with serving the state; in his time as *conseiller* (counsellor) to the parlement, as *maître des requêtes* (counsel to the Conseil d'Etat), then as *intendant* of the Limousin, he had but one passion – the public good. This passion had its source in his very strong intellectual convictions: Turgot was a philosopher in the service of the state. This exception to the rule which, in the eighteenth century, separated practitioners of politics and specialists in ideas, was a rare and fragile moment when, after Maupeou

[2] Edgar Faure, *La Disgrâce de Turgot*.

and on a quite different plane, the *ancien régime*'s other last chance was at stake – a monarchy that was both liberal and rational.

The heart of Turgot's philosophy belonged to the physiocratic school, of which he was one of the outstanding intellects. He held that there was a natural order of society, intelligible through reason, which it was consequently the duty and wisdom of governments to actualize: this was a way of thinking diametrically opposed to the idea so often nurtured among *parlementaire* opposition that, somewhere in the mists of time, there might be a royal 'constitution' containing all the original rights of the nation *vis-à-vis* the king. Turgot recognized no authority other than reason, which was the sole foundation for a true social order. Society would thereby be completely liberated from its past, with the idea of tradition emptied of all meaning, while the state, in contrast, would have the task of personifying that reason, which was simultaneously the public interest.

Royal absolutism for him was absolute only in the sense that its function was to institute the natural order: productive agriculture, booming land revenues managed by the owners, and all sectors of the economy stimulated through free trade. The old notion of 'fundamental laws' was turned from its original sense to mean the exact opposite: it no longer referred to history and tradition, but to reason, property and the rights of property-owners. By replacing the idea of privilege with that of ownership, physiocratic thinking in general, and Turgot in particular, introduced the protection of liberties into universal modern language.

The text which expresses this most clearly is the famous *Mémoire sur les municipalités* (Memorandum on the municipalities), written during the years of Turgot's ministry, under his authority, by his adviser and friend Du Pont de Nemours, who was also a staunch supporter of physiocracy. We know from Condorcet, who was also in the inner circle of the new Controller-General and a fierce supporter of his ministry, that Du Pont gave shape to an old idea of Turgot's, both fiscal and political. In order to transform the assessment and collection of taxes, and to assist the development of agricultural productivity and of the economy, it was necessary to set up a system of assemblies representing property-owning society, which would be given the task of carefully working out reforms, overseeing their implementation and replacing, at least partially, the King's *intendants*.

Turgot, who was more a disciple of Vincent de Gournay and *laissez-faire* than of the physiocratic sect in its strict sense, had never favoured the idea of 'legal despotism', according to which good monarchic power could not be shared since it was supposed to be the means of revealing reason. On the contrary, he had visualized a pyramid of elected assemblies, from the parochial *municipalité* to the 'general *municipalité*' of the kingdom, by way of two intermediate stages. In this four-tier arrangement, described by Du Pont, where each body delegates to the higher level, the electors are property-owners on a pro rata basis of the value of their property: the 'free citizen' fulfils the criterion of wealth which grants full suffrage, while the 'fractional' citizen must join a group of others to obtain the same electoral unit of power. There are therefore only a few members in these assemblies, which is a condition of their rational operation: theirs would be the task, each at its own level, of fiscal reform and administration. Turgot envisaged, for a future of which he would not be in control, one single general contribution for all incomes; but Du Pont's memorandum did not go quite so far, and was limited to a proposed reform of the *taille*, intended to make things easier for the farmers, hitting only the landowners, in order to increase crop productivity.

The most original aspect of the project identifies the representation of society and its administration with the ownership of property. Turgot's monarchy according to reason was also a monarchy of co-ownership between the king and all possessors of property. Within this concept, over and above a precise diagnosis of the crisis between state and society which was sounding the death knell of the *ancien régime*, lay a very modern line of thinking: it was a matter of representing the interests of society and not, as with Rousseau for example, the political will of those involved.

The parlements – those courts of justice peopled by judges who had purchased nobility together with their office – could not be the guardians of those interests, because they had their privileges to defend; therefore it was necessary to conceive completely new structures. The plan helps us to understand how the idea of the *tabula rasa*, which would have such a brilliant revolutionary career, emerged naturally from the *ancien régime*, which produced it.

In short, those interests which must be represented generate social unity, by the mediation of reason: a different concept from that of Adam Smith's 'invisible hand', although the problem is posed in comparable terms. The French version of liberal society did not include that miracle of final equilibrium which creates order out of disorder. It presupposed that all the participants, especially the state, were subject to a constraint which lay outside and above society – that of reason – and which would avert anarchy from a community defined in terms of individual interests. Du Pont's *municipalités* dealt in their own way with a question which would obsess Condorcet: on what conditions could a rational decision be obtained from an assembly? From its very origins, French thinking about representation guarded itself against the fear of social breakdown by having recourse to reason and science: an oscillation which would continually haunt and characterize it for a century, right up to the time of Guizot and Jules Ferry.

Here we have, then, ready to get down to work, the first and last team of *philosophes* peaceably preparing an assault on the *ancien régime*, with the shaky support of a young king. If the ideas were revolutionary, the means of implementing them were not. Condorcet, in the shadow of the Controller-General, began his apprenticeship in the world and work of politics, where he would never truly be at ease. Philosophy had finally encountered the state.

The promotion of 24 August 1774 immediately revealed the limitations of this economic and political experiment. The new Keeper of the Seals, Miromesnil, former first president of the parlement of Rouen – one of the most turbulent in the kingdom – had refused since 1771 to sit in the 'Maupeou parlement'. The dismissal of the chancellor had, moreover, aroused such enthusiasm in Paris that the consequences were almost inevitable: two months later, the parlements were reconvened, hereditary rights and the sale of offices restored. The 'guarantees' demanded in return by the young king – such as the prohibition of collective resignations and the interruption of justice – were so shaky that they immediately became the subject of complaints by the *avocat général* (government law officer), Séguier, at the registration session for the edicts of recall.

Turgot had taken no direct part in the decision, but he had given his agreement. Was this a tactical manoevre towards the young sovereign and Maurepas, who wanted to please public opinion? Was it the influence of his friend Malesherbes? At all events, the new Controller had always had his reservations about 'legal despotism' as described by his physiocrat friends, being imbued with the feeling that one should woo opinion in order to educate it rather than put obstacles in its way. In reality, as Condorcet had warned him, he had just given a hand to those who would be his most formidable adversaries. Did he foresee this? It is not certain. At least he could reflect that the popularity of the new ministry gave him a free hand in the immediate future.

In the financial area, nothing was urgent. Taking over from Terray, inheriting a management which was both efficient and unpopular, formed the best possible accession. Wisely, Turgot shelved his old project, ripened while he was *intendant* of Limoges, of improving the assessment for levying the *taille*. He handled the court with equal care; the only 'cutbacks' he operated on state expenditure were aimed at the costs of tax collection and the exorbitant profits of tax farmers.

This slowness, however, was not entirely tactical. Turgot was more of an economist than a financier. He believed less in budgetary techniques than in increased production. As a good physiocrat, he linked tax surpluses to the enrichment of the kingdom, which itself depended on the priority given to grain policy. He had made this clear in 1770 in his *Lettres sur la liberté du commerce des grains* (Letters on the freedom of the grain trade): annual fluctuations in the quantity and price of grain could be reduced only by free trade. The resulting rise in the average price would be slow and gradual, and would create more jobs and better wages; the broad trend of physiocratic prosperity would replace the violent cyclical contractions which periodically bred poverty and famine.

An initial liberal experiment had been attempted in 1763–4. Under the influence of the current situation and the economists, internal free trade and, to a certain extent, exports of corn, had been authorized. But the continuous increase in prices which had fed the euphoria of the landowners and the *laissez-faire* of the liberals had grown to such proportions that it had offered the sticklers for regulation their revenge. It was in the name of the wretched populace, in 1770–1, during the peak of a cyclical price rise, that Terray had returned to banning exports and to the traditional policy of corn provision by the state in order to stabilize prices. To this end he had re-established not the old policy governing the movement of goods between provinces, but complex market regulation.

Turgot suppressed that regulation by his edict of September 1774, the fine preamble to which is a long piece of liberal pedagogy, resuming the argument of his *Lettres*. Voltaire comments in a letter to d'Alembert: 'I have just read M. Turgot's masterpiece. What new heavens and new earths, it would seem!' But already general reaction was far from un-animous, and some words from Nicolas Baudeau, the physiocratic abbé, concerning this preamble throw light on forthcoming events: 'The two extremes of the people did not heed him, namely, those of the court and the leading townsmen and those of the populace. For a long time I have noticed a strong conformity of propensities and opinions between these two extremes.' The court – any step towards a liberal economy threatened the world of acquired rights. Leading townsmen – the representatives were hostile to the innovations of economists and *philosophes* alike. Lastly, the 'populace' lived in age-old terror of dear bread, which was imputed not to the nature of things but to the maliciousness of men.

The drama took shape in the following spring, with the exhaustion of the previous year's harvest. From eleven sous for four livres in weight, the price during the summer and winter, bread went up to fourteen sous; cheaper than at Terray's 'peak' period, but relatively dearer in that stocks had been exhausted by previous high prices. In the second fortnight of April 1775, a sort of generalized rioting developed around Paris, culmi-nating in the capital itself at the beginning of May.

This episode, known as the Flour War, indicated, in the less impover-ished France of the eighteenth century, the lasting nature of old popular emotions aroused during the gap between the exhaustion of stocks and the new harvest. Contemporaries in favour of Turgot believed some aris-tocratic or clerical conspiracy was at the bottom of it, though we have no proof of this other than a convergence of hostile intent towards the minister. Historians today insist that it was the 1775 forerunner of the rural revolts of July–August 1789: such comparison underlines the same-ness of popular mentality and reaction in the face of high prices and poverty.

There was the same kind of anarchistic rumour-mongering, the same spontaneous demands for state price-fixing and protection, the same train of violence and looting of markets and bakeries. On 5 May at Brie-Comte-Robert, to quote from the report of the tax inspector Dufresne, 400 people 'who appeared to be artisans from the villages around Paris' formed a mob outside his house; about forty got inside and demanded 'in furious tones' that he give them corn at twelve livres 'like at Choisy-le-Roi'. They added that 'if they were to be hanged they would suffer less than by dying slowly of starvation'.

Upheld by the king, Turgot gained the upper hand from early May, but his liberal experiment was ultimately brought into discredit. The parlement of Paris solemnly condemned his policy. At Versailles, the intrigues of the cliques resumed against the Controller: chiefly the Choiseulists, who had the important backing of the queen, unhappy about the appointment of Malesherbes to the king's household during the summer of 1775. Necker made history by publishing *La Législation et le commerce des grains* (Legislation and the Grain Trade), a counter-offensive in favour of economic controls. A whole society of monopolies and privileges united in opposition to liberal innovation.

Turgot, feeling himself threatened, chose a solution which worsened the situation; such audacity, or tactical imprudence, has nurtured the thesis that he was a doctrinaire minister, heedless of reality. In January 1776, he persuaded the king to sign a series of six edicts, which actually comprised two important reforms: of the *corvée*, which was replaced by a money tax on landowners; and of the trade guilds, which were purely and simply abolished.

The edicts appeared less daunting for what they contained than for what they foreshadowed. Turgot was suspected of wanting to do away with the traditional organization of the kingdom. It was feared that the end of the *corvée* might mean the end of seigneurial society: the disappearance of the guilds prefigured the confusion over 'rank' and 'status'. A whole range of society united against that prospect: clergy, nobility, magistracy and the organized sectors of traditional urban life – *basoche*, master craftsmen and merchants. Erstwhile enemies made a holy alliance, magistrature and clergy, Choiseulists and the *parti dévot*, financiers and the petty nobility.

On the opposite side, how much weight did Voltaire or Condorcet carry, the *philosophes* and the economists? The truth is that Turgot's reforms affected noble society enough to rouse it against him, and not enough to separate important strata of the bourgeoisie from it. They revealed the political deadlock of that society of propertied voters so desired by the physiocrats, and showed the resistance of civil society as well as the strength of the nobles' counter-offensive. From top to bottom, aristocratic society united around the same defensive reflex, admirably defined by an expression of Trudaine: they were not 'sure if they would wake the next morning to the same status'.

Nevertheless, the edicts got through, after a long battle in the parlement. But Turgot had been isolated in the ministry and at court. Everyone was against him: Maurepas, the queen, the king's brothers, his aunts, his kinsman the Prince de Condé. Malesherbes hesitated, and wanted to resign. Louis XVI yielded to the general wave of feeling and dismissed Turgot on 12 May 1776. In August, the guilds were re-established in new forms, and the *corvée* made subject to possible redemption by parishes.

Thus, after the downfall of the triumvirate's neo-absolutist attempt, came the failure of the philosophical and reforming monarchy. In six years, the two paths of state arbitration had been explored in vain. At the end of this double shipwreck there remained an ever more anti-absolutist public opinion and a monarchy which was falling apart.

LOUIS XVI

The King who mounted the throne in 1774 was the third son of the Dauphin, son of Louis XV.[3] His father had married Maria Theresa of Spain, who died in childbirth at the age of twenty, and whose death had left him inconsolable. He had been very quickly remarried to Marie-Josèphe of Saxony; even if he did not love her, he at least gave her a number of children: a first daughter, who died very young; then Louis-Joseph, Duc de Bourgogne, born 1751; Marie-Joseph, Duc d'Aquitaine, in 1753 (died the next year); then, in 1754, the child who would be Louis XVI, receiving the title of Duc de Berry.

His birth was followed by that of two brothers who would also reign, but over post-revolutionary France, between 1814 and 1830: Louis-Stanislas, Comte de Provence, born in 1755, and Charles Philippe, Comte d'Artois, in 1757. Lastly, two daughters brought the list to a close, Marie-Adélaïde Clotilde, in 1759, then Elisabeth Philippine Marie-Hélène, in 1764 – the Madame Elisabeth who would share her brother's captivity in the Temple prison. In this enormous family, which did not escape the curse of high infant mortality, the Duc de Berry became heir to the throne because of the death of his older brother, the Duc de Bourgogne, in 1761 at the age of ten. His father, the Dauphin, died in 1765. The future Louis XVI thus knew his destiny at the age of eleven; he would be king of France.

This hereditary devolution wrought by God's hand broke what God's hand seemed to have prepared: death had struck the child whom everything had destined for the throne, to the advantage of one who showed only ordinary aptitudes. Where Bourgogne had been lively, charming, adulated, precociously authoritarian and genetically a king, Berry was withdrawn, solitary, graceless. The grief of his parents and grandfather – papa-Roi, as he called him – brought no extra affection his way; it was the turn of his young brothers, Provence and Artois, to be the favourites. In short, Louis XVI was the unpopular member of the family.

That was a psychological misfortune which probably added its effects to his paternal heritage, and which distanced him from his grandfather and similarly from the task of kingship. For his father, the Dauphin, had been kept apart all his life from a political role or even apprenticeship. In fact, under Louis XV, the royal family had transposed a drama from bourgeois repertory to the court of France. On the one hand, the king and his mistress, Madame de Pompadour, who reigned at Versailles and even, if her enemies were to be believed, over the kingdom's politics: she was the protectress of the *philosophe* party, of Choiseul and the Austrian alliance. On the other, the queen, Marie Leczynska, ill and ageing, but drawing

---

[3] Here I am using part of an article on Louis XVI in Furet and Ozouf, *Critical Dictionary*.

strength from the outraged loyalty of her children, guardians of morality and religion.

The Dauphin had sided with his mother: he was the symbol and hope of the *parti dévot*, the Jesuits' man, a bitter adversary of Choiseul and the Austrian policy. This plump, almost obese, man, intellectually lazy, with the typically Bourbon combination of sensuality and devoutness, was carefully kept away from matters of the realm by Louis XV. He never forgot the respect he owed his father; but he was a living reproach and a potential rival. He died too soon – nine years before his father – to be able to reign. However, he had taken great care over the education of his children to prepare them for their future role, as if he had realized that the throne of France was going to 'jump' a generation.

When he died, in 1766, the Duc de la Vauguyon, governor to the Children of France, took charge of the new Dauphin without in any way modifying his programme of studies. It was a serious programme, with an industrious pupil, but perhaps neither deserves the excessive praise which whitewashing historiography has sought to shower on them. There were few innovations in the subject matter: the basis of the lessons and 'discussions' drawn up for the instruction of the future king remained a mixture of religion, morality and humanities, to which the shade of Fénelon lent an unreal quality and the ponderousness of the pedagogue-duke a touch of grandiloquence.

As far as the pupil is concerned, his work manifests a docile and un-imaginative way of thinking, reflecting only what he was being taught. His style, sometimes elegant, is more interesting than his thoughts, which are always banal; in these pastorals on paternal monarchy, superficial com-mentaries on Fénelon's *Télémaque* or the *Politique tirée de l'Ecriture sainte* by Bossuet the future king learned neither to conduct a reasoned argument nor to govern a State.

The great event – and the greatest failure – of his youth was his marriage, negotiated in 1768 under the influence of the Choiseul party, to an Austrian princess: the youngest daughter of Maria-Theresa, the Archduchess Marie-Antoinette. The union was celebrated in 1770; the Dauphin was sixteen, his bride fifteen. For seven years, until the summer of 1777, he would not manage to consummate the marriage. For seven years, the Court of Versailles, Paris, the entire kingdom and foreign courts, according to circumstance, would make this fiasco into a state problem or an object of mockery – the one not excluding the other. When he became king (1774), Louis XVI was the butt of this European vaudeville.

He was not impotent, properly speaking, like his brother Provence, but incapable of ejaculation – and, in any event, he was little inclined towards love and women. One can imagine that this anomaly would have intrigued his libidinous grandfather, quite apart from the harm it was doing to the future of the kingdom. There may well have entered into it a justifiable repudiation of his cynical and blasé grandfather, with his weakness for

Madame du Barry, and a sort of loyalty to his paternal heritage: through Louis XVI, the Bourbons would end in virtue, but without capitalizing on it, since that virtue had begun by being ludicrous. It appears that, in the end, a chat with his brother-in-law Joseph, who came to France incognito in 1777, freed Louis from his inhibition. In August, court correspondence mentioned the event, and the queen's pregnancy confirmed it the following year. The future emperor of Austria – perhaps with the help of a small operation (it is not certain) – settled the affair privately, but without being able to obliterate all traces of it in public opinion or in the royal couple themselves.

Thus, the still adolescent man who came to the throne on 10 May 1774, on the death of his grandfather, had already had long experience of loneliness, which the exercise of power would intensify. That was what gave his personality that 'indecipherable' quality remarked upon by his contemporaries, which Marie-Antoinette also wondered about in her letters to her mother.

When he became king of France at twenty, Louis XVI was a rather gauche young man, already tending to portliness, with a full face, Bourbon nose and a short-sighted gaze which was not without a certain gentleness. Michelet stresses the Germanic heredity (through his mother, daughter of the Elector of Saxony) of this heavy, slow, thick-blooded prince, who ate and drank too much. But it is equally easy to trace these traits back to his father, the Dauphin, son of Louis XV and Marie Leczynska.

The dominant motif of contemporary accounts of the young king, apart from his lack of grace, was his difficulty in communicating, and even in reacting. With no conversation, no distinction, he had good sense but was short on wit: the best document in this regard is the diary he kept of his daily activities, in which are noted, together with his hunts, his meals and his meetings, and family events. This list never discloses the slightest emotion, the smallest personal comment: it reveals a soul without any strong vibrations, a mind numbed by habit.

By contrast, what a lot of physical exercise! Louis XVI spent on hunting – which was his passion – the energy he saved in his contacts with men or his relations with his wife. He watched with meticulous care over the upkeep of forests and animals, knew the men and dogs of the hunting teams, and devoted long hours, often several times a week, to staghunting, a typically Bourbon pastime from which he would emerge exhausted but happy, with the evening in which to listen to discussions of the afternoon's exploits.

Another practice which was characteristic of his solitary and rather arid nature was manual work, tinkering about, locksmithing: above his apartment, Louis XVI had a little forge set up where, with a modest talent, he made locks and keys. From there he could ascend a further storey to reach his belvedere and watch through a telescope all that was happening in the gardens of Versailles. On some days he took the opportunity to wander through the attics of the château, chasing stray cats.

It is easy to see how historians have been able to turn this really very average man into a hero, an incompetent, a martyr or a culprit: this honourable king, with his simple nature, ill adapted for the role he had to assume and the history which awaited him, can equally well inspire emotion at the unfairness of fate or an indictment against his lack of foresight as a sovereign. Where personal qualities were concerned, Louis XVI was not the ideal monarch to personify the twilight of royalty in the history of France; he was too serious, too faithful to his duties, too thrifty, too chaste and, in his final hour, too courageous. But through his visceral attachment to tradition, the adolescent who had spent his youth clinging to his aunts' apron-strings and in the shadow of the *parti dévot*, would be the man of a monarchy which was no longer suited to him or the era.

Michelet grasped this well and truly, seeing in that royalty in God's image the supreme ill of the *ancien régime*. He recognized that Louis XVI was its poor, final symbol – too scrupulous, too domestic, too 'national' as well (because of the war against England, and American independence). He had, in fact, to pay the price for his grandfather's sins, for the harem of the Parc-aux-Cerfs and the alliance with Austria. For Michelet, the drama of the French monarchy had been played out under Louis XV. When his grandson mounted the throne, it was too late; the monarchy was already dead.

That profound intuition explains where Louis XVI's real failure lay: less in his day-to-day politics, at home or abroad, which did have some great moments, than in his powerlessness to resuscitate on any lasting basis the great moribund body of old royalty as it used to be. The new king received the consecration of his coronation at Reims in 1775, like his predecessors, but thereafter the only legitimate consecration would be by public opinion. For a brief while he obtained this by virtue of his youth, his good will, the reinstatement of the parlements, and Turgot; but all too soon he let this popularity be swept up into the unpopularity of the queen and the court.

MARIE-ANTOINETTE

The queen was an archduchess of Austria, daughter of the Empress Maria Theresa, married to the Dauphin after lengthy diplomatic manoeuvres by Choiseul. On her mother's orders, she was accompanied by the ambassador, Mercy-Argenteau, doubling as mentor and spy, who had been given the task of ensuring that the Austrian capital invested in the French marriage bore profitable fruit; but she did not succeed for very long in the difficult role assigned to her. She could find nobody to lean on at the court: hostile to Madame du Barry, Louis XV's last official mistress, she therefore became close to the *parti dévot* and the king's daughters, who would have liked to put an end to their father's misconduct; but she was Austrian, thus in the Choiseul camp, and found herself the very symbol of a policy which had been rejected, together with the minister, in 1770; its adversaries were in power, including, within the royal family, the aunts of the king and her own husband, the future king.

With little education, as badly prepared as could be for the role of Austrian 'antenna' at Versailles, which her mother would have liked to see her play, she had to live through those long early years with the court speculating every morning on what had happened – or rather, what had *not* happened – in her bed; gossip travelled swiftly from Versailles to Paris, and she was soon credited with lovers (of both sexes), since her husband seemed to be so inadequate. When children finally appeared (first a daughter, the future Madame Royale, in 1778, a Dauphin in 1781, another son in 1785 and a daughter the next year), the damage was already done: the image of the Austrian Messalina had been fixed by Parisian lampoons. On her side, there was a certain flightness, due to her temperament; she was a poorly educated princess, disliked, lacking understanding of events or men. But the world of Versailles offered this rootless foreign queen, who enjoyed no support, a virtually impossible role.

Her personality harboured an incurable impassivity, a lack of concern for advice and circumstances which made her behaviour difficult to fathom. The ambassador Mercy-Argenteau complained about it to Maria Theresa, to excuse himself for his failure to manipulate the young queen. Later the Comte de Mirabeau and Antoine Barnave had the same experience. They knew or guessed that Marie-Antoinette had the stronger character of the royal couple, but they came up against her secret. In her hour of tragedy, which she faced courageously, having matured in her loneliness, she was just the same as she had always been, rather indifferent to the outside world.

In contrast with Paris, at the time of Marie-Antoinette's arrival the court already presented the almost perfect image of what would a little later be termed the *ancien régime*. Absolutism had invented Versailles where, far from Paris and the people, Louis XIV had set up his undivided government, the instrument of an untrammelled authority. In addition, that government had surrounded itself with a parasitic aristocracy, dancing around the king the sycophantic ballet of the courtiers, half vice, half servility.

From being a means of taming the nobles, under Louis XIV, the court under Louis XVI had become the symbol of their dominance. The king no longer reigned over them – he obeyed them: in this telescoping of absolute monarchy and aristocracy was forged the overall rejection of what was no longer, in actual fact, either absolute monarchy or aristocracy, but something born of the decadence of the two principles and still surviving on their complicity, at the expense of the people.

Louis XVI contributed to this image concocted by the Parisian satirists through his lack of inclination for important matters and that slightly affected kind of spinelessness which was the most obvious trait in his make-up. But the king was always careful about the image of his calling, never compromised tradition and, by his serious-mindedness and personal virtue, would even be able to revive for both his person and his office a respect that the old Louis XV had not left intact. Now that novelty – a chaste Bourbon – itself became a butt: the faithful king was impotent; the virtuous sovereign had married a shameless hussy.

Yet he still maintained at least the façade of the court, and sheltered his shaky relationship with the world behind observance of etiquette, the ultimate legacy of tradition. His rash Austrian queen, on the other hand, elbowed aside this last rampart and revealed the rack and ruin behind the walls. She wanted, and obtained, private apartments; created a little court within the court, where she amused herself with selected friends, destroying the nature of the monarchy's public image offered at Versailles, and exposing only the aristocratic coteries. Public opinion deeply resented such dereliction of the duties and trappings of the reign: Marie-Antoinette presented a trebly vulnerable target – queen, foreigner and woman. The King's mistresses had been lampooned. The queen's lovers were even more detested. By making its object female, opinion's frustration changed into hatred. This was the hidden curse of Marie-Antoinette's life. Turning reality upside down, opinion condemned the queen for pleasures in which she had not indulged.

A scandal of the time gives some measure of Marie-Antoinette's unpopularity. The Cardinal de Rohan, bishop of Strasbourg, a luxury-loving *grand seigneur* who combined extreme ambition with extreme frivolity, longed to regain the favour of the queen, whom he had offended by his life-style and his *mots*. He made contact with a gang of adventurers who painted him a vivid picture of secret dealings at Court, and held out the prospect of a reconciliation: he handed over 150,000 livres to them, and they undertook to arrange a rendezvous, in a Versailles grove, with a 'queen' – in reality an accomplice – who promised him pardon. That was not all: he then had to buy, on behalf of a queen who was mad about diamonds, a necklace worth nearly two million livres – originally intended for Madame du Barry – which had become too dear even for the queen of France.

The plot was unmasked in the summer of 1785 when the jewellers vainly demanded the first payment. By then the necklace was out of reach, in London. The affair threw a lurid light on court life. The queen had tangled with crooks, including the alchemist Cagliostro; Rohan was the dupe, and won the sympathy of the public; handed over to the parlement, he was cleared of responsibility. The queen had sunk so low in public opinion that he was judged not guilty in having believed her to be promiscuous or (even worse) mercenary. Paris acclaimed him. The kingdom thought like the cardinal. When majesty ceases to be majestic, there can no longer be such a thing as *lèse-majesté*.

The verdict of public opinion gradually discredited everyone at court: the king's two brothers, the Comte de Provence, the underhand intriguer, and the Comte d'Artois, the queen's friend; his cousin the Duc d'Orléans, another shifty figure, biding his time at the Palais Royal;

the aristocracy, savouring the last happy days of what Talleyrand later called *la douceur de vivre*. To free itself from the external constraints of good conduct and piety, the court had effectively become a daily miracle of wit and pleasure. But it was rousing the entire town population against it. Jealous of a world from which it was excluded, enemy of a luxury which discredited its spirit of thrift, the bourgeois town – the laboratory of democracy, hard work and talent – threw its repressions and its hopes into the battle. The court, where nobles ruled, must be ruinous, reactionary and debauched, and reason, progress and morality must be mobilized against it.

THE FINANCIAL CRISIS

The last two charges of the indictment were more than justifiable. But what about the first? The collapse of public finance gave it a particular resonance. In reality, the court absorbed only 6 per cent of the Treasury's revenues – a relatively low percentage. Moreover, in its anathema, opinion constantly confused two kinds of expenditure: one relating to splendour and festival, and the other to official position. Financially, the second was the larger: not everything in it could be cut down – the king's household troops, for example, who drew their pay from the Versailles budget, could hardly be cut back after the 1775 reforms. But spectacular examples of waste abounded, so permanent was the confusion at Versailles between pensions and gifts, remuneration for public office, the speculative resale of the benefits of office, all kinds of financial devices. Finally, among Marie-Antoinette's entourage, the arbitrary nature of favour was more and more glaringly obvious. Madame de Lamballe, who already received 170,000 livres as superintendent of the queen's household, procured 600,000 livres on domains in Lorraine, plus 54,000 livres for her brother. Madame de Polignac and her family, other well-known protégés of the queen, were registered for a pension of 700,000 livres.

Had he attacked court wastefulness, Louis XVI would not have saved his finances, but he might perhaps have salvaged even more – the monarchy itself. His weakness in the face of the court was symbolic of the abdication of the monarchy before the aristocracy.

This erosion of royal power, marked by the nobles' victory at court, was not so rapid that it prevented Louis XVI from harvesting the last fruits of the century's progress, and of a better management of wealth and men. There are other examples of a power in decline and an enduring administration.

Since Choiseul, France had been preparing its revenge for defeat in the Seven Years War (1756–63). In 1775 – in the midst of the Turgot affair – the king summoned back to the War Ministry an old retired *condottiere*, the Comte de Saint-Germain, who in the space of two years 'Prussianized' the French military system, with efficient assistance from officialdom. He pruned the overmanned and over-costly corps, such as the king's household troops, whose expenses were the highest; he reduced the militias to the benefit of the regular army, whose numbers were doubled. Under the direction of Gribeauval, the French artillery became the best in Europe; on the advice of the Comte de Guibert, the light infantry updated military tactics: such were the two great debts that the Revolution owed to the *ancien régime*.

Finally, Saint-Germain attacked the sale of military posts. All his life he had pleaded the cause of the poor nobility; he was a man of Prussian-style military nobility, a specialist in the field of arms. As he could not redeem all posts at one stroke, he decided that they should lose one quarter of their value each time one was vacated, so that the financial value would be written off within four generations.

After Saint-Germain, Ségur pursued the work of technical renovation. He maintained its social inspiration, making further cutbacks by the 1781 regulation which reserved certain military ranks for sons who possessed at least four quarterings. But it was done rather grudgingly, for he declared to the Council: 'It would be better to tackle the unreasonable prejudice which is the ruin of the nobility by allowing it no other activity than the practice of arms.' While the attack on the sale of office pleased the poor nobles, who were rich in title alone and did not want to see its value diminished, the edict pertaining to the four quarterings united all the ancient nobility. It was in essence directed against the ennobled, since within the second order it disqualified all nobility after the middle of Louis XIV's reign.

This is significant evidence of the mechanism of aristocratic distinctions constantly in operation in old society, by which, among those who had held them for a long time, new privileges arrived to compensate for the risk of an upsurge in the number of titles, brought about by the financial needs of the monarchy. That mechanism, which split the second order into castes, created even more malcontents within the Third Estate than among the recently ennobled: by continually pushing farther back the barrier guarding the way to the highest social status, it made the way still less accessible to those who had not passed through the preliminary stages.

What the Third Estate bourgeois rightly took to be aristocratic arrogance frequently had its source in conflict between the nobles themselves. The 'feudal' *grand seigneur*, who despised the ennobled financier (though he might often marry his daughter), gave the tone to what Mirabeau called 'a torrent of contempt', the psychological mainspring of old French society. Adopted in order to reconstruct a military nobility, this edict aroused the Third Estate against 'reaction'. There was no state reform which could be compatible with the reinforcing of inequality, even if the intention was to replace parasitism and privilege with service to the state.

Under the long ministry of Vergennes (1774–87), a wise and methodical diplomat, the effort towards overseas recovery which had been made since Choiseul's time finally paid off: its aim at that time was revenge against Britain. At the same time, Vergennes did not abdicate from the European scene, where the partition of Poland had caused French influence to lose ground; he refused to help the Austrian ally in its German ambitions, and maintained a balance between the houses of Brandenburg and Habsburg. But the American conflict provided the opportunity for the great design against England.

In the conflict which developed in 1773–6, when American desire for autonomy had garbed itself in the Declaration of Independence (1776), French opinion had good reasons for taking sides: patriotism and philosophy, combined to form a new passion. An American office set up near Versailles enrolled volunteers with illustrious names – the Marquis de La Fayette, the Vicomte de Noailles, Ségur. In a strong position because of the family pact, Vergennes sought the support of Spain, then hesitated. At the beginning of 1778, he decided to sign a treaty of alliance with the new United States: this quickly led to war, in which Spain joined the following year.

While the naval war was going on, with great feats on both sides, and Admiral Suffren in the Indies was avenging the defeats of the Seven Years War, the decisive action took place in America itself: the relief army sent from Versailles to the American colonists, commanded by the Comte de Rochambeau, joined de Grasse's fleet and Washington's troops to obtain the capitulation of the British expeditionary force at Yorktown, in Chesapeake Bay (1781). The peace treaty was signed at Versailles at the beginning of 1783. France gained nothing from it but the freedom to fortify Dunkirk, plus Saint-Pierre and Miquelon, Tobago and the Senegal trading posts. But it had taken its revenge on Britain and erased the shame of the Treaty of Paris in 1763.

Nevertheless, the dynamic of weak governments is such that even their victories are turned into losses. The American war not only multiplied in the kingdom the numbers of admirers of the 1776 Declaration, soon to be known as 'patriots'; it had also cost, over five years, more than a thousand million livres and had aggravated the chronic malady of the country – its finances. It was a chronic disease, because no cure was possible, and one which became more and more serious as the urgency and impossibility of relief became more obvious. Public expenditure continued to grow in line with the obligations of the state. Under Antoine de Sartine, the reorganization of the Navy was swallowing up sums of money which swelled every year. Servicing the public debt became an ever heavier burden.

After Turgot, and some months of traditionalist reaction, it was Necker's turn. The monarchy stepped up its forms of therapy: after the liberal economist came the banker and economic planner. The choice, however, did not result from doctrinal alternatives. In reality, it marked a crucial watershed in the monarchy's policy: resort to pure financial technique and confidence in banks took the place of vague impulses towards fiscal reform. It was doubly a sign of the times, characteristic of the slackening hold of the government and the growing strength of banking capitalism. Not that Louis XVI's ancestors had never resorted to it, but *they* had not actually installed it in the post of Controller-General.

To be more precise, since he was not only a banker, but also Swiss and

Protestant, Necker did not receive the traditional title: first, he was Director of the Treasury, under the nominal supervision of an ousted Controller, and in the following year he became Director-General of Finance with sole authority. This only emphasized the technical limits of his powers: Necker had no right of entry to the king's Council, where the important decisions were made, notably about peace or war. He would not be able, as with Terray against Choiseul, or Turgot against Vergennes, to oppose war and its train of expenses: he was given the task of paying them off painlessly. To hark back to a classic distinction under the *ancien régime*, his advent marked the abdication of finance in the face of banking.

The great officers of the royal finances – known as *financiers* – were at the end of their wits and their resources; Terray's bankruptcies had ended by dealing a blow to the old system of borrowing against lifetime annuities. Now it was the turn of the banks, and of a private capitalist – without office and without country, but with a keen awareness of public opinion, and excellent at raising loans. After him, the great officers – Joly de Fleury, d'Ormesson, Calonne – remained trapped by these techniques.

It was a sign of the times that the abdications of the old monarchy in the face of money was greeted with joy by public opinion: mistrust of the government and the prestige of money joined hands. Moreover, there was Necker himself, eager to please, manipulated by family propaganda, naturalized by success and opinion. This banker was also a thinker, who would leave behind an important work, written mostly after this period, in leisure time left to him by political failure. But when he first came to power, it was not so much his thoughts that were fêted in Paris as his success and his image: that kind of overwhelming public approval was a very modern phenomenon.

Turgot had also received a similar welcome, but he had been one of the insiders naturally destined for the Control-General. Necker, though, having made a fortune in brilliant speculations on the Indies Company, had neither office nor even status, in a society where everything *was* office and status, and, apart from money, had but one other imponderable asset: the favour of public opinion.

On that he had built his road to power. Madame Necker's Fridays were one of the high spots of Paris, when the master of the house spent his money paying homage to sensibility and virtue in political and literary conversations. An *Éloge de Colbert*, a polemic against Turgot's *laissez-faire*, had further reassured traditional economists: Necker did not intend to abandon the poor to the cruelties of the market. In short, the Swiss banker was perhaps less revolutionary than the liberal *intendant*. Furthermore, at the court there was less to fear from a man whose best interests would be served if his past were forgotten, and who could reveal modern monetary secrets to the monarchy. Parisian *rentiers* living on their private means rejoiced as if they were the ones being put into power. That was why public opinion hailed a genius, where Maurepas had seen nothing but a banker.

His management would be rather in the form of administrative modernization. Orchestrated by fashionable philanthropic propaganda, the basic reforms of this saviour-minister mainly affected the running of the state's financial machinery: a reduction in the costs of tax collection, the termination of a certain number of useless offices, dismantling of the Tax Farm, attempts to improve public accountancy and, finally, in another sphere, the abolition of serfdom in the king's domains. Yet, for fear of the parlements and the clergy, this Protestant made not a single gesture on behalf of his fellow Protestants. For fear of the nobility's reactions, this commoner proposed no tax reforms. His most important idea in truly political affairs was once more to present to the king the concept of political representation.

He was unaware of the memorandum prepared by Du Pont for Turgot, but his project had no need of precise antecedents because it was so much in tune with the mood of the times. He had set out its principles in a confidential document to the king published in 1791: to entrust provincial fiscal and economic management to assemblies of property-holders, made up half from the Third Estate, a quarter from the nobility and a quarter from the clergy, voting by head. Necker preserved the distinction between the orders (doubling the representation of the Third, it is true), whereas Turgot (or Du Pont) had given consideration to property-owners only. He also abandoned the elective principle.

Four of these assemblies were created in 1779–80: one in Berry, the next in the Dauphiné, the third in Haute-Guyenne and the fourth in Moulins. The first members were appointed by the king, and thereafter co-opted their colleagues. Even this timid attempt, however, immediately ran into strong opposition: courtiers, *intendants*, parlements were all worried about these new powers; the institutions functioned only in Berry and Haute-Guyenne. This episode revealed once again the monarchy's inability to give the enlightened classes any organized means of being party to the administration of the kingdom.

Because he could not forge ahead with a policy of reforms, the banker Necker was administering a deficit and paying for the American war by way of royal lotteries and ever more costly loans. His main expedient was to increase state-guaranteed life annuities – manna for the bank, which specialized increasingly in the investment of public securities, thus foreshadowing one of its major later roles under the Restoration and the July monarchy. Not only did Necker obtain life annuity loans without making any distinction in interest rates according to the age ranges of the lenders, but he also left to the *rentiers* the choice of subjects on whose lives the interest would run.

It was a chance for lenders to think up almost endless variations on speculative schemes; the best-known was perfected by the Genevan banks, which gathered local capital together around thirty girls of tender age, selected on the best medical expertise for their optimal chances of survival. The figure of thirty met the need to find the lowest starting number on which to base the calculation of probabilities – the Dutch went as far as eighty.

Each of these young girls, surrounded by vigilant and single-minded solicitude on the part of everyone of importance in Geneva, concealed a fortune in each heartbeat. The town went into mourning at the early demise of one Pernette Elisabeth Martin, at the age of eight, on 16 July 1788, as she took with her a capital of over two million livres in life income. But that catastrophe was the exception, and the progress of the demographic forecast ensured the fortunes of the lenders and their banking intermediaries. It was the symptom of an entirely new mentality: the old tax expedients of the monarchy were being turned to the triumph of movable asset capitalism.

In total, between 1776 and 1781, 530 million in loans of all kinds fed the Treasury and financed a war which was all the more popular because it was painless. Money continued to flow in, and the resale of annuities enriched Parisian speculation. Even if the state was seriously compromising its future, Necker retained his popularity. In 1781, to counter-attack court intrigues to find his successor, he published the *Compte rendu*, a statement of accounts which concealed the expenditure of the extraordinary budget and revealed an apparent surplus revenue of ten million livres.

After three years of war and no new taxes, that was truly financial wizardry! But though this little book enjoyed immense public favour, it created conflict at court. The parlement drew up remonstrances on the provincial assemblies, the king's ministers were jealous, and the old *financiers* absolutely clear-sighted: the real deficit lay in the region of eighty million. Necker wanted to get the support of public opinion. He asked for the title of Minister of State, and also for general application of the system of provincial assemblies. On the king's refusal, he fell in May 1781.

His successors, Joly de Fleury and d'Ormesson, made mediocre, almost timid, use of the ordinary routine. Increases in taxes on consumer goods, a third *vingtième*, sales of offices, and, above all, massive borrowing: more than 400 million livres in two and a half years. When d'Ormesson came to grief against the Farm, suppressing its lease three years ahead of term in 1783, the fashionable Vaudreuil and Polignac coteries had their candidate, Calonne, accepted.

Calonne deserves better than association with those names; better, too, than his posthumous reputation. He is greater than the image of dishonest liquidator in which revolutionary historiography has imprisoned him. On many points he had ideas well in advance of his time: his plan rested chiefly on the modern concept that state expenditure should be favourable to the circulation of money, create purchasing power, 'initiate' an economic revival in order to boost the pool of tax revenue.

This interpretation of Calonne in a Keynesian light in fact rehabilitates part of his administration. The new Controller-General masterminded an entire economic policy: public works, fitting out of ports, a road network, various encouragements to industrial and commercial enterprises, the creation of a new Indies Company. He spent money in order to invest. He paid out in order to inspire confidence: annuity arrears (arrears on interest due) were honoured at term. To siphon speculative money towards the Treasury, he put an end to speculation in shares in the Discount Bank and on the import of Spanish piastres.

In the short term, however, this policy could live only on credit: on his installation as Controller, Calonne had found, out of 600 million livres in annual revenue, 176 million committed in advance, 250 million absorbed by debt service and 390 million in accounts in arrears to be settled. He borrowed money on all sides, even more and at a higher rate than his predecessors: 650 million in three and a half years. Necker had a good opportunity in 1784, in his *Administration des finances*, to explain to public opinion – which believed in his *Compte rendu* of 1781 – the mechanism of bankruptcy. For he was touching a sensitive spot: he was denouncing the last of the great court *financiers* to bourgeois *rentiers*, to an entire Parisian democracy for whom he, Necker, was the ideal man.

On this point, the hatred of the Jacobins – or, conversely, the friendship of the Polignacs – had not mistaken its object. Calonne's ministry belonged to the last fine days of the aristocracy. A true son of the times, the descendant of a long line of eminent lawyers, former king's *intendant* in Lille, he was the man of the *grands seigneurs*.

Historians have for too long paid too much attention to the polemics of the era and the little cliques of intriguers and speculators who hovered around Calonne anticipating with their pocket-books the decisions of the state. But the essence lies elsewhere, often concealed in the mystery of princely book-keeping, royal gifts and court speculation: one would need to reconstruct the entire circuit of the money borrowed by Calonne to understand how these years were without doubt the most dazzling in court civilization. Versailles fêted a magician who handed out money right and left – another financial wizard like John Law, in an even shakier world.

In 1785 the king spent 137 million in the cash settlement of debts to unnamed beneficiaries. During that time, he wrote off several princely bankruptcies: that of the Comte d'Artois, the second in six years: those of two great families, the Guéménées and Soubises. The 'enrichissez-vous' of Calonne was not that of the bourgeois king; he was addressing court society, princely and noble houses and, for the time being, the *financiers* in their service. It was neither a surreptitiously revolutionary attempt, nor an international banking conspiracy; it was the last great effort to restore *ancien régime* society in all its glory and splendour.

Sinking borrowed money into the parasitic round of court life proved eventually to be the downfall of this aristocratic sleight-of-hand: never had it been more apparent that the social and political structures of the *ancien régime* were compromising economic and financial stability. In a kingdom where, ultimately, everything depended on agricultural wealth and taxes levied on land, court nobles and the King – in short, the state – were increasingly living beyond their means; that was what the townspeople and the *rentiers* quite rightly perceived in their hatred of Calonne.

It is therefore true that the last great *financier* of the monarchy had helped to crystallize anti-aristocratic feeling, and had certainly brought forward by several years the moment of decisive choice. During the summer of 1786, the deficit was running at over 100 million livres, there were 250 million of debt in arrears outstanding, and half the income of the year ahead was spent in advance. Loyal to the only world he could imagine, which he loved, Calonne unearthed the greatest plan for saving the *ancien régime* that the century had produced: that of the physiocrats.

On 20 August 1786 he presented to the king his *Précis d'un plan d'amélioration des finances* (Outline of a plan to improve finances), built round the idea of fiscal reform. It comprised the replacement of the *vingtièmes* by a tax levied on all lands, without exception, and proportional to income. This was the 'territorial subsidy', which would be paid in kind; the physiocratic tax system had found a new follower. Calonne moreover advocated the reduction of the *taille*, the simplification of the *gabelle* (salt tax) and gradual cancellation of state debts by the transfer of royal domains. A second series of measures aimed at unifying the national market by freeing the grain trade, and the total abolition of internal Customs.

Finally, as with Turgot and Necker, the plan was crowned by a pyramid of consultative assemblies which were to give all property-owners a part in the government of the kingdom: they would have to be elected by suffrage based on property qualification (*censitaire*), without reference to the traditional orders of society. Calonne was thus closer to the *municipalités* of Du Pont's memorandum than to Necker's assemblies. Du Pont, as always, was still lurking in the wings. Never, even under Turgot, had such a vast and daring reorganization been proposed to Louis XVI. The king allowed himself to be convinced. In any case, he hardly had a choice any more, because he refused the bankruptcy which some of the privileged were seeking, in total indifference to the fate of the bourgeois *rentiers*.

But Calonne knew that there was no chance of getting such projects accepted by the parlement of Paris. He suggested to the king a procedure used in the past by Henri IV and Louis XIII: the meeting of an assembly of notables, appointed by the Crown, whose docility could be more easily relied upon. Despite Vergennes's misgivings, this plan pleased the king. As usual, execution was slow, while Calonne survived only by expedients. On 29 December 1786, at the end of a royal Council, Louis XVI announced his intention of 'assembling people of various conditions and the most qualified in my state, in order to inform them of my views on the relief of my peoples, the ordering of my finances and the reform of various abuses.'

He thought he was merely defining a procedure. In fact, he was setting in motion a system.

2

The Revolution of 1789: 1787–1791

THE ASSEMBLY OF NOTABLES

With the convening of the notables, the French monarchy had entered into the machinery of consultation: a strong government, a definite policy might have found support in that. But a weak and indecisive government risked exposing its isolation and hastening its own downfall; a single breach in the wall and a rout would ensue. Calonne's little artifice thus unleashed one of the most gigantic crashes in history. It inaugurated an acceleration of events in which the historian can with hindsight read the preface to a revolution.

It all started with the nobility. For those notables were nobles. When one considers how many of them were bishops, *parlementaires* and ennobled members of the Third Estate, noble privilege and the tradition of rank entirely dominated this small assembly, suddenly vested with a role that was too great for it: to represent the nation to the king. How strange was the spectacle of a Controller-General assembling the largest shareholders of a company in order to ask them to do away with the profits. But Calonne had overestimated the indulgence of his audience. Coaxed by Parisian opinion, the assembly of notables found it all the easier to refuse to submit, since Calonne's proposals effectively threatened tradition.

By opposing a single and proportional tax, they were protecting their own interests and at the same time gratifying public opinion. They had only to follow this trend to unite, in an anti-absolutist outburst, with the general feeling of nearby Paris, still hankering after the good Necker, and to make a scapegoat of the man who had sought their backing. In this manoeuvre, which backfired on him, Calonne became the personification of the deficit and a wasteful financial system. The shortfall of 113 million livres, to which he had admitted, was ascribed to his mismanagement alone. In April the King yielded to the notables and replaced Calonne with one of the most vehement among them – Marie-Antoinette's candidate, Loménie de Brienne, archbishop of Toulouse.

An intelligent and ambitious prelate, the archbishop began by giving with open hands. He took liberal measures, such as recognizing the civil status of Protestants, which annoyed the clergy. He persuaded Louis XVI to accept a fundamental reform of the state: just before its demise, the *ancien régime* professed to renounce one of its constituent principles, administrative centralization.

Brienne had inherited the idea of provincial assemblies from Calonne: set up in the *généralités* of the *pays d'élection* (areas in which provincial assemblies ceded their right to approve taxation) these assemblies, composed of the three orders (with a doubled Third Estate), would move in beside the *intendants* and would be called upon to replace them gradually in the country's administration. The king appointed half the members within each of the three orders: co-optation provided the remainder.

About twenty of these assemblies began to operate at the end of the year, leaving 'intermediary commissions' between the plenary sessions to keep an eye on grain, side by side with the *intendant* who, in theory at least, was largely relieved of his office. Thus a revolution had occurred before the Revolution, effected by the monarchy which, by renouncing its nature, was making way for society. Versailles no longer controlled very much, least of all the pace of change. The time of reforms from above had passed, to the benefit of public opinion, which paid heed to the demagogy of the parlements, the regional high courts.

It was necessary to get back to the heart of the problem: how to raise money. In certain periods of history there is a sort of inevitability attached to office: Brienne was forced to resume the idea of a land tax, to which he added an increased stamp charge. He aroused anew the hostility of his erstwhile colleagues, who declared themselves without mandate to vote on these projects; this was an implicit reference to another assembly which *would* have received such a mandate. So the Estates-General came about through the nobles' grand plan to regain control of the state. Everyone – reformist, conservative, bourgeois, aristocrat - rushed to welcome it in the name of anti-absolutism. Louis XVI, who had never understood how to divide and rule, was now up against the moment of liberal unanimity, or, one might as well say, of the parlements.

A sort of gradual widening of the campaign developed: the notables having been dispatched, the parliamentary relay transmitted the new watchword from the court to the Hôtel de Ville (town hall of Paris), and from Paris to the provinces. For some months the large towns in the realm regained their traditional spokesmen. In July 1787, after the dismissal of the notables, the parlement of Paris demanded an Estates-General, affirming it to be the only body with the power to agree to new taxes: that was why, in August, it rejected the financial part of Brienne's programme. Conflict, *lit de justice*, exile, recall: the classic scenario lasted barely a summer. In October, there was no longer any question of reform, but simply of borrowing: the reinstated parlement made registration conditional upon the convening of the Estates-General.

Enfeebled government made a last effort and imposed the loan. To the

Duc d'Orléans, who objected that this was illegal, Louis XVI retaliated with what he had always been taught: 'It is legal because I wish it.' He exiled his cousin and, at the very last, in May 1788, accepted a series of edicts from his Keeper of the Seals, Lamoignon, 'decapitating' the parlements: it was the story of Maupeou all over again. Taking the initiative, the magistrates had just reaffirmed the 'fundamental laws of the realm', voting on taxes by the Estates-General, the right of registration, and the liberties and rights of individuals and corporate bodies. The royal army surrounded the Paris parlement, which yielded only to force, after thirty hours of warnings.

The year 1788 thus saw the culmination of the old struggle which had begun after Louis XIV's death, between absolutist administration and *parlementaire* resistance. But it soon revealed to what extent the inequality of political forces had grown since Louis XVI's accession. Between a solitary and discredited monarchy, with nothing to offer but vague inclinations, and the great liberating watchword of the Estates-General, uniting all ambitions, public feeling did not hesitate.

The provincial towns were even more vociferous than Paris. High court magistrates flew to the aid of Parisian colleagues, enveloped in the same popular fervour. French clergy and local nobility were no less ardent in their battle for 'liberties', during this short year when no one could yet gauge the chasm which could separate the plural from the singular in such a word. In fact, the provinces in which the first two orders of the realm possessed the strongest political positions were the most relentless in combating the king's and Lamoignon's edicts. They were the ones who had Provincial Estates, or remembered when they had had them, and who now asked for their restitution: the eighteenth century briefly blossomed for the nobility for an instant before it vanished.

Unrest reached all towns with a parlement. Risings were especially violent in places where the conflict between the courts and the Crown was most long-standing, and where it had smouldered throughout the century: in Béarn, Brittany and the Dauphiné. In Rennes, where the nobility immediately declared its solidarity with the parlement, gentlemen, barristers and students held a combined demonstration on 9 May; the next day, the king's representatives were stoned by the crowd and forced to take refuge in the governor's palace. In Grenoble, the protesting parlement was exiled by the Duc de Clermont-Tonnerre, commanding the province. On the day fixed for the departure of the magistrates, 7 June, the tocsin was sounded, summoning a town already filled with people: it was market day. All the folk from the surrounding mountains came down to lend a hand. Clermont-Tonnerre's soldiers were pelted with tiles hurled from the rooftops. The revolt was so violent that the king's representative capitulated and allowed the parlement to be reinstated.

But it had also given rise to a revolutionary institution: a 'central committee', dominated by barristers like Jean-Joseph Mounier and Barnave, which on its own authority, at the end of July, convoked the

Provincial Estates. In the big château of the rich merchant, Claude Périer, where the three orders met together, the assembly of Vizille heralded a new era: contrary to what was happening in Pau or Rennes, the men of the Third Estate had the numbers and the authority: they did not confine themselves to demanding the restoration of old provincial franchises, but drew the nobles with them to the national level: in response to Mounier, they in fact voted that 'the three orders of the province shall not grant taxes, by free gift or otherwise, until their representatives have discussed the matter in the Estates-General of the realm.' Parlements and personal privileges were immediately superseded. A national will was taking shape behind anti-absolutist unanimity.

Louis XVI himself could do nothing but yield to the torrent; on 8 August, the Estates-General was convened for 1 May 1789. Not before time, because on 15 August state payments were suspended. The 24th saw the dismissal of Brienne. Necker had become the providential, or rather, inevitable man; his name alone deferred bankruptcy and set Lamoigon's efforts at naught. The wave of popularity which carried him back to power was far too strong to be controlled; nothing mattered any more in France except the imminent meeting of the Estates-General.

At that precise moment, the end of the summer of 1788, history unveiled its real significance to clear-sighted contemporaries, rather as, at the theatre, when the scenery shifts a little and discloses what is going on behind the façade. But what really *was* going on? The nobility and parlements refused to alter anything whatsoever in the traditional method of designation and voting of the Estates: one third of the representatives for each order, and voting by order, which automatically conferred the majority on the privileged. Now the Third Estate advanced the example of Vizille, where its representation had been doubled, and the orders held a common meeting; this was an admission that it wanted the means of dominating the common assembly, since it expected – with good reason – some backing from among the nobility and the lower clergy.

Besides, it had already received a certain amount: the 'national party' – the term 'patriot' also was already in use – which organized the campaign for the 'doubling' of Third Estate representation brought together a number of liberal aristocrats and enlightened bourgeois. The collective wave of hope was so strong that it transported many imaginations beyond social confines, towards a reconciled nation of 25 million citizens. Though the notables of the Third Estate, in towns throughout the kingdom, formed the nucleus of this vast movement of opinion, co-ordinated at the summit by a Committee of Thirty, they did not hold the monopoly: the culture of the century and a growing recognition of merit, which had been spreading for a long time, brought many instances of individual support from above.

The increased number of provincial academies, clubs and Freemasons' societies had foreshadowed the new world in which 'ranks' would henceforth fraternize. Thus, alongside Jacques-Pierre Brissot, Mounier or

Barnave, or the young *Parlementaire* Adrien Du Port, several heirs to the greatest names in the kingdom signified their support in advance for the end of privileges: La Fayette, hero of the war in America; Bishop Talleyrand, just appointed to Autun; the Duc de La Rochefoucauld, inimical to the morals of the court; his cousin Liancourt, the philanthropic agronomist; the Duc d'Aiguillon, one of the richest landowners in France.

All the same, some of these liberal *grands seigneurs* retained a sense of distance and conceived their action as an indispensable adaptation of the aristocracy to the new times: everything must change so that everything could stay the same. The Third Estate revolution would spontaneously feel itself closer to renegades like the Abbé Sieyès or the Comte de Mirabeau, elected on its own lists.

At the end of 1788, it put forward the quintessential revolutionary idea: going beyond liberal unanimity, it demanded equality. The fight against absolutism was already won – and had been for far longer than contemporaries imagined. It then discovered an essential element which had remained buried, undisclosed, like humiliation: the hatred born of a society of orders and a 'racism' of birth, exacerbated by the separation into the castes of the various ranks of society. Aristocratic society at the end of the eighteenth century, corrupt in its principle, suddenly revealed the psychological and political ravages provoked by the obsessive fear of differentiation: *bourgeois honour impugned had become equality*. History was already being accelerated in this cut-and-dried equation. It had made compromise between the enlightened classes very difficult; on the contrary, all parts of the Third Estate shared a common hatred of the aristocracy. That is evident from just one example: the Abbé Sieyès had become the man of the moment.

SIEYÈS

We must linger a little over the name of Sieyès – the best symbol of the French Revolution. Jacques Bainville observes that Sieyès punctuated the frenzied advance of the French Revolution with three utterances. At the beginning of 1789: 'What is the Third Estate? Everything. What has it been up to now in the political order? Nothing.' After 1793: 'I survived.' In the autumn of 1799: 'I seek a sword.' He was not the greatest man of action of the French Revolution; he was, however, its most profound political thinker. He gave it an initial impetus, in the winter of 1788–9, with three successive pamphlets: *Essai sur les privilèges* (Essay on privileges), *Vues sur les moyens d'exécution dont les représentants de la France pourront disposer en 1789* (Views on the means of action available to representatives of France in 1789), and lastly, *Qu'est-ce que le Tiers État?* (What is the Third Estate?), the most celebrated, which made his name renowned in the space of a few weeks.

They all appeared over two months, between November 1788 and

January 1789, at the time when Louis XVI and Necker were taking their
decisions on methods of convening and assembling the Estates, in the
throes of political crisis. Few books have acted with as much force on
major events as these three occasional pamphlets, written in haste but with
extraordinary power, in which a priest who had not been too badly treated
by the *ancien régime* developed a philosophy of revolution in the name of
the Third Estate.

Sieyès was a priest. Born in Fréjus into a modest bourgeois family which
was hard put to it to establish its five children, he followed the usual
ecclesiastical channels, without any special vocation but as an intellectually
gifted child. Taken under the wing of the Jesuits, those great unearthers of
talent, and then by the Congréganistes de la Doctrine Chrétienne, he was
in Paris in 1765 at the small seminary of Saint-Sulpice – the large one was
for young noblemen training to become bishops – where his teachers
found nothing to remark on, apart from his 'sly' nature, but his insatiable
appetite for books.

Ordained a priest in 1772, he had read everything about the philosophy
of the Enlightenment, both French and English. The notes he made
during those long years of study, preserved in the National Archives, show
evidence of an unlimited intellectual appetite, somewhat undisciplined,
ranging from literature to metaphysics, art and music, with an especial
passion for philosophy and political economy; Locke and the physiocrats
were the writers whom he constantly read, reread, discussed, challenged,
questioned.

In 1775 he wrote a *Lettre aux économistes sur leur système de politique et de
morale* (Letter to the physiocrats on their political and moral system),
which he did not publish. Everything in the mechanism of different
societies interested the young Sieyès: money, banking, labour, trade,
production, property, sovereignty, citizenship – everything, with the
exception of history. The basis of his thinking was political, in the widest
sense of the word, and conformed to the dominant trend of French
Englightenment philosophy: it was a question of thinking of society in
accordance with reason, whereas it offered only the spectacle of unreason.
From an early age Sieyès was fanatical about public happiness.

The potent and simplifying genius of this young priest could find no
outlet in the world of the *ancien régime*. First of all, he needed protectors in
order to get himself a post, to find a sinecure and help his family. A letter
of 1773 to his father – he was twenty-five years old – at the time when he
had just missed a coveted benefice, is very revealing both of him and of the
old society: 'If it had gone well, I would have been somebody, instead of
which I am nothing. Never mind, I cannot complain yet, because my
course is not yet run. I will either make my way in life or perish.' He
found that life in the train of an aristocratic bishop, first of Tréguier, then
of Chartres, Jean-Baptiste Joseph de Lubersac, a *philosophe* like himself,
and also like him an administrative priest. So the Abbé Sieyès was established, soon provided with a benefice, then becoming a canon of Chartres

in 1783, and finally Vicar General, the bishop's closest assistant and already a minor personality in the Church of France.

He had a fine status, but his real life lay elsewhere: not in religion (there is not the slightest evidence that he was ever interested in that) nor yet in his private life (everything indicates that he did not have one), but in his books and the intellectual life of the century, which he was continually debating, pen in hand, for his own satisfaction. When history's hour struck, this priest had published nothing but had written a great deal; he had lived nothing but meditated on everything: the *philosophes* Helvétius and Condillac, Rousseau, Turgot, the physiocrats, Hume, Adam Smith.

A contemporary, the Swiss Étienne Dumont, a friend of Mirabeau and one of the sharpest observers of the political world of 1789, has left the best pages yet on the subject of Sieyès, as witness this note, indispensable for anyone wanting to understand the nature of his intellect and the secret of his oracular behaviour in 1789–90: 'One day, having dined at M. de Talleyrand's, we went for a long walk in the Tuileries; the Abbé Sieyès was more communicative, more talkative than usual; in a burst of familiarity and openness, having talked to me about several of his works, his studies, his manuscripts, he spoke this striking sentence: "Politics is a science which I believe I have mastered."' Here was the rare coincidence of a man who had been unable to set down his ideas now finding a theatre where they could be enacted.

When he published his first pamphlet in November 1788, it was clear that this deviser of systems, the abstract intellectual, ideal prey for the great critics of 1789, from Burke to Taine, was also driven by a tremendous passion. The *Essai sur les privilèges* effectively set the tone for what was to be the motivating force of the Revolution several months before it broke out: hatred of the aristocracy. It is a short work of about twenty pages, violent, categorical, taut as an arrow winging to its target and piercing old society in its vital spot – privilege.

What is it, what else can it be, this privilege, if not the ultimate corruption of the concept of law, since it forms categories of individuals who are strangers to what makes the community? Sieyès at once establishes democratic universalism as the natural law of society, the only one which conforms with reason. Privilege removes its beneficiary from the public sphere of the state in order to define him by particular interests which keep him apart from it by placing him outside citizenship. It also brings in its wake antisocial psychological effects: the feeling of belonging to another race, the passion for domination, exaggerated self-esteem, etc.

Unlike Rousseau, Sieyès was not against modern society; if he occasionally speaks with Rousseau's accents, it is to denounce the moral corruption of aristocratic society alone. In that society, where privilege abounds, there is but one culprit, the very incarnation of evil: the nobility. The nobles have the monopoly of honour, the great driving force of every society; they cannot support their lofty position without money, the other great social reward; but, deprived by their very privilege of legal means of earning wealth, they live only as court parasites, estranged from the nation as a whole, their sole industry being a kind of high-class mendicancy.

Sieyès, who had taken such a long time to write anything other than notes on his reading, had reached the age of forty before circumstances drove him to publish his first twenty pages. But what pages they were! The nobility stands condemned there before the tribunal of reason, cast out from the nation, together with the court turned into the scapegoat of the movement of opinion in favour of the regeneration of the kingdom. The solitary abbé had guessed what was to happen, and suddenly took a hand in shaping events. His pamphlet even suggested what one year later would be called the '*ancien régime*' – that imaginary breaking point which consigned preceding centuries to nothingness: 'A time will come when our outraged offspring will be astounded to read our history, and will give that most inconceivable insanity the names it deserves.'

Sieyès's second pamphlet, *Vues sur les moyens d'exécution dont les représentants de la France pourront disposer en 1789* deals with the matter of the Estates-General from the angle of their necessary transformation into a 'National Assembly', vested with constituent sovereignty. The abbé was aware of the classic objection made to a republic, that is, a people's government, in a large country: the nation can no longer be assembled to allow it to discuss and vote on laws, as was done in the ancient city.

He got round this by way of a theory of representation, by which he extended to the political field the idea of division of labour elaborated by one of his favourite authors, Adam Smith. It was a question of 'selecting from the mass of citizens different classes of representatives who as a whole form, in their person and their kind of work, what we call the *public establishment*'. This 'establishment' is set up in accordance with a 'proxy' given by society to its mandatories, whether they be executive agents or legislators. In all cases, these mandatories do not therefore represent mere fractions of the social body (their electorate, for example) but the entire nation.

Moreover, the process of delegation of legislative power must not be handed on too far down the line, so that it can stay close to its source: 'Every legislature continually needs to be refreshed by the democratic spirit; it must therefore not be placed too far distant from the original initiators. Representation is there for those being represented; so the general will must not be lost, by passing through a number of intermediaries, in a disastrous aristocratism.' Thus Sieyès laid down the foundations of a theory of representative government, one torn from the start between the inalienable nature of the nation's rights and the delegated sovereignty of its representatives. Even before it had taken place, the Revolution had pinpointed what would be one of its greatest problems.

Shortly afterwards, in January 1789, *Qu'est-ce que le Tiers État?* resumed the argument of the *Essai sur les privilèges*, enlarging on it and being more specific. It is a longer, more complex pamphlet, simultaneously more theoretical and more practical, a treatise and a battlecry, a mixture which accurately presages the spirit of the Revolution. On a philosophical plane, the beginning of the text shows the extent of Sieyès's debt to the physiocrats and English political economy: society is approached from the viewpoint of the economic activity of its members, and as the place where the progress of civilization operates by the production of wealth. From all the useful classes that contribute to it by their labour, nobility is by definition excluded, since it cannot exercise a private profession; as for the public services which it is supposed to undertake, these could be more usefully carried out by men of the Third Estate. For it is absurd to place at the head of the state people who are defined by what separates them from the public good, these 'strangers in our very midst', says Sieyès, a 'caste':

That is the right word. It denotes a class of men who, without function and without usefulness, enjoy personal privileges merely by the fact of their existence . . . The noble caste has usurped all the good positions; it has turned them into a kind of hereditary possession and therefore exploits them, not in the spirit of social law, but for its private profit.

By this device, Sieyès extends the accusation to the monarchy, which is guilty of being the slave of that parasitic aristocracy: it is not the king who reigns, it is the court. The complementary nature of the nobility and the king, which Montesquieu had seen as a balancing act favouring the liberty of individuals, becomes for the abbé the combined domination of private interests over those of the nation: a forceful argument, with a promising future in that it shifts condemnation from the social to the political, including the old royalty in the curse hurled at the nobility. The court was there, close at hand, buzzing with intrigues and loaded with wealth, a very exclusive party for the privileged, perfectly illustrating the evil denounced by the prosecutor for the people. Monarchic centralization had produced both Versailles and Paris, *the* court and *the* town, as if to present two perfectly opposed embodiments – of privilege and public opinion.

What sort of society could be rebuilt upon this excommunication of the nobility, upon the ruins of that absurd regime? One dictated by reason, or science, which is its other name. Sieyès challenged every lesson drawn from the nation's past, and every example from abroad. Reading him, one realizes how revolutionary reason had been constructed, like an abstract deduction drawn from absolute and universal principles: as has been seen, he rejected any adjustment of the existing order, which stood condemned in its entirety; he denied the worth of any example in the English constitution, although acknowledging that it had a character 'astounding for the time when it was established'. But a century after 1688, the French were benefiting from the progress of the Enlightenment: 'Do not let us be discouraged if we find nothing in history to suit our situation. The true science of the state of society does not go back very far.' What he meant was that he had just founded it! A little later Mirabeau called him 'Mahomet'.

All those individuals, or the ensemble of those classes of individuals, engaged in the production of social wealth or in public service form a political community which Sieyès calls a *nation*: a cardinal word, one of the strongest in revolutionary vocabulary, but also one of the most enigmatic, because it reprocesses the 'flesh' of all the history constituted by the kings to form the basis of what is being born – the unique legitimacy of the community. The 'laws of the nation' in the face of royal 'despotism' had been a current theme of *parlementaire* opposition, by which jurists referred to the kingdom's customary 'constitution', buried in the mists of antiquity. For Sieyès, the nation means the community formed by the association of individuals who decide to live freely under a common law, forged by their representatives. It is the constituent will, the social contract itself in its founding act; the nobility has no part in it, since nobles escape the universality of the law and have their own private assemblies.

It was towards this founding act that the next Estates-General could and must proceed; the people already enjoyed a certain civil emancipation, through the progress of what the Scottish philosophers had called 'commercial society'. Now it had to constitute itself into a political society in order ultimately to form a nation. Only the Third Estate could do this, because it alone constituted in advance the body of those associated with the common enterprise.

It was nothing, yet it was everything: that was the famous phrase in which Sieyès gave a radically new meaning to the old institution of the Estates-General, and showed the future representatives of the Third Estate where their duty lay, as sole guardians of the national will. It was not enough that the numbers of members of the commons should be doubled or that voting should be by head: the privileged, for as long as they were defined by privilege, were not representable. The Third Estate must meet separately: 'It will not join with the nobility and the clergy, and will not vote with them either by order or by head . . . It will be said that the Third Estate by itself cannot form the Estates-General: it will make up a National Assembly.'

The argument of this celebrated book is such that it can be read at two levels. Sieyès presents a complex theory of the formation of the body politic starting from individuals in civil society; he combines a classically liberal starting-point, the multiplicity of private interests typifying modern man, with the construction – almost an obsession – of a unitarian general will, which is inalienably possessed by the nation, delegated to and subsequently exercised by its representatives.

But the triumph of the pamphlet lies less in this learned reflection than in what it offers, with brilliant simplicity, to anti-aristocratic passion. Public opinion is burying the years of contempt under a rediscovered equality, which has once more become the natural principle of every society. It excludes nobles from the nation. It celebrates the death of the court and its courtiers, the end of noble arrogance, and its own deliverance from social humiliation. *Qu'est-ce que le Tiers État?* offers us the French

Revolution's biggest secret, which will form its deepest motivating force – hatred of the nobility: as well as being a thinker, the abbé was a resentful man, settling old scores with the old society. In resolving his lifetime's quarrel with the well-born, he had touched the fiercest passion of public opinion, which found a voice in him.

Now, the king was seeking advice from that very opinion, though he believed he was still addressing the orders of the realm. This misunderstanding deserves some comment.

PREPARATIONS FOR THE ESTATES-GENERAL

The institution of the Estates-General had belonged to the tradition of the French monarchy since the end of the Middle Ages; it had often been used by kings of France between the fourteenth and sixteenth centuries.[1] Its purpose was to assemble round the monarch, when he so desired, the 'representation' of the kingdom, intended to assist him with its opinions and advice. 'Representation' must be understood in the old sense of the word – one of the most interesting in both ancient and modern politics – which goes back to the very nature of old society. The individual had no existence other than by membership and solidarity with units such as the family, the community, the corporate body, the order – defined by rights which were both collective and personal, since they were group privileges shared by each of the members. The social universe was thus formed by a pyramid of corporate bodies which had received their position and their titles from history and the king of France, according to a hierarchy in keeping with the natural order of the world.

The 'representation' of this universe to the king worked quite naturally from the bottom upwards: the upper level 'represented' the lower which, by its position, it incorporated and whose identity it took over. The king of France, at the summit of the pyramid, subsumed and embodied the ensemble of corporate bodies constituting the nation, to fashion from them one sole body of which he was the head; his consultation with the 'Estates' had as its only objective to set the seal on the unity-identity of society and its government. In the framework of this concept of the social aspect, the process of 'representation' was not intended to develop a common political will arising from the interests or wills of individuals, but rather to express and transmit from the bottom upwards, and right to the very top, the requests (by definition homogeneous) of the corporate bodies of the realm. That is why it was linked to the 'imperative mandate', by which every community delegated to the higher level representatives who were not

[1] In the following pages I summarize an article which I wrote for a collection entitled *The Political Culture of the Old Regime*, vol. 2 of K. M. Baker (ed.), *The French Revolution and the Creation of Modern Political Culture*.

entrusted with the task of 'representing' them in the modern sense of the word, but simply with being the faithful spokesmen of their wishes.

The rules of convocation had never acquired a fixed form. Electoral methods, right to vote, the number of constituencies and deputies – nothing more. If a systematic history of the Estates-General were to be made, it would offer an excellent illustration of the characteristic incapability of the *ancien régime* – in spite or because of its incessant legislative activity – to formulate fixed rules regarding public law and official institutions (a theme dear to de Tocqueville, who saw in it one of the origins of the Revolution's *tabula rasa*).

When, in July 1788, the decision was taken to convene the Estates-General to consult it on ways of resolving the crisis the kingdom was going through, no body of doctrine or statutory documents existed to help the royal administration define the rules of the electoral game. Moreover, that consultation procedure had fallen into disuse, at the wish of the kings, since the first half of the seventeenth century. If, for want of a doctrine, the King's jurists wished to find a legal precedent, they had to turn back to the Estates-General of 1614. The last sitting was already nearly 200 years old: there were no archives, not even an oral record. The victim of its own practices, absolute monarchy no longer possessed either heritage or tradition which would allow it to consult public opinion in indisputable form.

Therefore, by decree of the king's Council on 5 July 1788, the king asked his subjects to send to the court 'memoranda, information and clarifications' on the conduct of the Estates. He appealed chiefly to the learned societies, by the device of a tribute to the academies, which prompted ironic comment from de Tocqueville, who was surprised that such a topic had been submitted to them. But during those last years of the eighteenth century the problem of the vote and political representation – in the modern sense this time – had really become a philosophical question, discussed by the savants, as can be seen in the works of Condorcet, for example. Though tradition was silent, confused, too distant or too faint, philosophy could answer in its place, at the behest of the monarchy itself.

With the hindsight of two centuries of democratic practice, no government in the world today would engage, with this kind of innocence, in a problem with such far-reaching consequences as the methods of organizing a ballot. But that experience was precisely what the French monarchy lacked. It trusted in the new spirit, which was already prevailing, to return to an ancient institution with very few rules. Not that matters really had such clear-cut simplicity, because many political intrigues interfered with regulatory decisions: the royal entourage tried to settle old scores with the privileged, who were guilty of unleashing the revolt, while Necker, at least the most popular if not the most influential minister, cautiously explored the route towards an English-style monarchy. But in the two key texts of 27 December 1788 and 24 January 1789, as well as in all the documents relating to the organization of the impending Estates-General, the general management of thoughts and decision was certainly influenced by that dialogue of the new spirit with a lost tradition, which it permeated throughout without obliterating it.

On 6 November 1788, when Louis XVI met the assembly of notables to get their advice on the matter, Necker, opening the session, underlined the changes which had taken place since 1614, and put forward the idea of 'equity' of representation: that meant not only the doubling of the Third Estate, but also proportionality between the numbers of those represented and their representatives. The two proposals were justified by the recent transformations in the economy and in society. The implementation of the first would have the greatest bearing on the subsequent sequence of events, after the fusion of the deputies of all three orders into the National Assembly in June.

Intellectually speaking, however, the second idea is the more revolutionary. In fact, even if it seemed for the moment limited only to the Third Estate elections, it was inseparable from the modern idea of representation: in trying to set up a stable connection between every representative and the number of his electors, it came back to the concept of individuals possessing equal rights in the formation of political power and of a 'national' assembly. From what one can read of the deliberations of the notables, who were nobles, it is less surprising to find them on the whole hostile to the doubling of the Third Estate and innovations, than to see them devote so much comment to the idea of a necessary proportionality between the population of a constituency and the number of its deputies.

There are many quotations on this theme to be extracted from the records of a meeting which assembled the greatest noble names in the French monarchy. The importance attached to argument in opposition to its final decisions on the doubling of the Third Estate and proportionality between represented and representatives reveals how little assured the majority of those 'notables' were about the imprescriptibility of their rights. Furthermore, when it came to discussing methods of voting within the Third Estate, this assembly of the privileged came out in favour of universal suffrage, by a very large majority, without making any distinction between the right to elect and to be elected – whereas that distinction would be characteristic of revolutionary legislation.

Now at last, Necker's report of 27 December 1788 on the preparation of electoral regulation could allow the spirit of the times a major role. Recalled to power by opinion rather than by royalty, the philosopher-administrator finally had the chance to implement his ideas on the need to let elected assemblies participate in government, representing the wants of society. But the Protestant banker, mindful of his failure in 1781, also knew better than anyone that he would have to mollify the nobility and the '*grands*', handling their amour-propre even more delicately than their vested interests, as he had shrewdly noted in *L'Administration des finances* ('In France, distinctions of status form the keenest subject of interest; obviously, no one objects to the pecuniary advantages to be gained, but it is the tactful handling of ideas of superiority which satisfies the most active feeling.') From that stemmed the contradictory nature of his text, midway between tradition and innovation. Not in the sense that a political compromise would be effected within each of the points under discussion: certain questions were treated according to the spirit of innovation, others left to tradition – or, rather, to the prevailing understanding of tradition. Two spirits are in contention for the minister's document, but they are simply superimposed, with no attempt made to reconcile them.

They are both stated successively at the beginning of the report: the first rests on the precedent of 1614, the second on public opinion, which in so far as principles were concerned, was the minister's overriding reference, since it led him to make the fundamental recommendation of proportioning the number of Third Estate deputies to the size of the population represented:

There is only one opinion in the kingdom on the necessity to adjust, as far as possible, the number of deputies from each *bailliage* [bailiwick] to the size of its population, and since it is possible in 1788 to establish this proportion on the basis of certain knowledge, it would obviously be unreasonable to abandon these measures of enlightened justice merely to follow in servile fashion the example of 1614.

These few lines said it all, through the indirect praise for the statistical efforts of the *intendants* and their staff: drawing its unanimity from knowledge and justice, public opinion was paramount, while at the same time there was a kind of modern political representation, based on both the equal rights of individuals and technico-administrative rationality. Noteworthy also is the rejection of a 'servile' imitation of the 1614 precedent. Through the intermediary of its minister, the monarchy itself set reason and justice against tradition.

The recommendation for doubling the Third Estate was made, starting from an exposition of the order's motives. On that point – the most hotly discussed in the current national debate – Necker first prudently presented the list of supporters for each of the two arguments. But this double enumeration revealed the incomparable superiority in influence and numbers of the innovators, because when all was said and done, besides a minority of notables and nobles, they comprised 'the public wish of that vast portion of your subjects known as the Third Estate'. Lastly, for good measure, the minister invoked 'the deep murmur of the whole of Europe, which generally favours all ideas of common equity'. This was a way of introducing into the weighing-up of royal decision the key argument of the irreversibility of history – with whose future in the nineteenth century we are all familiar.

History versus tradition: through this contrast one can measure to what extent the French monarchy itself – contrary to what Burke would write – had stopped referring to a traditionalist vision of the kingdom's constitution, seemingly to open the way to reform, but in reality to a sub-version of its spirit and history. Into the necessity for changes acknowledged by the minister came not so much a concern for institutional renovation as a feeling of inevitable evolution.

However, while the December document contained this major shift in the idea of representation to the benefit of the Third Estate, in the name of the progress of civilization, it insisted more than ever on the separation of the orders in the consultation which was about to start and the meeting which must follow: a point which, theoretically, cancelled out the doubling of the Third Estate, since the orders would sit separately; then, whatever the number of deputies for each entity, the two privileged orders would be in a position to dominate the third.

In this connection, it is interesting that the separation of the orders should be recommended in a far more radical fashion than in the sixteenth century or in 1614, when the bailiwick assemblies had frequently mingled the nobility and the Third Estate. So that at the very moment when it was laying claim, at least implicitly, to a democratic conception of the vote within the Third, the royal government was on the other hand reinforcing its aristocratic character, falling back on its own tradition.

That central contradiction is to be found throughout the regulatory arrangements organizing the elections, as set out in the bill of 24 January. On the one hand, apart from the watertight separation of the orders, the regulations hark back to tradition, insisting on the idea of an assembly intended purely to advise the king, stipulating that in towns inhabitants should meet in corps and trade guilds, increasing the number of particular cases and exemptions in the name of acquired privileges. Above all, it preserved the traditional procedure of the *cahier de doléances*, or list of grievances, which was supposed to present the unanimous wishes of each community: a procedure inseparable from the concept of the imperative mandate, and incompatible with any public electoral competition according to the modern plan.

On the other hand, however, the text of 24 January – similarly prepared by Necker – made an appeal to the spirit of the age, to the development of mentalities, underlining the need to make the representation of bailiwicks more or less proportional to their population, and set itself the objective of 'an assembly representative of the entire nation'. All the regulations carefully worked out in the January bill and those which followed bore witness to the will to institute, as fully as possible, a 'fixed' principle, and to organize consultation with all the people of the realm, by transforming into a voter every adult Frenchman enrolled on the tax registers. As Michelet clearly saw, the French people – with the peasantry to the fore – were for the first time about to make their massive entry into a political ballot in the spring of 1789.

Over and above everything else, no distinction had been drawn between the right to elect and the right to be elected: every individual with access to electoral assemblies – that is, any Frenchman of age – automatically acquired the right to present himself for the votes of his fellow citizens. If one considers as a whole this dawning of political equality and the adjustment of the number of seats to the population of the bailiwicks, Louis XVI's electoral regulation – in regard to the Third Estate alone – was comparable to a modern district poll, slightly complicated by the different levels of election, from the parish to the *chef-lieu* (administrative centre) of the bailiwick.

Thus, in the organization of a consultation of its own devising, the French monarchy had combined the spirit of tradition and the spirit of geometry, a respect for precedent and democratic innovation. There is no reason for surprise that it should contrive, here and there, to remain faithful to its past: the structure of the society of orders was part of the very nature of the monarchic system. On the contrary, it is surprising that it should combine at one and the same time three consultations, which were distinguished from one another more carefully than ever and corresponding, with the three orders of the realm, with the general implementation of modern democratic principles, as if partial conformity to the traditional vision of government and society were meant only to imbue the conflict between aristocracy and democracy with its already revolutionary purity.

Historical truth invites us to attribute more innocence to the actors in this prologue. For what confers exceptional transparency on this sort of interregnum between the *ancien régime* and the Revolution is not the autonomy and the will of the government of the kingdom: on the contrary, its impact derives from the fact that the old monarchy was for the last time lending its presence to the ambiguities of society and the spirit of the era. It resolved upon the meeting of the Estates-General unaware that, though the *ancien régime* had a very long past, the monarchy had never had any tradition of representation – or even a real tradition at all – in the sense of the English constitution.

Incapable of building an institution on this void, it yielded to the two alternatives offered by its history and its current position: aristocracy and democracy. At the very moment when it was making distinctions within the nobility itself and separating it from the nation, it gave the Third Estate the means of embodying and uniting that nation. Not only did it bequeath democracy to the Revolution but, before expiring, offered it the means of forming itself into a national body politic against the aristocracy.

THE CRISIS OF 1788–1789

An element which, in itself, owed everything to chance added its measure of disorder to the situation. The political crisis was accelerated by one of the biggest economic and social storms of the century; the heavens also were revolutionary. It had all begun with the bad harvest; the storms and floods of 1787, then the drought, and lastly the hail of 13 July 1788, which ravaged western France – everything had conspired against the harvest, which was catastrophic.

Urban industry lacked rural outlets and laid off workers; the ability of business to resist was weakened even more by a Franco-British trade treaty in 1786 which, by reducing import tariffs on British products in France, had increased its vulnerability. This was true mainly of the textile trade, a great industry of the period and the unsurpassable domain of British progress; at the start of 1789, there were 12,000 out of work in Abbeville and 20,000 in Lyon. *Intendants* disclosed the increase in begging and vagrancy. A traditional signal of social crisis and alarm, an explosion of prices further cut back incomes already hit by unemployment; in Paris, at the end of spring, bread cost four sous a livre, where the precarious balance of the popular budget reached its top limit at about three sous.

Violence erupted everywhere; in the countryside, where the small peasant could no longer manage to feed his family from his crops, let alone pay his lord and the king; in the towns, where the lower classes were demanding work and a fixed price for bread. At the end of the 1788–9 winter, which had been so severe, trouble broke out from Provence to Burgundy, from Brittany to Alsace; peasants and workers raided grain stores, stopped the transport of grain, threatened lords who claimed their dues, and *intendants* who symbolized taxation. In Paris, in April, a crowd of poor wretches looted the big Réveillon wallpaper factory and were then massacred by troops.

In this great anarchistic movement, when authority melted away, the traditional elements of the *ancien régime*'s corn riots are recognizable. But its novelty lay in a sort of unanimous direction of the movement, born of the contemporary political situation. It did not matter that the urban masses' demands for regulation were contradictory to the *philosophes' laissez-faire*: that was a problem the future would pose, not the present. For the moment, the crisis united the entire Third Estate against seigneurial privilege, against tax assessment, and for a profound reform of traditional political society.

Food riots coincided with the political effervescence of the clubs and enlightened societies, the mutterings in the suburbs with the revolutionary speeches of the Palais Royal. In short, the uprising of the poverty-stricken provided revolutionary consciousness with the strength of numbers and a feeling of urgency. Throughout the entire period of elections to the Estates-General, the tone of the thousands of brochures and pamphlets addressed to the French had noticeably heightened: Sieyès had set the keynote.

The *cahiers de doléances*, drawn up according to custom by local assemblies of the three orders, presented a more delicately shaded picture. It is true that neither the wretched peasant nor the unemployed craftsman could express themselves directly, since they were unable to write and were almost as incapable of speaking in public. They probably had little in the way of spokesmen at these parish or guild assemblies, which met in the village or local district church. The old practice of the imperative mandate which underlay that of the *cahier* presupposed the unanimous agreement of the electorate on the missions given to representatives. That is what makes the ensemble of this multitude of documents, which emerged from the greatest public consultation in modern French history, difficult to interpret and probably misleading: under the umbrella of the people as a whole, it was really the lawyers who were expressing themselves; they had most often presided over the assemblies and drawn up the grievances.

Within the Third Estate, the existence of several electoral strata had also acted as a filter for the demands. The revolutionary radicalism of *Qu'est-ce que le Tiers État?* was not to be found in the *cahiers*, although it was acclaimed by a vast reading public. That divergence forewarns the historian against simplification and allows him to grasp, even if crudely, the existence of several kinds of public opinion. In Paris, revolution was already widely expected, but the French *en masse* still expected the reforms they considered essential to come from the king.

It is true that the reforms demanded constituted a formidable pro-gramme of change. Almost all the orders – the clergy less vehemently than the other two – called for the end of 'despotism' and for a controlled monarchy. The Estates-General had become quite a different matter from a mere financial resort. It had been given the task of 'regenerating' the kingdom through a liberal and decentralizing constitution, ensuring forever the natural rights of individuals as conceived by the philosophy of the century: individual liberty, property, intellectual and religious tolerance, compulsory voting on taxation by periodic meetings. The king, once freed from the evil influences of his entourage, remained the supreme guarantor of this new social happiness. The *cahiers* of the nobles were as reformatory on this point as those of the bourgeois.

Beyond this kind of national unanimity – which was already a revolution in itself – appeared the multiple social conflicts of ancient France: that society of 'status' and 'rank' was supremely one of particularisms. Many of the *cahiers*, for example, set rich and poor peasants at odds over the sharing of common pastures, shopkeepers and guild masters over freedom to work, bishops and priests over the democratization of the Church, nobility and clergy over the freedom of the press.

But the essential distinction was the one which separated the privileged orders from the rest of the nation. For the Third Estate was not only in favour of voting by head, which would establish its political supremacy, or of fiscal equality, to which the majority of the nobles' *cahiers* had in the end assented. It was also demanding full equality of rights, the admission of all to public office and military rank, the abolition of seigneurial dues, with or without compensation: in short, the end of the society of orders. Since it was no longer simply a matter of a new state government, but of a new civil law, the holders of privileges dug their heels in against this additional revolution for equality: most of their *cahiers* indicate this very clearly.

The revolt of the parlements, the resignation of the government and the convening of the Estates had thus already determined two major modifications. Little by little they had transferred public authority to the coming assembly, by the very fact of the unanimity which had been revealed regarding a liberal reform of the monarchy. At the same time, however, the methods of convocation and the electoral campaign had disclosed the deep and secret wound afflicting society: inequality of birth, which separated the Third Estate from the privileged orders. Already, any transformation of the monarchy, if it were to be accepted, would of necessity be accompanied by a total upheaval of aristocratic society: that was the price paid by absolutism for its systematic manipulation of status and rank.

The development is even more obvious if one moves from the *cahiers*, which are the visible part of the 1789 poll, to the election of the deputies, which is the hidden part. In effect, since electoral procedures had for the most part broken the traditional structures of the kingdom, and since no opposing debate of programmes or ideas had been foreseen before the vote of the different assemblies, the Third Estate deputies who emerged victorious from the interminable consultations were elected less by the people than by the intrigues and compromises preceding the vote. The victors were all declared enemies of the aristocracy, carefully selected from among the Third Estate, with a few rare exceptions like the Abbé Sieyès or the Comte de Mirabeau, who had broken their ties with their respective orders.

THE THIRD ESTATE

At the beginning of the twentieth century, Augustin Cochin's great contribution was to grasp this aspect of the 1789 elections, and to show their mechanisms by way of the Breton and Burgundian examples. In Burgundy, for instance, in the autumn of 1788 everything revolved around a small committee at Dijon, which worked out the 'Patriot' platform: doubling of the Third Estate, voting by head, and also exclusion of the ennobled and seigneurs' agents from commoners' assemblies – a significant and fundamental precaution against the risk of aristocratic contamination of the will of the Third Estate.

From this starting-point, the Patriot committee infiltrated all established bodies. First of all, the barristers, who had almost been won over in advance, then the minor members of the legal profession, doctors, guilds, finally the town hall, through the intermediary of one of the sheriffs and under pressure from 'zealous citizens': in the end, the document concocted in a small committee had become the unanimous wish of Dijon's Third Estate. From there, under the usurped authority of Dijon's municipal officers, the *corps de ville*, it reached other neighbouring towns, where a similar outflanking of constituted authorities by barristers and laywers took place. The *intendant*, Amelot, Necker's protégé, who was an adversary of the parlements, looked favourably on these events. In December, the nobles organized themselves around what had such a short time ago been

Dijon's *philosophe* and *parlementaire* party. This time they intended to resist
the egalitarian exaggeration of their erstwhile allies, the barristers, but they
were excluded from the Patriot camp, which held sway over the *cahiers* and
the elections.

Most of the history of the 1789 ballot has still to be written. It was long
concealed by examination of the *cahiers* only, which often masked the
truth. A whole network of propaganda and manipulation had an almost
obvious but still little-known hand in it. The historian can pick out certain
leading figures, such as the Committee of Thirty, which included many
great names of the morrow – Mirabeau, Du Port, Talleyrand, La Fayette –
or the small committee which formed around the Duc d'Orléans, with
Sieyès and Choderlos de Laclos, but details of intrigues and their results
are unknown.

For want of procedures and institutions, the dawning egalitarian
democracy developed by way of circuits of enlightened opinion which
characterized the century: clubs, Freemasons' lodges, groups of thinkers.
There was more deliberate and concerted action towards the incipient
revolution than history has recorded, yet no one imagined – or could
imagine – the unprecedented nature of what was happening. For the *ancien
régime* still appeared to be in place, and the king of France, as in the past,
was banking on regaining his authority through the very division of his
subjects. But it was only a matter of time. The deputies to the Estates
arrived in Paris at the end of April. The opening session was planned for 5
May at Versailles.

Now, between May and August 1789, the entire *ancien régime* came to
grief. In three months, the space of a season, in the most extraordinary
summer in French history, nothing was left standing of what the centuries
and the kings had constituted. The French had turned their rejection of
the national past into the principle of the Revolution. A philosophical idea
had become incarnate in the history of a people.

It all began with the deputies, who from the start refused to bow before
the king. On the day when the Estates met in the hall of the Hôtel
des Menus Plaisirs, the main problem was whether to vote by head or
by order. Louis XVI reiterated his choice through the protocol of the
reception of the deputies, which scrupulously respected the traditional
distinctions: at the opening session, he furthermore indicated his wish
to limit the competence of the Estates to examination of the financial
problems alone.

But he did not have the means to effect this policy. Faced with some 600
deputies of the Third Estate, he could not count on support from all the
members of the two privileged assemblies. Among the clergy, where
internal strife had been lively, there were only forty-six bishops out of 300
deputies, and many country priests were being attracted by their Third
Estate neighbours. One third of the nobility group had been won over to
liberal ideas, and was dominated by the reputation of the *parlementaire* Du
Port and the American prestige of La Fayette.

On the contrary, the Third Estate's large number of deputies was remarkable for its social and political homogeneity: no peasants, artisans or workmen, but a group of bourgeois, educated and earnest, unanimous in the desire to transform both state and society. The lawyers, who were the most numerous, were not conscious of any distinction between themselves and the merchants and shopkeepers; the local celebrities from the French provinces, whose shining hour had truly arrived, were not intimidated by Paris. The Bretons, Jean Denis Lanjuinais and René Le Chapelier; Jacques Thouret and François Buzot from Normandy; the Dauphinois, Barnave; Rabaut Saint-Etienne from Nîmes and Maximilien Robespierre from Artois were there on equal terms with Sylvain Bailly, the Parisian Academician.

Under the anonymous greyness of costume and origin was concealed the strongest collective will ever to have moved an assembly. The sole concession it made to the aristocratic times – but that, too, was a clever move – was to leave the limelight to two turncoats from the privileged orders: the Abbé Sieyès, elected at the last moment by the Paris Third Estate, and the Comte de Mirabeau, spurned by his order but welcomed by the Third Estate of Aix-en-Provence – the thinker and the artist of the Revolution.

The former we have already met, at the moment when he threw down the gauntlet to the *ancien régime* at the end of the preceding year. The latter, also just turned forty, was equally desirous of settling many an old score with the state of society. However, while the abbé was a studious man who had long cultivated a sort of cold rage against old society, Mirabeau had suffered its injustices from the inside, through the various troubles of his life. Born into a well-known family of Provençal nobility, the son of the famous physiocrat Marquis who was passionately interested in agronomy and political economy, his childhood and adolescence read like a chronicle of the *ancien régime* in which his battles with his father were punctuated by exiles, *lettres de cachet* and jail.

He had a volcanic nature: in early youth he deserted his regiment, ran up debts, compromised women – including his own wife – slept with his sister, fought his rivals. His father took more and more legal actions and prohibitions against him, and on several occasions had him imprisoned. The two men wore themselves out arguing family disputes in court.

Mirabeau emerged from this extraordinary and wretched life about 1780, earning his living by writing: despite his great name, he took on little jobs amid the numerous band who lived on the small change of the Enlightenment, as if that were the inevitable path towards the great roles to come. France was a literary country. Great works and great ideas received a warm welcome from a vast public, and were served by an army of fluent writers with a nose for the market. The old Marquis de Mirabeau, his father, had been a literary man and a crank; he himself acted like all the ambitious young commoners of his age and could imagine only one way to fame:

writing. What were the others doing at the same period – Barnave and Brissot, Camille Desmoulins and Antoine Saint-Just? Since literature had assumed a political function, it also found itself the antechamber to politics.

While he waited, Mirabeau sold his pen – and that of others – without much delicacy in his methods: he had never had any, and never would. In the last years of the *ancien régime*, this impoverished aristocrat wrote for the powerful men of the day, published in favour of Calonne against Necker, for the speculator Isaac Panchaud against his rivals, a series of dissertations often written by others – notably by his associate Etienne Clavière of Geneva, and by the young Brissot, another literary adventurer of lesser rank. Even his friend Chamfort had worked for him for a short while.

Mirabeau had failed at everything: with 1789, everything would smile on him. This disorganized, erratic, unfaithful, venal man grabbed at the opportunity of his life: to be elected deputy of the Aix-en-Provence Third Estate to the Estates-General, to offer his torrents of words to the new nation. Rejected by his own kind, the most despised son of the old nobility had all he needed to become the most brilliant figure in the revolutionary assembly. His talent for oratory, his quick-wittedness, his anger against the past, his temperament – none of which had so far found a use. But he had something else, more deeply concealed, which made him an exceptional person among all those Third Estate legal men.

One would look in vain, among the men of the Revolution, for a similar blend of high birth and unconventionality. Many of the leaders of 1789 would prove to be nobles – La Fayette, the Lameths, Talleyrand – but a liberal noble is not a noble who has lost his class. Quite the opposite: the spirit of liberty is a possession generously available to both bourgeoisie and aristocracy. As for the bohemian element, heaven knows it was well represented in the French Revolution; but in 1789 its time had not yet come: when it did, in 1792, noble birth had become a curse. On the other hand, in the spring of 1789 France was still groping amid the chaos of events for the constitution of an English-style political class, mingling liberal nobility with enlightened bourgeoisie. This fusion, which went back over several centuries of English history, now had to be taken on all at once by the old kingdom, by way of democracy and amid popular tumult. Who could act as its guarantor before the new-born 'nation'? Who was both democratic and aristocratic enough to make the France of yesterday bow before the Revolution? Mirabeau was the only noble sufficiently *déclassé*, and the only *déclassé* noble enough to link the past with this advent.

From that providential cross-breeding of status, like a great musician he would draw superb sounds. The Revolution showed him where his genius lay, providing him with a stage and a job. The assembly which met at Versailles in May 1789 included a number of intelligent and capable men who had made a name for themselves in their various callings, and some who already had a brilliant career. To that earnest community he brought flair, inventiveness and imagination. He produced the decisive words of the epoch. He would have been its leading light had he not dragged in his wake rumours of scandal and money troubles – his *ancien régime* legacy. Nevertheless, he would at least be its voice, and very frequently. This voluminous writer, this amateur, this tempestuous man discovered the strange power of incarnating the Revolution and threw all his formidable energy into it: he was one of the leaders of the great debates in those early months.

THE ESTATES-GENERAL

As from 6 May the Third Estate rechristened itself the 'Commons' (Communes), as if the new name washed it clean of old humiliation. Thus, in a single movement, it held firm against the king. For more than a month it refused to undertake the verification of credentials apart from the other two orders; because through sheer numbers it held sway over the great hall, it chose to wait and let its social weight exercise its attraction. That long month of May 1789 was one of passive revolt. Far from wearing out the commoner-deputies, it welded them together into one soul: on 10 June, at Sieyès's appeal, the Third Estate invited the other two chambers to join it in a communal verification of the credentials of 'all the representatives of the nation'. The roll-call began on 12 June; the next day, the first signs of weakening appeared within the clergy, and three priests from Bas Poitou, by joining the Commons, gave the signal for a support which increased in the following days. Strengthened by this clerical backing, the assembly on 17 June, at Sieyès's urging, declared itself the 'National Assembly'.

It had taken a long time debating this formula, in the consciousness that it was taking a decisive step. Mounier, already cautious and already unaware of what was going on among his colleagues, had argued for a definition which would open the door to a compromise with the privileged orders: 'a legitimate assembly of the representatives of the major part of the nation in the absence of the minor part'. Mirabeau had proposed that the meeting of the Third Estate should be formed of 'representatives of the French people'. But the word 'people' concealed a partial and inferior implication – that of the Roman *plebs* – whereas the term 'National Assembly' had no ambiguity.

By the use of this name alone, the Third Estate relegated to the past the whole of the society of orders, and created a new power, independent of the king. The next day, it assigned itself the vote on taxation and placed the state's creditors 'under the guard of the honour and uprightness of the French nation'. This was a clever way of telling the Parisian bourgeois, who were so near at hand, that if bankruptcy was a royal custom, then the protection of property-owning *rentier* democracy was a revolutionary innovation. Truly a different sovereignty had just been baptized: the Revolution had been born.

The Third Estate's daring move divided the other camp, but hardened the remainder. The mass of the clerical deputies swung towards the National Assembly; a third of the nobles also voted for 'union'. But in the hour of danger, the majority of bishops and nobles rediscovered their natural protector in the figure of Louis XVI. They hurried to Marly, where the king had withdrawn in his sorrow after the death of his eldest son; they preached resistance to him. At the same time, but from a different stand-point, Necker felt that the king must resume the initiative. He put forward the idea of a royal sitting of the Estates, at which the king would simply say what he would and would not accept.

But who was to define what was acceptable? Who would write the royal speech? In the meantime, on the pretext of making the necessary arrangements for this sitting, the large hall of the Menus Plaisirs was closed, and so the deputies of the 'National Assembly' found the doors shut on 20 June. They therefore took themselves off to a large building nearby, the Tennis Court, which they immortalized by their famous oath 'never to separate, and to meet wherever circumstances demand, until the con-stitution of the kingdom is established and affirmed on solid foundations'. At all events, the reply was given in anticipation of any potential threats from authority.

But what did the king want? For once in his life – the first and the last time – he expressed it clearly on 23 June, in the two declarations which were read out for him. Necker had prepared the first version, but his enemies, upheld by Marie-Antoinette and Artois, had the last word on the final text. On this occasion, Necker did not come. This royal testament granted approval of taxation and loans by the Estates, liberty for the individual and the press, and administrative decentralization; it expressed the wish that the privileged should accept fiscal equality. But it said nothing about equal eligibility to any office for all men, and did not envisage voting by head except in regard to certain limited problems, refusing it explicitly for anything connected with future Estates-General. Lastly, it expressly upheld the hierarchies of aristocratic society. In short, the monarchy acknowledged the liberal demands, but denied equality of rights: it accepted only the reforms which had the assent of the nobles. The threat of the barristers had for once united bureaucracy and the dukes; but only around the death-bed of the old monarchy.

As soon as the king had departed, followed by the deputies from the nobility and the prelates, the young Marquis de Dreux-Brézé, grand master of ceremonies, addressed the men of the Third Estate, who remained there motionless and silent: 'Gentlemen, you know the king's intent.' In the following minutes, the Revolution found three Roman phrases to express the new era. Bailly: 'The assembled nation cannot take orders.' Sieyès: 'You are today what you were yesterday.' Mirabeau: 'We shall not leave our places save at bayonet point.' The National Assembly decided to persist with the preceding resolutions and decreed the inviolability of its members.

Jacques Louis David The Tennis Court Oath of 20 June 1789, *Musée Carnavalet, Paris.*
(*Photo: Lauros-Giraudon*)

Had Louis XVI the means of imposing his policy in those decisive days? He did not even try. From then on, the resistance of the privileged was broken down by successive defections. On 27 June the King himself accepted the *fait accompli* by inviting 'his faithful clergy and his faithful nobles' to join with the Third Estate. In the evening, Paris was illuminated. The National Assembly had become a constituent body.

Two powers now had a presence; one entirely new, which had suddenly emerged from the Estates-General, the other bequeathed by the centuries: the Assembly and the king. What did this coexistence mean in actual fact? Absolute monarchy was dead, and the aristocratic monarchy outlind on 23 June was stillborn. Could a monarchy and a National Assembly live together? On what conditions? With this completely unprecedented constitutional matter, the first question in the immediate future was one of the authorities charged with public order. In principle, they were still entirely on the king's side, but that was in appearance only.

What did Louis XVI want, in those supremely important weeks? That was one of the questions on which the future would depend, and was already being asked in all its fullness. The historian, however, can merely provide probable answers: the to-ing and fro-ing of decisions and counter-decisions going on at court have left no trace. On 23 June Necker had been defeated by his adversaries, supporters of the confrontation with the Third

Estate barristers; there is no cause to doubt his evidence, which an examination of the speeches confirms.

Between the end of June and 10 July everything points to the fact that Versailles was looking for revenge, and Louis XVI allowed the development of a policy of military concentration around Paris. Was it against the Assembly or against Paris? The clearest outcome of this common threat, on minds which were in any case ready to brandish it, was to unite the fears of both the Parisian mob and the deputies at Versailles.

REVOLUTIONARY VIOLENCE

Paris was the scene of daily excitement, a permanent meeting-place. From the economic viewpoint, nothing was conducive to calm: bread had never been so dear, there were large numbers of unemployed, whose ranks were swollen by a population which rural poverty had recently driven to the capital. Shopkeepers and *rentiers*, the backbone of the urban populace, grew alarmed about the value of their credit on the royal Treasury: when Necker lost ground at Versailles, they too felt threatened. But neither the hardships of life nor worries about private interests can explain the general unrest, which was of a political nature. The Estates-General, the proclamation of the National Assembly, the Tennis Court oath and the victory of the Third Estate had crystallized revolutionary public opinion in Paris, both popular and bourgeois, which was fed by the constant coming and going to Versailles.

That opinion had its centre at the Palais Royal, where 'patriots' of all allegiances converged to listen to orators and agitators. Paris was at last having its revenge on Versailles, where it had its bridgehead, and had already been victorious at court. The news which came through at the beginning of July, and the arrival of the troops both gave signs of a noble counter-offensive, referred to as an 'aristocratic conspiracy' since the spring. With a feeling of having to vanquish a formidable enemy lurking in the shadows, the Parisian revolution was on its feet for several weeks before taking action.

Now royal authority was foundering over the discipline of the soldiers: coaxed by the Parisian bourgeois, unhappy with the harshness of their officers, and won over by an awakening public spirit, their hearts were with Paris. On 30 June a huge crowd opened the gates of the Abbey at Saint-Germain-des-Prés for a number of soldiers who had been imprisoned for indiscipline. It was in this climate that the troops summoned as reinforcements started to arrive: the atmosphere of the Palais Royal won many regiments, even foreigners. It needed just one spark for the blaze to ignite.

It came on 11 July. Even before all the troops summoned were present, the king exiled Necker and dismissed his liberal ministers. The new ministry, formed behind the scenes several weeks before, and whose

Campion The Taking of the Bastille, *Musée Rothschild, Paris.*
(*Photo: Lauros-Giraudon*)

moving spirit was Breteuil, was a declaration of counter-revolution; but the dismissal of Necker by itself said it all to public opinion, which immediately interpreted this as a doubly unlucky omen: of bankruptcy and counter-revolution.

Reaction was instant. On the afternoon of 12 July Paris rebelled; soldiers of the Garde Française (the palace guards) joined the rioters, who soon controlled the city. The Baron de Besenval, in command of Paris in the king's name, fell back to the Champ de Mars, from which he would not budge: on 13 July the wave of people broke down the tolls, hated symbols of the Farm General's tax collecting activities, and looted the gunsmiths' shops. A new power emerged from the shadows, which had been prepared by the notables of the electoral districts in the spring: this 'permanent Committee', whose first measure was to organize a volunteer militia, wanted both to encourage and to control the insurrection. During the night of 13–14 July all Paris – illuminated by order of the Committee – could hear the first patrols of the new social order on the move. The National Guard was born.

At dawn on 14 July the mob gained control of the Hôtel des Invalides, where it found 32,000 muskets; it was also with the intention of looking for arms that the crowd then thought of the Bastille. This remarkable collective intuition had another, quite different, motive: there was no better symbol of the enemy than the legendary prison which, with its eight large towers, blocked the entry to the faubourg Saint-Antoine. The end of this monstrous urban, political and human anachronism must by its very nature mark the advent of liberty.

The Bastille surrendered in mid-afternoon, after a bloody outburst of shooting, and faced with the cannon captured at the Invalides. The victors – all traditional people, shopkeepers, *rentiers*, artisans, journeymen – then inaugurated the bloodbath which would always be part of all the great revolutionary episodes. The governor, the Marquis de Launay, dragged along the quays to the Hôtel de Ville, was killed in the Place de Grève; the chief municipal magistrate, the *Prévôt des Marchands*, Flesselles, suffered the same fate. Their decapitated heads, stuck on pikes, were paraded all the way to the Palais Royal.

The fall of the fortress, which no one at the time considered to be the decisive event it later became, did not quell the rising: a week later, on 22 July, Joseph Foulon de Doué, one of the men in Breteuil's ministry, was hanged by the people in front of the Hôtel de Ville, together with his son-in-law, Bertier de Sauvigny, *intendant* of Paris, accused of 'having young corn cut' in order to starve the poor; the obsession with corn continued to be the principal cause of accusation and popular terrorism against the men of 'ministerial despotism'.

But it was really on 14 July that the decisive battle was played out: for Louis XVI, having taken the resolve on 11 July, had effectively abdicated on 14 July. At Versailles, the court plied him with contradictory advice: going against the Comte d'Artois, who was already counselling him to take refuge in Metz under the protection of loyal troops, he resigned himself to remaining, or in other words, to giving in.

On 15 July he announced to the Assembly the recall of Necker and the dismissal of the troops; on 17 July he went to Paris in the afternoon and acknowledged the new authorities born of the insurrection, Bailly and La Fayette, respectively mayor and commander of the National Guard. Popular welcome, at first very reserved, warmed up only at the Hôtel de Ville, when Louis put the red and blue municipal cockade in his hat – the cockade which would produce the revolutionary flag when La Fayette added to it the white of old France. In short, the crowds acclaimed the king's capitulation as well as his presence.

The victory in Paris brought in its wake that of the towns; everywhere the kingdom's bourgeoisie seized and channelled the torrent of urban emotions. As if naturally, they relieved *intendants* without powers and governors without troops, making general the Parisian example of the National Guard. It was the revenge of the communes against monarchic centralization, the end of those *corps de ville* in the hands of the monarchy. But the victory of liberty over despotism was not the same as that of the old franchises of aristocratic society. It had taken place in the name of new principles, and was accompanied by a very keen consciousness of the national unity enveloping those principles: suddenly ties of revolutionary brotherhood were woven between town and town, and 'federations' were set up, after the old Latin word. The idea of nation was inseparable from local democracy, which was its condition and guarantee.

The urban revolution joyfully celebrated its triumph. The sporadic outbursts of popular violence which marked this immense transference of power did not yet trouble the clear conscience of the bourgeois. The king appeared to have yielded. While the Bourse greeted regained confidence by resuming trading, the nobles were starting to leave. The court set the example. Those courtiers who had foreseen nothing had long since lost the habit of acting in concert and fighting.

A first wave of several thousands of departures took place in July–August. The Comte d'Artois, the Prince de Condé, the Duc d'Enghien, Breteuil, the Contis, the Polignacs, gave the signal the day after July 14. All the great names of the court abandoned the king and queen in their misfortune: they blamed them for a weakness which they themselves had helped to create and from which they had amply profited. They would continue, from the other side of the Rhine, to discredit both the monarchy and the nobility in the eyes of the new France. It was a role of which they had held the secret since the death of Louis XIV.

But neither the king nor the court had yet drained the cup to the bitter dregs. For the subversion of the traditional order was so general that, after the deputies' revolt and at the same time as the municipal uprising, it revealed a third revolution, emerging from the social depths of the kingdom: it brought to the Parisian Revolution, which had sided with the deputies against Louis XVI, the anarchic support of the vast peasant class. Everything had happened in Paris, and the *journée* of insurrection on 14 July had been the start of the long and exclusive dominance – which would last for a century – of the capital over French public life. But just for once – and it would not occur again – the country areas, instead of merely following, had also risen up with the same intent.

In the spring, the electoral situation had aroused in peasant hearts a hope as vehement as the despair born of the crisis: the injustice of seigneurial dues and the royal tax was a general complaint in the *cahiers*. At the same time, poverty was driving on to the roads and around the hamlets hundreds of vagrants, who aggravated the chronic insecurity of the countryside. Fear of brigands, harking back to the mists of antiquity, seemed more than ever to prowl round villages living in terror. Everywhere, rumour's mysterious voice murmured to the peasant that, come rain or shine, apocalypse or blessed event, it was a decisive moment.

Violence erupted in the second fortnight of July, and sometimes very clearly took the form of social warfare: in the *bocage* (farm enclosures) of Normandy, in Hainaut, in Alsace, in Franche-Comté and the valley of the Saône, armed peasants attacked châteaux and abbeys; in collective celebration they came there to burn the old deeds of their serfdom, as if the destruction of seigneurial archives would deliver them once and for all from the tithe and the field rent. But in the rest of the kingdom, the

peasant revolts took a more complex turn: Georges Lefebvre has reconstructed the paths taken by what was called the Great Fear.

The news of the taking of the Bastille was slow to reach the villages,
and assumed en route end-of-the-world proportions which increasingly
provoked reflexes of panic and defensiveness. It was also harvest time, a
major period of rural life, and destructive brigands were therefore all the
more to be feared. Peasant imagination and rumour, fascinated by echoes
of urban propaganda, saw them as the mercenaries of the enemies of the
people and of that aristocratic conspiracy with another face: foreign
invasion. In Limousin, it was supposed to be the Comte d'Artois coming
from Bordeaux with an army of 16,000 men. To the east, the fear was of
Germans; in the Dauphiné, of Savoyards; in Brittany, of the English.
From village to village the false news spread, grew fat on exaggeration and
tyrannized the countryside. The peasants kept watch and armed themselves as best they could. One can thus follow, from day to day and from
village to village, the route and ramification of the 'Fears': it was the
simultaneously panic-stricken and threatening form assumed by the former
jacqueries (peasant risings) in the hour of the French Revolution.

THE END OF PRIVILEGE

At Versailles, the deputies were surprised to discover the social frailty
of a civilization which had shone so brilliantly during the Enlightenment.
Bourgeois or nobles, they were all, to a greater or lesser degree, property-
owners in one way or another: seigneurial rights were a possession, too,
and it so happened that some commoners enjoyed them if they had
purchased a seigniory. But to re-establish order in the name of property
would shatter the unity of the Patriot group; the new bourgeois militias
would join with the royal mercenaries against the country folk, to the
greater advantage of the king. The other idea was to satisfy the peasants in
order to bind them to the revolutionary nation, but that would have to be
done more widely and more swiftly than had been planned; fiscal equality
would not be enough, nor the abandonment of what remained in France of
ancient serfdom. The entire regime of seigneurial and ecclesiastical dues
was brought into question.

After tending for a moment towards repression, the majority of the
Assembly realized its political impossibility and plunged headlong into
another strategy. On the night of 3–4 August about a hundred deputies
gathered together in a Versailles café by the 'Breton Club' (forerunner of
the Jacobins) decided to take the initiative on the inevitable reforms. In the
evening of 4 August the nobles gave the signal: through the voices of a
younger son of a poor family, the Vicomte de Noailles, and one of the
richest lords in the land, the Duc d'Aiguillon, the peasant uprising made
itself heard by the deputies. The philanthropic tone of that famous sitting

was imparted by those nobles who were sacrificing such ancient feudal titles on the national altar; gone was the oppression of the peasants, gone the 'gothic' distinctions, gone the divisive privileges.

Enthusiasm for civic equality, however, did not rule out a certain amount of calculation. Aiguillon concluded in favour of the need for fiscal equality, straightforward abolition of *corvées* and serfdoms, as well as the redemption of other feudal dues at interest of 'one denier to thirty'. This fairly low rate (3.3 per cent) clearly indicates that the great lord had been careful to set the highest value on the capital to be redeemed. It was a matter of converting the old seigneurial due into a sound bourgeois contract: the nobles saved the essential part, and the propertied men of the Third Estate had everything to gain from the equalizing of noble land and commoners' land. The tithe alone was abolished without compensation: in terms of revenue, the clergy were the principal losers on 4 August.

Abandoning the feudal principle was such an important step that the Assembly was gripped by a kind of magic of transformation: they vied with one another to be first at the tribune to renounce the privileges of the old world, amid general applause. The most famous parliamentary night in French history thus ended the sale of offices and instituted equality of eligibility for jobs, the abandonment of all provincial or local privileges and the triumph of the 'national' spirit. The old parlements, already forgotten, so quickly overtaken, suffered the common fate. The feudal regime was obliterated. At three in the morning, in order to associate him in due solemnity with the birth of the new world, the Assembly proclaimed Louis XVI 'restorer of French liberty', a phrase which indicated that there was still something in the nation's past worthy of being 'restored'.

The debates continued until 11 August, so that the exalted votes of the great night could be drawn up in right and due form. The final decree, written by Du Port, declared that 'the National Assembly completely destroys the feudal regime.' It established the end of personal privileges, the admission of all to any employment, free and equal justice for all, the abolition of any remaining serfdom and the suppression of the tithe, which laid such a burden on peasants' crops. By contrast, the majority of seigneurial dues and judiciary offices were declared redeemable: the Assembly had wanted to save all properties by integrating them into the new law.

In fact, the elimination of what the men of 4 August termed the feudal regime would take place more slowly than the decrees of 11 August would lead one to suppose. The laws were actually completed in 1790 and 1791 by several supplementary decrees. The redemption of suppressed judiciary offices was a long process, taking several years. In the rural areas, the redemption of seigneurial dues was too burdensome for the peasants, and there were sporadic outbreaks of unrest, in Quercy for instance. Finally abolition without compensation was voted in July 1793. Nevertheless, despite the wariness and long-windedness, there was something in the Assembly's and its contemporaries' perception of 4 August which, for the historian, remains fundamentally true: the notion of a break with the old society and the foundation of a new one.

The peasant felt himself victorious over the seigneur. The bourgeois had broken aristocratic privilege. What the deputies had termed feudal comprised an extraordinary variety of properties and rights, because they had included features which were really feudal legacies – such as the vestiges of mortmain (tenure in perpetuity), the residue of seigneurial justice, or the dues paid by the tenant to his lord – and elements which had nothing to do with feudalism – such as the ecclesiastical levy of the tithe – or which came after the feudal era, like the sale of offices. Basically, what the text of 11 August called the destruction of the feudal regime was the annihilation of the aristocratic society which absolute monarchy had patched together on the ruins of feudal society. What disappeared in August 1789 – and for ever – was a society of corporate bodies defined by shared privilege.

What came into being was a modern society of individuals, in its most radical conception, since everything which might come between the public sphere and each actor on the stage of social life was not only suppressed, but also roundly condemned. The Revolution rediscovered an idea put forward by Sieyès at the end of *Qu'est-ce que de Tiers État?* Within the modern individual there are two legitimate sides: the private one, which keeps him apart from others in enjoyment of himself, his family and his private interests, and that of the citizen, which he shares with all other citizens and which, in aggregate, forms public sovereignty. But the third side, that of the social individual who tends to create inter-social coalitions on the basis of particular interests, must be ruthlessly excluded from the state. Hatred of aristocratic society had led the men of the French Revolution to ban associations, in the name of radical individualism: two years later, Le Chapelier's law against trade unions and employers' associations would solemnly confirm this.

CONSTITUTIONAL DEBATE

Thus the laws of 11 August did not only, or especially, establish that property-owning society dreamed of by the monarchy's enlightened reformers in the eighteenth century. Nevertheless such a definition is not completely erroneous: provided 'property-owner' is not confused with 'capitalist' – France was an agrarian country at that time – it may well be said that the night of 4 August, by making all equal before the law, instituted the universal nature of the property contract: not a new economic society, but a new legal society. Quite simply, the nature of the decrees had another significance.

By the ban which they imposed, going beyond privilege, on all associations between private individuals, they excluded from the formation of sovereignty interests which any contracting individuals might have in common in civil society and might wish to see guaranteed or defended within the state. If, in order to have a legitimate existence, the public sphere must undergo such a radical denial of the interests at stake in modern society, that did not make the problem of its constitution and its authority any simpler: how was the divergence between social man and the citizen to be dealt with?

That was the chief question of the summer for the Constituent Assembly; by destroying the 'feudal' regime, it had redefined the French people as individuals who were free and equal in the eyes of the law. It then had to constitute them as such in a corporate political body. Two debates were crucial in this respect. The first concerned the Declaration of the Rights of Man, the principle of which had been accepted before 14 July. But the discussion, punctuated by so many spectacular events, lasted until the end of August. It was long, complex, contradictory, and passed through the filter of numerous preparatory drafts of the final text, which was agreed on 26 August.

The American Declaration of Independence in 1776 was present in all minds, but so was the chasm which separated the situation of the old kingdom from that of the American ex-colonies, peopled by minor land-owners with democratic customs, who from the start had cultivated the spirit of equality, unhampered by external enemies or a feudal or aristocratic heritage. As in the American example, the French declaration had to have as its aim the foundation of the new social contract within natural law, in keeping with the century's philosophy, and the solemn enumeration of the imprescriptible rights possessed by each contracting party, which entry into society guaranteed him.

In France however, those rights had not been in harmony beforehand with the social state: on the contrary, they would be proclaimed after a violent break with the national past, and against the corruption of an old society which had for so long trampled on the mere idea of a contract. This aroused many fears among the more moderate members of the revolutionary camp: Mounier, for example, was afraid of the anarchy which might spring from the contrast between the proclamation of theoretical rights possessed equally by all individuals and the actual social situation of those individuals – poverty, inequality, class distinctions. From that arose the compensatory demand for a declaration of the citizen's duties in order to underline his obligation at the same time as his liberty.

These debates, well known for their abstract quality, show evidence that the deputies recognized quite clearly the scope of the problem they were tackling. They had just declared the complete emancipation of the individual: what then would become of the social bond? Many among them wanted to affirm its equally fundamental nature. That discussion was the grand début of a famous *topos* of modern political philosophy. The idea that affirmation of the subjective rights of individuals as a foundation of the contract carried the risk of social breakdown has haunted European political thought ever since Burke, from conservatives to socialists; it was already fully present in the July and August debates of 1789 in the

Constituent Assembly, chiefly among those who were beginning to be called *Monarchiens*, but also outside.

However, it was the Patriots who easily won the day, and a simple Declaration of the Rights of Man, a preamble to the coming Constitution, was adopted on 26 August. It was a noble and well written text, often close to the American model. The essence was expressed in a very few sentences, leaving the way open to debate on their interpretation. Firstly, what had been done on 4 August: 'Men are born free and live free and with equal rights.' What rights? Liberty, property, safety and resistance to oppression, with all that derives therefrom: civil and fiscal equality, individual liberty, the admissibility of everyone for all employment, *habeas corpus*, non-retroactive laws, guarantee of property.

What most clearly differentiated the French declaration from the American text concerned the coupling of these natural rights with written law. In the American example, those rights were perceived as having preceded society and also being in harmony with its development; more-over, they had been inscribed in its past by the jurisprudential tradition of English Common Law. In the France of 1789, however, emphasis was placed on a certain political voluntarism: the law, produced by the sovereign nation, was established as the supreme guarantee of rights.

Article IV: Liberty consists in being able to do anything as long as it harms no one else. Thus the exercise of each man's natural rights has no limits other than those which ensure that other members of society may enjoy the same rights. These limits can be determined only by the law.

Article XVI: Any society in which guaranteed rights are not assured, or the separation of powers not determined, cannot be said to have a constitution.

So it was society's responsibility, through the intermediary of the law, to ensure the rights of individuals; that law which was constantly referred to in the articles of the declaration as the 'expression of the general will'. The dominant inspiration of the Constituent Assembly was centred on the law: its immediate highlights were the idea of 'general will', intended to define the extent and the exercise of rights, and the refusal to recognize any authority other than that of the sovereign.

Now, this 'sovereign', which was henceforth the people, or the nation, needed to be given a form, to be constituted: for a variety of reasons, that was an extraordinarily difficult problem. France was a modern nation, too vast for its citizens to be summoned together in a public square to vote on laws. It was also a very ancient nation, whose heritage included a hereditary king, at the head of what one of the deputies called 'the gothic colossus of our ancient constitution'. In three months, all of the complete sovereignty which he had held, over a kingdom represented in his person, had entirely disappeared. In its place was a society composed of free and equal individuals, on the one hand; on the other, a people who had reappropriated sovereignty: how was that to be organized? Ever since

Declaration of the Rights of Man and the Citizen, 1789, *Musée de la Ville de Paris, Musée Carnavalet, Paris.*
(Photo: Lauros-Giraudon)

Hobbes, philosophers of the Social contract had been puzzling over this problem, but it was now being posed for the first time in the existence of one of the oldest European monarchies.

To understand how the men of the Revolution tackled it, let us turn to the beginning of the great constitutional discussion at the end of August and start of September: having made the Declaration of Rights, they now had to organize the new public authorities by way of a real constitution. This could not be a shaky monument made up of ancient customs and haphazard revisions, like the *ancien régime* monarchy, but an ensemble of institutions based on the new principles, which were those of reason.

That definition already left outside the Patriot camp a small minority of former revolutionaries who, in fact, had been anxious since June about the way things were going and about the violence in July: among them were Mounier from Grenoble, Malouet, a naval *intendant* and liberal nobles like Lally-Tollendal and Clermont-Tonnerre. What united these *Monarchiens*, as they came to be called, was the desire to 'put an end to the Revolution' – a theme which was beginning its long career in French politics; there were, too, some fundamental convictions which drew them nearer to Necker and isolated them from the majority of the Assembly.

They were against the revolutionary *tabula rasa*, hostile to the reconstruction of a political society on the basis of will or reason. They believed that the extraordinary summer could be turned into no more than a fertile incident if it led to the reform, in a liberal, English sense, of what they called 'monarchic government', the heritage of the national past. Their vision was a joint sovereignty of the king and two chambers, breaking with absolutism but uniting with what a monarchy loyal to its origins ought to become.

A political and intellectual chasm thus separated the *Monarchiens* from what had, since June, been the overriding spirit of the Revolution. They were men who stood for continuity and the adjustment of institutions: this was the nearest that French political tradition came to Burke, and gives some idea of their political isolation in 1789. They battled in vain for a bicameral system, without realizing that, for an assembly which had struggled so hard to join three Estates into one alone, it was hopeless to try to recommend a return to a division between an upper and a lower chamber. The spectre of aristocracy would still stalk the Constituent Assembly without any need of them, but it had marked them out in advance as losers.

The same debate at the beginning of September, in which they were crushed, concerned another, more central, matter: the question of the royal veto and its right over the legislative authority, and therefore of the nature and attribution of sovereignty. On this subject, the Patriot orators were unanimous in excluding the king from either originating or holding sovereignty. The monarchy was merely a government which had just been constituted by the act of the Assembly itself, which had reinvented it by voting, without regard for its history. The prerogative of full and entire sovereignty thus belonged to the Assembly, which had been delegated by the nation to create a constitution; afterwards, once the authorities had been constituted, it would be embodied by the legislative power, of which the king, as head of the executive power, would merely be the secular arm.

Reading the debates, one is struck by the obsession with legitimacy which runs through them, the stress laid on the absolute transfer of sovereignty and the indivisible, ontologically unitarian nature of that sovereignty. Pastor Rabaut Saint-Etienne, the Third Estate deputy from Nîmes, spoke on behalf of all when he said: 'The sovereign is a single and simple entity, since it is all men collectively, without any exception: therefore legislative power is one single and simple entity: and if the sovereign cannot be divided, neither can legislative power.' Elsewhere, on the same day (4 September), like many others, he spoke of the 'general will'.

In these rather rustic phrases, which retain nothing of the complexity of Rousseau's concept, the words of the *Contrat social* nevertheless permitted the naming of the new realities, while concealing what they were unwittingly borrowing from the past: the indivisible and limitless nature of sovereignty was an absolutist inheritance which the 'general will' transposed in terms of the autonomy of individuals producing a collective autonomy.

From that democratic chemistry, which went straight from the individual to the universal, Rousseau had excluded representation as incompatible with the very principle of will. The Constituent Assembly, on the other hand, combined a certain naïveté about the mechanisms of representation with such a unitarian conception of the sovereign. Here again, the most systematic theory was advanced by Sieyès who, as we have seen, thought of this political representation, which was essential within bodies as vast and complex as modern nations, by analogy with the division of labour within the economy: the 'representatives' were appointed to legislative activity, acting by proxy for society, elected by virtue of their particular capacities by their constituencies, but holding their mandate from the entire nation, and thus collectively sovereign.

The Patriots in the Assembly did not espouse all the arguments of this complicated theory; but the common feeling was certainly to give the vote to those citizens who were enlightened and capable of autonomy, so as to make will and reason coincide, and together to resolve all the problems posed by Rousseau and the physiocrats. The general will of the Constituent Assembly went no farther than the sovereignty of a body which was supposed to concentrate in its bosom both free individual wills and the evidence of reason.

The eventual attribution to the king – despite Sieyès's advice – of a suspensive veto on the Assembly's decrees during two legislative sessions did not modify the general economy of the new constitution. For it was not a matter of a government constituted as a counterweight, American fashion, within a shared sovereignty; the king's provisional veto was conceived as a simple possibility of appeal to the nation, a right given to the head of the executive to verify that representatives were faithful to the general will.

It changed nothing in the nature of the constitutional system being set up, where the Assembly was sovereign and the king exercised only a secondary power which it delegated to him, as the president of a republic calling itself a monarchy. The consequences of this daunting ambiguity would dominate French political history from the summer of 1789 right up to the second half of the twentieth century, when the problem was settled by the 1958 Constitution, modified in 1962.

MONARCHY, CHURCH AND REVOLUTION

These consequences became obvious at once, at the end of September 1789, and confirmed the 'republican' interpretation of the laws already voted. Louis XVI was reluctant to give his sanction to the decrees of 11 August, to the Declaration of the Rights of Man and to the first constitutional measures. He tried to use subterfuge, while the Assembly regarded all these votes as so many shares in constituent power, outside royal sanction. As at the beginning of July, he opened up a political crisis from a position of weakness.

The outcome was all the more to be expected since unrest had hardly ceased in Paris, sustained by municipal elections and the revolutionary incitement of the newspapers, and it increased rapidly in September, nourished by the debate on the veto and the food crisis. For though the 1789 harvest was good, it had not yet been threshed and interim provision had not been made. The disturbances of the summer made the circulation of grain and the provisioning of markets more difficult than ever. Unemployment was brutally aggravated by the emigration of many aristocratic families, who dismissed their servants and threw out of work their suppliers among the Parisian craftsmen. Money went to ground while waiting for better days: the failure of the two Necker loans in August had revived the fears of bourgeois *rentiers*.

When, at the end of September, the Flanders regiment summoned by the king arrived at Versailles, all Paris felt a renewed threat of counter-revolution, and was already talking of the possibility of the king's fleeing to Metz. In this emergency, the entire Patriot party, united by the summer's events – Versailles deputies, National Guard, Parisian democracy – prepared for a new day of action to force the king to draw back. La Fayette and Bailly, who could not have been unaware of it, and who remained the legal resort in that urban anarchy, made no objection. Mirabeau, who was already in favour of a strong royal government, was not in the habit of going against the tide; moreover, having got the measure of Louis XVI, it is probable that he supported the Duc d'Orléans's intrigues for the succession, in the hope of reconciling monarchy and popularity.

In this dangerous situation, amid so many menaces, Louis XVI and Marie-Antoinette provided the rioters with a cause. On 1 October the officers of the king's bodyguard had invited the officers from the Flanders regiment to dine in the beautiful opera theatre at Versailles. At the end of the banquet, at which many toasts to the health of the king and the royal family had been drunk, the king and queen, appeared in their *loge* with the Dauphin in his mother's arms. An immense acclamation accompanied them back to their apartments, where the tricolour cockade was trampled underfoot. The insult aroused fury in Paris: the next Sunday, 4 October, the Palais Royal crowd demanded a march on Versailles. The king was to be brought back to Paris.

Was it in order to isolate him from the accursed court? or so that if Paris regained its king, food and work might also return? The French Revolution was beginning its tempestuous relationship with urban poverty. The revolutionary lower classes continued to confuse the grain issue with politics; on 5 October a long column, mostly of women, formed at the Hôtel de Ville and started out for Versailles. Shortly afterwards, the 15,000 National Guards forced La Fayette to follow them. It was raining on that autumn Monday, which was the king's last day at Versailles. Having returned in haste from the hunt, Louis XVI gave in, after contemplating flight: he promised the women to have Paris reprovisioned, and the Assembly that he would sign the August decrees. But the arrival of the second Parisian procession as night was falling gave the crisis a second impetus: two commissioners of the Commune, who were escorting La Fayette, demanded that the king should return.

Everything was postponed until the next day; but the people, who had camped on the *Place d'Armes* finally invaded the château early in the morning. La Fayette, having rushed to protect the royal family, had no choice but to sanction the people's victory: from the balcony of the marble courtyard, where he appeared with a silent and distressed Louis XVI, he made promises and calmed things down. Louis XVI himself announced his departure for Paris: as in July, it was the king's defeat which won him the people's acclaim.

The huge procession of men and women moved off at the beginning of the afternoon. Following the National Guards, bearing loaves impaled on their bayonets, and the armed women and disarmed soldiers of the king, came the royal carriage, as heavy as a hearse, with the deputies and the victorious crowd in its wake. The people had imposed the tricolour emblem, together with the other symbols of their revolt: they were bringing back 'the baker, the baker's wife and the baker's lad'. At nightfall, after stopping by the Hôtel de Ville, Louis XVI arrived at the Tuileries, a prisoner in his own capital. A second wave of émigrés promptly fled the country.

By leaving Versailles, the monarchy was obeying the force of circumstance: exactly one month after the deputies had placed it under the yoke of the new sovereign, it was brought back to Paris under their supervision. Those two October days, as decisive as 14 July, marked the end of the sunlike solitude in which Louis XIV had revealed his royal omnipotence to his subjects, the people. All at once, they destroyed in actual fact the little that had remained of that power; in the streets they demonstrated the unlimited strength of the people's sovereignty, decreed by the Assembly. In Paris, the vast, melancholy Tuileries, where the royal couple were installed, had been more or less abandoned since the young Louis XV had left it in 1722 to go to Versailles: since then it had given shelter to a succession of 'squatters' including the Opera and the Comédie Française for a while. The royal pair, together with a small Court, were as if in exile in Paris.

To finish with this year of 1789, and even to go a little farther, something has to be said on the Revolution's relationships with the Catholic Church and the traditional religion of the French, through which the Revolution added a major element to the unprecedented break it introduced into national history.

That break, however, had not been brought about deliberately. It is certainly true that the French philosophy of the Enlightenment was anti-clerical in spirit, sometimes antireligious, and that in the act of inaugurating its reign, democratic civilization substituted the rights of man for a world regulated according to divine order. On another level, the clergy had been the first order in the kingdom, and the Church the greatest partner of absolute monarchy. But if, for that reason, it was inevitably wounded in the destruction of the *ancien régime*, the Catholic religion as such was not threatened by the revolutionary majority of the Constituent Assembly.

Republican historians of the nineteenth century, such as Michelet or Edgar Quinet, frequently remarked quite rightly on this point (to deplore it, however) that the 1789 Revolution did not intend to substitute a new religion for the old. Its ambition was limited to the radical rebuilding of the body politic on universal principles. In that it included, at least formally, features which gave it similarity to a religious movement; but the Assembly had never taken the step which would have placed the revolutionary concept in competition or contradiction with the Catholic faith. Although it had quickly given rise to a crisis with incalculable consequences between revolution and Catholicism, it was by way of a political logic of struggle against the *ancien régime*. By uprooting the Catholic Church from society, depriving it of its stability and possessions, it had violently separated French democracy from Catholic tradition. Here began a conflict which was fundamental yet circumstantial, from which France is barely emerging two hundred years later.

Its origins can be pinpointed as far back as the summer of 1789, since the Catholic Church had the most to lose through the reforms of summer and autumn. It received the first blow on 4 August, as the owner of 'feudal' dues, but it had to be reimbursed for these, according to common law. A far more swingeing blow, in the days that followed, was the suppression of tithes, this time with no indemnity. That exception had shocked Sieyès – the personification of equality before the law – but Mirabeau had justified it as making up for the public nature of the services rendered by the Church: if the tithe was too dear a tax for what it served to finance (education, welfare), the nation had the right to make use of the revenues for itself.

There was worse to come. The Church was also going to have to pay off the deficit which had given rise to the meeting of the Estates-General. On 2 November 1789 on the proposal of Talleyrand, Bishop of Autun, the Assembly placed 'at the disposal of the nation' the wealth of the clergy, to be used to repay the national debt. There again, the explanation of the motives was drawn from the idea of public service: the Church should not be considered as a true property-owner, but merely as the steward of its wealth, which was intended to allow it to fill offices which were them-selves revocable. In any case, this type of confiscation was not unheard of in Europe's history, since the English crown and German princes had practised it under the banner of Protestantism, and Joseph II, Louis XVI's brother-in-law, had given a more recent example of it in Austria in the name of enlightened despotism. In the French instance, the men of 1789, who were not especially anticlerical, and were in no way antireligious as a whole, killed two birds with one stone: they resolved the problem of the public debt by dispossessing one of the privileged orders of the *ancien régime*.

That was without counting a third gain – the most important of all: by selling the Church's possessions to the public, by lot, they firmly bound a large proportion of the French people to the Revolution, by way of their new acquisitions. In a first stage (December 1789), the Constituent Assembly authorized the Treasury to issue 400 million notes (*assignats*) bearing 5 per cent interest, and with preferential entitlement in the purchase of ecclesiastical properties, which had become '*biens nationaux*'. This first issue would be used to discharge the most urgent of the state's debts. But the Assembly took a further step in autumn 1790: the debt had become worse because of the undertaking given in August to repay the capital of suppressed offices; the old taxes were no longer coming in, the new ones not yet, and the political situation offered nothing sure enough to discourage speculation.

In September, just after the dismissal of Necker, whose reputation had ebbed away during the past year, the assignat became paper money, with no interest, as legal tender, despite all the expert voices which were raised (Talleyrand, Condorcet, Du Pont de Nemours) to warn against its rapid depreciation in the face of metal coin. It would be the Revolution's great financial instrument, but also its political weapon: 'Assignats', said the Abbé de Montesquiou, 'will form the link between all private interests and the general interest. Their adversaries will themselves become property-owners and citizens by means of the Revolution and for the Revolution.' Thus the Revolution had provided itself with a tremendous political instrument to involve both bourgeois and peasants in its future, by the same act through which it ran the risk of ultimately alienating a large part of the Catholic population.

In the matter of relationships with the Church, the deputies had been drawn since the end of 1789 into a logic whose constraints they had certainly not foreseen. If the Church were merely a corporation under the jurisdiction of civil power, what was to be said and done about the corporate bodies existing within it, such as the monastic orders? The Assembly's Ecclesiastical Committee had a bill passed in February 1790 stipulating that the law no longer recognized monastic vows and authorizing freedom to leave monasteries for those who wished to do so. During the discussion, the bishop of Nancy wanted to obtain the Assembly's recognition that Catholicism was the national religion: the motion was rejected.

There still remained the question of who would take over the administration of the Church's property and possessions which had been 'placed at the disposal of the nation': this was a tense debate, rough at times – notably when the Assembly again refused to declare Catholicism the national religion – which concluded with the transfer of the property to the new departmental and district administrations. It was the moment of truth, which split the apparent unanimity of the autumn.

At that time, the mass of clergy and the faithful had espoused the Patriots' cause. Neither the suppression of the tithe nor the vote of 2 November had deeply affected the general enthusiasm, or yet called into question the relations between Church and state. The clergy had remained loyal to the national role it had played in the previous spring, at the time of the meeting of the orders. Moreover, it had gained something from the Revolution: during the beginning of 1790, when passions were running high, the Assembly had allocated to the Catholic religion a maintenance budget which, for the majority of priests, meant an improvement. The high dignitaries themselves, Boisgelin, archbishop of Aix, and Champion de Cicé, archbishop of Bordeaux, whose duties were more administrative than pastoral, had experienced less difficulty in entering into negotiations with the state because the entire *ancien régime* had well prepared them for it; although they lacked enthusiasm for the new principles, they had at least rediscovered in them, now transferred to the people, the temporal sovereignty they had been accustomed to acknowledge in the king.

It is true that for the jurists of the Third Estate this Gallican spirit was underlined by the memory of the parlements' battles against the papal bull *Unigenitus* of 1713 and by the Jansenist tradition. Hostility towards Rome and any papal intervention was very widespread among them, as was the will not to accept any authority of appeal against the Assembly's decrees: the sovereignty of the people was no more able to compromise in the matter of its omnipotence than that of the kings. But though the Catholic Church had been accustomed to this subordination to temporal power, it was still dependent on Rome in spiritual matters.

Thus the political ground which was common to the Revolution and the Church of France – the predominance of national sovereignty over Rome – could also give rise to a conflict of principles concerning the domain of the Catholic faith and the authority of the pope on the subject. The legal non-existence of monastic vows had offered a foretaste of this in February. Although French kings had frequently made laws on the religious orders during the eighteenth century, they had not destroyed their principle: with the Assembly's vote, was it or was it not a matter of unacceptable encroachment on the spiritual by the temporal?

Two additional elements, of a different kind but both of major importance, added their weight of uncertainty to the risks the Assembly was taking on the path which was gradually leading it towards legislative innovations regarding the Catholic Church. The first was that a section of public opinion was beginning to be disturbed by the blows struck at religious tradition, for instance in the Cévennes, where the Catholic population faced strong Protestant minorities and the Revolution reawakened old memories of the Wars of Religion. July 1789 had been celebrated on all sides, but since November the spectre of religious confrontation had been on the prowl, and that could offer the first piece of popular support for the vanquished aristocracy.

The rejection of Dom Gerle's motion, on 13 April – Dom Gerle was the monk, 'ardent Patriot, but nonetheless a good Catholic' (Michelet) who had wanted to have Catholicism declared the national religion – sparked off trouble at Nîmes and the surrounding area. A strong Protestant bourgeoisie, cautious but also firm, was confronted by a Catholic crowd, stirred up by demagogues; they might well have rearisen from the sixteenth century.

The other element, of course, was the attitude of the pope. Born into the aristocracy, a narrow-minded priest and ostentatious pontiff, Pius VI well embodied the Roman tradition, and that implies how far distant the Revolution was from his mental universe. He did not even have to wait for the night of 4 August (when he lost the *annates*, those dues levied by Rome on the occasion of the presentation of certain benefices) in order to feel hostile to the new spirit. But in 1789 events in France provoked revolutionary disturbances among his subjects in Avignon and, to a lesser degree, in the Comtat Venaissin: the Holy See was attacked not only through the Church of France but also within its estates. On 29 March 1790, on the advice of the French ambassador – the old Cardinal de Bernis, disloyal to his mandate – the pope condemned the principles of the Declaration of the Rights of Man in secret consistory. The conflict was as yet only latent.

In Paris, it was not perceived as imminent, or even certain. Neither the men of the Assembly's Ecclesiastical Committee, who at the end of 1789 were considering the reorganization of the Church of France, nor yet the prelates of that Church, who were not totally dedicated to the Roman Curia, had any presentiment of an out-and-out conflict. Historians have restored to that period of history what, for its contemporaries, had been unforeseen and unexpected. The Civil Constitution of the Clergy was not the work of anticlericals out to destroy the Catholic Church. Nor had it rudely aroused the French episcopate to a state of holy indignation. Although it marked the point at which the Revolution and the Church went their separate ways to become merciless adversaries, the men of spring 1790 were not yet aware of it. Through its decree, the Constituent

Assembly had gradually been brought into this conflict, without ever having desired its consequences.

From that, perhaps, comes the fact that the parliamentary debate from which the Civil Constitution would emerge – from the end of May to mid-July 1790 – frequently seems rather a disappointment to historians; it did not match up to the high stakes it was dealing with, which the future would reveal. 'The discussion was neither powerful nor profound', wrote Michelet, who extracted from it only one important thought – that of the Jansenist Armand Camus, one of the leaders in the debate: 'We are a national convention; assuredly we have the power to change religion; however, we shall not do so.'

In that moment of time which the Paris deputy allows us to glimpse, Michelet dreamed of the religion of the Revolution which, according to him, could then have seized its opportunity but failed to do so. He read into that claim – withdrawn almost as soon as it was put forward – the spiritual timidity of the Assembly which, like the kings, was obsessed only with its own sovereignty. In fact, though long and painstaking, the discussions on the bill which would produce the Civil Constitution of the Clergy evinced a drying up of ideas when faced with the immense question of the relations between the new principles and the old religion; they were discussions between politicians, jurists, quibblers over procedure; between an exhausted, subservient, almost secularized Catholicism and a Revolution huddled over its brand-new power, which had been conceived, however, on the absolutist model.

The bill comprised four headings. The first substituted new electoral districts for the Church's old constituencies, worked out on the recent division of France into eighty-three *départements*. There would therefore be only eighty-three bishoprics instead of 130, plus ten metropolitan *arrondissements*. Overall appointments of clergy were rationalized and simplified by the suppression of all traditional titles and offices – prebends, canonries, abbacies, chapters, etc. Episcopal authority was henceforth collective, each bishop having to be assisted by a permanent council of curates compulsorily associated with the exercise of his jurisdiction.

Article 5 of section I disengaged the Church from any submission to foreign bishops or metropolitans, that is to say, in the last resort, from Rome. Section II, still more innovatory, substituted election for the customary canonical formulae for the nomination of ecclesiastical incumbents. All electors could take part in the vote, which was equally necessary for bishops and priests. Paid by the state, bishops and priests must undergo the obligation of an oath of loyalty to the constitution. Section III fixed the remuneration of members of the clergy, reducing it noticeably. Section IV insisted on their residence, under the control of the municipalities.

The religious order was thus brought into line with the civil order, the edifice of the Church structured on that of the state, founded on a constitutional sovereignty deriving its legitimacy from election by the people, its links with the papacy were severed; now it depended entirely on temporal government.

Faced with a reform of this scope, the opposition, led by Boisgelin de Cucé, argued the incompetence of the state in matters spiritual. A law touching on such fundamental Christian traditions as the authority of bishops or the choice of priests must also be approved by a national council of the Church of France or by the head of the universal Church. The retort came next day from Jean Baptiste Treilhard, the Paris deputy. It extended to Church organization the curse which the Revolution had laid on the *ancien régime*, condemning it as a tissue of disorders and abuses which could be judged only by civil government: he immediately let it be clearly understood that what was going to cost the Church so dear, in this debate, was not religion itself, but its close involvement in the old order, its collusion with the power of yesteryear. In any case, who had defended the spirit of that religion better than the men of the Ecclesiastical Committee since, by the election of priests, they wanted to restore it to rules which were closer to its origins? There was therefore no reason at all to question the absolute right of the sovereign over ecclesiastical discipline: the constant tradition of the monarchy had vouched for it.

The discussion of the articles, which began on 1 June 1790, was interminable, grim and interspersed with other bills and debates which had also been planned for the agenda. However, the Ecclesiastical Committee finally managed to get the essence of its plan voted in mid-June. The whole was adopted on 12 July.

Although it overturned its entire organization, the law was not unacceptable to a Church which French kings had accustomed to the rough supremacy of political power. In any case, not so long before, its Austrian namesake had been subjected by Joseph II to reforms of comparable brutality. The majority of bishops had shown some reservations on the Civil Constitution, but the main body of the clergy seemed willing to accept. Nearly all the prelates, moreover, were playing a waiting game, uncertain about the ultimate incompatibility of reform with canon law; meanwhile they were not over-anxious to fuel the suspicions of aristocracy that their names aroused. On the advice of the bishops, with Champion de Cicé at their head, Louis XIV, more hesitant than ever, signed the decree.

But it was still necessary to obtain the support of Rome and, more importantly, once the effect of surprise had worn off, the firm and deep-rooted adherence of Catholic opinion. The Civil Constitution of the Clergy would not withstand the test of time.

PROGRESS OF THE REVOLUTION

Those nobles hostile to the new era had emigrated, were emigrating or keeping a very low profile. The abdication or dispersal of the different social groups composing the nobility is a quite surprising and relatively little known phenomenon. Doubtless it had its roots far back in national history, in the humiliation accepted under Louis XIV, the political abasement and the acceptance of sycophancy; and then, in the time of the Enlightenment, in provincial isolation or the irresponsibility of salon or court life. A great era for the nobility as regards the brilliance of the art of living, the eighteenth century had at the same time multiplied the proofs of the nobles' political incapacity: emigration was their ultimate penalty.

There is additional evidence of the way the nobles were dispersed: in the Constituent Assembly, a nobility that supported the Revolution was constructing the new France in company with the commoners of the old Third Estate. In the Patriot camp, two La Rochefoucaulds, a Montmorency, a Talleyrand-Périgord and La Fayette, at the summit of his popularity, heading the National Guard, or in other words, Paris. Among his rivals of the 'triumvirate', contesting his authority, were a member of the 'old nobility', Alexandre de Lameth, and the former *parlementaire* Du Port, side by side with Barnave, the non-noble barrister from Grenoble. Lastly, there was Mirabeau, superior to all by virtue of his genius, but for that very reason and for what was known about his past, suspected by all.

During 1790 something began to evoke an 'English-style' fusion between the revolutionary great nobility, which had maintained its social prestige, and the bourgeois revolution. The Festival of Federation, which celebrated the 'national' spirit as opposed to the vanished 'feudalism', was the outstanding testimony. It was the year of a very temporary – although they were unaware of it – reign of an Enlightened society which had been formed by the entire cultural evolution of the century, in which liberal nobles and successful bourgeois could share ideas. Salons, clubs and newspapers were the marvellously new means of spreading and discussing the great topics debated by the age, which had finally become reality. Even the Friends of the Constitution, established in December 1789 in the former Jacobin monastery and soon known as the Jacobin Club, took care to keep the poor at a distance by imposing a hefty subscription: here was a France of notables and property-owners replacing that of the seigneurs.

Was this the France that innumerable reformers of 'abuses', *philosophes* and physiocrats had so tirelessly mapped out? Was this the France that provincial academies' learned societies and Freemasons' lodges had tirelessly – and somewhat more timidly – argued about? Yes, certainly, to some extent: the idea of a property-owners' monarchy was older than the Revolution. But the way in which it had finally come to pass, in the abstractness of principles and a social storm, enveloped its birth in the ephemeral on both the monarchic and the property-owning side.

What had been most spectacular and profound about the event was related to the universality of its message, which had made it resemble a new religion. The 1789 Revolution had wanted to rebuild society and the body politic on the idea that the essence of man, and therefore common to all men, was liberty. It has emancipated the individual from the age-old bondage of dependence, simultaneously destroyed the power of divine right and aristocratic domination, rethought society on the basis of the rights of each contracting party, and the body politic on the free consent of the electorate, by means of representation.

It had in fact combined two inspirational sources: liberal individualism on the one hand, according to which the constituent element of the social pact is the free activity of men in the pursuit of their interests and their happiness; on the other, a very unitarian conception of the sovereignty of the people, through the idea of the nation or 'general will'. Those two sources had been violently separated by French philosophical tradition, since Rousseau's *Contrat social* can be read as a criticism of the first by the second. But the men of 1789 made a fragile synthesis of them, using the concept of reason, which allows one to pick out in each individual the share which he can contribute to collective sovereignty, and which, moreover, is educable; if man's universality was not yet quite ready for the exercise of all political rights, at least it might be in the future.

In the Constituent Assembly's debates and the laws it passed, one may thus endlessly follow that tension between the universal principles on which it prided itself and their adjustment to the current situation of the old kingdom, which was a product of its 'gothic' past. The idea of '*ancien régime*' explained what it could not yet do; that of 'revolution', by contrast, meant being torn away from that accursed past by the advent of rational legislation. The new rights of the French had been stated negatively on 4 August, by the destruction of 'feudal' law, and positively, on 26 August, by the Declaration: now it remained to define them in statutory law.

The universality of civil laws encompassed all Frenchmen without exception. The Constituent Assembly had wavered a little before the question of Alsatian Jews, who were less 'assimilated' than the Bordeaux Sephardim and were the victims of a strong local anti-Semitism, which had its spokesmen in the Assembly. To begin with, in integrated the second group into civil equality before the first group, which it emancipated 'in extremis' in September 1791, during the last days of its session. Even the 'Mosaic religion', that cement of Alsatian ghettos which seemed so strange to this old Catholic country, was in the eyes of the law no more than a private affair of individuals, to be absorbed into the legal equality of citizens, which was a constituent of national unity.

Classic ground for this tension between philosophical abstractions and political realities was the redivision of national territory. The Assembly wanted to give a rational basis to both the representation and the administration of the old kingdom. The session of 4 August had done away with the tangle of 'feudal' electoral districts. At the end of September 1789, Thouret, for the Constitution Committee, had proposed his geometric plan for eighty-one *départements*, composed of absolutely regular squares. As each representative of the people held his mandate not from his personal electorate but from the entire nation, the best equivalent of this wholeness of the nation was to have each part of it exactly equal to all the others.

To that logic, history, geography and economy opposed theirs: the reality of national space, composed of such differing populations, traditions and activities. Mirabeau countered the committee's idea with one of demographic equality, and Barnave invoked the weight of customs and 'usages'. A debate started in those days to which, by letter and by delegation, communities from the heartlands of France would contribute in the name of their preferences, customs and ambitions. The final division of the territory emerged from a compromise between rationalism and empiricism, the spirit of unity and that of local government. The new France was divided into *départements* of comparable size, mapped out by deputies in accordance with reason and history, and baptized by their natural elements, such as rivers and mountains; each of them was sub-divided into districts, cantons and communes. All were provided with elected administrations.

Elected by whom? Political citizenship is a complex affair. Its regulation by the Assembly explains how 1789 also belonged to the bourgeois order, even if the ideas which had inspired the Revolution burst right through that reality to which so many historians have tried to reduce them. The Constituent Assembly had decreed equality, but it had also learned from the century's books that aptitude for government and public life was born of independence and education, and therefore from property and affluence. Hence arose a complex stratification of political rights according to tax thresholds, which contributed again to social inequality.

The precautions taken against the poorest acted both ways, as much against the aristocrats as against the multitude, who would both be equally capable of trying to exploit their ignorance. Another indication of the time: domestics, who were particularly numerous in the service of noble families, were excluded from the right to vote on the grounds that they were not independent citizens. Nevertheless, right at the bottom of the pyramid, there were still more than four million 'active citizens' – an enormous, audacious figure when contrasted with the 200,000 electors in Louis-Philippe's France, fifty years later.

Above them came the second-degree electors, then those who were eligible, who formed the new framework of the country. Theirs was the new, elected administration – municipality, district, *département* – liberated from the detested and centralizing *intendant*; theirs was the new justice, independent of the government; theirs was the new army, the National Guard, which had sprung from the events of 1789 and was guardian of the new order. Enlightened society was a revolution of occupations.

Another aspect of bourgeois ascendancy was the freeing of economic interests. The Assembly abolished monopolies, regulations, industrial and commercial privileges. It instituted the freedom of internal trade and also, in 1791, eliminated the democracy of corporate interests by Le Chapelier's law – which extended to the labour contract the equality of individuals before the law. No one had any thought of defending the right of employees to form a coalition; that would have been to recreate the corporations and trade guilds.

In the countryside the new liberal orthodoxy, learned from François Quesnay, Gournav and Adam Smith, clashed with the old community system, the psychological and economic importance of which for the small peasant has been demonstrated by Georges Lefebvre. The big farmer beloved by the physiocrats had for a long time been demanding the opening up of markets and prices, the end of village constraints, freedom to rotate crops, the right to enclose fields and meadows and the end of collective grazing: rural capitalism was the condition of better productivity. In the end, the Assembly compromised. On the one hand, it instituted freedom of prices and, on the other, authorized that of crops, for the benefit of the needy and poverty-stricken. Similarly, Enlightenment France gave way to popular France over international free trade: despite the good harvest of 1790, it prohibited the export of corm: the old fear of famine still ruled people's minds.

Nevertheless, the important measure which welded the French peasantry to the philosophy of the Enlightenment was the sale of the Church's possessions: the municipalities' action of putting them up for sale by auction in small lots which might go as low as 500 livres, with ample facilities for deferred payment, put the seal on what Michelet called 'the wedding of the peasant and the Revolution'. With the exception of regions such as a good part of the west (with the Vendée to the forefront, of course), it also marked the alliance of the rural world with the bourgeoisie, which derived the greatest profit from the sale of the *biens nationaux*.

All the beneficiaries, both large and small, were henceforth united, equally irreconcilable to the *ancient régime*. The break of 1789, which was so potent in national imagination, had another equally deep-rooted foundation in the private interests of innumerable families. Up until at least the middle of the nineteenth century, the question of *biens nationaux* would form one of the centres of gravity in French politics. It also played an essential, though less spectacular, role in the country's economic history: by multiplying peasant ownership, which crowned and accelerated a movement that had been going on for several centuries, the Revolution consolidated a pre-capitalist rural France – history thumbing its nose at the creation, at the same moment, of 'bourgeois' economic institutions.

However, the ordinary people of France, both peasant and bourgeois, who had celebrated the first anniversary of 14 July in apparent unanimity, split in 1790 over the religious question.

The Church and the king had accepted the Civil Constitution only subject to approval by a spiritual authority. The Assembly had rejected a national synod. There remained the pope, who was grappling with the matter of Avignon, a papal fief which was demanding unity with the France of 1789 and, both on principle and in the current circumstances, was little inclined to moderate his condemnation of the Revolution by making a fine distinction between the spiritual and the temporal. From prudence, both because of Avignon and in order not to expose the French bishops too soon, he did not condemn the Civil Constitution until 10 March 1791; but his opposition was known as early as May 1790, and widely used, chiefly through the self-interested channel of the tireless Bernis.

In any case, Catholic France was stirring ahead of its priests, mobilized by intolerance and intrigue, alarmed by all the novelties regarding Protestants and Jews, and annoyed that the Assembly should have re-fused to concede to the old religion a 'national' status which would have allowed it to retain a sort of privilege. The tradition of intolerance had resumed where it was strongest, in the towns of the Midi where Catholics and Protestants confronted one another: Nîmes, Uzès, Montauban. In Nîmes, in the middle of June, during the Assembly's discussion on the Civil Constitution of the Clergy, civil war raged for several days, to the great detriment of the Catholic forces, who were beaten and massacred.

At the end of the summer, the situation hardened everywhere. The Civil Constitution had been published in the *départements*, and was benefiting from the sometimes aggressive support of the new administrations elected in the spring. Popular clubs and societies were agitating for the immediate application of the law. On the other side, Catholic opinion was increasingly hostile. The bishops who were members of the Assembly broke their silence and on 30 October published, under the title *Exposition des principes sur la Constitution civile du clergé* (Exposition of principles on the Civil Constitution of the Clergy), a formal refutation of the law passed in July. Faced with this situation, where violence was still the exception but calm was precarious, the Assembly chose to go ahead: a decree of 27 November allowed practising priests two months in which to take the oath of the Constitution, and consequently of the Civil Constitution of the Clergy which had been included in it. This proved to be both the signal and the start of the schism.

One third of the Assembly's ecclesiastical members agreed to take the oath in January 1791. Only seven bishops, three of them without dioceses, took the oath. But the Assembly no longer counted: it was the country that mattered. Almost everywhere, the publication of the 27 November decree, followed by the ceremony of the oath in January 1791, gave rise to troubles on both sides, for and against the Civil Constitution. These disturbances were all the more serious when parts of the populace upheld or even anticipated refusals to take the oath.

In Paris, of course, it was the opposite: organized popular pressure was brought to bear on priests who wavered or jibbed, to force them to take the plunge. On the Sunday planned for the swearing of the oath, a huge crowd invaded Saint-Sulpice and threatened the recalcitrant curé, who managed to escape, to cries of 'Swear or swing'. But in Alsace, in the Massif Central – notably in the Catholic highlands of the Velay and Rouergue – and in the west – especially in what would become in 1793 the 'military Vendée', the region of the armed insurrection – the crowds forcibly opposed the ceremony of the oath: quite often it was the local authorities, the mayors and municipal officers, who had to give in.

These cases of resistance proved so strong and so widespread that the Constituent Assembly had to make concessions: having chosen intransigence on 4 January 1791, it climbed down on 21 January, authorizing refractory priests to remain in their parishes until replaced (and in all cases guaranteeing them a small pension). On 7 May it voted the decree known as the *'tolérance'* decree, giving the force of law to a measure taken in April by the directory of the Paris *département*, according to which refractory priests could celebrate mass in 'constitutional' churches.

This measure 'froze' the situation rather than sought to find a remedy for it. It simply took note of the political and religious impasse to which the Constitution had brought the Revolution. Indeed, at the beginning of the summer, the pope's hostility to the Act had become obvious to all, and the position of the 'public ecclesiastical officers' was unambiguous: the refractory priests had been replaced, or were on the point of being. But they stayed on in the villages or suburban districts, and the Assembly, in its desire for stability, finally had to accept the existence of two Churches, of which only one complied with the law. The Constituent Assembly wanted to put an end to the Revolution: it had provided counter-revolution with its officers and troops.

The numerous efforts of the past quarter-century to find social or socio-economic causes for rural counter-revolution have yielded only negative or very tenuous conclusions. The regions and social groups which rose up in 1793 against the Revolution were not, in 1789, any more favourable to the *ancien régime* than the rest: the *cahiers de doléances* of the future insurgent areas or of the parishes in the 'military Vendée' were as hostile to feudal rights as the other texts drawn up in the name of French rural communities.

It is hardly possible, either, to attribute the peasant counter-revolution – where it can be observed with hindsight starting from the events of 1793 – to a particular antagonism between town and country, bourgeois and rustics. For however spectacular that antagonism seemed to be during the war in the Vendeé, it was fairly general and took vastly different forms: the peasants of Quercy, for instance, well after 4 August 1789, continued the struggle for their own claims for abolition of seigneurial dues without compensation, defying the authority of the new urban administrations; but Quercy did not rebel against the dictatorship of Paris and the towns in 1793. It was more to the north, in Lozère, that an uprising began at that time. Furthermore, the antagonism between town and country might well have been more political than social, had not the cultural arrogance of the new gentlemen of the *chefs-lieux* in regard to the country regions proved more unbearable in practice than the seigneur's paternalistic extortions.

In the interpretation of the factors contributing to the counter-revolution, it does not seem that the religious element can be reduced to another level of reality. What is clear, on the other hand, is that this religious element was immediately transformed into a political problem, in that first the absolute monarchy, then the Revolution, had turned the Catholic Church into a body which was subordinate to the state. The crisis of the oath revived, in a more acute and infinitely more massive form, episodes from the history of relations between the old monarchy of the seventeenth century and the Jansenist clergy, such as the proposal to make them sign *billets de confession* renouncing their Calvinist doctrines. In 1791 the entire Catholic Church had to pay the price for its pact with the absolutist state: Jansenist revenge, in the name of Gallicanism, had only accentuated its political subordination. Henceforth, all its priests were obliged to choose between Rome and Paris, the Church's universality and French citizenship, inner conviction and the authority of the state. And behind the priests, or with them, the Catholic country's millions of faithful understood and espoused that dilemma, which was inextricably religious and political.

If one wants to understand the depth of the conflict which started on this dual level in 1790–1, one has only to consider how long it was destined to last: the map showing religious practice in mid-twentieth-century France – which, incidentally, is the least inaccurate approximation to that of the political right wing – is also very similar to that of the refractory priests of 1791. This bears witness to the fact that the national crisis begun by the Civil Constitution continued to dominate the nineteenth and a large part of the twentieth century in France.

The Revolution had struggled against the Catholic Church without breaking with Catholicism. Too close to the Jansenist and Gallican legacy to conceive of a secularized democratic state, it was also too far removed from it to imagine the start of a new Protestantism. Quinet was the most profound commentator on that impasse from which, without any deliberate intent, would arise an antireligious revolutionary culture still imbued with the spirit of a worn-out Catholicism.

Until the clerical schism, counter-revolutionary emigration had scarcely found an echo in France. The Comte d'Artois's little court at Turin, where Calonne had taken up service and gained promotion, had begun its long career of plots and counter-plots, but it tried in vain to revive the war of the Languedoc Catholics against the sons of the Calvinist *Camisards* of the Cévennes. Before mid-1790, the *ancien régime* had no popular banner. The religious affair provided them with one.

In Paris, it reactivated debates on the king, 14 July and the October days. The Assembly, since then, had organized its own royalty. It was sovereign itself, since Louis XVI was subordinate to it. He was no longer anything but the nation's first servitor, bound by the oath of fidelity to the constitution. The holder of a provisional veto, which was more theoretical than actual, he remained without authority over the majority of his officers, who were elected. He retained control over his ministers, but they were regarded with suspicion by the Assembly, where the real power lay.

There he was, subjected to the surveillance of the National Guard, which in turn was closely watched by Parisian activists, at Jean-Paul Marat's command. The days of action in July and October 1789 henceforth acted as models of revolutionary political behaviour: the king represented the heart of the plot, and the people the arm which broke the plot. A powerful image which, in the name of the people, superimposed on the legal sovereignty of the Assembly the organized or brute force of the sovereignty of the people, plain and simple.

It is too often forgotten that the Assembly itself had to hold its sittings under a hail of vituperation from the galleries, where every day there were crowds of readers of Marat's *L'Ami du peuple*, and vociferous extremists. As a way of compensating for the deputies' monopolizing of the general will, the people themselves were supposed in this way to keep an eye on the deliberations of their representatives: that was the double pathology of modern 'representation', the inconveniences of which mounted up rather than neutralized one another. In actual fact, the authority of the 'nation' tended to be exercised by two oligarchies: that of the representatives and that of the Parisian activists.

In this France without an executive, this constitutional monarchy without a constitutional king, a revolutionary dialectic was a quite natural response to royal resistance; that was the role of Paris, where three powers held sway – the municipality, the National Guard and the *sections*, or administrative divisions. The first two, elected or recruited on the basis of property qualification, were in the hands of the Assembly's patriots, La Fayette and Bailly. But the forty-eight *sections*, which in 1790 succeeded the sixty districts, played a more popular and autonomous role: through their primary assemblies, through their committees which enjoyed police powers, through their petitions, their addresses, their decrees, they were popular sovereignty in the flesh.

The unrest over corn had subsided with the good harvests of 1789 and the following years; revolutionary vigilance roused the *sections* against Marie-Antoinette, the 'Austrian bitch' who was hatching her intrigues in the secrecy of the Tuileries. In the winter of 1789–90 a violent conflict had set the Cordeliers district, presided over by Georges Jacques Danton, against the legal jurisdiction of the Châtelet of Paris, which wanted Marat arrested for his incendiary articles. The Assembly legislated under the constant pressure of this demagogy, which declared itself the guardian of the new legitimacy: that was already the revolutionary tradition.

In 1791, at the same time as the political climate worsened, urban anticlericalism made its appearance: one would have to look for the roots of this phenomenon, which antedated the Revolution, in the crises of Parisian Jansenism in 1720 and 1730. The democratic movement got under way through the creation of popular clubs and fraternal societies where, by candlelight, men joined together in the public reading of truly 'patriotic' leaflets. Marat and Danton ran the Cordeliers, on the left bank, and many local societies federated in 1791 around a central committee.

The revolutionary forces, which were critical of the Assembly's moderation thus made ready for their coming role by organizing the *sections* and the street mobs. But in order to be in the right, to win, they needed royal treason, just as the Assembly would have need of the royal word in order to contain Parisian extremism and revolutionary passion. But what if Paris and the king were in accord – even if from opposite directions – against the Assembly?

While its commissions, filled with earnest and competent men, accomplished an immense amount of legislative work, the Assembly, already in a doubly precarious position, had furthermore been continually split by the jealousies of its leaders – none of whom had been able to gain the upper hand. Mirabeau, the thundering orator of 1789, the bourgeois Assembly's *déclassé* aristocrat, was soon suspect in the eyes of Parisian democrats; it was not long before he was in the king's pay, vainly advising him to accept the new rules of play, and he wore out his genius in a double game of politics, dying in the spring of 1791. It was the same story for La Fayette – though he was less venal and less of a genius: the commander of the National Guard did not have the ear of the royal household, who could not forgive him for the October days, and on the other side Marat continually denounced him to the Patriots.

The 'triumvirate' (of Barnave, Du Port and Alexandre de Lameth) was under suspicion. The 1791 colonial debate showed that clearly. In the West Indies, the treasure-house of eighteenth-century France, news of the Revolution had exploded the fragile social balance between colonists, free mulattos and black slaves. The former wanted to take advantage of the opportunity to free themselves from the metropolitan 'Exclusive' rule and trade freely with all countries. But they had no intention of giving up any part of their local and racial proponderance, at a time when the mulattos were pleading the 1789 principles in order to claim political rights. Jean Jaurès has admirably recounted and interpreted those long debates in which the Lameths and Barnave supported the colonists, and Robespierre the mulattos.

Backed by Parisian societies – one of which was called Friends of the Blacks – the mulattos' cause finished in triumph. No one in the Assembly had really posed the problem of slavery; but the political dividing-line which had been established went beyond the mulattos, because it was a matter of the application of democratic universalism defined by the Revolution. It showed that, after Mounier, after Mirabeau, it was the turn of Barnave, Du Port and Lameth to do battle with the extremism of Parisian societies and the little group acting as their spokesmen in the Assembly. In truth, was Paris overstepping the mark, or was the triumvirate retreating? The very nature of the revolutionary imbalance explains that both were true: in this triangular debate, fear of Parisian excess brought successive waves of quite a few Patriot deputies closer to the king's cause. Speaking to the Assembly, Du Port stated quite clearly: 'The Revolution is over. It must be settled and protected by combating excesses. We must restrain equality, reduce liberty and settle opinion. The government must be strong, firm and stable' (17 May 1791).

A DEMOCRATIC MONARCHY?

After the *Monarchiens*, this was the second version of the need to 'terminate the Revolution'. But like their predecessors in 1789, the triumvirs of 1791, in order to achieve it, needed royal authority which was both strong and frankly committed to their side – that authority which they had destroyed two years earlier. It had resisted them then; it was no more favourable to them because it had been broken. A secret letter exists from Louis XVI to his cousin the king of Spain, written in October 1789, in which the phantom king of the Tuileries protests against all the edicts which had been wrung from him since July.

Between 1790 and 1791 there was Mirabeau's admirable secret correspondence with the court, the great man's extraordinary monologue to a king who paid for the advice of the genius without even being able to understand it. The deputy from Aix argued that the Revolution had carried away the *ancien régime* with no hope of return, but that it was not by any means incompatible with a renewed monarchy: the existence of a society composed of equal individuals, as opposed to the former corporate society (Richelieu would have liked the idea, writes Mirabeau, looking for illustrious sponsors), was actually favourable to a strong royal government. Mirabeau had never felt at ease with the idea of a virtually absolute sovereignty attributed in actual fact to representation; he had always denounced the danger of its handing over the will of the nation to a parliamentary oligarchy. Against a slide in that direction, the presence of a strong king was a guarantee: in any case, was he not the personification of national history, coming from the mists of antiquity, uniting the past and the present, and giving modern democracy the firm anchorage of tradition? Mirabeau was Chateaubriand thirty years in advance: it was just a question of 'nationalizing' the monarchy.

The monarchy, on the contrary, chose to offer the spectacle of its separation from the nation. Louis XVI's reply to the policy proposed by Mirabeau, who died in April, was attempted flight in June. It would not be fair to ascribe sole responsibility to the king for the failed dialogue and the untried policy: we have seen that the spirit of the Revolution left hardly any room for even a partial retrocession of public authority.

The circumstances of spring 1791 were less accommodating than ever: in April, Louis XVI had been prevented by the crowd from leaving the Tuileries to perform his Easter duties at Saint-Cloud and to receive communion from the hands of a priest of his choice. In the mind of the king, who was deeply Christian, the religious schism added impiety to all the other reasons he had for hating the Revolution. Captive in Paris, a stranger in the midst of a people who no longer recognized him, the king had wanted to flee, leaving in the Tuileries a solemn declaration of his hostility towards the Revolution. He was counting on the French undergoing a change of heart once he was out of the country; in reality, he made his own contribution to the death of the monarchy in public opinion.

Perhaps nothing speaks such volumes on revolutionary France as the tocsin at Varennes, that mobilization of a remote little village on the arrival of the strange carriage – and the silent crowds on the return trip, watching bare-headed over the convoy: Louis XVI started to die on 21 June 1791. He was not yet a hostage, but he was already little more than a stake in the game. For his flight tore away the veil of that false constitutional monarchy and once more confronted the Patriot party with the whole problem of the Revolution's future.

The watchword 'republic' was launched by small enlightened circles gathered around the Marquis de Condorcet and Jacques-Pierre Brissot. Robespierre mistrusted a republic which might lead to oligarchy. Together with the Assembly's left, and the popular societies and clubs, he contented himself with demanding the trial and punishment of the king: he made himself spokesman for the punitive reaction of the people faced with this proof of an 'aristocratic conspiracy'. The king was no longer sacred, but the fact was that he was guilty; the father of the nation had become its executioner.

How, then, was the Revolution to be 'settled'? The moderate Patriots of the Assembly tried desperately, though at the price of a fiction which would cost them dear in the future: La Fayette, Bailly and the 'triumvirs' persuaded the deputies to vote on a version according to which the king had been 'abducted'; dominated by fear of renewed revolutionary fervour, they pleaded the constitutional law, the king's inviolability, respect for what had been voted. Barnave acted with the most intelligence, explaining that the choice must by definition remain independent of the qualities of the monarch:

Either the constitution you have created is wrong, or he whom the chance of birth has given you for king, and whom the law cannot touch, must not, by his individual actions or his personal faculties, be important to the stability and soundness of the government . . . I will say to those who are holding forth so furiously against the one who has sinned: Would you be at his feet if you were satisfied with him? (15 July 1791)

The argument had its vulnerable side, however, since it acknowledged Louis XVI's faults as transformed into buttresses of the law. Paris was more sensitive about the flight than about the constitution. A vast campaign of petitions for the King's punishment climaxed in a central demonstration at the Champ de Mars on 17 July. One year after the great misleading festival of national unanimity, and on the very spot where he had been acclaimed, La Fayette gave the National Guard the order to shoot into the crowd. This was an important date. For the first time, the authorities who had emerged from the Revolution did what they had not dared to do against the peasants in August 1789, or against Paris in October: they turned against the 'people', on the side of the king. They had booked their places on the morrow's scaffold.

They were temporarily the victors, but at the cost of a new and serious split among the Patriots. Deserting the Jacobins' club, the moderates installed themselves in the Feuillants' monastery, whether they were followed by nearly all the deputies, while Robespierre went out of his way to keep the affiliated provincial societies true to the Jacobins – they would prove a formidable instrument for the future.

For the time being, the Feuillants seemed to be triumphant: they had some Parisian agitators arrested, maintained order in the streets and voted for several cautious alterations to the constitution. The property qualification for electoral purposes was raised, the eligibility rating was decreased. The Civil Constitution of the Clergy lost its character of constitutional law, so that it was not unassailable.

But the crucial vote for the future had been obtained by Robespierre one month before the flight to Varennes: the deputy from Arras, who had already seized control of the court of public morality, had had members of the Constituent Assembly decreed ineligible for the next Assembly. It was a decision which it was diffult to fight, on pain of passing for a self-interested Patriot, and which pleased a good number of tired deputies who were keen to return home; yet it was a demagogic decree, since it instituted a second revolutionary *tabula rasa*, more limited, it is true, than that of 1789, but nevertheless affecting all the parliamentary personnel who had had two and a half years of experience in the political arena. The constitution was deprived in advance of the support of those who had formed it.

Robespierre began his dual career of moralist and tactician. The ineligibility of the Constituents allowed him to marginalize experienced adversaries, like the chief Feuillants, and at the same time to give additional weight to the militants of the Parisian Revolution, who alone would keep the advantage of length of service: since he paid court assiduously to the clubs, his own influence would thereby be reinforced, including his influence over the brand-new deputies.

On 14 September 1791 Louix XVI – as in February 1790 – solemnly swore an oath of loyalty to a revised Constitution which he accepted no more sincerely than before, and the Constituent Assembly proudly proclaimed before parting: 'The end of the Revolution has arrived.' But its words were firmer than its convictions. In reality, it was bequeathing to the new men of the coming Assembly, in addition to its lasting achievements, the ephemera it had reconstructed.

The historian who seeks to understand why can begin from the extraordinary ease with which, on 4 August, the fate of old society had been sealed and civil equality inaugurated, in order to contrast the violence and uncertainties of political reconstruction. In fact, what had been accomplished in the civil sphere in 1789 was irrevocable, at the same time as, in the political sphere, there was an end to the absolutism of divine right, which was swept away with the whole of the *ancien régime*. On the other hand, the Revolution came up against the reconstruction of public

authority: no one could believe, in the summer following the Varennes
expedition, that this *de facto* republic, accompanied by a former absolute
sovereign, instituted by the constitution, could be destined for an easy
future.

Edgar Quinet put forward an interpretation of this contrast: the 'difficulties' – as he called them – of the Revolution were not in the civil order,
where 1789 simply accomplished, or crowned, so to speak, the work of
centuries. 'Not a voice was raised', he writes regarding 4 August, 'to retain
civil inequality. There was the unanimity imposed by necessity. Men took
stock of the ruin, rather than brought it about.'[2] The civil Revolution was
thus almost a natural product of the *ancien régime*, a simple updating of
history, conceded as a necessity even by the privileged, an invention of the
time; the political Revolution, being devised by men, was infinitely more
difficult precisely because its object was the free participation of citizens in
the new sovereignty.

The strong point of Quinet's theory is that it allows one to consider the
two faces of the same event: one looking towards the past, the other turned
to the future; one showing its determination, the other revealing its chancy
nature, in both the exact and the popular sense of the word. Basically,
when the Thermidorian successors of Robespierre, some years later, contrasted the *good* results of the Revolution with its *bad* development, they
would say more or less the same thing in other words: what had been
necessary in 1789 did not extend to what had followed.

Nevertheless, neither type of reality – civil or political – nor the
two successive stages of the Revolution can be separated by such fine
distinctions. History does not present, in order, first a civil society which
was immediately revealed to itself, in July–August 1789, in its modern
true form of free and equal individuals, then a state reconstituted with
great difficulty, at the cost of a flood of events which began only in that
year and would prove uncontrollable. On the contrary, we have seen that
in 1789 everything had been put in place together in the name of the same
universal principles, and that this ambition for radical construction from
scratch was the dominant feature of the six extraordinary months of spring
and summer, in both the civil and political spheres.

Society, and that society's government, were replaced together. By
placing the rights of man as the foundation of the social contract, the men
of 1789 had no difficulty in instituting civil equality, since they repaid in
capital most of the possessions connected with the previous aristocratic
social state. The movement of ideas and passions did the rest. But radical
philosophical individualism, which could not be divorced from the uprooting of orders and corporate bodies, made the construction of the new
body politic infinitely more difficult.

How, in fact, was it possible to envisage sovereignty, starting from
a society of individuals, and how could its representation be formed?

[2] Edgar Quinet, *La Révolution*.

Imagining it presented no problem: there was a single, all-powerful, inalienable general will. But as for its organization, in this ancient, vast, populous nation-state . . . It was necessary to pass via the idea of delegating the sovereignty through the representation of individuals, even if it meant in theory leaving the nation entitled to regain its rights at any time – rights which could not be alienated once and for all.

The year 1789 had caused the appearance, on the one hand, of *homo democraticus* in his modern purity, free in all things not forbidden by law, equal to any single one of his fellow men; and on the other, a new sovereign power constituted from that basis, forming a general will as absolute and autonomous as all the individual wills from which it proceeded. The Revolution had avoided the risk of the atomization of individuals in society by reinventing a sovereignty as indivisible and inalienable as that of the former king, but even more powerful since it had nothing – not even God – above it: henceforth it issued from the people, or from the nation, where it remained latent until the moment of the constituent contract.

But once 'constituted', in and by the National Assembly in May–June 1789, it had instituted representation: a major institution, under which the law was not agreed directly by each citizen, as in Rousseau, but through the mediation of representatives. These were not elected by the universality of citizens, but chosen by the more enlightened, in accordance with a double fiscal selection. Certainly, the electorate envisaged by the 1791 constitution was incredibly vast for the era; none the less, it rested on a distinction between civil rights, which were universal, and political rights, which were not: to that democratic man who was the central representation of the Revolution it added a contradictory element, at the sensitive spot. It was not by chance that Robespierre built his reputation as defender of the people on criticism of the *censitaire* electoral system.

In the new institutions bequeathed by the Constituent Assembly, there was therefore a dominating spirit of 'pure democracy': Burke had made no mistake when he wrote using these terms in 1790. He had thus designated the revolutionary *tabula rasa*, the universalist abstractness of the Rights of Man, equality, the destruction of aristocratic bodies, the turning of royal sovereignty to the benefit of the people. But the Assembly had preserved the king in a republican constitution, and had placed the universality of rights alongside representative government chosen only by a class of citizens. The royal problem would outlast it, although that had been decided in advance by the subordinate role given to the former sovereign in 1789.

For a time it would be a thorn in the flesh of the revolutionary movement. In depth, however, it was the tension between the idea of democracy and the extent of inequality retained by the Constituent Assembly in the new body politic which formed the mainspring of the Revolution. Anti-aristocratic feeling could just as easily become anti-bourgeois: it could be transferred all the more easily from breeding to vested interests, and even property, since it had the more vigorously embraced the abstract idea of equality. By the same movement, it could the better ignore representative government because the concept of a general will and a sovereign people inevitably evoked direct democracy. At all events, battle lines were being drawn up; on the other side, the religious quarrel had provided possible popular support for nostalgia for the *ancien régime*, and an entire 'Feuillant' bourgeoisie was beginning to worry about the consequences of 1789.

The Constituent Assembly had destroyed corporate society and instituted civil equality in the old kingdom. It had not settled the question of its government. The problem was to last for a hundred years.

3
The Jacobin Republic: 1791–1794

Between 1787 and the autumn of 1791 the unprecedented fluctuations of the French upheaval were due entirely to internal reasons: the legacies of aristocratic society and absolutism, the power vacuum, the king's resistance, the intellectual and political daring of the deputies of the Third Estate, Parisian and national agitation. The welcome given by Europe to 1789 – enthusiastic among intellectuals and the public of the Enlightenment, somewhat lukewarm in royal courts – had not turned the Revolution towards Europe. Furthermore, the 'Internationale' of the kings and the great had in the end managed to endure the fall of French aristocracy and the woes of Louis XVI without too much distress: they had made no move, despite appeals from the émigrés. For the sovereigns of continental Europe were counting on gaining territorial advantages from the disorder they saw in France: Austria and Prussia in Poland, and Russia in the Turkish empire. As for Britain, it was simply rejoicing in the enfeeblement of its rival.

Several events – consequences of what was taking place within the country – had contrived to upset this spirit of coexistence which, though disapproving, was peaceable and cautious. Between 1789 and 1791 the word 'patriotism' meant first and foremost attachment to the new France, even if those proclaiming it went on to celebrate the progress of the great principles of 1789 beyond French borders. As if hesitantly, and taking pains to avoid any conflict, the Constituent Assembly had been led gradually to proclaim a new international law extending the liberty of citizens to other nations.

To the German princes holding possessions in Alsace, who were demanding their feudal dues, maintaining that they were not subject to French laws, the Assembly replied, while offering them compensation as it had to the landowning seigneurs, that Alsace was French not by right of conquest, in accordance with the Treaty of Westphalia, but by its voluntary membership of the great 'Federation' of provinces of 1789–90.

In the old papal territory of Avignon, it had waited until September 1791, right at the end of its mandate, to declare an annexation that had been ratified beforehand by the population who had been demanding it for two years: it was the clash with the pope over the Civil Constitution of the Clergy which led the deputies to confirm the right of peoples to self-determination.

This was a formidable threat to international order and dynastic Europe, but it was still only implicit. Although they worked hard at it, the émigrés alone would not be able to open the road leading to war between the Revolution and Europe. In the end, it was the king who unwittingly showed the way, and quickly became its symbol and its chief stake. He was constantly writing to his cousin, the king of Spain, and to his 'brother' in Vienna, to whom he imparted his plans for flight. If the Parisian press, with Marat in the forefront, so frequently denounced those plans, of which it really knew nothing, and the *sections* mounted guard around the Tuileries – as in war one guesses at enemy movements – it was because of a presentiment that in Louis XVI they held a hostage against the European monarchies.

In fact, the people immediately saw his attempted escape in June 1791 as a prelude to invasion; the arrest of the king at Varennes and his return under guard seemed a victory over the foreigner. The Patriots were already at war before the kings gave any serious thought to coming to the assistance of their cousin in France: after Varennes, the Emperor Leopold and the king of Prussia limited themselves to signing the declaration of Pillnitz, which made any intervention subject to a general agreement of the European sovereigns. But if the Parisian clubs were mistaken about the diplomatic reality, they correctly read the wishes of the royal couple. They knew instinctively what the European chancelleries had not yet been able to grasp: when war came, it would be a war between two ideas. Louis XVI knew this too: the shared secret established a kind of complicity, an ardent wish held in common, but in opposite directions.

In the march towards war, therefore, there was no technical calculation or territorial ambition on the French side; none of that Machiavellian and princely rationality, those diplomatic or military calculations which typified war under the *ancien régime*; no evaluation of chances and risks. In this period France's strength lay in the century's demographic growth, the impetus given to society by the Revolution, and good technical reforms carried out in the military field by the *ancien régime*'s last ministers.

At the same time, however, the army was disorganized by the emigration of numerous officers and the subversion of discipline by democratic ideas; the volunteers levied after Varennes were still low in number. But this mixed balance sheet misses the essential point, which is that war with Europe would constitute the new form and intensification of the revolutionary explosion with all its contradictions.

Sieyès and the men of the Revolution had conceived the nation from the starting-point of the expulsion of the aristocracy, who were outside the community. When they drew, within the social body, a dividing-line which had hitherto separated Frenchmen only from foreigners and potential enemies, they replaced the traditional membership of all in the nation-state built by kings with a definition of the new nation, which was both wider-ranging yet more restricted: wider-ranging because it was rooted in democratic universality; more restricted because it cut into the historic community, from which the privileged were now excluded.

This idea, which was the fount of revolutionary hatred for the aristocracy and the secret of its violence, would find a sort of natural confirmation in war. Already the émigrés had occupied the place beyond the frontiers marked out for them in advance by *Qu'est-ce que le Tiers État?*: they were the perfect embodiment of the nobility according to the revolutionaries, even before they began to fight alongside the enemies of the nation. Armed conflict would thus superimpose internal and external enemies, civil and foreign war, aristocracy and treason, democracy and patriotism, around the same images, feelings and values. In this set of identifications the historian can discover much of the secret which made war so popular with the Revolution, and made it such a powerful instrument of political acceleration.

For centuries, under the kings, the nation had been formed in an antagonistic relationship with neighbouring dynasties and territories, at the cost of long wars and shared dangers. The French were not a new community, like the young American republic, whose citizens faced no external threat and were united in the desire to live in peaceful happiness. Like other European peoples, and perhaps *par excellence* among them, the French were accustomed to define themselves in relation to an enemy, to close ranks in the hour of invasion and to respond to the sovereign's appeal when 'public safety' was in jeopardy.

It was not so long since the ageing Louis XIV had appealed to the entire nation for its aid. Now that assortment of memories, habits and emotions could be mobilized against the monarchy which had been, for so many centuries, both their catalyst and beneficiary. The Third Estate had only had to brandish them against the aristocracy to bring down the king as well. By placing Louis XVI in the émigrés' camp, war would finish what 1789 had begun: it would strip the monarchy of its share in French history. The Republic, already implicit in institutions, would be inscribed in people's minds.

How could Louis XVI possibly understand this process, and thus avoid becoming its unwilling accomplice? He contented himself with playing his usual part in the symphony of escalation. After Varennes, the royal couple had hoped for war as their last chance for restoration. They imagined France as enfeebled, torn apart by the Revolution and incapable of resisting the professional armies of their cousins and brothers-in-law. In fact they strengthened the forces of the Revolution, offering the latter exclusive rights to their ancestral heritage transformed by 1789 – the nation. This enigmatic and all-powerful word effected the devolution of the collective patrimony from the monarchy to revolutionary democracy. It had defined the citizens' sovereignty; now it would feed their patriotism against the treason of the aristocrats and the king.

The concepts of democracy and nation, which had come together in 1789, forged around the war which began in 1792 a body of very strong feelings, welding together classes and the Revolution itself in a common passion. The philosophy of the Enlightenment, so cosmopolitan and European, had won over only a limited public, aristocratic and bourgeois, and almost entirely urban. Here, in its most democratic form, it was penetrating the mass of the people in both town and country through an unexpected channel: national sentiment. It was thereby simplified and radicalized to a point where very soon the Europe of the Enlightenment no longer recognized 'its' philosophy.

But what did that matter to the French revolutionaries? They gave the peasants and *sansculottes* leaving for the frontiers the chance to democratize glory – that caress of life which for so long had been reserved for the nobility – and to win in their turn a marshal's baton. By the precocious synthesis – destined for such a great future – which it effected between intellectual messianism and national feeling, the Revolution had integrated the masses with the state, and created to its own profit the modern sentiment of collectively belonging. In this sense, the French experience turned that of enlightened despotism upside down: democratic nationalism had taken up, against all the kings of Europe, the universal message of philosophy.

From then on, the Revolution's objectives received a new dimension, and its rhythm added acceleration, which its partisans hoped for and counted on: there was no foreseeable end to the war with Europe. Natural frontiers? Albert Sorel's brilliant and systematic book[1] seeks to portray them as the French goal in the conflict: the Girondins had said so, and Danton, and also Jean François Reubell, under the Directory. But Brissot, in a letter to Joseph Servan, also spoke of 'setting fire to the whole of Europe'. And the Montagnard Pierre Chaumette expressed even more vividly the almost emotional excesses of the revolutionary crusade: 'The land which separates Paris from Petersburg will soon be Gallicized, municipalized, Jacobinized.'

In fact, the revolutionary war had no definite aim because it sprang from deep within the Revolution itself, and could only end with it. That is why even French victories could at best result only in truces; to look for peace was as suspect as being defeated – both were betrayals of revolutionary patriotism. This is a measure of the extraordinary power of internal instability the war would have in all its phases – defeats and victories. It would bring three groups in succession to that ephemeral power conferred by a dominant role in the Revolution: the Girondins, the Montagnards and the Thermidorians. It would provide the backdrop for two successive types

[1] Albert Sorel, *L'Europe et la Révolution française*.

of republican regimes, on either side of 9 Thermidor 1794: dictatorship by the Terror, also called 'revolutionary government', and the Thermidorian republic, which would survive only by repeated coups d'état from start to finish.

Since the flight to Varennes and the Declaration of Pillnitz in August 1791 (an acceptance by the Austrian and Prussian Sovereigns that the safety of Louis XVI was a matter of concern to them), the French Revolution had clearly become a European question. Louis XVI had set the example by fleeing towards the frontier, towards the Germany of the princes and his brother-in-law the Austrian emperor, where the majority of French émigrés had already gathered on the banks of the Rhine. The Legislative Assembly, which succeeded the Constituent in Paris, immediately turned its attention towards these groups of 'ci-devants' who had left the country uttering threats to return on the morrow as the king's avengers.

The Assembly was made up of men who were new to parliamentary office, which is not to say new to revolutionary politics, since nearly all of them came from various administrative bodies elected in 1790 and 1791, chiefly from the districts and *départements*. The primary assemblies had for the most part voted in June, before Varennes, and the major electors had elected the deputies, in each *département*'s main town, in the summer during the crisis brought on between Feuillants and Jacobins by the king's flight.

The two clubs, which had been rivals since the split in July 1791, could both claim their share of the new deputies, 250 to 300 Feuillants, 140 Jacobins. These figures have only a relative significance: revolutionary events, by definition, could not obey the laws of a parliamentary arithmetic. Even more than the Constituent, the Legislative Assembly would have to sit under pressure from the people in the galleries, in a constant uproar, and amid the exaggerations of popular newspapers and societies. The Jacobin Club, kept going by Robespierre in the summer of 1791, brought together the most advanced Patriot leaders and formed the federating element of the movement. The Revolution would slip rapidly towards the government of minorities.

The most illustrious figure in this Legislative Assembly was Condorect, who had just managed to get elected in Paris, where the Feuillants had controlled most of the electoral choices: he was one of the few republicans of July 1791, at the time when Barnave and his friends had rescued Louis XVI, and was ahead of the Revolution before becoming too late for it. Apart from him, the newly elected members were not nationally known: minor provincial notables, they were mostly young, and were a less homogeneous group than the 1789 Third Estate.

For example, there was Brissot, a future Girondin leader, and already a kind of authority in the Parisian clubs, where he had been one of the destroyers of the Feuillants, notably Barnave. The son of a Chartres caterer, he had not succeeded, under the *ancien régime*, in his many enterprises. He had gone bankrupt in the bookselling business (hence a short spell of imprisonment), before becoming a hired article writer, dealing with topical subjects. He had Mirabeau's unconventionality, without Mirabeau's genius, and was the embodiment of the kind of political personnel through whom the Revolution would map out its course in 1792 and 1793. The men of 1789 had for, good reason, had no experience in such matters. He had what he had learned in revolutionary activism since 1789: ultra-patriotic rhetoric, superimposed on a politico-literary culture, the whole enveloped in daring oratory, a vigour born of confidence, a sort of ice-cold fever, which made him one of the Assembly's leaders in October, when he spoke against the emigration.

In fact, the spirit of revolutionary overstatement dominated the first debates; it led the deputies to take up the royal challenge on its own ground: war with Europe. In November, decrees against the émigrés, who were summoned to return, and an ultimatum to the German princelings – the Electors of Trier and Mainz – ordered them to break up the gatherings which had formed on their territory. That was the start of the conflict.

THE FALL OF THE MONARCHY

The royal family had painted things as black as possible. They had tried everything to get La Fayette beaten in the municipal elections and thus to place the Jacobin Jérôme Pétion in command in Paris. They wanted war, which they could not envisage as victorious. That was a secret calculation, since it could not be admitted, yet it was public because it was so obvious. In this encounter between the Revolution's suspicious mind and the secretive mysteries of royal policy lay a tragic complicity which led to war as if to a test of truth.

However, the kind of unanimity in the revolutionary camp was less clear than the wishes of the royal couple. Fresh claimants to the role of princely advisers, pushing their men into the ministries, the Feuillants, with a few intelligent exceptions (including Barnave), encouraged bellicosity: La Fayette was counting on getting command of an army, and the entire group hoped that a short and limited war would bring internal stability, through the power it would give to the generals. But these inaccurate calculations were secondary.

The main fact of the matter was that war was popular, advocated by the Assembly's left and waved like a flag in the faces of the Jacobins. The reasoning behind Brissot's great speeches is well known: on the one hand, to destroy Koblenz, the home of the émigrés, would mean putting an end to Louis XVI's double game and forcing him to choose; on the other, the war against the kings was won in advance, since the French army would be welcomed as liberator of the peoples. The increasingly isolated resistance of Robespierre in the Jacobin minority group is equally well known.

For once, the Incorruptible not only cut himself off from the revolutionary camp but also took a stand against excess and the relentless pursuit of the same policy. With his genius for mistrust, he had seen right through the objective complicity which the political situation had started between Louis XVI and the Brissotins. The king desired war because it would bring him allies who were much more powerful than the Revolution; Brissot sought it as a road to power; he had uttered this extraordinary phrase, which reveals all: 'We have a need for great betrayals.'

Robespierre had understood this language: it was also his own; but he turned it against his rivals. Betrayal, in fact, was already their crime if their wishes matched those of the king. In those great debates in December 1791 and January 1792 the two principal actors played opposite roles. Robespierre clear-sightedly denounced the perils of military messianism ('no one likes armed missionaries') and the danger that a conquering general might take away French liberty. Brissot, for his part, had sensed that war with Europe would speed up revolutionary radicalism; he was unaware that he would be the big loser in the venture.

Brissot played the role of sorcerer's apprentice. Revolutionary opinion backed him. What has been little studied yet deserves attention, is the social echo awakened by the talk of national messianism in revolutionary France – how the patriotism of 1789, fed by the violent split with the aristocracy, was transformed into the missionary zeal of 1792. It is easy to see what brings the two together, but the second stage is so immense and vague that it is difficult to imagine today how the French at the end of the eighteenth century could use it both as a slogan and as a political and military programme. Swept along by Brissot and his friends, the Legislative Assembly's greatest original act was to make this transformation clear and to give the unstable blend of the national and the universal an obviousness which even now seems a creation of the recent past. Every Frenchman can still, two hundred years later, recognize the similarity of present attitudes to those of 1792.

Louis XVI yielded to the tide the more willingly because he had already given his agreement, though for opposite reasons. In the spring he set up a 'Brissotin' ministry, losing what little autonomy remained to him as regards the Assembly, in the hope of regaining everything. The accession of Francis II of Austria, who was also determined on war, led in the same direction. On 20 April 1792, on the king's proposal, an almost unanimous Assembly (with seven dissentients) voted to declare war on the 'king of Bohemia and Hungary' (who was also emperor of Austria). That was a major decision, which would have consequences quite opposite to the intentions of those who had taken it: war would be the undoing of Louis XVI. It would break Brissot and his friends. It would bring Robespierre to power, before leading him to the scaffold, like the two others.

From that date on, Parisian and more generally urban popular riots would find a new catalyst – defeat. Not that the previous ones had disappeared: on the contrary, the inevitable depreciation of the assignat (it had already fallen to 60 per cent of its nominal value) and the rise in prices renewed outcries against the dearness of goods. The 'aristocratic conspiracy' was blamed more sharply than ever. But what better proof of treason could there be than defeat? If the revolutionary army retreated before the enemy, it was because the king, the nobles, the generals and the rich were betraying the nation: so it was necessary to punish in order to conquer, as it was necessary to punish in order to eat.

By radicalizing the popular militants' latent Manichaeanism and investing it with the aura of public safety, war gave a fearful impulsion to the terrorist idea, which was an extreme form of revolutionary political involvement. The ambiguous behaviour of La Fayette, who did not discount the idea of using his army to help the Feuillants, awoke the Parisians' worst fears: it was proof of the 'aristocratic conspiracy' and its infiltration into the heart of the Revolution itself. One of the great figures of 1789, the former idolized head of the National Guard, was nothing but a counter-revolutionary! Thus the Revolution progressed, leaving men and epochs crushed in its wake.

The bad news of the first engagements near Lille again triggered the already classic mechanism: mobilization of the *sections*, clubs and popular societies, denouncing the 'Austrian Committee' of the Tuileries. There was anxiety in the Assembly, which voted to call up 20,000 National Guards for the defence of Paris, at the same time making a decree against refractory priests, which was vetoed by Louis XVI, who moreover sacked his Girondin ministers in order to recall the Feuillants. In contrast with 1791, but as in 1789, it would be the street mobs who would deliver judgement: it was a sign of the times. The 'repression' of July 1791 had merely been an isolated episode.

On the first occasion, on 20 June 1792, the revolt which gained control of the Tuileries did not manage to break the king's resistance. The initiative had not come from the Brissotin group, or from the Jacobins or from Robespierre, playing his waiting game and still loyal to his post-Varennes position – the whole constitution and nothing but the constitution. The *journée* was organized by local agitators in the working-class suburbs to the east and south-east of Paris, Saint-Antoine and Saint-Marceau. The crowd of sansculottes (breeches with silk hose had become the sartorial symbol of aristocrats) forced the Assembly to receive its petitioners, then invaded the nearby palace, where Louis XVI, wedged into an embrasure, had to drink to the health of the people. But he would not give in about either the ministry or the decrees.

The failure of 20 June turned to success seven weeks later, on 10 August 1792, with the help of the revolutionary provinces. The distinctive nature of this decisive period lay in the contribution to a Parisian *journée* made, for the first time, by provincial *fédérés* (soldiers of the National Guard) chiefly from Marseille. The tenth of August thus marked the crowning achievement of an entire patriotic stirring against betrayal: France was threatened with invasion (the Prussians had entered the war in July on Austria's side) and the Assembly had declared *la patrie en danger* (the country in danger).

Against this background, demands for a Republic returned and developed, put forward by the Parisian *sections* and upheld by the Jacobins. The great Parisian club, at the centre of a national network, had since the preceding summer abandoned any reference to constitutional law in its struggle against the Feuillants. In July, it recommended the election of a new Constituent Assembly, that is to say, a Convention, and therefore a second Revolution. Robespierre backed the movement behind the scenes, before giving it its full direction on 29 July, in a great speech in which he dropped his position of 'defender of the constitution' (the title of a newspaper he had published at the start of the Legislative Assembly).

Those fiery weeks of summer 1792 set the seal on the alliance between the Parisian popular movement and the great bourgeois club where Robespierre was not yet absolutely dominant, but was becoming the principal authority: he built a bridge between democratic escalation of the principles of 1789 and sansculotte extremism, and at the same time between the past and the future. There are no written traces of the Jacobins' participation in the insurrection of 10 August, though such participation seems likely, by means of a clandestine directory: too many club militants made their mark on the day for there not to have been any consultation beforehand, and after the fall of the Tuileries, Jacobins were to be found in the command positions.

As always, the 'day' had benefited from an involuntary contribution from the foe: that was the Duke of Brunswick's manifesto, as commander of the enemy troops, enjoining the French not to harm their king. The text became known in Paris during the first days of August, and the uprising made ready in broad daylight while the authorities remained powerless. The *fédérés* played their part, but the Parisian *sections*, invaded by 'passive' citizens – a sign of the times – provided the main impetus.

In the early hours of 10 August an insurrectionist Commune (government of Paris) was formed by deputies of the *sections*, and the legal municipality was eliminated. Two columns of very large numbers of demonstrators marched on the royal palace, one on the right bank, coming from the suburb of Saint-Antoine, the other on the left bank and from Saint-Marceau, swollen by men from Marseille and Brest. Louis XVI and his family took refuge in the Assembly, just before the Tuileries were taken by storm by the rioters, at the cost of a fusillade from the Swiss troops whose duty it was to defend them.

Royalty, the stake in the battle, could not survive the victory of the people: the Assembly, surrounded and invaded by the victors of the day, had no other choice than to suspend Louis XVI and substitute a provisional Executive Council for what was no longer anything more than the phantom power of past centuries. In accordance with what the Parisian *sections*, together with Robespierre and the Jacobins, had demanded at the end of July, it convoked a new Constituent Assembly, the Convention, which was to be elected by universal suffrage.

The day of action thus tore out the last of the monarchy only by debasing the Assembly. The Brissotins had vacillated, trapped between the logic of their own policy and fear of an insurrection taking place without them – therefore against them; they were obliged to defend the throne without really wanting to, since in the denunciation of royal treason which the Parisian mob used as a sort of battle-standard, Brissot, Pierre Vergniaud and Armand Gensonné (soon to be called the Girondins) had set an example several months ahead of the time.

On the eve of the decisive uprising, they had not dared to accuse La Fayette. The latter, however, had appeared in the Assembly on 28 June, indignant – almost threatening – about the *journée* of 20 June. On 7 August the Commission known as the 'Twenty-one', elected by the Assembly to serve as a deputy executive, and presided over by Condorcet, had voted for his indictment, but on the following day, the Assembly had refused to pursue it, Brissot's and Vergniaud's friends voting with the Feuillants. La Fayette went to Luxemburg and fell into the hands of the Austrians on 19 August; the shadow of his 'treachery' extended not only to the Feuillants but also to the Girondins.

The deputies finally suspended Louis XVI only under threat of arms. The street crowds that had saved the Constituent Assembly three years before, condemned the Legislative. In July and October 1789, the poor of Paris had come to the aid of the National Assembly: not that this motive, or pretext, is enough to define the two insurrectionary *journées*, the second even less than the first; but in the end, 14 July had probably rendered irrevocable and put out of reach of a royal counteroffensive the title 'National Assembly' adopted by the deputies of the Third Estate. After 6 October 1789, forcibly brought back to Paris, Louis XVI had had to accept the Declaration of Rights, just as he had to acquiesce in the measures of 4 August and the lowering of his role before the sovereignty embodied in the representatives of the people. In both cases, the intervention of direct democracy – insurrection in the name of the sovereign people – had occurred in the sense of support for national representation: different, even heterogeneous, the two 'wills' had remained parallel.

By contrast, 10 August 1792 went further than the Assembly and forced its hand. It was not a matter of helping representatives to resist the king, or even to put paid to royal betrayal; it was a matter of taking to the streets to proclaim the end of royalty, and therefore of the Constitution and the Legislative Assembly. Direct democracy intervened *against* the representatives.

In this respect, the *journée* of 10 August demonstrated the fragility, in revolutionary opinion, to say nothing of any other, of the political concept envisaged by the Constituent Assembly: the power of representatives is sovereign, although it is only secondary (constituted) in relation to the constituent will, which is the prerogative of the nation. Consequently, national representation is both omnipotent and fragile: fragile *because* it is omnipotent. Since it belongs entirely in a single, indivisible body of deputies, with no external ties, it is also entirely dependent on its sole possessor: the people. They have the constant, indefinite power to re-possess it. The tenth of August illustrates this primitive scene of democracy. The Feuillants had wanted to bring the Revolution to a close. On the contrary, it had to be recommenced, to be taken back to its origins, in accordance with its spirit.

What changed on that day, even more than the political form of the regime – it has been seen that the constitutional monarchy of the Constituent Assembly was broadly republican – was the core of its nature: after 10 August the Revolution tended to disappear as a means of instituting a new order through the law; it existed increasingly as an end in itself. The Republic designated the way in which the revolutionary militants expressed their search for a political government with the same identity as its constituent element – the people. The Revolution became the theatre for the dilemma of democratic representation explored by Rousseau. Sieyès thought he had resolved it, but history had rediscovered it: in a large country, direct democracy in the style of classical antiquity was impossible, and without it, how was it possible to avoid usurpation of the sovereignty of the people by the deputies?

This political transformation by no means concealed, as Albert Mathiez has written, a social revolution: in this regard, the summer of 1789 is still the fundamental episode of French contemporary history. But it is true that the guiding forces of the Revolution had changed. Ex-nobles had become rare, notables with an *ancien régime* career less numerous, and the dominant tone was set by fairly unknown men of letters like Brissot, Marat and Desmoulins.

It would be wrong, however, to think of all the principal actors in the period just beginning as marginal or embittered. It is a useful explanation, but only in small doses. Neither Vergniaud nor Robespierre had exactly failed in their lives before 1789, to say nothing of Condorcet, who had been a member of the Academy of Sciences at the age of twenty-five. The truth is that the personnel of the 'second' Revolution comprised not only fewer nobles, but also fewer bourgeois examples than that of 1789, which it nevertheless resembled by virtue of the large number of men from the bar and the legal fraternity, and because it was dominated by a daunting involvement in political extremism, which formed the prevailing climate. Demagogues excelled – Marat, for instance.

In short, the factor these men had in common, for the most part, was not to have played a star role in 1789. They were not so much sons of the *ancien régime* as of the revolutionary years, having done their training in administrations and clubs. Since then, they had been biding their time, schooled in the particular discipline of revolutionary language and less distanced from the people than their predecessors. They had learned

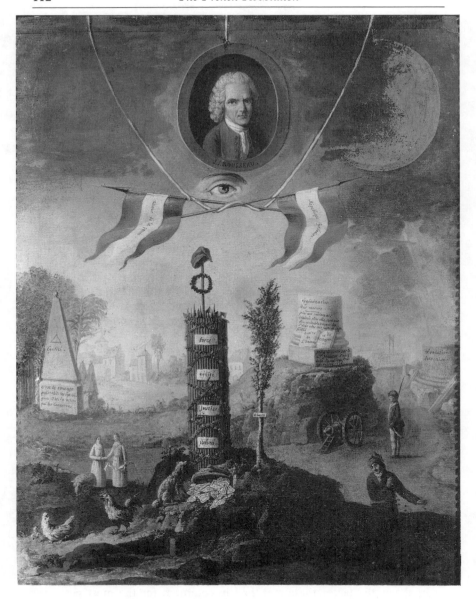

Nicolas Henry Jeaurat de Bertry Revolutionary Allegory, *1794, Musée de la Ville de Paris, Musée Carnavalet, Paris.*
(Photo: Lauros-Giraudon)

respect for property in the century's books, but needed to form an alliance with the 'lowly' in order to win and exercise power, or what remained of it. That was also what would divide them.

The period following 10 August and preceding the meeting of the Convention (21 September) was marked by a duality of power: Paris and the Assembly. The legal government of the Legislative Assembly, which had only a month more to run, was counterbalanced by the urban dictatorship of an insurrectionist Commune which had emerged from 10 August. The Parisian *sectionnaire* movement of local revolutionary committees had found its spokesman, and its constant pressure forced the Assembly to back a policy foreshadowing the Terror. The *sections'* surveillance committees increased the number of searches, corn requisitions and arrests of suspects; the Assembly appointed an Executive Council of six members to replace the imprisoned king, set up a special tribunal and worsened the penalties against non-juring priests.

On the Executive Council, which the Girondins had hoped to control through their three former ministers, Clavière, Servan and Jean-Marie Roland, the chief personage was Danton, because he was the link with the Commune – the real power in the summer. Like Robespierre, snatched away from the bar by 1789, he was one of the conspicuous men in Parisian activism, based in the Cordelier Club, which had a stronger working-class membership than the Jacobins. From 1790, his role was as leader of the Parisian *sections* petitioning the Constituent Assembly against the king's ministers. The following year, after Varennes, he was one of the chief agitators for the suspension of the sovereign. His role on 10 August has been the subject of celebrated controversy among historians. According to Alphonse Aulard, he did almost everything; according to Albert Mathiez, almost nothing. Nevertheless, he was among those who profited greatly from that day, and was the symbolic figure of 1792.

Feature for feature, he was the complete opposite of Robespierre, although not yet politically separated from him: in style, temperament and type of talent. Danton was what is called a 'natural', an instinctive orator, the antithesis of the studious, retiring Robespierre the 'Incorruptible'. But he lacked continuity in his planning, and that impressive economy of means to be used for a project, which characterized Robespierrist strategy. He was erratic, a pleasure-lover, familiar with money worries and the value of private happiness; in short, as has often been said, a popular version of Mirabeau, to whom he was much inferior in intelligence. His demagogic talent found ample scope in the circumstances of summer 1792. Danton personified both the *patrie en danger* and the first version of the Terror.

Not eveything depended on circumstance, however, in the revolutionary thrust of August–September. The longer-term legislative work was similarly speeded up by the situation: the secularization of the clergy, the institution of divorce, and new concessions to the peasantry. Émigrés' properties were put up for sale in small lots, and compulsory redemption of seigneurial dues disappeared, except on production of the original deed.

Portrait of Maximilien Robespierre, *Musée Carnavalet, Paris.*
(Photo: Lauros-Giraudon)

Thus 10 August 1792 completed the great measures of 1789 and hastened seigneurial dispossession: that was one of the Parisian revolution's trump cards with regard to the rural world. The dying Assembly had allowed the Terror to be set up in Paris, under the iron rule of the insurrectionist Commune. But in those terrible circumstances it still pursued its legislative work, by which it instituted a new civic society maintaining the spirit of 1789, a contrast destined to be perpetuated with the Convention.

However, neither the Assembly nor the Executive Council, nor even Danton, who was the outstanding voice of the summer, managed to channel – let alone control – insurrectionist pressure which, on the contrary, was magnified by the bad news from the fronts (the fall of Longwy and Verdun). The organized massacres perpetrated in the Paris prisons between 2 and 5 September bear tragic witness to the chain of images dominating terrorist ideology: defeat, betrayal, punishment. But by their savagery – between 1,000 and 1,500 victims, mostly common law prisoners – they also reveal to what extent these bloody excesses had risen since the spring. Danton, the Minister of Justice, had kept quiet; the Girondins were paralysed with fear: Robespierre had already accused Brissot of treason. In the Commune, a complete style of rhetoric had developed to justify the event. The struggles of men and groups to gain power henceforth borrowed the language of terror from the *sections*.

Portrait of Danton, *Musée de la Ville de Paris, Musée Carnavalet, Paris.*
(Photo: Lauros-Giraudon)

On the very day when the Convention was constituted (20 September), victory at Valmy saved France from invasion: this was both a political and a psychological triumph, because the army of volunteers had held fast in the face of the best soldiers of the era, but from a military point of view it was only half a victory, followed by negotiations whereby General Dumouriez allowed the Prussians to go peacefully back to their winter quarters. The famous artillery duel had therefore settled nothing in the long term, and 10 August had been followed by a flood of diplomatic breaks with Europe.

The Convention, which met on 21 September, had thus been elected in conditions which had nothing to do with a free ballot in peaceable circumstances, as seen in modern democracies. It was the advent of universal suffrage in French history, but only militant revolutionaries dared to make an appearance in the assemblies. Everyone demanded Louis XVI's dethronement. The decisive ballot took place at departmental level, in the assembly of electors of the *chef-lieu*, among supporters of what had happened on 10 August. In Paris and several of the *départements*, election took place in the Jacobin Club, in public and out loud.

The Convention had therefore been elected by a small minority of the population, but those who were the most determined. That explains the ambiguity of the word 'popular' when it is applied to this period: 'popular' the French Revolution was certainly *not* in the sense of participation by the people in public affairs. Michelet stressed this, to contrast the period with 1789: the end of 1792 marked the beginning of the withdrawal of public opinion, when the people 'went home';[2] fear had commenced its reign. But if the word 'popular' is taken to mean that revolutionary policy was formed under pressure from the sansculotte movement and organized minorities, and received an egalitarian impetus from them, then yes, the Revolution had well and truly entered its 'popular' age.

However, the Convention – 749 members strong – was a bourgeois assembly. It comprised nearly half the deputies who had sat in the Constituent or the Legislative Assemblies, the same weight of lawyers and barristers, the inimitable style of the epoch which the years had intensified. All these men had three or four years of political battles behind them but, in that era, experience was exactly the opposite of practice in these matters. There was a marked and increasing separation between intellectual and actual politics.

By recommencing the Revolution, the *Conventionnels* escalated the spirit of 1789. For the moment, they had a tendency to decide their voting in the light of the most recent events: that period from 10 August to 20 September when the Paris Commune, born of insurrection, had overridden a Legislative Assembly which was doomed from the outset. The Girondins did not form an organized group in the modern sense of a party, nor did the Montagnards. But Brissot and his friends, Vergniaud, Buzot, Roland and Jean Louis Carra, formed a focus of opinion (more than reluctant when faced with the consequences of 10 August), while the Paris deputies often came from the headquarters of the insurrectionist Commune: Robespierre, Collot d'Herbois, Billaud-Varenne, Camille Desmoulins, Danton. Events yet to come, and firstly the king's trial, would crystallize these two antagonistic groups on one or other side of the divide which already separated Robespierre from Brissot, or Roland from Danton.

At the time it met, the mass of the Convention contained men who had not taken sides: they were referred to as the *Plaine* (or *Marais*). It would be a misinterpretation to infer from those contemporary names an idea of centre politicians, accustomed to the safe subtleties of parliamentary compromise. The Conventionnels of the Marais were men of the 10 August Revolution, 'patriots' of the revolutionary war, bitter adversaries of the *ancien régime* – including the monarchy. Certainly, they were still bourgeois supporters of freedom of contracts and trade, and counted property among the foundations of the social order; but that did not make them any the less deputies engaged in irrevocable conflict with old France and the Europe of the kings. They included the indestructible Sieyès, faithful to his post, slightly less to the fore than in 1789 but constant in his hatred of the aristocracy.

---

[2] Jules Michelet, *Histoire de la Révolution française*, book IX, ch. 1.

THE EXECUTION OF LOUIS XVI

After its inauguration on 20 September, the Convention met on the 21st. It marked its advent by two significant votes; one to its left, the other to its right. It was simultaneously decreed that the future constitution would be submitted to the people, and that 'all territorial properties, both personal and industrial, shall be maintained in perpetuity.' But above all, in an atmosphere which harked back to the night of 4 August, it declared unanimously that royalty in France was abolished: the other part of the *ancien régime*, the monarchy after feudalism, was buried amid the same enthusiasm.

The word 'republic' had not been uttered, as if the Assembly were hesitating on the brink of the first precipice to be tackled: a republic, likened at the time to direct democracy (as can be seen in the Sieyès of 1789), was a regime belonging to antiquity, possible in city-states but incompatible with the vast populations and huge territories brought together in modern monarchies. However, the Convention took the plunge the next day. It accompanied its decision with a major consequence of a symbolic nature: the advent of the Republic would also be the date of the first day of Year I of liberty. The year 1789 was cast back into the *ancien régime*! To a member (Dr Salle) who indeed proposed Year IV, instead of Year I, to place the event in continuity with 1789, Marc-David Lasource replied: 'It is ridiculous to date it Year IV of liberty; for, under the constitution, the people had no true liberty . . . No, gentlemen, we have been free only since we have no longer had a king.' His words were greeted with applause.

What was to be done with the king? The Commune had placed him with his family in the keep of the Temple, in the heart of Paris, but it was for the Convention to decide the fate of this person who had no precedent in French history – a deposed king. The Convention had wrested from the Commune the papers seized in the Tuileries, and appointed a Commission to examine them. It had begun to discuss the conditions of the monarch's trial when, 20 November, the accidental discovery of a secret cupboard which had been contrived in one of the Tuileries walls delivered to the Commissioners part of the king's confidential correspondence – mainly with his Austrian in-laws.

If it was not enough to prove treason in the strictest sense, this correspondence nevertheless formed a dossier about counter-revolution which allowed the king's duplicity to be established on documentary evidence: Mirabeau's letters, in revolutionary opinion, dishonoured the greatest man of 1789 while at the same time bearing witness to *ancien régime* corruption at work in the failed regeneration of that celebrated year. Such contamination revived a crucial question: which Louis XVI was to be tried? When it destroyed the *ancien régime*, the Revolution had preserved the king; it had reinvented and rechristened him, turning him into the nation's first servant, in the terms of the 1791 constitution. It was that king who had been suspended on 10 August, and deposed on 21 September, and who therefore had to be tried; but he had also personified the *ancien régime*, which his ancestors had embodied for so many centuries.

Of those two images superimposed in one man, the Convention retained only one: that of the constitutional king, established by the Act finally voted in September 1791. The court's task was not made any easier thereby, since the constitution had guaranteed inviolability to the king, as to the deputies. Moreover, Barnave and the Feuillants had used the argument in July 1791 to save Louis from deposition after Varennes. The law had provided for only three possibilities of this guarantee being called into question: if the king left the kingdom, placed himself at the head of a foreign army or refused to take the constitutional oath.

In November 1792, none of these was demonstrable from the documents in the dossier, although every deputy was personally convinced that Louis XVI had toyed with all these plans: he had been caught just in time at Varennes, and the letter of the law put Louis XVI out of reach, although he was guilty in the eyes of all. From that arose the predicament in which the Convention found itself during the whole discussion on inviolability in November and December.

That predicament also expressed a scrupulous regard for legality which was enough to place the king's trial outside the revolutionary institution of the Terror, which came afterwards. The Conventionnels had in mind the English precedent of 1649, when an improvised court of deputies appointed by Cromwell had brought a botched action against a Charles I who was very sure of his law. They, on the other hand, represented national sovereignty, and intended to judge Louis XVI according to the law which both they and he had shared in common: that of the constitution.

In fact, they could not do so. Firstly, because the obstacle posed by inviolability was impossible to remove legally as things stood. Then, above all, because the legitimacy – or the crime – of Louis XVI had its roots far beyond that date of 1791, and called into question infinitely more than an argument about constitutional law. The fact remains that parliamentary debate during the last two months of 1792 – as Jaurès, one of the few great commentators on the debate, has noted – went deeply into those fundamental questions. One may think, in company with an American philosopher,[3] that the Convention wanted to cover with a 'maximum of legality' a decision which could not find its source in the Constitution. That was a sign that it had not yet reached the stage when it identified law with power.

For all the orators, the image of the *ancien régime* king was never far away; even for those pleading the 1791 text as jurists (for and against inviolability). All the force of Saint-Just's speech, on 13 November, went into showing its radical incompatibility with revolutionary citizenship. The young deputy from the Aisne, author in 1791 of a fairly moderate little

---

[3] Michel Walzer (ed.), *Regicide and Revolution: Speeches at the Trial of Louis XVI*.

book, had chosen to make his entry into the Convention as an extremist: he brought the sovereignty of the nation face to face with that of the king, legitimacy with usurpation; he declaimed against the nullity of the 1791 contract, denied the existence of any legal relationship between a king and a people – and therefore even the possibility of a trial: Louis XVI was a criminal simply because he had been king and, as such, should be killed, not tried.

Robespierre, a little later (December 3), adopted the same tone in building a more political argument, holding that the respect for judicial formalities displayed by the Convention implied doubt about what the people had done on 10 August: if the king could be brought to trial and therefore presumed innocent by a court, could the hypothesis be made that the Revolution was guilty? That was a formidable trick question, elaborated by his Machiavellian mind which always steered a middle course between principles and objectives; it was addressed to the Paris activists, and pointed out to them their new enemies in the Assembly.

The Convention's debate, however, remained centred on the interpretation of the 1791 constitution and inviolability. To try the *ancien régime* king would go against the principle of non-retroactive laws. Jean Mailhe, the *rapporteur* presenting the recommendations of the Legislation Committee, had said very early on all that could be said against inviolability: the latter ceased to apply when acts were committed outside legal functions; Louis had now become an ordinary citizen, and thus liable to prosecution. Furthermore, if he had committed none of the three crimes for which inviolability could be suspended, he had frequently, as king, put himself in breach of the law, immediately coming within the scope of laws which targeted corrupt officials.

Today's historians, reading this long legal quibble over a dead constitution, are astounded by its strangeness: the deputies argued over the king's inviolability, while Louis XVI languished in prison. Nevertheless, if the situation, rather than the law, indicated the fatal outcome of the discussion, it is very important to understand the Convention's interrogation of itself and the Revolution, on the brink of events which would carry away part of its authority.

The king was declared able to be brought to trial on 3 December, and the Convention transformed itself into a court of justice, deeming itself the only tribunal equal to this national act. Then the trial proper began, the king making two appearances, on 11 and 26 December, the day after Christmas. These were unhappy debates, in which the former monarch – deprived of his royal majesty, lacklustre, tragic because so out of his element – retreated with his lawyers into a narrow system of defence, incapable of pleading the cause of the French monarchy and even of personifying its memory.

The indictment's reference to the 1791 constitution effaced everything that had happened before. After that date, Louis XVI, whom the judges addressed as Capet, his family name, just like any other citizen, sheltered behind his ministers, or took refuge in his poor memory, or yet again denied everything – even the evidence, such as the documents signed by him. The secret of this sad farewell lies not only in his political mediocrity, his taciturn nature or his solitariness; above all, it was due to the fact that he was being interrogated in a world quite foreign to him. The king of England, Charles I, had outclassed his judges in 1649; but he had been on his own ground; he had brandished the English Constitution, by virtue of which he was king, to demand of Cromwell's judges by what right they judged him.

In the France of 1792 the situation was reversed. The ex-king did not have in common with his judges a royal constitution which he could use against them. The Revolution had created the one of 1791; how could he defend what he was, on the basis of that Act which already made him entirely dependent on it, and by which he had given his support beforehand to the curse laid on the *ancien régime*? Louis XVI kept silent because he had nothing to say in answer to the questions he was being asked; his shared history with France had ceased earlier. His counsel, Raymond de Sèze, François Tronchet and old Malesherbes, would plead such a meagre case that Jaurès – an unlikely defender of the old monarchy – rewrote their script: one of the most moving passages in the admirable *Histoire socialiste de la Révolution française* is the imaginary speech for the defence, in which the writer, who belonged to so different a tradition, renders homage to the fallen king.

The monarchy was dead, but the Girondin deputies wanted to save the king, to spare him from being sentenced to death, or at least from having the sentence carried out. The outlines of the group in the Convention become more clearly discernible around this common desire. Brissot, Vergniaud and their friends, after being the chief instigators of the war with Europe, and enemies of the court, had become moderates – a change of front found throughout the course of the Revolution among those in command, but which, for them, had happened very quickly, between July and November. Not that they had become royalists, as their adversaries would inevitably maintain. But they feared Paris and Parisian revolutionary extremism. Memories of the summer were one of their obsessions: the dictatorship of the insurrectionist Commune, the prison massacres – which had gone unpunished and were therefore excused – and the passion of the crowds that continued to intervene in the Assembly's debates.

All those second-generation provincial bourgeois, such as Vergniaud, Buzot, Gensonné and Guadet, had dreamed about revolutionary France more than they had actually known it. Rather like their oracle, Madame Roland – a sensitive and earnest woman, but enclosed in a literary relationship with the times she was living through – they lacked any real political strength: detested by the right, hated by the left, caught between two lines of fire, retreating from what they had undertaken. Those who had been the great apostles of the war to free the peoples now feared that the king's death might bring in its wake a rupture with Britain and Spain.

But that was a secondary argument, which derived from their parliamentary conflict with the men who had backed the Commune in the summer, Robespierre and Marat to the fore.

They had manoeuvred in vain to delay the trial. The idea which brought them together in December was to submit the Convention's judgement to the primary assemblies, thus to the people: this idea was apparently irrefutable, since it drew directly on the core of revolutionary argument, going from the representatives back to the nation which had constituted them. The first great parliamentary battle between Girondins and Montagnards took place with each side reversing its expected stance: Vergniaud based the appeal to the people on a criticism of representation, and Bertrand Barère, speaking against an appeal to the people, extolled the sovereignty of the Convention. The conflict of principles exposed the uncertainty of ideas, but chiefly the political stakes.

The weakness of Girondin argument lay in the fact that it left its supporters open to the accusation of royalism. The *appelants* (they would keep this name) were those deputies who appealed for help from the *départements* against Paris in order to save the king's head; their desire was less to consult the people than to rally moderatism against the victors of 10 August. Against them, Barère, the son of a notary from Tarbes, who was not a true-blue Montagnard, gained the ear of the Assembly by his decisive speech at the beginning of January: he described the circumstances, demonstrated the lack of realism of a national consultation, the risks of civil war and the equivocal nature of Girondin intentions. Finally he argued for the Convention's responsibility: you must not, he said to his colleagues, 'throw back on the sovereign the task the sovereign has given you to perform.'

Voting was by name, a defeat for the clemency camp, since every man had publicly to mark out his place for the morrow. Three questions were put: first that of guilt; then whether there should be an appeal to the people; and finally that of sentence. The Montagnards gained a new advantage, since the first vote, which was almost unanimous, would weigh on the other two. An appeal to the people was then rejected by 424 votes to 287; death was decided upon by a small majority. But because forty-six deputies wanted to suspend capital punishment, with various demands for a reprieve, the Convention voted a fourth time on a reprieve, which was rejected by 380 votes to 310.

Louis XVI was executed on the morning of 21 January 1793, in the Place de la Révolution (today Place de la Concorde). He had been a poor defendant; he died with simple and majestic courage: 'His royal and Christian upbringing, which had not provided him with the wherewithal for a political defence, had taught him how to die. This he did as a very Christian King, thus transforming regicide into deicide, as Ballanche saw so clearly.'[4] A great throng of people attended his execution; but, contrary

---

[4] Mona Ozouf, 'Procès du roi', in *Critical Dictionary*.

to that of Charles I in seventeenth-century England, his death prompted no visible movement of opinion in the weeks that followed. The peasants of the Vendée, who rose up in March, did not take up arms in the name of the guillotined king.

The important, and still mysterious, question is whether the Revolution, in bringing Louis XVI to the scaffold, cut the thread of a living royalty, or put an end to an institution which, in public opinion, was already dead. A view of French public life in the nineteenth century would incline one towards the second hypothesis: as opposed to the English revolution, the French Revolution killed not only the king of France, but royalty itself. In this sense, even if the Conventionnels had only transformed into a national tragedy what the last century of absolutism had already marked out as inevitable, they had at least accomplished their aim: to strip royalty from the nation's future. By executing the king, they had severed France's last ties with her past, and made the rupture with the *ancien régime* complete. Michelet, giving the republican regicide its deepest meaning, wrote:

It was necessary to *expose to the light* that ridiculous mystery which barbaric humanity had for so long turned into a religion, the *mystery of royal incarnation*, that bizarre fiction which imagines the wisdom of a great people concentrated in an imbecile . . . Royalty had to be dragged into the daylight, exposed before and behind, opened up, so that the inside of this worm-eaten idol could be clearly seen, full of insects and worms, giving the lie to its beautiful gilded head.[5]

Michelet, however, would have preferred, once the demonstration by public trial had been carried out, that Louis XVI should not be executed, for fear that his punishment should transform him into a martyr and revive the monarchy. By contrast, in deciding on his execution, the Conventionnels had intended to prevent for ever the return to the throne of any of his family, to strike out the institution of royalty from the pages of the future; and they had put their lives on the line. All who had voted for the king's death had been fully aware of it: there could be no royal restoration in France which would not turn them into criminals. They had burnt their boats. So had the Revolution.

CIVIL WAR

After Valmy and the retreat of the Austro-Prussian armies, the French had advanced beyond the frontiers: in Savoy, to Nice, on the left bank of the Rhine. General Dumouriez, who owed his new career to the Girondins, occupied Belgium following the victory of Jemappes: pieces of territory which, in wars of yesteryear, could have been used as bargaining points in an advantageous negotiation. But the Convention remained true to the

---

[5] Michelet, *La Révolution*, book IX, ch. 7.

spirit of the new times when it annexed Savoy, by voting for 'brotherhood and help for all peoples who wish to enjoy liberty', by introducing into the conquered countries French principles and legislation, together with the assignat and compulsory taxation. The king's death radicalized the conflict, as the Girondins had at first keenly desired, and then feared: spring 1793 witnessed the entry into the war of Britain, the pope, Spain and German and Italian princes.

However badly organized it may have been, that immense coalition soon caused the spectre of defeat and the threat of invasion to reappear, renewing in 1793 the situation of the preceding year, which had been the backdrop to 10 August. The Prussians reconquered the left bank of the Rhine; beaten in Belgium, Dumouriez plunged into political intrigues and ended by going over to the Austrians, as had La Fayette a year before. The latter had dishonoured his Feuillant friends, the former discredited his Girondin protectors. But the war brought to the rising revolutionary wave even more massive proof of the internal betrayal and secret corruption which were ceaselessly at work within the body politic of the Republic: the insurrection in the Vendée.

The revolt began in March as a rejection of conscription. To reinforce the Republic's military numbers, the Convention had voted in February for a levy of 300,000 men, to be chosen at random among the unmarried men of each commune. The arrival of recruiting officers, which brought to mind the monarchy's procedures, gave rise almost everywhere in French rural areas to resistance and even signs of sedition, which was swiftly put down. But matters took a particularly grave turn to the south of the lower course of the Loire, in the Mauges and the farmlands of the Vendée.

During the first few days of March, at Cholet, a large textile township at the junction of the two regions, young people from the surrounding communes, peasants and weavers together, invaded the town and killed the commander of the National Guard there, a Patriot manufacturer. A week later, the violence spread to the western fringe of the farmlands, into the Breton marshes: hundreds of Patriots were massacred there. To the north, near the Loire, a large band of peasants took possession of Saint-Florent-le-Vieil, under the leadership of a carter, Cathelineau, and a gamekeeper, Stofflet.

On 19 March a small republican army of 3,000 men, which had left La Rochelle to go to Nantes, scattered at Pont-Charrault in the Vendée, under the attack of a rural band. Rioting had turned into insurrection. This covered a four-sided area which it was impossible to demarcate in administrative terms: it straddled the *généralités* of Poitiers and Tours – according to the *ancien régime* classification; or the *départements* of Maine-et-Loire, Loire-Inférieure, Vendée and Deux-Sèvres – according to the 1790 redistribution. The heart of the movement lay in the Mauges and the *bocage*, a vast area about one hundred kilometres square, with Cholet at its centre. The periphery of this zone, chiefly to the west, in the Breton marshes, between Montaigu and the sea, would never be completely controlled by the insurgents, but would be endlessly torn between the two camps, depending on the luck of the battle.

The 'Vendée militaire' which, for the space of a few months, would totally evade Parisian authority, in 1789 had not been a region in moral secession from the rest of the nation: at least, there are no noticeable traces of it in the parishes' *cahiers de doléances*, which were quite 'normally' hostile to seigneurial rights, and reasonably reformist in matters of justice or taxation. It was therefore not the fall of the *ancien régime* which roused the populace against the Revolution, but the setting up of the new one: the unprecedented mapping of districts and *départements*, the administrative dictatorship in towns and villages and, above all, the affair of the clergy's oath to the constitution, which presented clandestine resistance with the banner, the faith and the additional backing of the refractory priests.

In August 1792 there had already been the beginning of a revolt, quickly repressed. But in 1793 it was not the January regicide which unleashed the rising: it was the return of forced conscription. This is further proof of the fact that, though the people of the Vendée inscribed 'God and the King' on their flags, they were endowing those inevitable symbols of their tradition with something other than simple regret for an *ancien régime* whose death they had witnessed without any feelings of grief.

The Convention, viewing a rising of the people againt the people's Revolution, could only read into it a new aspect – perhaps the most serious – of the 'aristocratic conspiracy' to restore the old world on the ruins of the Republic. On 19 March it voted an initial decree instituting capital punishment within twenty-four hours for anyone taken carrying arms or wearing the white cockade. In its own way, it too provided the insurrection with a banner. The die had been cast in the space of two weeks.

Thus, by force of circumstance, the war in the Vendée became part of the merciless conflict between revolution and counter-revolution. In Paris, the Convention had no other way of analysing the situation: the idea of a vast conspiracy intended to destroy the Republic simultaneously from within and without united the Montagnards with the militants of the *sections*, and cemented their alliance. On the opposite side, the old nobility saw this uprising as an unexpected windfall. Cut off since 1789 by the inglorious emigration of its best-known names, it now regained the opportunity – with a providentially counter-revolutionary part of the populace – to wage war on the Revolution from elsewhere than abroad. Everything conspired to endow this uprising with a fearful echo of the civil war between the *ancien régime* and the Revolution.

However, in 1789 there had been nothing to foretell the call to action of the Vendéen peasants. What appeared in their recent history was rather a growing political hostility to the upheavals inflicted on their daily lives by the Constituent Assembly's reforms: the creation of *départements* and districts, new taxes, the massive purchase of '*biens nationaux*' by the town-dwelling bourgeois. To those upheavals much was contributed by equally new administrations, organized and staffed by bourgeois readers of

Voltaire and the *Encyclopédie*, large purchasers of Church estates, who flaunted an air of conclusive superiority regarding the backwardness of rural areas. In many of the western *départements*, the age-old antagonism between town and country assumed an unprecedented vigour when there were clashes between the interventionism of brand-new administrative authorities and rural communities jealous of their autonomy and little inclined to innovation.

Beginning with the Civil Constitution, the burning question was the religious issue. The March 1793 insurrection was preceded by a series of local incidents arising from the obligation to take the oath and the division of the Church into two inimical sets of clergy. Everything points to the fact that the mainspring of the Vendéen revolt was religious, and not social or simply political: just as the nobles appeared as latecomers on the scene, royalism came only second, in the wake of the call to God and the Catholic tradition. Lastly, the insurrection's military heroism – when there was any, because the Vendéen army was also subject to panics – was fed by religious fanaticism and the promise of paradise. That collective attachment to the old faith and the old Church, which were seen as inextricably threatened by the Revolution, exceeded the limits of conflict between town and countryside. It explains why the royal and Catholic army also included artisans from the towns, not to mention notables, both great and humble.

To get things in perspective, one must abandon the 'republican' obsession, inherited from the Enlightenment and so much in evidence in Michelet, about manipulation of half-civilized peasants by refractory priests. The Vendéen people must be given back their faith and their traditional forms of worship, with which revolutionary reorganization – so swiftly perceived as antireligious – had crossed swords. It is a little-known, still mysterious, and perhaps unknowable story, probably because there are so few sources of information.

The Counter-Reformation had given the population of the Mauges and the Vendéen *bocage* a religious tradition which was both clerical and popular, centred around frequent and regular devotions, supervised by a Church with large numbers of priests. That tradition, which was doubtless not so ancient or 'feudal' as they believed, but which they were so little prepared to understand, the bourgeois revolutionary administrations in the towns regarded as mere superstition, obscurantism and brutishness: they were disciples of the *philosophes*, not of Catholic reconquest. The war in the Vendée arose from the head-on clash of those two worlds, which knew nothing of each other, set in motion by the Revolution and, in the space of a few years, revealed to each other in a difference which war turned into radical antagonism.

The patriotic unity of the Federations in the summer of 1789, and the great national brotherhood of 14 July of the following year had therefore not survived the Revolution. The Revolution of 1789 had been able to exclude the aristocracy from the nation because the monarchy itself, over the preceding centuries, had prepared the ground for that uprooting; 1793 was able to separate part of the French peasantry from the national body politic only at the price of liquidating a conspiracy, which led to the mass terror.

In this sense, the Vendée revealed at the deepest level the dual nature of what had been attempted since 1789: the Revolution had founded the modern nation on the universality of citizens, but at the same time had torn history and society to pieces. That was why the rural uprising of March 1793 threatened it more profoundly than the situation abroad, however bad that might be. It was also why the Convention could find no other way of overcoming or even thinking about it than by putting it purely and simply in the same category as the enemy: a new and lethal version of *Qu'est-ce que le Tiers État?*

FALL OF THE GIRONDINS

Now this national crisis in spring 1793 found the Revolution once again without a real government, torn between the generals, the Executive Council and the Convention. The latter was itself divided between a Gironde and a Montagne which grew daily more antagonistic, and was subjected to pressure from the Parisian sansculottes who had allies on the spot, such as Marat. Quite independently of men, the very situation manufactured remedies which aggravated it, and added viciousness and resonance to the slogans in the *sections*: Girondin treason, public safety, terror, price-fixing, requisitioning.

In the same way that religion and politics could not be dissociated in the Vendée, in Paris the social question could not be separated from the revolutionary activism of the *sections*. The Montagne armed itself with it and the Convention followed suit, voting the assignats to be legal tender, imposing price controls (the *Maximum*) for grain, dispatching representatives with full powers to the armies, setting up a revolutionary Tribunal and a new executive authority, elected by the Convention, the Committee of Public Safety. To start with, in April, it elected to the Committee only deputies who were not too involved in the row between Gironde and Montagne, and who desired unity, men like Barère and Danton.

It was the Girondins, however, who unwisely engaged in an internal battle for power, by seeking to mobilize the *départements* against the Parisian authorities. They had been unable to get Marat condemned by the revolutionary Tribunal. They succeeded in having a commission elected to inquire into the Commune's activities, and in placing under warrant for arrest two chiefs of the 'popular' party, Jacques Hébert and Jean Varlet. In Lyon local supporters of the Girondins seized control of the town by force from the Montagnard municipality on 29 May and were soon joined by the remaining royalists: another civil war was starting.

Robespierre would doubtless have liked to rally a majority in the Convention to eliminate the Girondin deputies: thus national sovereignty would have remained master of its fate, by a sort of self-purging of the parliament of the Revolution. But events took another turn, more in keeping with what was already revolutionary tradition: two Parisian *journées* decided the Girondins' fate, organized like the others by local ringleaders, launched by the *sections* and an insurgents' committee formed on 30 May, which met in the bishop's palace.

Neither the Convention, where Robespierre remained cautious, nor the Jacobins, who hesitated, nor the Paris Commune where Hébert, who had been freed, tried to instil moderation, gave any encouragement to this movement. Moreover, on 31 May the Paris *sections* wavered between the bishop's palace committee and the authorities constituted after 10 August. Nevertheless, the news was bad: Lyon in the hands of a revolt, the Vendée on the offensive, France wide open to foreign armies.

On 31 May the sansculotte agitators already had enough followers to surround the Convention and present their demands: the arrest of those Girondins most hostile to Paris, a tax on the rich, the creation of an army of revolutionary militants to punish suspects, the right of suffrage for sansculottes only. The Convention voted only for the suppression of the Girondin commission of inquiry on Paris. But everything started up again two days later, on Sunday 2 June, and this time in earnest.

The *sections* had mobilized large numbers of people around the Tuileries, where the Convention had been meeting since 10 May. The day had been methodically planned, but no one knew by whom. Had the leaders of the Montagne taken a hand in it? There is no evidence. The sansculottes had brought with them the National Guard, under the charge of François Hanriot, one of their men, a former toll clerk turned captain, a loudmouth from the Mouffetard quarter who had just recently been promoted to general-in-command by the new insurgents from the bishop's palace.

One hundred and fifty cannon barred the exit from the Convention, where one of Danton's friends, Hérault de Séchelles, was presiding over the gloomy sitting. The deputies – apart from about thirty Montagnards, Robespierrists and Maratists – tried to leave: Hanriot demanded that the guilty should be handed over. There was a tremendous scene, where for the first time there appeared, in razor-sharp clarity, the confrontation between national representation and direct democracy personified in the brute force of the poorer classes and their guns.

Did the representatives yield to force or to the people who had constituted them? To both at once: if they had no other choice for the moment than to yield before Hanriot's artillery, their legitimacy was too frail and too recent to give the necessary weight to a feeling of obedience to the law. Born of 10 August, which had shattered the 1791 constitution, what could be more legitimate for the representatives than the people who had carried them into power? With greater internal strength, Hérault and the Conventionnels might perhaps have broken the blockade of cannon; but they went back into the meeting hall to obey Hanriot's ultimatum and hand over, by acclamation, twenty-nine Girondin deputies into custody.

That was therefore the end of the Girondins politically, and the prelude to their end plain and simple. It was also an important date in the history of the Revolution: the Montagne had paid for its victory with a popular coup d'état against the national representatives. This feature had already existed in the *journée* of 10 August, which had dismissed both king and Legislative Assembly. But it had been concealed by the overthrow of the monarchy, which had really brought to term the Revolution's victory over the *ancien régime*.

The taking of the Tuileries had obscured the violence done to the Assembly: recommencing what 1789 had not been able to carry through to the finish, it had cloaked itself in the legitimacy of the Revolution and the need for its intensification. But less than a year later, on 2 June 1793, there was no longer a king to be conquered. The Convention itself, elected by universal suffrage, had to lower its flag in the face of the Parisian *sections* and their cannon. It was the national representatives who had been vanquished, those who had been entrusted with the task of forming the Republic's new constitution and who had just begun debating it.

The Revolution could no longer come to an end within the law. Cut off despite itself from part of its members, the Convention was now merely a rump parliament sharing its sovereignty with the street mobs. Public Safety, the Terror, speeches about civic virtue might well, for the moment, cast a veil over this public anarchy, but the day of 2 June would nevertheless extend its disastrous shadow over the concept of national representation. Edgar Quinet saw it as the sansculotte version of Napoleon's coup d'état of 18 Brumaire.

REVOLUTIONARY GOVERNMENT

The men of June 1793 could not see so far. The French Revolution had once more torn itself apart, in the most spectacular fashion, at the moment when it faced the gravest situation in its history. There was a link between the two sets of circumstances: national territory was being invaded on all fronts – to the north, on the Rhine, in the Alpine valleys and the Mediterranean south – and civil war had spread. After 2 June the Norman and Breton *départements* had formed a federation against Paris under the Girondin banner. Bordeaux expelled the Convention's representatives. Lyon gradually went over to overt royalism, which had also won towns in the south-east, in August opening the port of Toulon to the English. Refractory priests were busier than ever sowing the counter-revolutionary message, and further 'rural Vendées' were hatching in the Catholic lands of the old kingdom, alongside villages and towns held by the Patriots: in the whole of the heart of the west, in Lozère, on the borders of the Margeride and the Rouergue.

I shall illustrate the danger incurred by the Revolution with an example borrowed yet again from the region where the depth of the civil and military crisis found particular expression – the Vendée. Though the

Girondin revolt was limited, caught in a pincer movement from right and left, the counter-revolution, for its part, was waging a veritable war. The peasants, who had adopted as leaders nobles who had withdrawn to the country, like d'Elbée or Lescure, but also Cathelineau, the Pin-et-Mauges carter, and Stofflet, the Maulévrier gamekeeper, had finally organized a 'royal and Catholic army' which formed the main body of their forces.

Operating on the borders of Poitou and Anjou (while Charette de la Contrie carried on the war on his side more to the west, in the Vendéen marshes), this army, at its best, numbered 40,000 soldiers; it controlled the Mauges and the *bocage* in April 1793: villages and towns, lacking republican garrisons, had fallen without resistance. To the west, Les Sables d'Olonne fought back, but in the east, even the towns were conquered: Bressuire, Parthenay, Thouars and Saumur on 9 June, when the town royalists gave the peasants a helping hand.

From there, the chief rebels decided to go and take Nantes, that rich metropolis of the west, and there to open up the republic to the English and the émigrés. The town, defended every inch of the way, remained in Patriot hands. But the rural uprising maintained its mastery over a vast quadrilateral, on occasion beating Republican columns of troops which were even more disorganized than their own. The threat hanging over the Revolution and Paris lasted the entire summer.

In these circumstances, revolutionary opinion restored extraordinary force to one of national history's old ideas, the classic resort of the monarchy – public safety. Kings had frequently made use of it in justification of 'extraordinary' measures – both military and fiscal; the men of 1793 enlarged the scope of the royal 'extraordinary' to turn public safety into a regime which suspended constitutional laws and was entirely directed towards the rebuilding of a strong central government which would be obeyed unquestioningly. Public need was placed above the law, and the state's arbitrariness accepted in the name of its efficacy.

The contrast was all the keener with the Convention's original mission, and even with the bills debated and voted on by the Assembly. For prior to 2 June Condorcet had proposed a plan for a constitution intended to avoid popular insurrections like that of 10 August by giving the people themselves, in their primary assemblies, control over the laws and the appointment of the executive. After 2 June the Montagnards had not dared completely to go back on that democratic utopia. On 24 June they too had voted their constitution, with a new Declaration of Rights which differed little from the previous one (though citizens' equality, the guarantee of rights by society and the indivisibility of power received additional emphasis). The role of primary assemblies in the development of the law was limited but maintained.

As soon as it was voted, however, this somewhat slapdash text had its application suspended until peace was restored: nevertheless, the Montagnard constitution of June 1793, which had never even begun to be implemented, would be an essential reference point for nineteenth-century republican tradition, as if it had been the sacred ark of the Convention. At the beginning of the Third Republic, Aulard still placed it at the heart of Montagnard conceptions. Nothing speaks more eloquently of the lasting nature, in French history, of that separation between political ideas and realities created by the Revolution.

So, in June 1793 the principles were safe but suspended; the nation's government would be arranged by other means: the dictatorship of Public Safety, which was set up in the summer.

There existed therefore a *de facto* regime, the nature of which was defined from the start by forces rather than by institutions: the Assembly, purged on 2 June, and thenceforth dominated by the Montagnards, provisionally shared power with the Parisian sansculottes. During the summer of 1793, the Parisian *sections'* movement reached its apogee at the same time as the national crisis, and not by chance. Its victory on 2 June caused it to play a temporarily decisive role in the situation: it could not do without the mediation of the Montagnards in the Convention, but neither could the Montagnard deputies, who were indebted to it for the Girondin expulsion, afford to ignore its demands.

Today the revolutionary government no longer appears as the most 'advanced' point of the Revolution, but rather as the arbitrator of an alliance combining deputies of the Plaine and the urban lower classes: those who were called the sansculottes. If modern historiography has preserved the name given to them at the time, it is not for want of seeking another denomination more in keeping with the collective dignity of a class; but this negative sartorial designation still gives the best definition of the mixed character of that population. Poverty-stricken – their numbers swollen by rural immigration into Paris since the 1789 crisis – factory workers, those who worked at home, journeymen, but also artisans, shopkeepers or 'ex-bourgeois of Paris' from the *ancien régime*, sansculottes are better defined by a political state of mind than by economic status. They often invoked Rousseau because they liked direct democracy, but they had not really gone deeply into the concepts of the *Contrat social*. They also doubtless drew on the old Christian millenarism: the cruel yet exhilarating times they were living in represented the advent of brotherhood.

An age-old religious sensitivity had been invested – or perhaps inverted – in a return to its sources and the image of a 'sansculotte Jesus': in opposition to the Church, which had betrayed its mission, it nurtured a new eschatology, secularized by the cult of the Revolution's saints and martyrs. One can also detect the psychological signs of the more recent past: the red bonnet, the pike in hand, the use of '*tu*', virtue – the sansculotte personified the reverse of aristocratic society. He was the very embodiment of equality. His enemies? the enemies of equality and that poor and virtuous community he dreamed of: not only nobles and the rich, but also the powerful, whom it was essential to keep constantly under the threat of the guillotine, that 'scythe of equality'.

The passion for punishment and terror, nourished by a deep desire for revenge and the overturning of society, thus complemented direct democracy as practised in the *sections*, which the sansculottes wanted to extend to the Convention by permanent control of the deputies: not through the old idea of the imperative mandate, but by making elected members subject to removal.

In the social and economic field, there was the same belief in interventionism and supervision, the latter inherited from the *ancien régime*, and diametrically opposed to the principles of bourgeois liberalism which were shared by the whole Convention: the government must hold prices (in the inflationist storm of the assignat), keep an eye on stocks of provisions, and give to the destitute what it took from the rich. Urban unrest was still defined by the egalitarian distribution of hardship, not by the solidarity of producers.

In 1792–3, there was even the traditional character of the revolutionary *curé*, the priest who was a friend to the poor and faithful to Jesus against the Church – the figure who passes through the history of European popular revolts: this was Jacques Roux, an unfrocked priest from the Gravilliers *section* of Paris, leader of the extreme revolutionary *Enragés*. The sansculotte movement was inextricably anti-liberal and extremist; the bourgeois in the Convention, with the Montagnards to the fore, were all *laissez-faire*, *laissez-passer* men in economic matters. At their side, the Parisian revolution had set up the first great collective actors in what would later be called the 'social question'.

During 1793 – mainly up till the semi-failure of the demonstration of 5 September (see p. 133) and the end of the permanent session of the *sections'* assemblies – those popular demands would be taken into account by the Montagnards, to whom the revolutionary government would owe a number of its features. Links existed between the *sectionnaire* movement and the central institutions: firstly, Marat, whose newspaper had affected and mobilized the public since 1789, making endless appeals for vigilance, suspicion and violence. He was assassinated in July, but he left plenty of emulators and even rivals to take over from him. Collot d'Herbois and Billaud-Varenne were the members of the Committee of Public Safety who were closest to Parisian ultra-revolutionary 'maximalism'. In the Paris Commune and in the Ministry of War, the sansculottes were there in force, protected by personalities like Hébert or Jean Pache, the mayor of Paris, who vied with the leaders of the Enragés, Jacques Roux and Varlet, for an extremist following.

But although the Montagnard group was sensitive to the pressure from the streets and from its own 'left', and though it brought in the Terror and planned economy, it also needed to retain the support of the Convention which, without daring to say too much, was already blaming it for giving in on 2 June. In control of the Jacobins, and soon of the Committee of Public Safety, it had no intention of yielding entirely to the demands of the streets; it drew its strength from its position of temporary arbiter.

The Constituent Assembly had legislated through its commissions. The Convention governed by means of its committees. Two of them were of essential importance: Public Safety and General Security. The second, which had formidable police powers, is less well known than the first, which was the true executive authority and was armed with immense prerogatives. It dated from April, but its composition was thoroughly reshuffled during the summer: Danton resigned from it on 10 July, and Robespierre joined it on 27 July.

This exchange recalls the long-lasting argument which, in French historiography, has divided partisans of Danton and of Robespierre, notably Aulard and Mathiez, at the beginning of the century. In so far as the two men had real value as symbols, in July 1793 it was certainly less a matter of moral opposition between corruption and integrity than of a conflict between two policies; Georges Lefebvre has clarified that point very convincingly.[6] The elements which make Danton's venality more than likely have been put forward without, however, showing the services he had rendered the counter-revolution in exchange.

Of more importance was his policy during spring 1793, when he dominated the brand-new committee: the most moderate of the Montagnards secretly explored the possibility of a compromise peace, doubtless prepared to exchange the queen for European recognition of the French Revolution. But he came up against the military situation, which was unfavourable to the French armies, and he was equally unable to break the internal machinery of the revolutionary war. His resignation from the committee marked the failure of his policy.

Paradoxically, it was Robespierre who, because he possessed great influence over public opinion and the knack of adapting to circumstances, had become the key man of a messianic war he had originally opposed. He was certainly, at the beginning, the key figure of the great Committee of Public Safety, although he did not yet dominate it as he would some months later: he brought to it his conviction that only an alliance between the bourgeoisie and the people could save the Revolution, together with the image of living embodiment of the great principles which he had so cleverly built up for himself since the Constituent Assembly.

Flanked by his supporters, Georges Couthon and Saint-Just, he was the necessary 'bridge' between Paris and the Convention. As a consummate parliamentary tactician, he conveyed this fact to the Convention: the committee was renewable each month. But the Robespierrist group was not enough to define the committee, which was always managed collegially, despite the specific nature of the tasks of each director: the division of its members into 'politicians' and 'technicians' was a Thermidorian invention, intended to lay the corpses of the Terror at the door of the Robespierrists alone.

Many things, however, set the twelve committee members at logger-

---

[6] Georges Lefebvre, 'Sur Danton', *Annales Historiques de la Révolution française* (1932).

heads; Barère was more a man of the Convention than of the committee, and was a link with the Plaine. Robert Lindet had qualms about the Terror which, by contrast, was the outstanding theme of Collot d'Herbois and Billaud-Varenne, latecomers to the committee, forced on it by the sansculottes in September; unlike Robespierre and his friends, Lazare Carnot had given his support only provisionally and for reasons of state to a policy of concessions to the people. But the situation which united them in the summer of 1793 was stronger than those differences of opinion; the break-up of the Montagnard group, which would lead to the dictatorship of the Robespierrist group alone (April-July 1794), occurred only after the relative re-establishment of the situation at home and abroad, in the autumn and winter of 1793-4.

The dictatorship of the Convention and the committees, simultaneously supported and controlled by the Parisian *sections*, representing the sovereign people in permanent session, lasted from June to September. It governed through a network of institutions set up haphazardly since spring: in March, the revolutionary Tribunal and representatives on mission in the *départements*; followed the next month by the Convention's representatives to the armies, also armed with unlimited powers; enforced acceptance of the assignat as the sole legal tender in May, price controls for grain and the forced loan of a billion livres from the rich.

The summer saw sansculotte disturbances reach a peak, under a double banner: price-fixing and terror. In the name of the wretched poverty of the people, the leaders of the *Enragés*, Jacques Roux at their head, called for a planned economy from a Convention with no liking for the idea. But the revolutionary logic of the mobilization of resources by national dictatorship was infinitely more powerful than economic doctrine: if Robespierre and the committee managed to make Jacques Roux retreat, it was by adopting part of his programme. In August, a series of decrees gave the authorities virtually discretionary powers over the production and circulation of grain, accompanied by ferocious punishments for fraud, with the inevitable reward promised to informers. 'Granaries of plenty' were prepared, to stock corn requisitioned by the authorities in each district. On 23 August the decree on the *levée en masse* turned able-bodied civilians into soldiers, and multiplied the number of mouths to be fed by the state. It was a mixture of national lyricism and social utopia.

The Parisian disturbances did not stop; they were inspired by the threats hanging over the nation and by their earlier successes. On 5 September Paris tried to recreate 2 June. Armed *sections* again encircled the Convention to demand the setting up of an internal revolutionary army, the arrest of suspects and a purge of the committees. The Revolution was a theatre where the tune of the sovereign people was endlessly replayed in the streets.

It was probably the key day in the formation of the revolutionary government: the Convention yielded, but kept control of events. It put the Terror on the agenda on 5 September, on the 6th elected Collot d'Herbois and Billaud-Varenne to the Committee of Public Safety, on the 9th created the revolutionary army, on the 11th decreed the Maximum for grain and fodder (and general controls for prices and wages on the 29th), on the 14th reorganized the revolutionary Tribunal, on the 17th voted the law on suspects, and on the 20th gave the local revolutionary committees the task of drawing up lists of them. But at the same time, it had the chiefs of the *Enragés*, Jacques Roux and Varlet, arrested: once it had endorsed their programme, it had removed the source of their strength.

The 'revolutionary government' was thus born of a gradual but rapid institutionalization by the Convention of the main demands of the *sectionnaire* movement. It was written into the logic of Montagnard policy, which had needed the sansculottes in order to break the Girondins in the spring, and wanted to retain them as allies without in any way handing over to them the essentials of government. That was what allowed it, through the Convention's deliberations, to maintain a connection, albeit truncated, with the inherent legitimacy of the Revolution, after giving their due – in the name of direct democracy – to the many *de facto* powers which dominated the Paris streets. Saint-Just made that balance of forces the subject of a decree on 10 October, although his rhetoric did not mitigate its legal flimsiness, even if Article 1 of the decree assigned it a closing date: 'The provisional government of France is revolutionary until there is peace.'

The ensemble of institutions, measures and procedures which constituted it was codified in a slightly later decree of 14 Frimaire (4 December), which in an overall Act set the seal on what had been the gradual development of a centralized dictatorship founded on the Terror. The debate, introduced by Billaud-Varenne, lasted eleven hours, and had as its aim the simplification and tightening-up of the system's 'intermediate mechanisms'. In the centre was the Convention, whose secular arm was the Committee of Public Safety, vested with immense powers: it interpreted the Convention's decrees and settled their methods of application; under its immediate authority it had all state bodies and all civil servants (even the ministers would disappear in April 1794); it directed military and diplomatic activity, appointed generals and members of other committees, subject to ratification by the Convention. It held responsibility for conducting war, public order and the provisioning of the population. The Commune of Paris, famous sansculotte bastion, was neutralized by coming under its control.

THE TERROR

In order to govern, the committee relied in the provinces on the districts (departmental authorities, suspected of federalism, were short-circuited), municipalities and revolutionary committees, which were given the task of applying public safety measures. Its direct spokesmen with these local authorities, apart from representatives on mission, were a body of 'national agents' chosen locally by a 'purging ballot' (which meant by local activists) and vested with authority by the Convention.

Technically, authority was less centralized than it appeared on paper: just like former absolutism, the government of the Revolution came up against the slowness of communications and the inertia of habits and mentalities. In order to overcome this, it relied, on the one hand, on fear of the guillotine and, on the other, on a huge propaganda effort ranging from the introduction of the revolutionary calendar to systematic coverage of the territory by the Montagnard press, in which the Jacobin Club played an important role through its hundreds of branches. Revolutionary government was inseparable from ideological orthodoxy, which forbade plurality of opinions.

In other words, it ruled through fear, making the threat of death hang over all servants of the state and citizens alike. At the summit of the apparatus of the Terror sat the Committee of General Security, the state's second organ, consisting of twelve members elected each month by the Convention, and vested with security, surveillance and police functions, over civil and military authorities as well. It employed a large staff, headed the gradually constituted network of local revolutionary committees, and applied the law on suspects by sifting through the thousands of local denunciations and arrests which it then had to try.

The dossiers to be investigated and the people to be sent for trial were passed to the revolutionary Tribunal: reorganized in September, this displayed considerable and expeditious activity from October onwards. In the *départements*, the situation was more varied. When there had been civil confrontations, the representatives on mission had superimposed *ad hoc* legal commissions on the ordinary criminal courts, in order to direct repression against the Revolution's adversaries: in Lyon, Marseille, Nîmes, Toulouse and in all the west. The revolutionary government had therefore generally suspended the rights of man in the name of reasons of state.

Finally, it exercised full power over the economy. That prerogative remained rather theoretical in financial matters, in that the administration set up by the Constituent Assembly, largely staffed by *ancien régime* specialists, did not undergo any great changes: throughout the period it came under the control of Pierre Joseph Cambon, president of the Finance Committee of the Convention. But in the economic field, properly speaking, where it was occupied by the old regal obsession with feeding the population – and chiefly those in Paris, in order to avoid an uprising – the Committee of Public Safety had installed a completely new administration, headed by the subsistence commission (22 October). Directed by three Patriots, this body, armed with the law of the general Maximum, had the task of regulating production, transport and consumption.

Under its jurisdiction it had sectors as varied as foreign purchases, internal requisitions, price control, the provisioning of Paris and the armies, not to mention the progress of agricultural production, forests, mines, etc. Divided into three large departments, and employing about 500 people, the subsistence commission revived the statistical and regulatory spirit of the former Control-General. But despite the Terror, despite the hunt for 'hoarders', the state's enterprise of directing the national economy by means of requisitions and controls ran headlong nearly everywhere into a general spread of fraud through all classes of the population.

The revolutionary government, by resuming the state's centralizing and regulatory tradition, which had been briefly interrupted by the Constituent Assembly, was the source of a great increase in the number of administrative jobs from which revolutionary personnel benefited. Whereas records show only 670 posts in the ministries in 1791 (a number comparable to that of the last years of the *ancien régime*), there were 3,000 at the beginning of 1794 and nearly 5,000 at the end of the year (for the fall of Robespierre did not reverse the trend).

When they were not in the armies, the sansculottes staffed police offices or those concerned with war or subsistence. At the very time when Robespierre and Saint-Just were accusing these same 'bureaux' (the term, as it is accepted today, was spreading at that period) of being just so many screens between the committees and the people, the representatives and their mandate, by their action they increased the bureaux's influence, role and number. The revolutionary government's political rhetoric thus collided with its sociological truth.

That rhetoric, however, is crucial to an understanding of the motivating forces and passions linking this period with the history of the Revolution in general. The regime of Year II in effect constituted the application – paradoxical, but full and complete – of what was perhaps the French Revolution's supreme principle: the absolute and indivisible sovereignty of a single Assembly, deemed to represent the general will stemming from universal suffrage. It is a paradoxical application, because the Convention after 2 June was not the Convention of universal suffrage, and the 'revolutionary government, was a political concept cobbled together under pressure from supporters of direct democracy.

Yet, it was a full and complete application in so far as the Convention was the sole centre of government and the Committee of Public Safety, the true organ of the dictatorship, was not an executive power distinct from it, but merely one of its committees – a part of itself and therefore sharing the same identity. It was not by chance that Billaud-Varenne, in his introductory report of 28 Brumaire (16 November), had criticized as criminal the Constituent Assembly's organization of an executive power distinct from itself.

Thus, at the moment when the Revolution seemed farthest away from its early aim of founding society on the universality of the law, it was also most faithful to its concept of sovereignty: which shows that 1789 and 1793 may be contrasted or linked, as the case may be. In Year II, the power of the people finally rested on a pyramid of identities: the people were in the Convention, which was in the Committee of Public Safety, which would soon repose in Robespierre. The Terror and virtue, each in its own sector, had the task of making this stream of abstractions hold together.

The 'revolutionary government's' most elaborate 'theory' was probably the report presented by Robespierre to the Convention on 5 Nivôse Year II (25 December 1793) on behalf of the Committee of Public Safety. An unprecedented form of government, which the 'political writers' had consequently neither anticipated nor studied, it contrasted with constitutional government in that it obeyed 'less uniform and less rigorous rules' – which was a way of saying that it was outside the law. Nevertheless it was a kind of prelude, since its aim was to 'institute' the nation against its enemies on whom it waged a war of liberty: 'The objective of constitutional government is to preserve the Republic: that of revolutionary government is to establish it.'

What did 'establish' mean? First of all, to preserve its existence not only against the enemy without, but also against the 'factions' within: Robespierre held the old idea that the greatest risk encountered by the sovereignty of the people was of being usurped by groups pursuing private interests. That justified the beginning, in the winter of 1793–4 of the struggle against the *Indulgents*, who wished to end the Terror, and the Hébertists, who aimed to extend it. What was to draw the line between the people and the factions, good and evil? 'Love of one's homeland and of the truth'. In the last resort, it was therefore a moral criterion which dominated political life, and if the French people recognized themselves in the Convention, it was less according to the law than the 'character' of the action taken by the Assembly.

What permitted the temporary suspension of the law, and for example the rights of man, was therefore something even beyond public safety – the loftier need to establish society on the virtue of the citizens. The Revolution had inherited from the *ancien régime* corrupt men who had distorted the nature of its very actions; before ruling by the law, it had to regenerate each actor in the new social contract. What, for Rousseau, constituted the transition from man to citizen – a difficult, perhaps almost impossible passage – had become the Revolution's goal, through the radical action of the revolutionary government.

Behind the politico-philosophical façade of the revolutionary government, local stories of the period underline the total diversity of situations, according to circumstance and also the dictatorship's available communication network. Civil war was latent, or overt, only in the west and south-east: elsewhere, there were villages where the Revolution had meant only the abolition of feudal rights, the end of the *taille* and conscription. Revolutionary authority took various forms, and the Convention's directives were modified by the nature of local people's societies and district administrations: the rule of acting minorities was far from uniform.

Furthermore, deputies sent as 'representatives on mission' by the Committee of Public Safety, armed with full powers, reacted according to both local situations and their own temperaments: Lindet pacified the

Girondin west in July without a single death sentence; in Lyon, some months later, Collot d'Herbois and Joseph Fouché relied on frequent summary executions by shooting because the guillotine was not working swiftly enough. The same thing occurred in the economic sphere, where the bureaucratic utopia instituted by the Convention's decrees created a steep decline in good citizenship, immediately feeding the guillotine, wherever it passed, accompanied by the 'revolutionary army'.

The reason why the improvised administrative and political system of summer 1793 left a legendary trace in the Republican tradition, was because revolutionary France had loosened its mortal stranglehold at the beginning of autumn, and the gloomy start of the epoch could be covered over by the poetry of national vigour, itself enveloped in universality. Indeed, by force of circumstance, the Revolution had now carried its glory to the frontiers. It had not yet overturned the rules of conventional strategy and, like its enemies, retained the old superstition about siege warfare and line formation; but it had a new army, amalgamated with the old, under the undisputed authority of the civil government, and the Convention kept an eye on developments through its representatives to the armies.

Victory or death: the terrible rule did not belong only to the Terror, but also to patriotism. It had allowed renewal of command and promotion to young generals like Hoche and Jourdan: the nation's war belonged to the children of the people, as the kings' wars had to the aristocrats. At the beginning of September the Anglo-Hanoverian army was beaten at Hondschoote, which liberated Dunkirk from enemy pressure. In October the battle of Wattignies freed Maubeuge from the Austrian army. The Sardinian army was driven out of Savoy, and the Spanish withdrew across the Pyrenees. In the autumn, on the eve of withdrawal to winter quarters, the situation at the fronts was thus redressed.

At the same time, the areas of civil war were reduced, but at a very high cost, in no way related to the need for public safety. The Revolution no longer struck at foreigners, but at those Frenchmen who had defied it, or simply those suspected of doing so: an unlimited category which merely indicated government by fear. The Terror was being installed, no longer a spontaneous reaction of the masses, as in the September 1792 massacres, but a judicial and administrative institution set up by the Convention and the committees. The central repressive apparatus had been in place since March, because the revolutionary Tribunal had been created at that time. But the activity of this Tribunal had been restricted until September, even though its character was already in evidence, by allowing judges to choose only between acquittal and the guillotine.

The sharp rise in the number of the Terror's victims began in October: precisely at the moment when the situation was improving. The phenomenon was very clear in Paris: almost 200 guillotined at the end of 1793. Not only did these include Marie-Antoinette and the ex-Duc d'Orléans, who had in vain called himself Philippe-Egalité, but also the groups defeated by the Revolution: the Girondins who had been arrested or under suspicion since spring, notably Brissot and Vergniaud, plus the remainder of the Feuillants, Bailly and Barnave. The guillotine simultaneously wiped out the *ancien régime* and the first years of the Revolution.

The Terror operated from preference in towns and zones which had risen against the Republic, coming after victory, as a sort of punishment-cum-obliteration of the insurrection. The Girondins had taken control of Lyon on 29 May, at the very time when they were about to be eliminated in Paris. It was a town of merchants and silk workers, where Jacobinism had taken on the aspect of a class war between the poor silk workers and the merchants. From the Girondins, the town had gone over to the royalists, who had reigned there all summer; but it was retaken by the Convention's troops on 9 October. Like so many others, it was 'dechristened' and given a new name, becoming Ville Affranchie, symbolically torn from its accursed past and destined by a Convention decree to partial destruction, limited to the 'houses of the rich'. In November, Collot d'Herbois and Fouché commenced massive repression. The great mansions on the banks of the Saône began to be destroyed. Several thousand suspects were guillotined, shot or collectively gunned down in order to speed things up. The Terror lasted until March 1794.

The history of the revolutionary Terror in the Vendée followed the same reasoning and chronology. This also was a matter of putting down an insurrection – the most serious that the Revolution had had to confront. As in Lyon, repression not only followed victory, but was going full blast several months after victory. Indeed, the Vendéen revolt began in March 1793, and news of its triumphs filled the spring and the beginning of autumn. But, starting from mid-October, it ebbed when the peasant army was crushed at Cholet, and passed to the north of the Loire in the hope of joining up with an English fleet at Granville, before what remained of it was wiped out in December in the battles of Le Mans and Savenay. The revolutionary Terror – which must be distinguished from the atrocities and massacres committed in the heat of battle – raged between February and April 1794.

If the war had been merciless on both sides, what began afterwards was of a different nature: it was mass repression organized from above, on the orders of the Convention, with intent to destroy not only the rebels but also the population, farms, crops, villages – everything which had formed the home ground of the 'brigands'. The guillotine could not cope with such a task: in December, the Convention's representative, Jean-Baptiste Carrier, resorted to collective drownings in the Loire. Starting from January, there came into action a decree brought by Barère to the Convention on 1 August, ordering the 'destruction of the Vendée': the Republican troops were divided into several columns, each entrusted with a particular itinerary, with the explicit mission of burning every dwelling and exterminating the population, including women and children. This appalling operation lasted until May 1794, and its sinister balance should be added to war casualties proper: the 'military Vendée' territory lost 20 per cent of its housing and a large percentage of its population.

Numerical estimates of human losses remain a subject for argument. It is impossible to calculate them with even a modicum of precision: on the one hand, no specific sources exist, and the historian must resort to comparisons between earlier and later censuses, which are hypothetical. On the other hand, these documents do not enable one to make a distinction between three types of death: those killed in the war (on both sides), those who died as a result of terrorist repression (sentenced by a court or simply massacred), and finally the decline in the birthrate and increase in mortality following the war years. So it is not possible to put forward a precise evaluation of the Terror's victims in the Vendée; but taking into account both the victims of Carrier's repression in Nantes and those of General Turreau's fiendish columns, the number is in the order of several tens of thousands, perhaps more than one hundred thousand.

Thus the Terror struck out blindly during the last months of 1793 and the first few of 1794, after the dramatic situation of the summer had been put to rights and after the worst times of pressure on the Convention by the Parisian *sections*. It also formed part of the deputies' political culture, as all the parliamentary debates bear witness so prolifically. For it would be wrong to think of it as simply the product of sansculottes' pressure or the bloody excesses of certain representatives on mission. In reality, it was inseparable from the revolutionary universe, of which it had constituted one of the potentialities from the very beginning.

As early as 1789, the French Revolution could envisage resistance – real or imaginary – only as a gigantic and permanent conspiracy, which it must ceaselessly crush, by means of a people constituted as a single body, in the name of its indivisible sovereignty. Its political repertoire had never given the slightest opening to legal expressions of disagreement, let alone conflict: the people had appropriated the absolutist heritage and taken the place of the king. As a result, there was only one way to think of them in their regained legitimacy, and that was to imagine them as one, and as independent of the private interests characterizing each of their individual members.

Conspiracy was the other face of that vision, a counter-revolution that was concealed and evil, in contrast with the people who were public and good, and nearly as powerful as they, for it had to be overcome again and again. For Sieyès, the aristocracy – that wrong side of the nation – had still been defined legally by its hereditary privileges. The category had since gradually extended to all those conquered by the Revolution, who were stigmatized by their conquerors: the Feuillants were aristocrats, and after them, the Girondins.

The Terror was a regime where men in power designated those who were to be excluded in order to purify the body of the nation. The Vendéen peasants had had their turn. Danton awaited his. This analysis does not imply that there was no difference between 1789 and 1793. The circumstances were not comparable, and naturally played their part. But the political culture which could lead to the Terror was present in the French Revolution right from the summer of 1789.

However, it had not had the whole-hearted support of all the Montagnards, since at the start it had been a sansculotte demand, passed on by the Jacobin Club and by the left of the Montagnards and the committees. This would later allow Michelet, for example, to approve of Public Safety, but not the Terror, the Montagnards but not the Jacobins, Carnot but not Robespierre. That distinction was too biased to be truly in keeping with the facts, as has been seen: no voice was raised against the Terror when this was placed on the Convention's agenda on 5 September 1793, or with regard to any of the great terrorist decrees of the autumn. With the improvement of the situation, at the end of the year fresh conflicts began within the Revolution, in which it was at stake. The Parisian *sections* no longer played a central role; that was now assumed by the Paris Commune and the Cordelier Club, and above all by the Jacobins and the Convention.

After September, Parisian extremism had found a new outlet in the person of Jacques Hébert, who had made a speciality of gathering together round his newspaper, *Le Père Duchesne*, those customers left stranded by the demise of Marat's *L'Ami du peuple*. He was a less spontaneous, less genuine spokesman for the militant people than the leading *Enragés* in the summer, but more influential and better placed; the campaign he launched in November over the policy of the committees did not directly concern the Terror, but dechristianization. Representatives on mission, like Fouché in Nevers, were briskly taking the guillotine into the town centres, carrying out a campaign of extirpating the Catholic form of worship, which was tainted no longer only as a Church but as a faith, by the curse levelled at the *ancien régime*. The Paris Commune had also taken a part in it, by antireligious masquerades and then by closing churches. A whole popular and urban anticlericalism, the origins of which were less clear than its future, temporarily found a substitute cult in the Revolution.

The majority of the Convention, which had voted for the Republican calendar, was antireligious. But, being more realistic than the dechristianizers, it saw in Hébertist exaggeration an additional and gratuitous motive for civil dissension. Robespierre, moreover, detested atheism – that legacy from aristocracy and the rich – which was why, at that period, he moved closer to a more moderate group among the Montagnards who wanted to halt the machinery of the Terror, and to which some credit could be restored by the improvement in the situation. It was the moment of a very temporary alliance with the man who sought to personify that turning-point, Danton.

The Committee of Public Safety therefore allowed an anti-Hébertist offensive to develop, brilliantly orchestrated by Camille Desmoulins's *Le Vieux Cordelier*, which appeared in December; going beyond dechristianization, this aimed at the Terror itself. Perhaps Danton also remained loyal to his dream of a compromise with Europe; in this area, the Committee of Public Safety was more cautious than the Girondins. Robespierre himself, in his November and December speeches, introduced distinctions between the nations which had formed a coalition against the Revolution.

That policy, however, which at least was Danton's, could not be professed in public. In the France of 1793 the quest for peace clashed head on not only with the Paris *sections* but with all the recently promoted revolutionary personnel, who were bound to the Terror and to war. Furthermore, Danton was compromised through certain of his friends, who were suspected of corrupt practices in the liquidation of the former Indies Company.

In January 1794 Robespierre backed off, abandoning Danton, and developed the 'centrist' theme of the 'two factions' threatening the Revolution. In order to break the Hébertist offensive which developed at the end of the winter, originating from the Cordeliers, he urged the Committee to strike first at the extremists, Hébert and his friends; in exchange, he left Danton and Desmoulins to the Committee of General Security. Cleverly amalgamated with the corrupt deputies, they were guillotined less than two weeks after their adversaries, at the beginning of April. Hesitantly, the Convention had ended up by following Robespierre's line.

Now it was the hour of the Committee of Public Safety's absolute dictatorship, which the Parisian activists no longer disputed. For the tumbril which had carried Hébertists to the guillotine had reduced revolutionary Paris to silence. Thenceforward the Commune obeyed, societies and clubs held their tongues or disappeared, and Saint-Just would remark, with his gift for a phrase, 'The Revolution is frozen.' The Convention was the prisoner of the Terror, which had just struck at national representatives; it obeyed the Committee of Public Safety, whose members it had elected and re-elected.

In the bosom of the Committee, the winter's internal events and the two purges of the Hébertists and the Dantonists had definitively closed the book on a collegial executive: Robespierre was, in fact, the head of the Republic's government. In those times, that meant infinitely more than a phrase borrowed from constitutional vocabulary. In this personal dictatorship, the old revolutionary dilemma of 'representation' of the sovereign people found an unprecedented solution: the source of Robespierrist power lay both in the Convention and in the sovereignty of the people. It can be better expressed in monarchic vocabulary, provided 'revolution' replaces 'kingdom': the Incorruptible had ended up by personifying the Revolution.

ROBESPIERRE

It was an immense, though fleeting, victory. It was enough to isolate Robespierre from the politicians of the epoch and make him a figure apart, which he remains to this day. As Michelet understood so well, the French Revolution had not had any really great men, a Cromwell or a Washington: since 1789, it had involved many actors, but swept them along in its wake, and not one of them was capable of taming its fearsome advance. It was the event which was 'great', without precedent and without equal: it had cast into the void all those who had come forward in succession to put an end to it, *Monarchiens* and Feuillants, Girondins and Dantonists.

If, however, the historian wants to single out certain men among that cohort caught up in the tide of events, he can cite Sieyès and Mirabeau, and add Robespierre, but not Danton. Sieyès, because he had the presentiment about the Revolution, formed its philosophy and anticipated its features and passions; but never did he take the leading role, even in 1789. Mirabeau had been the most brilliant of the Constituents, before becoming secretly the most lucid commentator of his time; but he had had to retire into the wings because he could not even dominate the Assembly, let alone Paris. As for Danton, who had lent his great voice to *la patrie en danger*, but who also, in the Ministry of Justice, had covered up the massacres of September 1792, he was too erratic a politician to give true consistency to a more moderate version of Montagnard politics. If he enjoyed frequent popularity among nineteenth-century Republican authors, it was just because he seemed to offer a less bloody image than Robespierre, owing to the last months of his life. But at no time did he play a role comparable to that of his famous rival. Robespierre's greatness in the French Revolution – tragic, but unique – was to have gradually assumed power and, for a few months, exercised it.

He is not an easy man to portray, for he had no private life. His existence prior to the Revolution remains rather mysterious simply because it was so commonplace: Maximilien Robespierre appears in Arras as a barrister who has done pretty well, living amid his sister and aunts and spoilt, as his sister would say in her memoirs, 'by a host of little attentions of which only women are capable'. Without deep feeling, holding only the ideas of his era, protected by the women of the family, with a steady clientele, a member of the local academy, he is the exact opposite of Mirabeau, and the counterpart of Sieyès: during his *ancien régime* life he showed no sign of what would turn him into the Revolution's greatest spokesman.

His case is even more mysterious since, although he had published nothing, the abbé had at least written a great deal for himself: all those notes on so many subjects and authors which bear witness to a split personality and to his revolutionary turn of mind prior to the revolutionary years. There is nothing remotely like this in the pre-1788 Robespierre: a smooth, almost empty, existence; a professional life developing along classic lines; the ideas of the Enlightenment tinged with *fin-de-siècle* moralism – just like almost everyone else in his profession, generation and social circle.

With the Third Estate elections in Arras, a new person was born. In one sense he remained entirely true to himself: he would stay a deputy, an austere, self-controlled politician, rather stiff and starchy in both his attire and his tone, and ever chaste. Much feminine jealousy would surround him, but only over who would keep house for him: that was the domestic side of his existence, when he had to choose between his sister and the carpenter Duplay, his landlord, who had daughters. Like the Arras barrister, the Robespierre of the Revolution put no energy into private intercourse with his fellow men. But the new times revealed that he possessed a formidable power of identification with the public good. Maximilien Robespierre, lacking any other private existence than that which he had received willy-nilly, had found himself truly at home among the principles of the French Revolution. From the emptiness of his private life he derived the strength of his political action.

That was the first of his secrets, which Mirabeau had summed up in the witticism: 'He will go far, because he believes everything he says.' Mirabeau was in a good position to grasp this, since he lived several lives, spoke at least two tongues – one to the king and the other to the Assembly – did not say everything he believed and did not believe everything he said. For Robespierre, the political ideas and the principles which he constantly invoked were deeply rooted in universal morality, itself based on the existence of a 'Supreme Being'. He had a kind of circular conception of politics by which action legitimized itself as good solely from the fact that it could be deduced from principles which it had to translate into reality. His reasoning never emerged from a world where a kind of transparency had to exist between history and morality: a patently absurd supposition, but extremely potent in revolutionary France, which had inscribed it on its banner. That was Robespierre's 'Rousseauism', far more than his admiration for the *Contrat social*, to which his politics referred only by opportunism. The deputy from Arras endlessly extolled virtue: a quality which was no longer simply the civic selflessness of antiquity, but which constantly mingled with that heritage the subjective feeling of modern morality. Robespierre shared the same sensitivity with the France that had raved over *La Nouvelle Héloïse*.

The influence over opinion, which he gradually acquired with the Jacobins and in Parisian societies between 1789 and 1792, he drew from the inevitable tension between those rights proclaimed as belonging equally to all and the true state of society. His words tirelessly returned to that flaw, a component of democracy itself, with a vigour and consistency of thought which no doubt could assail, because the principles of 1789 had been finally decreed only so that they should be applied. In the Constituent Assembly, for example, one of his favourite topics had been criticism of the *censitaire* electoral system (based on property-owning qualification): not only were the French split into three categories (those who voted, those who could be second-stage electors, and those who were eligible); but in the end, one had to be rich to be elected by the people. Jean-Jacques, his beloved Jean-Jacques, could not have been!

This deputy, with his tendency towards the abstract, who identified so completely with the idea of man's universality, also possessed immense talent as a tactician. That was Robespierre's second, and probably principal, secret; at all events the less known. For the first immediately strikes anyone who reads his speeches, and was not linked to a great intellectual originality: the Arras deputy was not a true thinker. On the other hand, if viewed from the aspect of the conquest of power, he was a great strategist and a profound politician.

In his public life during those years, his moralistic turn of mind had instilled in him a veritable obsession with suspicion, through which he encountered the distinctive spirit of revolutionary democracy; thence he obtained unlimited scope for manoeuvres, punctuated with insinuations or accusations according to circumstance, but always used with consummate art to weaken his adversary before destroying him. Robespierre ceaselessly mapped out his route to power by continually denouncing power.

During the Constituent Assembly, filled with men not so new to the game as he, he was not a candidate for anything, yet he gradually played an increasingly central role – becoming the personification of principles in the Assembly and the Jacobin Club, and weaving his web in the heart of the political scene too. It was he who in May 1791 moved the vote on the ineligibility of deputies for the new Assembly, by which means at a single stroke he cleared future ground, for his own advantage, in the name of civic virtue.

Varennes happened, and the crisis following the enforced return of the king, during which he played a masterly game. He kept himself apart from the republican campaign, careful not to place himself outside constitutional law; but against the Feuillants he supported the clubs and popular societies demanding the punishment of Louis XVI. He took no part in the *journée* of 17 July 1791 on the Champ de Mars, during which the National Guard fired on the people. But he made great capital, on his own account, of hostility to Feuillant repression, and in 1791 made it the banner of the Jacobins who remained loyal to the old club when Barnave and his friends had left it.

This sequence of events is of value as an example. Robespierre was not a leader of *journées*: he did not participate on 20 June or 10 August 1792 or 2 June 1793. He had a studious temperament, and gifts of strategy. Popular for the doctrinal purity of his speeches, he drew on this capital by a subtle mixture of daring and caution: he accompanied the Parisian revolutionary movement, uniting it and giving it direction.

That doctrinal purity was bound to be fictitious, even though he had the art of preserving an illusion of it, doubtless within his own heart of hearts as well, because of his obsession with morality: for instance, this 'Rousseauist' took a succession of inconsistent stands on the question of representation. In 1792, he remained true for a long time to his position as inflexible defender of the constitution, and thus of the Assembly's inviolability; then, on 29 July, following the *sections* and widening their audience, he argued in a great speech to the Jacobins for the deposition of the king and the election of a Convention by universal suffrage.

The same thing occurred on 2 June 1793: he had taken no part in the sansculotte movement, and there is no evidence that he had encouraged it secretly; but he stayed inside the Assembly when most of his colleagues went out to try to break the encircling ranks of Hanriot's cannon, and he was one of those who benefited most from the anti-parliamentary coup d'état which eliminated his Girondin foes. Immediately afterwards, he became once again the herald of national representation, the man of the Convention, elected and returned by it to the Committee of Public Safety. His power came from the representatives of the people, but also from the people themselves. Such was the strange chemistry which allowed the two features of his talent to combine and lets us understand the secrets of his dominance. His ideological mastery offers a means of reconciling the two democratic legitimacies.

The idea of 'revolutionary government' was the field in which he excelled, for it freed him from all reference to the formalities of the law, leaving only principles and men on their own. The Revolution would at last come into power through him, but it no longer had any other end but itself: it was that gap that he pathetically tried to fill by talking of the absolute necessity for the regeneration of individuals through virtue, which was the condition of a Republic of true citizens. In 1794, however, this national pedagogy was effected by the Terror, a regime with no fixed laws, defined by a moral mission – to separate the 'good' from the 'bad'. That is why the Incorruptible's enemies had so often been mistaken when they credited him with a particularly repressive nature. Many of his proconsuls and his future conquerors tragically outdid him in that respect: Collot, Fouché, Carrier, for example. For him, the bloodiness was abstract, like the political system: the guillotine was fed by his moral preachings.

When he finally attained sole power, surrounded by his faithful supporters, with Saint-Just and Couthon in the forefront, two batches had gone to the scaffold: the Hébertists and the Dantonists. But the first carried off with Hébert the remainder of the *sectionnaire* movement, thus putting him at the mercy of the Convention, still trembling for having abandoned Danton. So the revolutionary government attained its dictatorial fullness of authority at the moment when its Parisian bases disappeared: at the same time the Committee of Public Safety had crushed the extremists of the guillotine and threatened Danton's fate to anyone seeking a policy of clemency. It no longer directed anything but a vast terrorist bureaucracy, which governed by arrests and fear.

One year after the creation of the revolutionary Tribunal, spring 1794 was the period when the Terror became institutionalized as an administration. A decree of 27 Germinal (16 April), introduced by Saint-Just, had centralized revolutionary justice in Paris. Then came the terrible law of 22 Prairial (10 June). Its novelty lay in the redefinition of the mission and the expeditious all-powerfulness of that fearsome court. Article 4 of the law stated that 'the Tribunal is instituted to punish the enemies of the people', a definition which heralded somewhat more than summary procedures. The Act suppressed investigation, at the same time allowing indictment to be based on a simple accusation; it denied the accused the assistance of a lawyer, and did away with the point of an open hearing by also authorizing judges not to hear witnesses. The draft of the bill is in Couthon's hand; Robespierre, who presided over the Convention on 22 Prairial, came into the debate to back his lieutenant against some deputies who were disturbed by the nature of the law: 'We shall defy the treacherous insinuations by which some would ascribe excessive severity to those measures which the public interest prescribes. Such severity is to be feared only by conspirators, only by the enemies of liberty.'

In fact, the two Acts of Germinal and Prairial sum up the mechanism of that bureaucratized Terror. The increase in executions in Paris, which may be seen from the monthly figures of those guillotined in spring 1794, arose partly because repression was now centralized in the capital. But it came about also because the revolutionary Tribunal hardly pronounced anything but the death sentence any longer: nearly 1,500 executions in seven weeks, between the law of Prairial and the fall of Robespierre, on 9 Thermidor (27 July). Parisian prisons were overcrowded: they harboured more than 8,000 'suspects' at the start of Thermidor. Historians generally apply the term 'Great Terror' to this period of revolutionary repression.

Almost at the moment when he had put the law of Prairial to the vote, two days beforehand (8 June), Robespierre had presided over a ceremony of a very different nature, the Festival of the Supreme Being, anticipated in his great Floréal text, with the magnificent title: 'On the relationships between religious and moral ideas and Republican principles, and on national festivals'. On that morning, processions from the forty-eight *sections* converged on the Tuileries, men and boys on the right with their branches of oak, women and girls on the left with their bouquets of roses and their baskets. At noon, the Convention made an appearance, looking magnificent in the costume which Jacques-Louis David, the great pageant-master, had determined in such detail that, of the three coloured feathers adorning the hat, one learns that the red one 'must be the tallest'.

Facing the Convention's stand stood an arrogant statue, Atheism, emerging from an enigmatic group in which ambition, discord, selfishness and false simplicity were supposed to be recognizable. The star of this first act was Robespierre, president of the Convention since 16 Prairial (4 June), who appeared with a torch in his hand. The main attraction was the setting fire to the group, which disclosed Wisdom, with a slightly blackened nose. Robespierre's speech revealed the meaning of the scene: by burning Atheism, man could be rescued from the desolating Hébertist creed (that death leaves nothing but 'separated molecules') and returned to the belief that it is possible to 'link this transitory life to God himself and to immortality'. 'Man, whoever you are', concluded Robespierre, 'you may still conceive great ideas about yourself.'

After this, the Convention moved off, flanked by the *sections* – twenty-four in front and twenty-four behind – and itself surrounding a sort of chariot of the national heritage, laden with 'produce of French territory'.

Draped in red, it was pulled by oxen with gilded horns towards the festival's second venue, the Champ de Mars, where a 'mountain' awaited it, dotted with 'accidents of nature', grottoes, boulders, brambles, and crowned with the tree of liberty. The Convention took its place on high, musicians half-way up, mothers to the left, and old men and adolescents to the right. The different groups, each in turn, intoned a verse of the hymn dedicated by Marie-Joseph Chénier to the Supreme Being. The last one, sung in unison by all those assembled on the 'mountain' announced the final scene: the adolescents brandished their sabres, the old blessed them and the young girls threw their flowers to the Supreme Being. However, the last cry of the participants was not addressed to him after the final artillery salvo: the fête, like so many others, ended with a cry of 'Long live the Republic.'

On this famous day, which took place all over France, historians have formed differing judgements which frequently tie in with their feelings about Robespierre. Some have seen no more in it than an additional means of crowd manipulation in the hands of the master, while others view it as an initiative dictated by his deep convictions. As the Incorruptible's personality precisely combined these two kinds of reality, the two inter-pretations are not incompatible. There is no reason to doubt Robespierre's sincerity, since he had always hated atheism as a destroyer of morality, loathed the *Encyclopédistes* and extolled Rousseau; even in his condem-nation of the dechristianizers in November 1793, there was more than mere political concern to handle the traditional faith of the people care-fully. In him, however, this fundamental feeling is as hard as the rest to distinguish from political strategy. Through this Festival of the Supreme Being, he was also trying to terminate the Revolution in his own way and to his own advantage – in the utopia of a social harmony in tune with nature.

The event produced something more enigmatic than its instigator had intended: the crowds who attended, dressed in their Sunday best, taking an active part and in very large numbers. Accounts agree on this point, which is hard to comprehend, since the Terror was going full swing and the dread machine had been still for only a day. Was the public at the fête simply because of the lovely June day, or was it too, in imagination, laying the first stone in the building of the future? After all, the spectacle presented was that of the religion of the century, and those who had read a little knew its repertoire in advance. If they could add a thought to exorcize the present, the idea of an end and a fresh beginning, the *journée* had truly found its public. Charles Nodier, who gave an admirable account of the festival, wrote that 'to appreciate it, one must take the trouble to go back to that time. Nothing was left. Here, therefore, was the cornerstone of a nascent society.'[7]

---

[7] Charles Nodier, 'Recherches sur l'éloquence révolutionnaire', part II, 'La Montagne', in *Souvenirs de la Révolution et de l'Empire*.

In any case, the illusion did not last very long – the bloody law of Prairial followed in a couple of days. Nor did the festival have a favourable effect on the Conventionnels, who had seen in it only its political, and even personal, aspect. The Supreme Being did not have the same hold over them as the Committee of Public Safety. War and fear remained the political and psychological mainsprings of the revolutionary dictatorship. War, at that time, was beginning to loosen its stranglehold.

Carnot had laid the plan of campaign at the moment when operations recommenced: the idea was to take the offensive on the northern frontier, by the co-ordinated action of three armies – those of Flanders, the Ardennes and the Moselle. In the end Saint-Just imposed a strategy which caused the principal effort to fall on the Sambre, at the centre of the front, where the Duke of Coburg was putting on the pressure. Sole command of the armies of the Ardennes and Moselle was entrusted to Jourdan. The Sambre et Meuse army hammered the Austrians at Fleurus on 26 June: it was a victory which opened Belgium to the French. On 10 July they got through to Brussels where Pichegru, commanding in Flanders, linked up with Jourdan.

Revolutionary expansion began, but victory abroad was a defeat at home for Robespierre and the Robespierrists. For if France was victorious, why the guillotine and why the dictatorship? That question was asked only within the revolutionary system of reasoning but, for that very reason, touched the right spot: if the Terror was detested by public opinion, as was demonstrated by the enormous collective relief at Robespierre's downfall, it could be overturned only by the Convention, which had given it life before becoming imprisoned by it.

There was no other power left standing which could confront Robespierre: the generals were under close supervision and the army had not yet entered politics. Within the country, fear prevented any public demonstration of opposition. Because of this, the *journée* of 9 Thermidor (27 July) which, in the days that followed, met with such spectacular assent, established the victory of a parliamentary conspiracy hatched amid intrigues of which, in the nature of things, no trace has been preserved.

Two active nuclei may be discerned, very different from each other in all respects. Firstly, the former extreme left of the committees and the Convention, which had kept silent since the execution of the Hébertists: Collot d'Herbois and Billaud-Varenne on the Committee of Public Safety; André Amar and Marc Guillaume Vadier, on the Committee of General Security, who had been keen 'dechristianizers'; and ex-terrorists on mission like Fouché, Louis Fréron, Jean Tallien or Paul Barras. Scenting a change, they wanted to maintain the initiative. They had seen the Festival of the Supreme Being as nothing more than a dictatorial masquerade; the Terror frightened the terrorists too, many of whom had been less incorruptible than the tyrant they wanted to bring down. At the other end of the spectrum were the moderates of the Committee of Public Safety: Lindet, who had refused to sign the order to arrest Danton, and Carnot, at loggerheads with Saint-Just over the conduct of the war. Then there were the former Dantonists, Louis Legendre, Thuriot de la Rozière.

Who was the conductor of this orchestra? Probably no one. The essence of the matter is that when these two oppositions united, they became a majority in the Convention; the famous Plaine, which had followed Montagnard policy since the king's trial and 2 June 1793, turned against the Robespierrist dictatorship, which was its ultimate expression. Everyone wanted some breathing space to ward off the fear that stalked abroad – in short, to enjoy life. Fleurus had struck the hour of a return to liberty. Thus passed the month of July 1794 in the Convention.

Nobody had any inkling of what Robespierre had sensed, or what he planned to do. Since the beginning of July he had been very distracted, very silent, in both the Assembly and the committee. On 8 Thermidor (July 26), from the rostrum of the Convention he denounced his adversaries, without naming them, and called for 'unity in the government'. Intimidation hovered over everyone. The reply came next day. The men of the extreme left played the leading roles: Billaud-Varenne, who attacked, and Collot-d'Herbois, who presided. Robespierre and his friends were not allowed to speak, and their indictment was decreed. In the same movement, the Conventionnels, who knew the score, relieved Hanriot of his command of the National Guard.

The last scene was played out in Paris, at the Hôtel de Ville, during the night of 9–10 Thermidor (27–8 July). The Paris Commune, loyal to the man who had inspired it, had released the arrested deputies in the evening and mobilized two or three thousand militants. The Convention outlawed the Robespierrist groups and its liberators. That was the crucial moment. But decisiveness had deserted the insurgents, and the Convention had mobilized, under the command of Barras, National Guards from the rich quarters of Paris, making a reappearance in the history of the Revolution. They recaptured the prisoners in the middle of the night and made a round-up of Jacobins in Paris. Robespierre shot himself in the jaw with a pistol, without managing to kill himself. He was guillotined the next day with his chief companions, Saint-Just, Couthon and nineteen others; two cartloads followed on the next day, and the one after that.

4
The Thermidorian Republic: 1794–1799

In the Convention's proclamation to the French people, read by the omnipresent Barère on 10 Thermidor (28 July 1794), celebrating the downfall of the new 'conspirators', there is a sentence which makes no sense and yet says everything: 'On 31 May the people had their revolution; on 9 Thermidor the National Convention had its own; liberty acclaimed both equally.'

What, therefore, had happened between 31 May and 2 June 1793? A violent take-over by the armed Parisian *sections* against the Convention, forcing the national representatives to rid themselves of twenty-nine Girondin deputies. The 9 Thermidor, on the other hand, was a victory for the Assembly over the Parisian street mobs, the first since July 1791. A double victory even, since the deputies has overthrown Robespierre and subsequently enforced their decision against the Commune and the remainder of the sansculottes.

The *journées* of spring 1793 and 9 Thermidor (1794) had in common a resort to violence: in both cases a group of deputies was arrested, then guillotined. However, they reveal a break in the history of the Revolution, since on 9 Thermidor the Convention had imposed its law, while on 31 May–2 June it had capitulated. It is this break that Barère's proclamation is trying to conceal, by spreading the common benediction of liberty like a veil over two contrasting events.

Nevertheless he was telling the Convention the psychological truth of the time. For those men who had decreed the arrest of Robespierre on 9 Thermidor were the ones who had elected him and returned him each month to the Committee of Public Safety since July 1793. They were the same men who, shortly before, had allowed the days of 31 May–2 June to occur, had abandoned to a Terror imposed by the Parisian *sections* their Girondin colleagues, elected by the people like themselves. Certain among them had done so from revolutionary fanaticism, but the majority from a sort of bowing to the inevitable: the parliamentary coalition of 9

Thermidor had brought together the extreme terrorist left and a crowd of deputies whose desire was to put an end to the Terror; Carnot numbered among the latter. Moreover the situation of the first group was complex, because even pronounced ex-terrorists like Tallien, proconsul of the Bordeaux scaffold, wanted to end the Terror.

At all events, by whatever routes they had followed, fanaticism or cowardice, the Thermidorian Conventionnels had had the same history and shared the same memories. They had founded the Republic; they had voted for the death of the king; they had excluded the Girondins and set up the revolutionary government; they had abandoned Danton to the guillotine and had finally sent Robespierre there as well. Quite a dramatic journey in less than two years; the country was rid of the enemy and victory was on the horizon. That served as a pardonable excuse, but provided no explanation for the deadly struggles in which they had confronted one another. If Robespierre, who had denounced so many conspiracies, was himself a 'conspirator', and the most dangerous of all, if he was merely the last of an interminable list to which he had already added a host of momentarily famous names, how could the Revolution make any sense?

Barère's wording offered no explanation; it was purely incantatory. The interest lies in its indication of the question present in the minds of Robespierre's conquerors: they could not begin the Revolution once again, starting from 9 Thermidor, reinvent a Year I by destroying the pages they had just written, as they had done on 21 September 1792. They had to shoulder that history, and allocate the parts to be remembered and those to be forgotten: a sign that the revolutionary concept had at last begun to lose whatever utopian content it had had since its formation.

They had a muddled, chaotic, contradictory and bloody history, but they were convinced they were its sons. They had put Robespierre to death, but they had not overthrown the Revolution, quite the contrary; that was the kind of speech which recurred endlessly during the days and weeks following 9 and 10 Thermidor. How in fact could they indulge in this repudiation of their past when they had all played an essential role as legislators, either since 1789, like Sieyès or Boissy d'Anglas, or since 10 August, like Fouché or Barras? Their lives were their sole link with that recent past. They had successively destroyed the old society and the old monarchy, they had cast down the aristocracy, and most of them had voted for the death of Louis XVI, while yet others had been pitiless agents of the Terror: among Robespierre's victors were, for instance, Carrier and Collot d'Herbois, and Barère, who had had the terrible decree of extermination in the Vendée voted in August 1793.

They shared different solidarities with the different ages of the Revolution; but their interests bound them to it as to a unique and liberating event. Many had purchased *biens nationaux*; all were uncompromising over the destruction of privileges and the creation of a society of civil equality. The Revolution had seen various governments follow one another, but its assemblies had never stopped legislating in the spirit of 4 August 1789: liberty of individuals and contracts, equal rights of succession, the institution of divorce, the suppression of compulsory compensation for seigneurial dues, etc.

Of that upheaval, the Conventionnels were both the latest authors and the heirs. They cherished it. They were the new breed of owners, freed from all seigneurial, 'gothic' servitude on what they owned or had acquired. The return of aristocratic society was unacceptable in their eyes. The Thermidorians brought back and would give lasting life to that new race of political men that the Feuillants had managed to personify for one summer alone – conservative revolutionaries. The Revolution was leaving the shores of utopia to discover the strength of personal interests.

Reality reimposed itself. All these men – who were not so very old – felt as if they were survivors. They had just lived through some terrible years, subjected to the tensions of overwork, exacerbated emotions and the threat of the guillotine. They were so enclosed in that world of terrorist politics that it took them several days after 9 Thermidor to comprehend what they had done. But they were soon informed by a public opinion which was being reborn as if by magic, sending them delegations and beginning once more to express itself in public nearly everywhere in the towns: Robespierre's fall swiftly signalled the opening up of prisons, the end of arbitary arrests and the tyranny of surveillance committees, the cessation of the guillotine.

Within a few weeks, 9 Thermidor restored to its former self a French society which had been alienated in the bloody and fictitious political unity of the revolutionary government. But it also roused or rekindled against the Terror feelings and passions which hardly distinguished 1793 from 1789, and thereby called into question the Revolution as such. The latter relied on a variety of new political and social interests, which continued to feed hatred of the aristocracy and the *ancien régime*; but the Republic had replaced liberty with the Terror. The Thermidorians were caught up in this contradictory legacy. They too had to 'terminate' the Revolution, to root it definitively, no longer in a regenerated citizenry, but in society and the law, as in 1789–91; at the same time exorcizing, no less definitively, the tragic memories it had left in national opinion.

If the fall of the dictator marked the end of the Terror, it did not signal the end of the Revolution; it merely opened up the possibility, should the Convention finally manage to give the Republic a constitution. However, the return to liberty revealed the spectacle of a country more divided than it had ever been since 1790, for the Terror and the end of the Terror had brought to a head the civil struggles born of the conflict over religion; Thermidor began an era of score-settling in towns and villages while the state remained impotent.

Abroad the émigrés still embodied the threat of counter-revolution, with the two brothers of the martyred king, Provence and Artois; they had in no way considered Robespierre's end as the end of the Revolution. Lastly, the war was still going on. By the summer of 1794 it had begun to be a victorious war, but had not changed its character: it remained a mixture of military domination, economic looting and social emancipation. In conquered territories the French armies abolished seigneurial rights and the tithe, but they lived off the inhabitants. When things went badly, the war had been the pretext for dictatorship. When it went well, it remained indivisible from the Revolution in that it was invested with the same national consciousness, surrounding the figure of the new France with a halo of universality.

If revolutionary patriotism had stopped rallying the street mobs, it lost none of its immense force by being channelled towards military glory. But it made the war difficult to check, as it was also – though for opposite reasons – on the counter-revolutionary side. Neither Danton nor Robespierre had dared openly to seek an end to it. It was a legacy from the Girondins, which they had passed on to the Thermidorians. The Plaine, that majority of the Convention dominated since its inception and successively by the Girondins and the Montagnards, at last found its true political place and autonomy with Thermidor. Its time had come. The war of the Revolution belonged to it.

Revolutionary history too rarely stresses that continuity from one side of 9 Thermidor to the other. Broadly speaking, the same parliamentary majority had successively supported – or rather, given free rein to – the Girondins, the Montagnards, and then the Thermidorians during the Convention, later perpetuating itself, as we shall see, in the leadership of the Directory. These Conventionnels of the Plaine, neither Girondins nor Montagnards, of whom Sieyès once again provides an excellent example, personify a fundamental loyalty through so many vicissitudes; they wanted to build a great Republic, without nobles and without a king, to stand against monarchic Europe. They had paid a high price for it with the Terror. They had put an end to that, but were not prepared to buy peace at the cost of compromising their ideas or denying their past. If peace meant the return of the Bourbons and the old order, rather even than the law they would prefer to have the revolutionary war, which kept them in power in the name of the principles of 1789.

To understand this, it is enough to observe the care taken by the men governing France between Robespierre's downfall and the advent of Bonaparte (1794–9) to keep power in the hands of the regicides; the votes of January 1793 denoted the demarcation line between the sure and the unsure, between those who could not betray the Revolution because they would be risking their lives, and the others who could, because they were not risking everything. After the Convention, from autumn 1795, the group of Conventionnels who had voted for the death of the king continued to govern the Directory, often in defiance of the constitution. In that sense, they were faithful to the Girondin promises in all their original ambivalence; the war of liberation was also a war of conquest.

Robespierre's victors held two additional trump cards over the Girondins and the Montagnards – they arrived after the Terror and they were victorious. They could thus substitute messianism abroad for activism at home, and free their oligarchic rule from the extremism of the mobs. But by carrying on and extending beyond the frontiers a war which they could not arrest, they would create – like Brissot, Danton or Robespierre – the conditions of their downfall. It was additional proof that this war had become consubstantial with the Revolution, almost its second nature. By halting it, the Revolution would be repudiating itself; but by pursuing the war, it would also open the way to its conqueror.

This described the political situation dominating those Thermidorians, who came to be known as the *Perpétuels* (Perpetuals) under the Directory, and whose symbolic figure is Barras. Squeezed in between Year II and Bonaparte, they do not enjoy a good press in French history; they do not contribute anything to the chronicle of national glories. Compared with the heroes of the Committee of Public Safety and the legendary genius of Napoleon, they present a picture of corrupt intermediaries clinging on to power with no scruples about their methods. The left disliked the world they made, one dominated by pleasure and self-interest, and the conservatives were content to settle for that password of 18 Brumaire: Bonaparte has put an end to corruption and disorder.

However, when one analyses those regicide representatives, those former servants of the revolutionary government, those generals risen from the ranks, those men grown rich in the business of war and the state, they present no less interesting a picture than that of the preceding regime: not the reign of public-spiritedness but, on a quite different level, government by a political class still defending a threatened Revolution while it is already the offspring of a Revolution which has succeeded. The historian can thus compare the Republic of self-interest with that of virtue, and try to understand why the one did no better than the other in establishing itself.

The Conventionnels who had overthrown Robespierre took several weeks, even months, to draw their conclusions from the event of 9 Thermidor. The 'revolutionary government' was at cruising speed, the war continued, the Republic had no other organized government. Moreover, any blunt challenging of the past raised only too clearly the question of the Convention's responsibility, over which the deputies were deeply divided. There were too many ex-terrorist *exagérés* (extremists) among them – Collot d'Herbois, Vadier, Billaud-Varenne, Fouché, Tallien etc. – to make the problem easy to formulate, even if some like Tallien, whose mistress 9 Thermidor had saved from the scaffold, went to the other extreme. Anyway the main body of the Convention remained cautious, following the example of the most moderate member of the old Committee of Public Safety, Lindet, who advised: 'Let us not reproach ourselves for either our misfortunes or our mistakes!'

Nevertheless the parliamentary debates of the period make very exciting reading, in which one can trace the birth of the first interpretations of the terrorist dictatorship: the Robespierrist 'conspiracy' against the Revolution, Robespierre's monarchic ambitions, the excuse of circumstances (destined for a long future), the oppression of the Assembly by the 'tyrant' and his accomplices. In a report written by Courtois in January 1795, commenting on the inventory of papers found in the conspirator's home in the carpenter Duplay's house, there is even the germ of a philosophic idea; the former dictator's confusion of public happiness with private pleasures, and his attempt to force individuals into egalitarian austerity.

If this debate rumbled on within the Convention almost in spite of itself, the reason was not an obsession with old memories but because public opinion imposed it. Totally repressed by force since 2 June 1793 and the setting up of the dictatorship, it had burst out after Robespierre's fall in a sort of immense collective relief in which the strength and vitality of French urban society reappeared, as spectacularly as in the last years of the *ancien régime* and the first of the Revolution.

As always, Paris led the way, mingling politics with the liberating of morals. It was as if opinion were living the anti-Robespierrist reasoning which Courtois would present in January 1795, before it had actually been formulated: the dictatorship had preached austerity, the summer of 9 Thermidor wedded rediscovered freedom with pleasure. The salons began to reopen, fashion and conversation to reign once more, and the growing number of balls held in August and September were like so many political allegories: it was the summer of the opening of prisons and the dismantling of the revolutionary dictatorship.

A new press accompanied the movement, and even the mobs went wild with anti-Robespierrism. The Thermidorian 'reaction' found its sanculottes in little bands of young people from the smart districts, the dandified *muscadins*, who specialized in anti-Jacobinism and operated on behalf of Tallien and his friends. This movement of opinion, which was so spectacular that it gave rise to innumerable accounts of it, was not yet royalist, but in its way it evidenced the relative isolation of the Convention, an old power worn out by a too difficult past and now without support from the left, discredited on the right, and yet still the only government, since it had gathered to its bosom the prerogatives of the committees through the intermediary of its commissions.

Nevertheless the Convention manoeuvred wisely. It yielded to the tide, but slowly. It had to let go of those of its members most compromised under the Terror, but purges were kept to a minimum: Carrier, the man of the Nantes drownings, was condemned and executed in the autumn; then, in the winter, Barère, Collot d'Herbois, Billaud-Varenne and Vadier were charged. But the right of the Convention, led by penitent former Montagnards, such as Tallien and Fréron, raised another ghost from the past: what about the Girondins whom violence had excluded from the Assembly? That was a far-reaching question, as one orator said, because quite simply it cast doubt on the validity of the laws voted since 2 June 1793.

Here again, the Convention made a realistic decision. There were three categories of Girondins: the principal leaders, arrested in June and guillotined in October 1793; twenty-one deputies who had taken flight on 31 May and had been outlawed, and seventy-one other ex-Conventionnels, imprisoned for having signed a protest against the coup d'état of 2 June. The reinstatement of the last two groups – the third first (as it had not been 'outlawed') and then the second, in March 1795 – has been admirably commented upon by Mona Ozouf.[1]

This painful rehabilitation once again brought face to face the Convention and its past, the Revolution and its law: the collective capitulation before Hanriot's cannon on 2 June 1793 was a constant source of remorse for the Convention and re-emerged in a bitter debate between left and right, to such an extent that, on 18 Ventôse (8 March 1795), to conclude the discussion, Sieyès deemed it necessary to add a postscript intended for the deputies who were to be reinstated:

It seems to me that, in a kind of preamble to the decree or, if you prefer, a letter from the president, a few words should be added to let it be known that if, since 9 Thermidor, we have appeared to waver in recalling our colleagues, it was due to considerations which they would themselves wish to respect. We have not wanted to deny their powers; that would have been to wish to destroy our own; we have not repulsed them – we did not have the right; but in reciprocal trust, you in their republican virtues, they in our legislative wisdom, we have presumed that they have voluntarily consented to that prolongation of their honourable exile until common opinion, more enlightened, more just, should itself have determined the time when it was permitted to announce and effect their return, with all the advantages that this measure must have for the nation.

Excuse, advice, warning, of which those returning took good note: in their name, Louvet de Couvray soon replied: 'Let us draw an impenetrable curtain over the past. May it conceal from history, if possible, the errors to which the Convention and the entire French people have been party.'

Easier said than done; the Conventionnels were far from being off the hook. The revolution in the faubourgs came knocking at their gate one last time in spring 1795, set in motion as before by the exposure of the illusions of equality. It had been stunned by Robespierre's ovethrow, and the remainder of its leaders had momentarily been caught up in the wave of Thermidorian opinion: dyed-in-the-wool sansculottes like Varlet or François Babeuf in the summer of 1794 had joined in the chorus of malediction against the 'tyrant'. While gradually dismantling the revolutionary government, the Convention had also returned to its long-held convictions in economic matters; between October and December 1794 it had restored freedom of trading and prices. In fact the relaxation of

---

[1] Mona Ozouf, 'Thermidor ou le travail de l'oubli', in *L'Ecole de la France*.

government control over the economy had begun earlier, in the spring, with the fall of the Hébertists and the disbanding of the revolutionary army at the end of March; shortage reigned in Paris, and Robespierre had taken advantage of the elimination of Hébert to cheat a little over the general Maximum. In fact, the economy was profoundly disorganized by the consequences of the Revolution: money went into hiding, taxes were not coming in, there was the need to feed vast armies, and the country as a whole was converting fraud into a new industry.

The end of the Terror brought with it a return to *laissez-faire*, but the most immediate effect of the abolition of the general Maximum in December 1794 was a terrible burst of inflation; goods certainly reappeared a little in the markets, but at astronomical prices well out of reach of the majority of buyers. The scapegoat was soon trotted out; it had existed for centuries – the state. From December onwards, the crowds no longer blamed regulations or requisitioning, but bourgeois selfishness, taking advantage of unrestricted prices and wages.

FACING THE FUTURE

The beginning of spring 1795 saw the rebirth of a classic situation, but in a very different context from that of 1792 and 1793. The Convention had executed Robespierre, who had executed Hébert. Parisian powers had died twice; in putting an end to the Terror, the Assembly had brought back to itself the public authority of the Revolution. The few remaining Montagnards in its bosom, ready to side with an insurrection in order to relaunch the mechanism of 1793, were insignificant: the Thermidorian bourgeois were afraid of their past; they wanted to end the Revolution, not start it again.

Because of this, the two great Parisian *journées* in the spring – their failure assured in advance by the new balance of power – assumed an unprecedented character, although the combatants were the same as before: it was less a battle for power-sharing than a social war. The poor against the rich. Later on, the Conventionnel René Levasseur, deputy of the Sarthe, would write in his memoirs: 'One saw Paris divided into two nations: on the one hand, the people; on the other, the bourgeoisie.' The two great antagonists were named for the coming century. Before it had definitively vanquished the *ancien régime* and the aristocracy, the bourgeoisie was already standing alongside the accused in the court of revolutionary equality.

The first of these two *journées*, 12 Germinal (1 April 1795), was a copy, in a minor key, of 31 May 1793. The mobilization points were classic: the faubourg Saint-Antoine, the central and eastern *sections* of Paris. The 1793 constitution (the second, that of the Montagnards), a rather fetishist reference – since it was the first, Condorcet's, which contained most direct democracy – began its long career in the extreme republican left.

The armed mob also demanded bread. It invaded the Tuileries and the Convention, where it had petitions read out for several hours, while the majority of deputies made themselves scarce. At the end of the day, battalions of the National Guard from the west of Paris evacuated the old royal palace without incident. It was a victory for the Convention, which took advantage of it to vote for the deportation to Guiana of Collot d'Herbois, Billaud-Varenne, Barère and Vadier. Barère escaped from prison, Vadier hid; the other two started the history of the penal colony of Cayenne.

Some weeks later, on 1 Pairial (20 May), events took a tragic turn. It was the same crowd, roused against the Convention by the same hunger, the same memories, shouting the same slogans, better armed than in April, men and women together. The same scenario, as well, in keeping with tradition: in the middle of the day, the insurgents from the suburbs and the eastern *sections* marched on the Convention; they overran the buildings, killing Jean Féraud, a representative who tried to intervene. His head was presented on a pike to the president of the session, Boissy d'Anglas, but only a handful of deputies supported the rising. It remained without objectives and without leaders, entirely caught up in interminable discussions and petitions, while the Convention, with the strength of experience, succeeded – not without difficulty, and late into the night – in getting the National Guard battalions to intervene on its behalf.

Strictly speaking, the victory was less military than political, 'which shows in retrospect', as Denis Richet has observed, 'how much influence was wielded in Year II by bourgeois, Montagnard or Hébertist leadership'.[2] That was the moment when the Convention exorcized its past in deeds, after spending so long debating about it: in the days which followed, it arrested and condemned the remaining Jacobins and Montagnards in Paris (including those within its own bosom), 'purged' the *sections* and sent an army of 20,000 carefully picked volunteers to remove the cannon and arms from the faubourg Saint-Antoine. The greatest twentieth-century historian of the Jacobins in the Revolution casts a melancholy eye on this moment: 'This date should mark the end of the Revolution: its mainspring had been broken.'[3]

Lacking that 'mainspring', had the Convention placed itself at the mercy of the right and the bands of *muscadins*, through whom there inevitably advanced the idea of a royal restoration? The deputies of the old Plaine might well fear so at this period, because they were already caught between two stools, too bourgeois for the faubourg Saint-Antoine, but too revolutionary for Bourbon supporters. In February, they had agreed to give their authority to an armistice in the Vendée, by which the remaining guerillas of Stofflet and Charette 'recognized' the Republic. But the said

[2] François Furet and Denis Richet, *La Révolution française*, ch. 8: 'Thermidor ou l'impossible oubli'.
[3] Georges Lefebvre, *La Révolution française*, book IV, ch. 3, 'La réaction thermidorienne et les traités de 1795'.

Republic had pledged itself to accept refractory worship and not to levy soldiers or taxes among the insurgents for ten years.

During this era, while egalitarian extremism was being reborn in Paris, the violence of anti-Jacobin revenge took hold of the country – called by historians the White Terror. It was also characterized by almost savage outbursts of violence and a trail of massacres in towns and villages, chiefly in the south-east, in those places where confrontation between partisans and adversaries of the Revolution had been so strong since 1790: for example, in Nîmes, Tarascon, Aix and Marseille. The hunting season for Jacobins was open: a reversal of the situation of 1793, revenge taken against the surveillance committees of the period and their militants. In this sense the two Terrors were truly opposite and comparable, and the blood spilt gives some idea of the extraordinary social violence which runs through the years of the Revolution.

However, there is something misleading in the comparison. The White Terror was never institutional; it had no courts and no administration; it was never sanctioned by instruments of justice or law. In this regard, it was nearer to the massacres of September 1792 (it also invaded the prisons) than to the Terror set up by the revolutionary government. Furthermore, the Convention reacted rather like the public authorities (or what stood for them) in 1792: it just let things happen. For it was more obsessed by past than by present violence. In 1795, as we have seen, the faubourg Saint-Antoine was again the focus of its fears.

Could it, would it, take the risk of favouring the return of the royalist idea in post-Thermidor France? The question arose principally after the anti-Jacobin repression of Prairial (see p. 159). But what had become of the royalist idea in 1795? Recent history presented at least two versions of it: that of pre-1789 and that of 1791. The first took up again with absolutism and the *ancien régime*; the second might correspond with a development of what had been missed by Mirabeau, La Fayette and the Feuillants between 1789 and 1791. The first rejected the entire Revolution out of hand, including 1789 and civil equality. It was largely held by the émigrés, who had assumed the role cut out for the nobility by Sieyès. It made war on revolutionary France in the army of the princes. Louis XVI's two brothers, Provence and Artois, were its chief figures, each with his little court – the former in Verona, the latter in England.

As for the other royalism, it was still only a vague project, though none the less powerful, in bourgeois opinion: precedents were not lacking, from *Monarchiens* to Feuillants. They had failed, but at a time when the revolutionary tide was rising. On the ebb tide, they could benefit from the discredit into which the Jacobin Republic had fallen, gain the support of disappointed Girondins or repentant Montagnards. If a republican regime were truly impossible in a big country, as the wisdom of the century had predicted before the Terror confirmed it, what else was left but a king wedded to civil equality? But the idea did not receive influential support among the émigrés, where a hierarchy of seniority had been established among the counter-revolutionaries: those who had left in 1789 disliked those who had joined them later.

Moderate royalism had no king: Louis XVI's young son had died in the Temple prison on 8 June 1795, and Provence lost no time in proclaiming himself Louis XVIII. Thus in the months of spring 1795, the problem that 1789 had not been able to resolve took shape again: a restored monarchy might perhaps, this time, take advantage of the weariness of the country, but it would have to meet it half-way. Louis XVI's brother and his circle were not willing to do so. A royal proclamation signed at Verona placed on the agenda for their return the punishment of the regicides and the re-establishment of the orders of society.

Moreover, in June, the British – Pitt had hesitated – financed and transported émigré troops to the Breton shores; the plan was to link up the two extremes of the counter-revolution, émigrés and insurrectionary royalist *chouans*, nobles and peasants, to turn them into a civil war army against the Convention. But the expedition only managed in the end to isolate 4,000 *chouans* and a few hundred émigrés in English uniforms on the peninsula of Quiberon. Hoche surrounded them like mice in a trap on 21 July. The military commanders – in whose ranks Tallien resumed service – had the 748 émigrés shot as traitors. The Thermidorian regicides continued to show no sentiment towards the counter-revolution. They were fighting on two fronts, against the residue of Jacobinism and against the aristocracy in association with the Europe of the kings. They spoke most about the first battle, because it penetrated their lives and their memories. But it was the second which continued to be the main front, as all their history would show.

They launched themselves into a daring foreign policy which linked up again with the Girondin dream of 1792, but changed its character. The French were victorious. They had been in the act of conquering Belgium when the Convention had overthrown Robespierre; in the autumn, the Sambre et Meuse army was advancing in Prussian territory towards the Rhine, and in January 1795, making use of the ice to cross the rivers, General Pichegru had mastered Holland. France and the Revolution therefore faced a new situation: spread out as far as Amsterdam, occupying the left bank of the Rhine, while Holland had capitulated and Prussia, totally engrossed in its rivalry with Austria and Russia over the new partition of Poland, was ready to make a separate peace in the west.

What did the Convention and its committees want? Opinion desired peace, even a partial one, but what would be its political and territorial conditions? One could imagine a prudent policy of gains limited intentionally so that they could be accomplished more easily. A man like Carnot at the time personified that old realism of the kings of France: the Meuse could provide a good frontier. But the Revolution had dreamed dreams which were too grand for those careful calculations of a hereditary prince. At the moment when it was losing its internal fire, it had all the greater need to invest its loyalty to itself in other issues.

As usual, Sieyès, who had been at war with the nobles since 1789, showed his colours by putting forward a policy of 'natural frontiers'. Together with many other Thermidorians, like the Alsatian Reubell, he made himself one of the principal advocates of that policy. But because it incorporated in the new France (liberated from aristocracy and kings) the entire left bank of the Rhine, from Strasbourg to its mouth, the formula clothed in geographical terms the French Revolution's European ascendancy. It was Girondin messianism rewritten in Thermidorian language: a revolutionary heritage composed of ideas and interests, uniting the nation around its conquests and its glory, since it was unable to unite it in a civil consensus on the years it had just lived through.

Therefore, the two advantageous treaties obtained by the Convention in 1795 – one with Prussia, which ceded its share of the left bank of the Rhine, the other with Spain, which evacuated French Catalonia – reveal only the division of external enemies, or the temporary withdrawal of the less determined. In matters of foreign policy, the most significant event of the year was the transformation of Holland into the Batavian Republic, soon bound to its big French 'sister' by the hard reality of an economic and political protectorate: forced to relinquish some territory, obliged to provide for the upkeep of an army, to pay a huge indemnity and to submit to the pillage of its works of art. Belgium was purely and simply 'reunited' with the French Republic a little later. The Thermidorians thus inaugurated a foreign policy destined for far-reaching repercussion which they could not gauge, any more than could the Girondins; they would, however, have control over its development for somewhat longer.

THE CONSTITUTION OF 1795

Finally they had to face up to the great day of reckoning at home. The Convention had been elected in September 1792 to set up a constitution, after the people had taken the Tuileries and overthrown the king. It had voted for one which was immediately invalidated by the sansculottes; then another, which was straight away suspended. Now was the time for the third, the good one – or, if the adjective seems excessive considering the short life of that document, at least the one which would determine the features of the Republic's government until the coup d'état of Brumaire (November 1799).

It was voted on 22 August, having been the subject of a long and gripping discussion. All the fundamental problems debated in the decisive months of 1789, between June and October, resurface in it. In this way, the historian has the unexpected chance of seeing a second run of the film, in its emended version, and of being able to measure the weight of events on consciences. Amongst the principals, certain actors have not changed. Boissy d'Anglas, *rapporteur* of the Constitution of Year III, had in 1789 been the deputy to the Estates-General for the seneschalship of Annonay, and had won renown in June of that year by backing the designation of 'National Assembly' for the meeting of the Third Estate. During Louis XVI's trial, he had voted for an appeal to the people, detention and reprieve.

Sieyès, however, was a regicide: on 2 and 18 Thermidor (20 July and 5 August 1795) he gave two of his greatest constitutional speeches. Unable to have all his recommendations put to the vote, he refused to have anything to do with the final bill, as with the first constitution after the summer of 1789. But his interventions in summer 1795, perhaps too philosophical for the occasion, remain essential for anyone wanting to understand the questions raised.

The third great name in the debate was Daunou, the deputy from the Pas-de-Calais, an ex-Oratorian, in favour of the Civil Constitution of the Clergy. He had proposed the trial of the king by a special High Court, before voting for his imprisonment and banishment. He was one of the seventy-three deputies arrested for protesting against 2 June 1793, and among the first to be reinstated in December 1794. He typified the dominant political tone: very hostile to the Terror, very closely bound to the Revolution, which now needed to be implanted in the law and in men's minds. It was up to legislation and philosophy to signpost the new road which had been opened in 1789 and lost in 1793.

The Revolution retraced its steps. It reopened the discussion about the Declaration of Rights, the sovereignty of the people, representation. It sought to write a document which would render impossible any return to the revolutionary government, which it branded 'anarchy', the lawless regime, and finally to bring 1789 to an end by a Republic governed by reason and property-ownership. The new declaration, like the two preceding ones, was included in the constitution. It contained the supremacy of the law, which was an expression of the general will of the people, as the guarantee of rights. But the right of 'resisting oppression' (1789) or of 'insurrection' (1793) had disappeared, to prevent any challenge to what had been instituted according to law.

Equality was still within the rights of man, together with liberty, safety and property, but it retrieved its 1789 status, defined by the same rights for every citizen before the law: there was no more reference, as in 1793, to the right to work, aid or education. Finally, the 1795 declaration contained a second addendum entitled 'Duties': it was the very one that the Constitutent Assembly had refused the *Monarchiens* in July–August 1789. It laid down, together with the obligations of legislators, those of the citizens, namely, obedience to the laws, productive labour and service to the *patrie*. It was all aimed at avoiding the tension between the unlimited nature of rights and the necessity for social order based on the law: since 1789, the internal revolutionary dynamic had found its source in that gap, which the Conventionnels could not fill but which they tried to narrow.

Another great question was the sovereignty of the people. The deputies were by now well aware that a much more oppressive government than the old absolute monarchy could reign in its name. Between 1792 and 1794 they had discovered the fearsome and literally boundless power concealed within the democratic idea of sovereignty: had it not attempted, under Robespierre, to engulf citizens' private lives, even their thoughts?

Comparison between the old absolute power of the kings and the Robespierrist dictatorship cropped up constantly in political discussion after 9 Thermidor. It gave Sieyès the opportunity, in his speech of 2 Thermidor (1795), for an explanation which has lost none of its historic value:

This expression [the sovereignty of the people] has loomed so large in imaginations only because French minds, still filled with superstitions about royalty, felt duty-bound to imbue it with the entire heritage of pompous attributes and absolute powers which gave the usurped sovereignties their glitter; we have even seen the public mind, in its immense liberality, become angry that it could not endow it still further; men seemed to think, with a sort of patriotic pride, that if the sovereignty of great kings is so powerful, so terrible, then the sovereignty of a great people should be something else again. For myself, I maintain that, as men become enlightened and distance themselves from the times when they believed they had knowledge, but in reality had only the desire, the concept of sovereignty will return to its rightful confines for, once again, the sovereignty of the people is not limitless, and many honoured and lauded systems – including the one to which we believe we still have the greatest obligations – will come to appear as mere monastic conceptions, poor blueprints for the '*rétotale*' rather than the '*république*', and equally disastrous for liberty and ruinous for both the public and the private.

Thus, according to the former Vicar-General of Chartres, the Revolution's mistake lay in having transferred the power of the king to the people. The only way to rectify that error was to entrust to them only the amount of power necessary for the existence of a nation of free and equal individuals, defined first and foremost by what belonged only to each one of them. Here began a long liberal tradition of reflection on the concept of sovereignty, to be found in Benjamin Constant, Madame de Staël, Royer-Collard and Guizot.

For the moment, one of Sieyès's ideas for limiting sovereignty was to have a *jurie constitutionnaire*, a special body which would have the task of judging complaints against any attack made on the constitution: this was the first appearance in French history of the notion of a jurisdiction superior to the legislative power, since it would exercise control over the constitutionality of laws and administrative regulations. With Sieyès, this was not born of a reflection on Montesquieu or on the necessary balance of powers. On the contrary, the *jurie constitutionnaire* was only one of the 'representative' authorities of society, armed with the special *procuration* to watch over the constitution, alongside several other *juries*, endowed with other *procurations*: Sieyès never considered the organization of public power in terms of weight and counterweight, American fashion, but – good French rationalist that he was – as a clockwork mechanism.

As in 1789, The Assembly adopted the spirit rather than the letter of his advice. To limit sovereignty by dividing it, while at the same time founding the Republic on the enlightened 'representation' of the people, charged with delegating its executive power to a college: such were the aims of the majority of deputies. The new constitution comprised two assemblies vested with legislative power: an innovation in revolutionary history, because since 1789 the two-chamber system had been tainted with 'aristocracy'. But it was now only a matter of dividing up the tasks: the Five Hundred, with a minimum age of thirty, discussed and voted on resolutions which the 'Ancients' (250 deputies aged at least forty) transformed into laws, or not, as the case might be.

Sieyès's constitutional jurisdiction had disappeared, not understood by his contemporaries: the sovereignty of the people was represented by two assemblies, but remained without total control. In the end, the deputies sought to moderate, rather than limit, it by specifying electoral rights, as in 1791. Voting continued to be two-tiered. All Frenchmen enrolled on the tax lists voted, but could elect only well-to-do electors (the rating conditions varied according to the size of the townships): this is where the *propriétaires* had such an advantage in national representation.

Executive power was in keeping with what might be expected in a republic: elected and collegial, therefore relatively weak – five Directors, chiefs of the Executive, and ministers chosen by the Ancients from a list of fifty names put forward by the Five Hundred. The assemblies were replaceable by a third and the Directory by a fifth each year. Executive power in the hands of the Directory was extensive, almost by nature in the France of 1795: war, diplomacy, police, administration.

The limiting factor was the existence of a college of five Directors, plus the rebirth of the elective principle for departmental and municipal administrations, which were nevertheless placed under the control of agents of the central government. But the most acute constitutional problem facing the Constitution of Year III concerned the relations between the legislature and the executive. The assemblies made and voted on laws, elected Directors but did not control their actions, except that they could indict them. Powers were separate, and how their co-operation was to be organized had not been precisely established.

As soon as it had completed the constitution, the Convention moved on to another debate, entitled in the *Moniteur*, the official journal of the time, 'Discussion on the means of ending the Revolution.' The question implicit in this already classic wording had been put clearly by Baudin, deputy for the Ardennes and a member of the Constitution Committee, on 1 Fructidor (18 August): it was less the end of the Revolution than its continuity that was in question.

The withdrawal of the Constituent Assembly is enough to teach you that, if an untried constitution is set in motion, a totally new legislature is an infallible means of overturning it . . . The Legislative Assembly, bound to uphold the monarchy as it had pledged with such ceremony, perhaps itself contributed to its rapid under-mining, and did not believe it was acting disloyally by saving the country. You should fear lest the establishment of the Republic encounter the same hazards, if you risk putting it to the same test, and that after so many jolts and wrenches and convulsions, liberty may succumb in a new revolution which you would have made possible by an act of weakness.

What was he trying to say, through this appeal to memories? This: the Convention had to do the opposite of what the Constituent Assembly had done, and keep control over what was to follow. By leaving the people to elect freely the two assemblies whose formation it had just decided upon, it was running the risk of a royalist majority which would imperil revolutionary ideas and interests. His speech was understood, because it was followed on 5 Fructidor (22 August) by a vote for a decree on the 'formation of a new legislative body'. Article II, section i, stipulates: 'All members presently active in the Convention are re-eligible. Electoral assemblies may not take fewer than two-thirds of them to form the legisla-tive body.'

That was the famous law of the Two-Thirds, followed shortly after by a supplementary safety clause: if the quota was not observed, the re-elected Conventionnels would co-opt their former colleagues. In May 1791 Robespierre had had the ineligibility of the Constituents voted in order to give forward impetus to the Revolution. In August 1795 the Convention perpetuated itself in order to preserve it. It paid a heavy price, for in doing so it inflicted a congenital weakness on the institutions it had just developed, and destroyed what had been at the very heart of its plan – a Republic founded on law. The entire history of the Directory had already been cast: all that was missing was the victorious general who would, as if by chance, make his appearance in the political crisis instigated by the cynical decision of the Perpetuals.

The decree went down badly with an urban opinion that had 'gone royalist,' and for which the Convention remained associated with the Terror. All the elements of French bourgeois life that had been reborn since the summer of 1794 – the new salons, the new newspapers, the new gentlemen and the beautiful ladies dressed in Roman fashion – had impatiently awaited the departure of those Public Safety veterans who should have taken the bad memories away with them. Now here were those same discredited men about to fill the new institutions, in the name of their worst habits, nullifying in advance the feeling of the country. Through them the Revolution would pursue its dictatorship. As Robespierre had suspended his constitution to make his power absolute, they had decided to abolish in actual fact the elective principle they had just sanctioned.

However, confronted with the moderates' anger (echoed by a minority on the right) the Convention had the logic of the situation on its side. Revolutionary France had a foreign war on its hands, and was increasingly detested by the émigrés and men of the *ancien régime*; the country was in a state of bankruptcy and unpopularity, which still carried the risk of re-igniting the sparks of the great *journées* of earlier days. The Perpetuals were the product of these circumstances, according the sovereignty of the people only the share which the situation allowed: that was a completely empirical strategy, which made such a sharp contrast with the abstractions of revolu-tionary government, and which would win for that very reason. The Convention and its committees had the power, and made use of it. They managed to get all the *départements* to accept the new constitution and the decrees of the two-thirds.

In Paris, on 13 Vendémiaire (5 October), they crushed a rising of the moderate *sections* of the west, led by the privileged youth. These last had rather played the role of sorcerer's apprentice in trying to repeat, to the advantage of the right, the great scenes of crowd-rousing against the Assembly. It was a scenario that the deputies of the former Plaine knew better. They even knew it by heart. And the *muscadins* were easier to bring down than the sansculottes. The Convention had entrusted the affair to Barras who, in order to crush moderate Paris, had recruited a young unemployed general, a former Robespierrist, who was trailing along in his entourage: Napoleon Bonaparte. All the same, there were 20,000 insurgents on the streets, but the cannon were in the Convention's camp and decided the matter without further ado near the church of Saint-Roch.

At the time when it dispersed at the end of October, the Convention was therefore more than ever the incarnation of the Revolution and its power; so that no one should remain unaware of it, on 3 Brumaire (25 October), at its penultimate sitting, it passed a law which reaffirmed and extended the curse laid on the aristocracy since 1789, because it forbade relatives of émigrés to hold public office. Not that the émigrés at that time were all nobles – far from it. But the idea of emigration was inseparable from that of aristocracy, and the Revolution continued its mission, extended to Europe. It was under this banner that the Thermidorian bourgeois put the finishing touch to their work by a last law of exception, before installing themselves in the Directory in the places they had reserved for themselves in advance.

The elections would therefore bring back 500 Conventionnels out of 750 deputies divided into two chambers. As many of these veterans had been chosen by several constituencies, their numbers were short and their old and new colleagues had to co-opt about a hundred more. So there were three categories of deputies: the elected Conventionnels, the co-opted Conventionnels and a final third, the most moderate, freely chosen by the electoral assemblies. Lots were drawn among the over-forties to pick the 250 who would form the 'Ancients'. This personnel was still perforce dominated by the majority of the old Thermidorian Convention, amongst whom the great names still appeared: Sieyès, Carnot, Treilhard, Jean-Jacques de Cambacérès, Barras.

They were not all former members of the Plaine who had once given the support of their votes to the Montagnard dictatorship; there were also reinstated ex-Girondins, like Louvet and Daunou, who were more deeply attached to the Republic than to their bad memories of post-2 June 1793. The right was composed mainly of the newly elected, but also included some former members. It was even more different in its loyalties, because it contained men of the old Feuillant group, Barbé-Marbois, Tronson-Ducoudray, Du Pont de Nemours – a lot of royalists without a king; and there were some supporters of the royal cause, like Henry-Larivière, an outlawed ex-Girondin, reinstated with the last group in March 1795, but not at all keen to 'draw a veil over the past', and a bitter adversary of the Republic.

The chief concern was the election of the Directory. It was prepared in a series of secret meetings of the Five Hundred, intended to pass on to the Ancients a broad list made up in such a way that the five desired names would impose themselves by virtue of their renown. They were – in order of votes received – five Conventionnels, La Révellière-Lépeaux, Reubell, Sieyès, Charles Letourneur and Barras. All regicides, save Reubell, who had been on mission to the Mainz army at the time of the king's trial. Sieyès declined, pleading his lack of enthusiasm for the office, and also aggrieved that his plan for the constitution had not been accepted. The Ancients replaced him with Carnot, another great name of the Revolution, another regicide, who had succeeded in personifying the glory of the Committee of Public Safety without its crimes.

In this team which had emerged from 1793, only La Révellière-Lépeaux was a former Girondin, proscribed by the Terror but still Girondin, that is to say, anticlerical and annexationist. Barras and Reubell were ex-terrorists who had little regard for means but were uncompromising over the revolutionary heritage. Barras, an ex-Vicomte, had saved the Convention on 13 Vendémiaire. He was a corrupt but energetic sensualist, the strong member of the team, protector of all the surviving Jacobin personnel in the administration, and watchdog over royalist intrigues. Letourneur, a captain in the Engineers, was an understudy for Carnot, the moderate member of this first Directory; the man who had sat with Robespierre and Saint-Just on the Grand Committee surely did not welcome the idea of the return of the kings, but above all he feared social disorder.

The Directors shared responsibilities: the Interior went to Barras, War to Carnot, Diplomacy and Finance to Reubell, Public Education to La Révellière-Lépeaux and the Navy to Letourneur. They appointed ministers, who were no longer anything but top civil servants, to head their administrations. The Republic was in place. It soon gave itself another ministry, also supervised by Barras – that of Police. There was certainly a need for it: barely established, it was already a discredited regime. The contrast which would be its undoing, between the glory of France abroad and the contempt in which the government was held at home, existed from the moment it took its first steps.

CONSTANT

One can better understand the reasons if one listens to a young Swiss who had just arrived in Paris, in the middle of 1795, in the train of Madame de Staël, with whom he was in love: Benjamin Constant. He was a child prodigy of Enlightenment Europe, who had studied classical antiquity, history and philosophy in the best universities of the era, in Germany and Edinburgh. He was twenty-eight years old. Here he was at last in Paris, the centre of universal history since 1789. There was no sharper observer of the political situation.

He had begun by writing an article against the decree of the two-thirds, before rallying to its support shortly afterwards: his life would offer other examples of that kind of about-face, but like those which followed, this can be explained by reasons which are not all circumstantial. For the young Swiss was a supporter of Year III of the Republic, yet at the same time aware of the threats hanging over it. He had absolutely no attachment to the aristocracy, for whom he had fewer regrets – if possible – than his famous friend, Necker's daughter Germaine de Staël.

His entire thinking, even ahead of his ambitions and interests, drew him to support the new world born in 1789. But from his vast range of studies he had also retained the classic impossibility of establishing a Republican government in a large country: modern nation-states were too immense for the people to vote on laws, as they had in Athens. In Thermidorian France, facts seemed to have endorsed that politico-philosophical dilemma, since the 1792 Republic had been unable to apply its own constitution, and had degenerated into a terrorist dictatorship. In doing so, it had added an element of emotive revulsion to what had hitherto been merely the philosophical acknowledgement of a contradiction. Benjamin Constant did not truly belong to the Thermidorians, because he had not shared their past, having lived outside France until 1795; but this young man would be their profoundest thinker.

In April 1796 he published a pamphlet entitled *De la force du gouvernement actuel et de la nécessité de s'y rallier* (On the strength of the present government and the need to support it). A significant title, which meant the opposite of what it proclaimed, at least in its first part: the government was weak, therefore it needed support. In fact, Constant was attempting to reply to the wave of reaction which had shown itself on 13 Vendémiaire and continued to accompany the first steps of the new regime. He had buckled down to a daunting, almost impossible, task: to establish the Republic in public opinion, in order to root it firmly in the law, two years after the Terror and several months after the decrees of the two-thirds.

The heart of the argument lies in making the French Revolution a part of historical necessity. Constant refutes Burke, who had become the source from which all counter-revolutionary thought drew its nourishment, and at the same time transforms the problem of the causes of 1789. The

break with the *ancien régime* did not represent a sudden eruption of the
'natural rights' of individuals, or their rediscovery in a society corrupted
by 'gothic' institutions. It demonstrated the operation of a historic reason
which had been at work from the very beginning – the concept of equality.
'The origin of the social state is a great enigma, but its progress is
simple and uniform . . . Emerging from the impenetrable cloud which
covers its birth, we see humankind go forward towards equality over the
ruins of institutions of all kinds. There has been no going back on any step
taken in this direction.'[4] Thus, the end of the *ancien régime*, foretold
by Enlightenment philosophy, wipes out what he calls the system of
'heredity', in which the destiny of individuals is written in their birth: it
inaugurates modern equality, whereby everyone receives his due according
to his merit, by virtue of a law which is common to all and in accordance
with reason.

There was therefore no sense in opposing an inevitable history, as
the counter-revolutionaries were doing, and being all the more harmful
because they were anachronistic. The Revolution was modern France,
born of a general shift in public opinion, and firmly implanted in new ways
and new interests: assent was not only wise, it was inseparable from public
peace, which the French so ardently desired. It alone could rebuild a
united opinion around the principles of 1789. However, that was to suppose that the problem of the Terror had been settled, which it certainly
was not. How could the renascent Republic in Year III be separated from
its first two years, when all the efforts of reactionaries and neo-Jacobins
were working in the opposite direction? The former cast the Revolution
as an indivisible whole, entirely to be damned; the Terror providentially
revealed the true nature of the event while forming its very heart: it was a
thesis which Joseph de Maistre argued in the next year (1797) in his
Considérations sur la France.

On the other hand, as has been seen, the 1793 constitution was beginning to be the subject of a special cult: among those nostalgic for Year II,
the term in reality covered the entire revolutionary programme, equality of
poor and rich, the Maximum, the guillotine, dictatorship. In order to
conquer the émigré and royalist right, Constant had not only to emphasize
the historic necessity for the Revolution, but at the same time to sever the
Republic from its revolutionary origins. That was the condition for the
institution of the law and the rallying of public opinion. He was the first
to grapple with a problem which all nineteenth-century liberals would
encounter, whether monarchists or republicans. There is no other modern
political heritage in France but that of the Revolution; that heritage
includes a portion which is not compatible with liberty, and which it is not
possible to 'forget', because 1793 also has its heirs.

In Constant's language, used by his contemporaries as well, the Revolution was a good thing, but its development had been uncertain, chaotic,

[4] *De la force du gouvernement actuel de la France et de la nécessité de s'y rallier*, p. 96.

sometimes detestable, because the revolutionary Terror duplicated the arbitrary nature of absolute power and caused the reappearance of an *ancien régime* characteristic. Constant endlessly explored the reasons for that contradiction between a necessary event and its mysterious course, even if he was unable to explain its nature. He would devote two further pamphlets to the subject in 1797. He could see the role played by the heritage of the past and the counter-revolution, but clear-sightedly refused to explain the Revolution's crimes only by reference to those of the *ancien régime*. He was the first to point out that the scaffold had most often followed Jacobin victory, instead of being its prerequisite. Finally, he put forward an explanation by anachronism. Revolutions were intended to reconcile the institutions of a people with its 'ideas', when the former lagged behind the latter; but the dictatorship of Year II had gone beyond the said 'ideas', threatening property; that was why it had provoked a sort of backlash movement of political 'reactions' which might well bring back the Revolution short of its principles, and serve the enemies of 1789 without really meaning to.

That explained the fragility of the regime of Year III, demonstrated by the decree of the two-thirds. For Constant, the young Republic was haunted by the spectre of arbitrary rule. The *ancien régime* had been subject to the whim of the king, revolutionary dictatorship had been lawless; and very soon, if 'reaction' triumphed, it would put the finishing touch to this tragic sequence: 'Those who seek to overthrow the Republic are strangely taken in by words. They have seen what a terrible and dire event a revolution is, and conclude that what they call a counter-revolution would be a happy one. They do not realize that this counter-revolution would itself be only a new revolution.'[5]

In order to break out of the fatal sequence, there was but one remedy; to rally general feeling behind the Republic of Year III, to entrench the principles of 1789 in a peaceable, durable political regime, which would be accepted, that is to say in both public opinion and the law. Benjamin Constant had not yet completely developed his theory of 'representative government', which he was nevertheless already hailing as the great modern invention; but he was the first to map out the republicans' and liberals' questionnaire on the Revolution. And he had put his finger on the nub of the French political problem, which would last for a hundred years: restoration of the monarchy brings back the *ancien régime*, but the Republic is indivisble from dictatorship in French history and French memories.

BABEUF

The French formed a nation of bourgeois, peasants and landowners. But not entirely. Almost at the very moment when Constant's first booklet made its appearance in April 1796, the Directory dramatically eliminated a

---

[5] *De la force du gouvernement*, p. 21.

communist conspiracy aiming to set up an egalitarian dictatorship in France. This chronological quasi-coincidence speaks volumes about the extraordinary segmentation of political traditions all harking back to the Revolution, and the precocity of their development on the very heels of that Revolution: 1789, 1793 – they were only yesterday; Robespierre's death had not reached its second anniversary when the revolutionary adventure found its heirs not only divided but enemies. Constant tried to justify the Revolution, Babeuf wanted to start it again.

The concept had as its background the spectacle of poverty, rendered even more cruel by the blatant luxury of the few. The parvenus of the Revolution, the Thermidorians, were also frequently made wealthy by it. The nobles had gone, or were in hiding; the court was nothing more than a distant memory. The bourgeois dominated Parisian society, where *biens nationaux* and public bankruptcy had offered the opportunity for profitable speculation, adding its effects to more traditional forms of profiteering – augmented by circumstances – such as army supplies and state markets. The *financiers* of the *ancien régime* had found their heirs.

This bourgeoisie had been liberated from aristocratic arrogance since 1789, but it had been separated from the people since 1792. The terms aristocracy, bourgeoisie, people, must be taken both in their very general social acceptance and as political categories defining extremely strong class feeling, inherited from the *ancien régime* and intensified by the Revolution. Post-revolutionary society unwittingly combined equality, which had remained its banner against the nobles, with the aristocratic heritage, turned against the people. To put it into an imprecise but clear nineteenth-century vocabulary, the *ancien régime* and the Revolution had cut the middle class off from both the upper and the lower classes.

The economic and financial situation constituted a permanent incitement to the resentment of the poor and intensified memories of Year II. The Directory had inherited a financial mess, and continued to honour settlements with increasingly devalued assignats. A feeble government, lacking credit in the country as a whole, or even among the wealthy, in March it botched an operation for financial stabilization, which ended up in the squandering of two billion of *biens nationaux*, sold for a song to the joyful speculators. Moreover, it had very bad luck: the harvests of 1794 and 1795 were poor, and the icy winter of 1795–6 was the hardest of all in the revolutionary years. Parisian police reports of the time, which were already adopting the modern practice of keeping note for the government of movements of opinion, all speak of the bad state of mind; one of them, on 2 January 1796, reports that the 'societies of patriots' coming into being again 'are made up only of terrorists and revived Jacobins whose influence and pernicious maxims are a threat'.

It was in that context that the Conspiracy of Equals was formed by Babeuf. For a time it lacked any great importance since it did not really threaten the government. Nor is it certain that its principal hero deserves, for the profundity of his writings, the attention he has received in the twentieth century. However, that very attention, notably on the part of communist historiography, indicates Babeuf's egalitarianism was more than a failed conspiracy: it was the basis of a tradition whereby the French Revolution entered the extreme left in the nineteenth and twentieth centuries.

An ex-militant sansculotte who in 1793 had passed into the revolutionary administration, participating for some months after 9 Thermidor in anti-Robespierrist reaction, Babeuf had soon returned to egalitarian extremism and had been imprisoned in February 1795 for 'incitement to rebellion, murder and the dissolution of national representation'. It was in prison – first in Paris at the Plessis, then in Arras, where he was transferred – that the nucleus of the future Conspiracy of Equals was formed, with the ex- and neo-terrorists that he met there: Germain, Bodson, Debon and Filippo Buonarroti. The last, a descendant of a great Pisan family, an intellectual nurtured on the philosophy of the Enlightenment and a loyal Robespierrist who became a naturalized Frenchman in 1793 – also the future historiographer of Babouvism – was able to play an important role in the doctrinal redevelopment of the group. At all events, when he emerged from prison in October (after the Vendémiaire royalist uprising, amnesty was granted to all Republicans) Babeuf, now transformed into *Gracchus* Babeuf, was the man whose new Roman forename evoked the sharing out of lands and the egalitarian distribution of wealth. That was the new banner of his newspaper and his activities.

In the terrible winter of 1795–6, Babeuf's group came across a group nostalgic for 1793, ex-Hébertists, ex-Maratists, ex-Robespierrists, brought together by the general misfortune of the times and seeking a popular platform against the newly established Directory. They all regrouped around the former Conventionnel Amar, famous for his role in the Committee of General Security, and met in clubs, the most active of which, the Panthéon, was gradually radicalized under the influence of Germain, Buonarroti and Darthe, one of the most extreme terrorists of the heroic epoch. From the fusion of these groups and men would emerge, in the autumn of 1796, the idea of the need for clandestine and direct action as a substitute for popular apathy.

After the Directory had had the Panthéon Club closed in February, the conspirators in their turn formed a 'secret Directory of Public Safety', consisting of seven members. Participating were communists like Babeuf and the amiable publicist, Sylvain Maréchal, who had strayed into this tragic sheepfold; he was the author of the *Manifeste des Égaux*. On the side of the neo-Robespierrists dating from the great epoch were such as Félix le Peletier, brother of the Montagnard Conventionnel assassinated in 1793, a rich banker who had possibly sponsored the team; finally Buonarroti, who exactly personified the transition from Robespierrism to Babouvism. This 'Secret Directory' put its agents in place for the day of action: one per *arrondissement* and, in the army, one per unit of troops. In the provinces it relied on the support of a certain number of nostalgic Conventionnels. It

Louis Lejeune Battle of the Bridge at Lodi, 10 May 1796, *Musée Versailles, Paris.* (Photo: Photographie Bulloz)

adopted as its banner and its programme the 1793 constitution, the return to the sovereignty of the people. The rest was known only to a small circle of conspirators.

But the other Directory – the real one – was well informed. Barras knew a little of what was being plotted through his informers and the relationships he had kept up with former friends. He took no action, fearing, since Vendémiaire, the royalists more than the sansculottes, who had been crushed in Germinal and Prairial. He was also a 'wait and see' specialist. Carnot, by contrast, knew every detail of the conspiracy, thanks to one of the conspirators, whose treachery he had bought. The former member of the Committee of Public Safety almost obsessively exorcized his own past through his combat against the Equals. Backed by Letourneur and La Révellière, while Reubell did nothing, he became the figurehead of the Directory against the terrorists and 'Levellers'. Through him, certain bourgeois members of Year III tried to turn the Babeuf affair into something of a bogey.

The conspirators were picked up by the police on 21 Floréal (10 May 1796). Of this new tumbril-load public opinion knew only the names of the old Conventionnels, Jean-Baptiste Drouet (the man of Varennes), Robert Lindet, Vadier, Amar. It saw this episode as the fall of a new terrorist faction, the final spasm of Jacobinism. Less famous, the 'Equals', strictly speaking, were masked by memories of 1793. Nevertheless, at the trial in Vendôme the following year, of the sixty-five accused who had decided to deny the conspiracy despite the evidence, only Babeuf and Darthe were sentenced to death and executed; seven, including Buonarroti, were sentenced to deportation; all the others were acquitted: from this judgement one may infer the solidarity of the ex-Conventionnel circle.

The affair had not therefore been very serious; first and foremost, it gave Carnot the chance to organize the first 'red peril' in modern history, which would know plenty of others. But it was important chiefly for the ideas it left. Buonarroti would make a book about them, published at the end of the Restoration: through this 'Constitution of Equals', the most egalitarian version of the Revolution would transform the great memories of 1793 into visions of the future.

The heart of the conspiracy was the concept of equality, glorified as the aim of the Revolution, since it was the law of nature and man's prime need and *therefore* – that was the crucial word – society's ultimate goal.

The French Revolution had seen the target, but had not been able to reach it. The historic development of the reasons for this failure is to be found in Buonarroti's book, but the idea was implicit everywhere in the texts of 1795, and served as a link between Babouvists and neo-Robespierrists: the Revolution had been taken over in its early stages by the aristocrats, whom Buonarroti likened to supporters of English political economy and self-centred individualism. But the 1793 constitution (the second, after the defeat of the Girondins) and Robespierre's revolutionary government had restored power to the people and to equality. Alas, not for long, since 9 Thermidor brought back their adversaries. Babouvism had thus formed the early ground for a Robespierrist historiography of the Revolution destined for a bright future, critical of both 1789 and Thermidor. But in Year IV, if one listens to the *Manifeste des Égaux* again, it was more a matter of an agenda: 'The French Revolution is merely the forerunner of another bigger, much more solemn, revolution, which will be the last.'

What revolution was meant? What could make equality 'real'? The suppression of private ownership? In this regard, Babeuf's contribution seems to have been decisive, in so far as his pre-1789 correspondence already bears witness to his interest in a general plan for social reorganization founded on the equal distribution of possessions. The leader of the 'Equals' was not a great thinker, and all his life remained more of an ideologist than a philosopher. He was an innocent and sentimental autodidact, an admirer of Rousseau and the Abbé Mably, advancing the idea of splitting up large farms for the benefit of the poorest people, commenting passionately, in his letters of 1787, on a work on the means of stamping out pauperism. His *Cadastre perpétuel* (Perpetual Land Register), which appeared in 1789, revolved around the same question. During the revolutionary years, Babeuf finally put forward not the idea of 'agrarian law', which suggested an egalitarian distribution of lands among individuals, but a community of land, which would rule out all private ownership, and an equal sharing out of its produce among all citizens who would be equally conscripted to work on it. Such sharing agrarian communism was not unknown in the store-house of eighteenth-century literary utopias, but in Babouvism it presented the new characteristic of constituting a revolutionary programme. It undeniably marked the entry of communism into public life.

The last distinctive feature of the conspiracy concerned its conception of politics; it owed more to Jacobinism than to Enlightenment philosophy. In 1794–5 Babeuf and his friends had adopted, as a unifying slogan, the watchword of a return to the 1793 Montagnard constitution. They praised its practice of direct democracy (by referring laws to primary assemblies), although they secretly criticized it for guaranteeing the right of ownership. But behind this exaltation of the one and indivisible will of the people lay, as with the Jacobins and perhaps even more so, the justification of dictatorship: that of the only true interpreters of that sovereign will, the purest revolutionaries – the Equals.

Like the Jacobins, Babeuf exaggerated the power of political action to change society and to maintain its strictly egalitarian nature when it had done so. According to Buonarroti, the distribution of possessions was to be carried out under the control of magistrates appointed, over a long period, by the members of the 'Secret Directory'. The revolutionary tradition of political voluntarism thus blossomed with the Conspiracy of Equals; in this respect, it is significant that the majority of Babouvist documents eschew the term liberty in favour of the word equality.

What should have followed success by the conspiracy can be seen in its concrete preparation. Babeuf borrowed his idea of political action from Marat and the Hébertists: the people who had been subjugated and deceived (this time by an evil conspiracy of the wealthy) could be freed from their chains only by a clandestine insurrectionist minority, organized along military lines, and determined at all costs to institute, at least temporarily, a dictatorship in the name of, and to the benefit of, the people.

That vision surely reveals the inability of the conspirators, in the circumstances of Year IV, to stir up the resigned mass of the people to recover the atmosphere of the great revolutionary *journées*. But it was infinitely more than this sad reflection of their isolation; it was the ultimate expression of the revolutionary belief that political will could achieve everything. The last wave of Jacobin extremism – and doubtless the only political synthesis of the passion for equality of those time – here elaborated the theory of the revolutionary *coup*, which had no real support in Thermidorian society, but was at least appropriate to the nature of a centralized state: he who conquers the ministries in Paris could be master of the country.

THE DIRECTORY

For the time being, however, in the year 1796, which witnessed the ruthless elimination of the Babouvist conspiracy, the danger for the Perpetuals did not lie on their left. It was precisely where Constant had foreseen it, on their right, in the disaffection and even contempt felt by 'enlightened' opinion for the regime of Year III and its men. Autumn saw the arrival of the first electoral date: one third of the Councils would have to be replaced, and the new Councils would then elect one new Director out of the five. How could they avoid a royalist success, which would open a dangerous breach in the Republican fortress?

Barras and Reubell had moderated the repression of Babouvism because they were the protectors of the revolutionary heritage. They had filled the new administration with former Jacobins, with whom they shared the will to oppose by all possible means a royalist restoration, including one by stealth. In opposition to them, Carnot sniffed the prevailing wind, as in 1793, but this time from the other direction, sensing the conservative trend of bourgeois opinion, like most of the two councils. But the parliamentary right, composed chiefly of deputies who had not sat in the Convention, was demanding more than they were prepared to give. It wanted the abolition of the law of 3 Brumaire (25 October 1795), which prohibited émigrés' relatives from holding public office.

All it obtained was an extension of the ban to the sixty-eight Conventionnels pursued after 9 Thermidor, who had been amnestied after 13 Vendémiaire and once again renegotiated like hostages in the shifting

balance of forces: it was a strange decision, which reveals much about the
spirit of the era, the influence of symbols and the powerful effect of
memories. In order not to have to relinquish them, the old Plaine temporized by extending to terrorists laws of exclusion aimed at émigrés'
families.

Neither counter-revolution nor Terror. This combat on two fronts could
still be defined only in relation to civil war, and could still express itself
only by exceptional laws. Nevertheless, if it allowed the government to
continue without lapsing into tyranny, it was firstly because it found
backing in private interests; the government was post-revolutionary and
bourgeois, wedding politics and money, guaranteeing assets, reassuring the
owners of *biens nationaux*, opening careers in the administration and the
army. It kept going almost uniquely because it was the embodiment of that
social continuity with 1789, and the heart of the country, including the
peasantry, was not prepared to re-exchange the Revolution for the *ancien
régime*. But it also presented a fragile governmental version of 1789, in the
hands of an oligarchy without credit even in the eyes of those citizens it
was protecting. In post-1793 France, private interests were very demanding in the matter of political guarantees. It was the Directory's good
fortune not to have on its right a royalist opposition which could make this
France a more secure offer.

Not that there were no moderate royalists seeking to reconcile the royal
family with civil equality. On the contrary, the country was full of them,
because it was a question of linking up with 1789 and not with the *ancien
régime*, and of rediscovering a *Monarchien* version of royalty which would
include the sale of *biens nationaux*, which had been decided upon two
months after the defeat of the *Monarchiens*. That, roughly speaking, was
the programme of the moderate notables who met together at Clichy in the
mansion of Louis XVI's ex-minister, Bertin, under the leadership of
General Mathieu Dumas, veteran of the American war, La Fayette's
former right-hand man in Paris and Feuillant ex-deputy to the Legislative
Assembly.

These men, who formed the right wing of the councils, felt that they
were carried by public opinion, by that very numerous class which, in
1790 and 1791, had staffed the administrations of the new *départements*
before being eliminated by the 1792 Republic and the 'revolutionary
government'. They disliked the Perpetuals, detested Barras, and had
hardly more confidence in Carnot, who had sat so long with Robespierre
on the Committee of Public Safety. They did not believe, like Constant,
that the Thermidorian Republic was capable of restoring concord in a
country which was gradually sliding towards a sort of soft anarchy. France
was too vast a country, where the roots of royalty were too ancient for any
power other than monarchy to be able to bring back order and revive
respect for property.

But which monarchy? The drama of these 'constitutional royalists' of
Years IV and V, also known as the Clichyens – unlike the 1789 *Monarchiens*,

or even the 1791 Feuillants – was that the regime they envisaged would again mean the subversion of institutions; and, supposing this subversion should take place, it would restore to power not a constitutional king, but the family of the martyr-king and his train of émigrés.

Certainly, since 1792, emigration had ceased to be essentially aristo-cratic; fear and events had driven tens of thousands of Frenchmen of all classes out of the country, especially from *départements* near to frontiers. But, just as for Madame de Staël the only good emigration was the one following 10 August, so for the aristocracy, monarchist loyalty was measured by the earliness of the date of exile, and it continued to mount a close guard around the king's brothers. It surrounded Provence and Artois with little courts more finicky than ever about etiquette, and all the great roles were played out in the minor key, including those of favourites: Madame de Balbi for the former, and Madame de Polastron for the latter.

The most terrible indictment brought against the aristocracy was written by one of the most ardent advocates of the counter-revolution, Joseph de Maistre, who took up his pen just at that time to reply to Constant's pamphlet of spring 1796.

One of the laws of the French Revolution is that émigrés can attack it only for their misfortunes, and are totally excluded from whatever work is being under-taken. From the first wild dreams of the counter-revolution, right up to the ever-appalling Quiberon enterprise, they have never undertaken anything which has succeeded, or even which has not gone against them. Not only do they not succeed, but everything they turn their hand to is stamped with such a mark of impotence and uselessness that opinion has finally become accustomed to looking on them as men who stubbornly persist in defending an outlawed party; that puts them in a disfavour which even their friends notice. And such disfavour will not occasion much surprise among men who believe that the principal cause of the French Revolution lay in the moral degradation of the nobility.[6]

It was all well and good for Maistre to explain in his book that the re-establishment of the monarchy would not be a counter-revolution, an 'opposite revolution', but the 'opposite of a revolution'; the émigrés gathered about the king's brothers would in fact prove Benjamin Constant right. Artois's entourage was even more reactionary than Provence's, and the old *Monarchiens* were indeed starting to provoke, in the circles surrounding the future Louis XVIII, a debate on the nature of monarchic tradition, in which men such as Jacques Mallet du Pan, Malouet, Lally Tollendal and Montlosier acquired some renown.

Nevertheless, since its origins, the restoration project had been marked throughout by a radical hostility to the Revolution: Burke's *Reflections* had been the seminal reference work in this respect. As can be seen in Bonald (who in 1796 published his *Théorie du pouvoir politique et religieux*), counter-revolutionary thought borrowed the criticism of revolutionary

[6] Joseph de Maistre, *Considérations sur la France*, part X, ch. 3.

'abstractness' from the British liberal, but it added to the political heritage of the ancient Gallican monarchy an unprecedented theocratic vision of royal government, and at least an implicit criticism of the secularization of which French kings had made themselves the instruments. For Bonald, as for Maistre, the whole truth of politics lay in the religious sphere: this feature gives some measure of the drift of counter-revolutionary thought, or rather its novelty, in relation to absolutism. Moreover, French aristocracy had returned to religion, with which in any case common misfortunes had reunited it, and which additionally offered it a means of expiating its eighteenth century.

It was thus the bad luck of constitutional royalism, which was putting down deep roots in moderate opinion at that period, to be without any constitutional king. The Comte de Provence had assumed the name Louis XVIII, while abroad, but his actual re-establishment on the throne would not mean a return to 1789; it would inaugurate a revenge of which the White Terror had given some idea: a resumption of violence, instead of a pacification. The Clichyens dreamed in vain of a new Henri IV, capable of reconciling the nobles' France with the France of those who had bought *biens nationaux*. Lacking a liberal prince, they were inevitably led to place themselves at the mercy of the princes available, who were Louis XVI's two brothers; this both perverted their plan and also made it more threatening for the Thermidorians.

In fact, Provence and Artois made great efforts and succeeded in getting their own men put in charge of the vast opinion campaign organized by the royalists of the councils in the summer and autumn of 1796 with a view to winning the next elections. They found support in the remaining counter-revolutionary rebelliousness in the west: the *chouannerie* in Brittany, Normandy and around Le Mans, those spasmodic guerrilla wars which lasted like so many vestiges of the great uprising of the Vendée. But their principal support remained in the Catholic Church, cleft in two by the oath of 1791, whose persecution during the revolutionary government had aggravated the trend hostile to the Revolution. Borne on the wave of Thermidorian reaction, the Church was – depending on the area – more than ever at the heart of moderate opinion and counter-revolutionary hopes. Its unresolved dispute with the Revolution, which Carnot – fortified by Bonaparte's Italian conquests – had for a while hoped to settle with Rome, proved insoluble, since it would be necessary to obtain from the pope, after the event, acceptance of the Civil Constitution of the Clergy.

Besides, the majority of Thermidorian personnel, especially the Directors, were both anticlerical and anti-Catholic; they were eighteenth-century-style deists, loathing priests and 'superstition', wanting to give the Revolution roots not only in education, but also in the civil religion of *décadaire* ceremonies, when the feast of the *décadi*, every ten days, was substituted for Sunday Mass. One of the Directors, the former Girondin La Révellière-Lépeaux, even wanted to implant a cult of his own devising, theophilanthropy, which was not very much different from the *décadaire* meeting, except that authority had no hand in it. It was the religion of Voltaire, rather than of Rousseau, a cold rationalist deism, that had had its images banned (they were covered with veils in the churches), a cult of the Great Architect of the Universe.

When the Directory held its first elections in Germinal (March–April 1797), they revealed the disparity of strength in public opinion between the moderates, whose ranks were swelled by extreme royalists, supported by the Catholic Church, and the anticlerical and republican bourgeoisie who supported the Perpetuals. They also showed the fragility of electoral rights, because in certain *département* capitals the Republicans did not even have access to the second-degree assembly. Nearly all the *départements* had swung to the right, and the Conventionnel majority artificially maintained by the two-thirds disappeared. On 7 Floréal (26 May) fate chose Carnot's friend, Letourneur, to be the one to leave the Directory, where he was replaced by a lacklustre Clichyen, Barthélémy.

Royalists took control of the assemblies, General Pichegru presided over the Five Hundred and Barbé-Marbois over the Ancients. They voted for the abolition of the law of 3 Brumaire Year IV, and several measures alleviating the fate of refractory priests; moreover, émigrés had started to return in small numbers, taking advantage of a process of being struck off the fatal list which made them liable to the death penalty imposed by one of the Convention's laws. Were things leading to a restoration? A large part of the country feared so: first and foremost, those who had acquired *biens nationaux*; next, the army, which had carried the Revolution's flag so high and so far.

The men of the new majority were divided over the nature of this restoration, since the so-called 'white Jacobins' – Pichegru, Imbert-Colomès, Willot – had decided on a coup d'état to bring back Louis XVIII and the émigrés, while the moderate royalists, like Portalis, Mathieu Dumas and Royer-Collard, held fast to the basic tenets of 1789 and to the respect for legal procedures. 'There is no one more dangerous', wrote Mallet de Pan at this period, 'than those who are known in France today as "decent people": were they to fill the legislative body for thousands of years, they would never decide to vote on an effective method of restoration unless they were totally sure in advance that there would be no risk involved.'

In the Directory, Carnot was the chief of those Republicans who had become conservatives, but in losing Letourneur he had lost an ally: Barthélémy did not belong to his political persuasion, and hardly counted anyway. By contrast, the other side of the Executive was ready for a coup d'état to defend the Revolution: Reubell first of all, in March. Colmar's former Third Estate deputy to the Constituent Assembly, who had spent a large part of his Conventionnel mandate as a representative to the armies, brought to the defence of the Republic and the natural frontiers a violent nature and stubbornly held convictions. He was joined by Barras, who had waited for a while and negotiated secretly with the other camp to see what their game was, but who had everything to fear from a return of the Bourbons; Bonaparte's former protector had made contact with the army of Italy and his choice was decided in spring 1797, when one of his friends brought back from Milan the news – passed on by the General-in-Chief – that Pichegru was in the service of Louis XVIII. As for La Révellière-Lépeaux, the theophilanthropist, he was outraged by the measures taken by the councils announcing the return to grace of refractory priests. There was therefore a majority in the Directory which could break the new royalist majority in the councils.

With whom? Where could they get their support? The sansculottes were no longer available and had, in any case, become unacceptable allies in post-Thermidor bourgeois France. Barras still looked after them, on occasion, when they became functionaries of the Republic, police *commissaires*, national agents, administrators. But the republican state was feeble. By this time, the only great popular force in the service of the Republic was the army, which had just covered itself with glory in Italy. Owing to its regimented structure, the army offered the additional, inestimable advantage of being unlikely to take an egalitarian tack, as on 10 August or 2 June. It could come to the aid of republican order without creating disorder. Of the three great military chiefs, Moreau, with the army of the Rhine, was not completely reliable; he did not commit himself to the royalists, but he agreed to listen to them. In Italy, Bonaparte was in favour of the Directory's 'triumvirate', but he did not wish to stick his neck out; he was lukewarm about putting his victories at the service of the Paris Lawyers; he would send one of his lieutenants, Augereau.

It was Hoche, at the head of the Sambre et Meuse army, who gave the decisive helping hand by having 9,000 men marched towards Paris in July, on the pretext of a transfer of troops to Brest, destined for an expedition to Ireland. Under this new protection, then, the triumvirs proceeded to hold a ministerial reshuffle on the left, with Hoche going to War and Talleyrand, returned from exile in America, to Foreign Affairs. It was open crisis with the Councils, refereed by Hoche's soldiers. In the night of 17–18 Fructidor (4–5 September 1797) Paris was occupied by the military. Augereau arrested Pichegru and his friends in the councils. Carnot, who was in neither camp, went into hiding before getting out of the country. No one had made a move. On the morning of 18 Fructidor, a great poster proclamation of the Rump-Directory informed the Parisians and the country that a royalist plot had been broken up, and that any individual guilty of wishing to re-establish royalty or the 1793 constitution would be shot without trial.

Those members of the councils who could be assembled sat during that day and the ones that followed, to vote on measures of 'public safety': the invalidation of 'bad' elections, which excluded one third of the legislative body, deportation to Guiana of fifty-three deputies and two Directors, Carnot and Barthélémy, plus several notorious royalists. The Directory, or what was left of it, quashed the elections of administrative authorities and local judiciaries, thenceforth to be at its discretion. The press was muzzled. Lastly, a series of laws hit émigrés and refractory priests once again, rendering them liable to the death sentence or deportation. The law of 3 Brumaire Year IV, only just abolished, was re-established, as if to show that the war against the aristocracy was still the Revolution's ultimate cause.

Like 2 June 1793, 18 Fructidor Year V (5 September 1797) was an anti-parliamentary coup d'état, a purging of the people's representatives in the name of public safety. As on 2 June, the operation was accompanied – though in a minor key – by a revolutionary Terror. The principal difference was that, in the role of secular arm of the Revolution, the sansculottes had been replaced by the army. Barras and Reubell triumphed, but were indebted to the generals. Hoche died suddenly in September, but a little Corsican general, who had already become one of the nation's glories by conquering Italy, could in his turn be looked on as its saviour.

THE RISE OF NAPOLEON

If one considers the destiny that awaited him, Napoleon was born at the right time,[7] twenty years before the Revolution; but not in the right place, a small outlying island, only recently incorporated into France and not at all happy about it. The Bonapartes were an entirely Corsican family, numerous, tribal, grubbing a living from a few vines and olive trees near Ajaccio, whose patriarch had the bright idea of rallying to the support of France and deserting the flag of independence brandished by his friend Paoli. For although the Bonapartes were poor, they were gentlemen, and for that reason could claim the benefit of the royal edicts of 1776, which had provided for the free education of impecunious nobility in the new military schools.

The two eldest, Joseph and Napoleon, obtained these new grants which constituted passports for a career in France, and through which Louis XVI offered the assistance of the old monarchy to the one that would follow. Napoleon studied at Brienne (1779–84), where he received a good education, which Stendhal would deplore later on as too absolutist: 'If he had been brought up in an establishment not run by the state, he would perhaps have studied Hume and Montesquieu; he would perhaps have understood the strength which opinion gives to government.'[8] Perhaps; but at Brienne Napoleon learned French, which he spoke all his life with an Italian accent; history, which filled his imagination as a child of the Mediterranean, and mathematics, at which he was good. In 1784 he was admitted to the Ecole Militaire; in 1785 he was graded forty-second out of

---

[7] This portrait of Bonaparte is an enlarged version of the text written for Furet and Ozouf, *Critical Dictionary*. Cf. also ch. 5, below, pp. 218–19.

[8] Stendhal, *Vie de Napoléon*.

fifty-eight, and taken on as sublieutenant of artillery at La Fère. Ségur's *Mémoires* attribute the following appraisal to his history teacher: 'Corsican by nationality and by temperament, this young man will go far, if circumstances are kind to him.'

The strange part of the story of his early years is that for a long time he continued to be a 'transplant', without any interest in what was going on in France: someone whose life was elsewhere, a poor scholarship student, then an idle soldier, thinking about what he had left behind, his family and his island. He was 'Corsican by temperament', traditionalist, touchy, somewhat shy, with none of that worldly apprenticeship which at the time typified the upper-class Frenchman. No officer could ever have been farther removed from court civilization. 'Corsican by nationality' as well: he went back on his father's choice and rejoined the Paoli clan.

During his garrison life, he spent every leave in Corsica; he seemed to want to confine himself to this tiny theatre. His encounter with France did not take place in 1789, and even that momentous year did not touch him. Little is known of him between the ages of nineteen and twenty-four. Michelet pictures him as a royalist because, according to Bourrienne, one of his Brienne schoolfriends, he exclaimed that Louis XVI should have fired on the rising of 20 June 1792. In reality, nothing linked him to the Revolution's losers, but there is no evidence of any enthusiasm on his part for the victors. He spent a great deal of time in Corsica, as he had before 1789. When the cannon thundered at Valmy in September 1792, he was still waiting for a boat to take him back to his island. But in Ajaccio, his brother Lucien was a leader of the local Jacobins (while the eldest, Joseph, failed in the elections to the Convention).

The family returned to the French side when Paoli considered opening the island to the English: the victorious insurrection of April 1793 broke the Bonapartes' links with their ancestral land, and Napoleon's with his childhood. The Bonaparte tribe, exiled as pro-French, had to leave Ajaccio. The family disembarked at Toulon with all their worldly goods: Madame Letizia, a thrifty and colourful widow who had inherited the patriarchal authority, the girls, who were pretty, and the boys, ambitious and active; the two eldest (Joseph and Napoleon), being familiar with mainland France, were able to cushion the family's feeling of disorientation.

It was in June 1793, after the purging of the Convention under the threat of Hanriot's cannon, in the terrible summer of the Revolution, that the family entered French history, at the moment that would forever mark off true partisans of the Revolution, those who had staked everything on it, from its lukewarm sympathizers. Coming from another world, brought up in another language, the tribe of islanders had nothing in common with the old France, whereas the Republic offered them the opportunity of finding their fortune, with the country in danger, open to any and every talent, where one could be on familiar terms with ministers almost as soon as one had arrived.

A compatriot, Saliceti, a Montagnard deputy to the Convention, dutifully opened some doors for the three oldest, Joseph, Napoleon and Lucien. Through this protection, Napoleon became not only a Montagnard, but also a Robespierrist. Captain of artillery in the army of Italy, given a mission in Avignon in August, he composed a topical pamphlet against the federalists who had brought civil war into the Midi: it was a work lacking in originality, consisting of a conversation between a soldier, a Nîmois, a Marseille shopkeeper and a manufacturer from Montpellier on the federalist revolt in Marseille; in it the soldier has the best part, arguing the cause of public safety. But it was a key document, because it marked the entry of the Corsican artillery captain into revolutionary politics with a Jacobin passport.

What did this young officer find to please him so much in those terrible months? Things that coincided with his temperament, his tastes, his career: a crudeness of manner that suited the brutality of his native island; a government with an antiquity-like energy, the limitless authority of national power; and higher rank open to merit, where a military talent would be honoured if victorious; the promise of equality in a profession where, as a young man, he had met only snobbery and discrimination. By serving the Montagnard dictatorship under the leadership of Saliceti, who was the Convention's representative on mission to the south-east, Napoleon Bonaparte was following both his inclination and his personal interests. In December 1793 it was he who devised the plan for regaining Toulon from the British. Almost immediately afterwards, he was a brigadier, earning enough to support his mother and sisters. The family was nicely settled in the Republic: Lucien had become one of the Jacobin personalities of Saint-Maximin; Napoleon took his young brother, Louis, with him to the army of Italy, to which he was appointed at the beginning of 1794, and waged war on the Austrians; the last brother, Jerome, was still at college.

Then came 9 Thermidor. Temporarily casting aside the young brigadier, who even spent a few weeks in prison, Robespierre's conquerors confirmed his Robespierrist reputation. But the Convention carried on the Revolution in its own way, and the following year gave him the chance to make a spectacular comeback on the *journée* of 13 Vendemiaire (5 October 1795). After Toulon, this was the second central scene of his marriage to revolutionary France: on that day Barras was at the head of an 'extraordinary commission' with full powers to crush a royalist rising in the fashionable districts of Paris. He assembled a small republican army, with Bonaparte commanding part of it, which raked the *muscadin* ranks with cannon fire, in the environs of the church of Saint-Roch. This easy victory had another aspect: the brigadier became one of the close associates of Barras, the great political chief of the regime then coming into being. For Napoleon, the Directory began under the best auspices; he had become one of the personalities of the new Parisian society.

That society was an odd blend of revolutionary *nomenklatura* and the rule of money, a world simultaneously very closed, because it was dominated by shared memories, and very open, because it contained nothing old enough to be truly definite. The modern pact between government and finance had replaced Robespierre's virtuous Republic. It was the time of private interests and pleasures, well personified by Barras, once a Vicomte, a former terrorist, cynical and corrupt, surrounded by a Byzantine court, but gifted with real political talent and keeping a watchful eye on what the Revolution had already won. In this milieu, the Corsican general cut an unusual figure, bony, emaciated, taciturn. An islander who had just come from his native scrubland, with his yellowish face dominated by huge eyes, framed by long hair falling to his shoulders in 'dog's ears'. The salons of the parvenu revolutionaries where the brilliant Madame Tallien reigned smiled a little over this soldier who had inherited nothing of the ways of the world, and did not even appear to want to imitate them.

The story of Napoleon's marriage to Josephine de Beauharnais, some months after Vendémiaire, says everything about what bound him to that society which was so foreign to him. It can be told as comedy. He married a ruined *demi-mondaine* (whom Barras had put in his bed), believing he was joining his destiny with that of a rich heiress of the old aristocracy. For once he hid from his family, because he had roused a storm among them which did not die down until the divorce: not only had he added to the Corsican clan a somewhat faded, wily Parisian woman who was too old for him, but also another family, for this widow had two children. Yet the marriage can also be painted in colours more touching and no less true. It bound together two people whose lives originally had very little chance of crossing; in the great upheaval of Thermidorian mores, Napoleon married for love. The burning passion he felt for Josephine had its source in everything that his wife's name led him to believe about her past; it was fed less by the vulgar ambitiousness of the era than by the way it erased, through the beloved object, his humiliation as a scholarship student at Brienne.

This little Corsican was a stranger to the world of the bourgeoisie, but he shared its most deep-rooted collective feeling – a love-hate for the aristocracy, that passion for French-style equality, an inheritance from the old court in its post-revolutionary guise, which could be appeased only by an acquired, acknowledged, guaranteed, almost obsessive recognition of superiority over the 'equal', the neighbour, the brother. Stendhal called it, as Napoleon did, 'vanity'. Little Bonaparte, who married the widow Beauharnais, was indeed, through her, truly naturalized a Frenchman.

For him, however, that national passion was transfigured by his imagination. At the time, such was his love for Josephine – pathetic, because it was not returned – that it was perpetuated by the dreams it fabricated. In the same way, his ideas of 'success' did not lie in money or power, as it did for the Thermidorian bourgeois. He derived it from political and military history (Alexander, Caesar, Charlemagne) and combined it with his recently acquired ambition – with was still in keeping with those great men of the past – to control the most tremendous event in modern history.

To control the Revolution: he had had numerous precursors – Mirabeau, La Fayette, Barnave, Brissot, Robespierre, Barras; but this rational Mediterranean dreamer had the advantage over them of arriving on the scene young in the later stages of a political drama on which he could impose his own script. Like the rest, he stood for 'equality', but he came from elsewhere; he was better then they, because he wanted to transform revolutionary passion into a means of authority. That idea alone would not have sufficed to take him where he was going, if he had not also contributed the awesome brilliance stemming from his own genius to the glory of the nation.

The army of Italy formed part of Josephine's dowry: at least, Barras suggests as much in his memoirs, but La Révellière-Lépeaux, in his, recalls that Napoleon was the unanimous choice of the Directory. The winter of 1795–6 was ending. Three armies were to advance against the Austrians: in Germany, the Sambre et Meuse under Jourdan, the Rhin et Moselle under Moreau; lastly, starting from Nice, the troops of Italy, placed under Bonaparte on 2 March. Since the short campaign in 1794, he had dreamed about waging war in Italy: it was, after all, in a way his country, his language, and the ideal theatre in which to unite his two homelands in victory. He had submitted his plan a long time before: to separate the Piedmontese from the Austrians by a rapid offensive, then to force the Turin monarchy to make peace and, if possible, an alliance with the French; lastly, to drive the Austrians out of Lombardy.

He did not have the best army, and there have been many descriptions of the barefoot, undisciplined cohorts (45,000 men, nevertheless) which he took under his command. But, with the aid of victory, he straight away demonstrated that plebiscitary quality of authority which was his hallmark: within one month, the little civil war general and protégé of Barras had become a military glory. It must also be said, he left no one else the task of publicizing him: his dispatches, his proclamations, his correspondence with the Directory all reveal an extraordinary talent for getting himself noticed. At twenty-six, this man possessed military genius combined with taste and an intuitive understanding of public opinion: that of the soldiers, as he well understood that they formed his first public, and that of the French, the great driving force of modern political power. The spectacle of a general speaking a language half civic, half praetorian, was entirely new, and one which he had invented; he retained the basic rhetoric in favour of the emancipation of the people, enveloping it in promises of glory and riches.

The first part of the military programme was thus achieved in April: it was the easiest. Bonaparte based his strategy on rapidity of movement, concentrated attacks and local numerical superiority. He managed to separate Colli's Piedmontese from Beaulieu's Austrians, and forced Colli to yield by the converging offensive of his generals, Masséna, Augereau and Sérurier. On 28 April King Victor-Amadeus signed the armistice of Cherasco, defeated and worried about the first stirrings of Italian Jacobins for a 'free Italy'. The Austrian army under Beaulieu fell back to the left bank of the Po, leaving on the river at Lodi a rearguard which the French armies beat on 10 May, but without getting through to the main part of the enemy forces. On the 14th Masséna occupied Milan, and on the next day Bonaparte made his triumphal entry. May 1796: one might cite this month, and his provisional installation as General-in-Chief in the Lombard capital, as the turning-point in his life.

The Directory was not yet as weak as in the following year after the royalist elections to the councils: but it no longer had control of the army of Italy. From Paris, Carnot had written to his chief of staff to urge him to abandon pursuit of the Austrians for the time being, in order to make some gains in central Italy: this was a movement Bonaparte favoured, but he attributed a different interpretation to it. Personally he wanted a policy of emancipation in the Italian states; against orders from Paris, he let the Jacobin and patriotic elements go ahead. Furthermore, Carnot had made a move to hand Lombardy over to Kellermann, while Bonaparte was to ransom off central Italy. He received a categorical refusal from the General-in-Chief, in the face of which the Directory gave way.

Was it because the Paris government could not survive financially without Italy's treasures? In fact, it had even greater need of victories and glory. There was an unequal balance between Carnot and Bonaparte. For example, Bonaparte wrote to him on 9 May, shortly before his entry into Milan:

What we have taken from the enemy is incalculable. I shall have twenty paintings by the greatest masters sent to you, from Correggio to Michelangelo. I owe you special thanks for all you are doing for my wife. Look after her: she is a sincere patriot, and I love her to distraction. I hope things are going well, and am sending you twelve or so million to Paris; that should be useful to you for the army of the Rhine.

One cannot fail to see that, behind this outpouring of gifts, power is starting to change hands.

Bonaparte was not yet king of France, but from that May on, he was king of a poor, subjugated, pillaged Italy – reinvented, so to speak, as if the land of ancient Rome and the villas of the Renaissance were part of his heritage. He lived in the palace of Montebello in Milan, more like a sovereign than a general of the Republic, surrounded by a little court, protected by strict etiquette, starting to live in the world of omnipotence. Josephine had come to join him, deceitful as ever, accompanied by one of her lovers. The brothers and sisters had got there before her, trafficking in his victories, thirsty for honours and profit, making money hand over fist: this Balzacian side of his parvenu life would never come to an end.

He just let it happen, and even condoned these sordid little games, provided he was their originator: these were the sidelines of his glory, the prizes offered to those who served him. But he was already in a different world, separated from his most celebrated generals by their acknowledgement of his superiority, holding discussions on an equal footing with the

Directory, and imposing his views on it because of his power over public opinion, receiving France's most esteemed thinkers and men of science: Gaspard Monge and Claude Berthollet were his guests of honour. He already possessed an idea of what life held, together with the certainty that he would achieve it; that his 'destiny' – according to one of his later expressions – 'would not be able to withstand his will' – which may be a definition of modern happiness.

The most interesting part of what he said at Montebello – already reported by numerous attentive witnesses – lies in this confidence:

What I have done so far is nothing. I am only at the beginning of the career that lies before me. Do you suppose that I have triumphed in Italy for the mere aggrandizement of the Directory lawyers, the Carnots, the Barras of this world? What an idea! A republic of thirty million men! With our habits, our vices! How can it be possible? It is a wild dream, with which the French are infatuated, but it will pass like so many before it. They must have glory, the satisfactions of vanity. But as for liberty, they understand nothing about it.

Indeed, in those sentences lies much more than the avowal of an ambition, none the less evident at that time; there is what he learned from the century's literature about the impossibility of a republic in a large country, aggravated by a pessimistic view of Thermidorian society, whose citizens presented quite the reverse image of republican virtue. Enclosed in the selfishness of private interests and pleasures, their abiding passion was vanity: individual vanity, which demanded 'toys' – the tiny differences in status and prestige indispensable to the world of equality; collective vanity, jealous of national glory and the greatness of the new France. Let the government satisfy those interests, and the French would forget about republican liberty. Formulated very early on, this philosophy of government reconciled national passions with the ambitions and character of the General-in-Chief of the army of Italy. It was simple, almost simplistic, and yet magisterial. It was the formula for revolutionary dictatorship, based no longer on virtue but on interests. Bonaparte alone, among the great generals of the Republic, showed such understanding of the motivating forces of national politics.

After holding to ransom all central Italy as far as the Papal States in June and July, he had soldiers who were paid in cash, rich generals, Paris receiving its share and, perforce, leaving him with a free hand. But he still had to conquer the Austrian army, part of which was entrenched in Mantua, north of the Po. He could pursue Beaulieu more to the north towards the Alpine slopes, but since neither Moreau nor Jourdan had succeeded early enough in the breakthrough in Germany planned by Carnot, Napoleon was afraid to start an engagement on his own without numerical superiority. The summer battles therefore took place around Mantua: they were difficult combats, for he had to lift the siege in order to confront several Austrian armies which had descended from the Tyrol.

In the autumn, his situation was not good: Italy was not inexhaustible and the army was showing signs of fatigue after several months of campaigning. Moreover, the Republic was in a difficult pass, for the Sambre et Meuse army, under Jourdan, victorious in July, withdrew across the Rhine in September; and the Rhin et Moselle army, which had reached as far as Munich, also beat a retreat in the autumn. The defeated generals were scarcely more obedient to Carnot than the conqueror of Italy had been; but their failures enhanced the glory of the Proconsul of Milan, who became more and more king of Italy: in October, he got rid of the Directory's *commissaires* and took it upon himself to form a Cispadane Republic, with Modena and the Legations taken from the pope.

Nevertheless throughout the autumn the military situation remained uncertain in the territories around and to the north of Mantua. At Arcola, on 15 November, Bonaparte had to set an example to check panic among the soldiery. He had to take the troops in hand again, and modify their command, while from Paris Carnot sent General Clarke to make a report on the army of Italy, and to explore the possibilities of a compromise with Austria at the cost of leaving Lombardy and the Cispadane Republic. The victory at Rivoli in January 1797 was decisive, with the rout of General Alvinczy's Austrian columns, followed shortly by the capitulation of Mantua on 2 February. After several very difficult months, Bonaparte triumphed, at the very moment when the authorities needed him most in Paris.

It was the period when Barras and Reubell were apprehensively watching the approach of the regime's first electoral date, and fearing that Carnot was ready to compromise with the royalists at home and the Europe of the kings. By contrast, as a good ex-Girondin, the hesitant La Révellière liked the policy of sister republics, and even more, as a good theophilanthropist, the dismemberment of the Papal States. The republican triumvirate in Paris could gain support against the royalists only by the amount of freedom it left to the victorious general. The latter, engrossed in his definitive victory over Austria, indulged himself by not following its instructions to destroy the seat of Catholic unity; once again he contented himself with a ransom.

After Rivoli, it was clear to everyone that he held the Republic's principal command. The makeshift troops he had been leading for a year were reinforced by other contingents coming from the Rhine: the heroic period was over, when his almost superhuman energy, his omnipresence, his capacity for endless activity and his power to intimidate had finally compensated for the improvised nature of his armies. In March 1797 he launched an offensive towards Vienna, across the Alps, with rested and reorganized troops. On the last day of the month, from a position of strength, he proposed an armistice to his adversary, the Austrian Archduke Charles, on the following conditions: either Austria ceded Belgium and Lombardy, acquiring in exchange most of the Veneto (excepting Venice); or it abandoned the Rhineland as well as Belgium, regaining Lombardy, with some Venetian territories. The terms of the choice dictated the reply, which formed the basis of the armistice of Leoben on 18 April. Austria left Belgium and the Milanese region to France, but kept the left bank of the Rhine, and its domain in the Veneto. It was the republic of the Doges which paid the dearest price, for it was conquered, occupied and soon wiped off the map, following a popular rising in Verona against the French troops.

The armistice, laying down the conditions of peace with Austria – the first since 1792 – had been conceived, negotiated and signed by Bonaparte, who thus took over the Republic's foreign policy. In Paris the Directory was in the worst of political situations, just after the elections had brought a royalist majority to the councils. It was therefore less than ever in a position to discuss initiatives and decisions with the conquering general. Carnot and his shadow, Letourneur, were not interested in the left bank of the Rhine: the right of the Parisian Executive had no reason to dislike Leoben. The triumvirate, on the other hand, was in favour of 'natural frontiers', and therefore the Rhine, but they also liked the idea of sister republics, particularly La Révellière; he would gladly have taken all together, Rhineland and Lombardy. In the end, he settled for Lombardy as a consolation for the Rhineland. Anyway, he had no choice, for the idea of an army-aided republican coup d'état was already in the wind.

The Leoben armistice was therefore an important turning-point for revolutionary policy abroad. Initially, because its negotiation had for the first time evaded the civil government, and then, because it designated war aims which went well beyond 'natural frontiers'. Holland had already been transformed by the Thermidorians into a sister Republic, but in essence it could be considered as part of the left bank of the Rhine. With the Po valley came the start of another story: that of French expansion and domination in Europe under the impetus of a genius who had inherited the spirit of the Revolution while at the same time transforming it.

Bonaparte, in effect, refashioned Italy, which was a prey to disturbances on all sides – pro-French, anti-French, Jacobins and Catholics. He took up his quarters again near Milan, this time in the castle of Mombello, and redesigned the map of his second homeland. With Lombardy he formed a Cisalpine Republic, to which in July he gave a French-style constitution, with institutions similar to those of Year III, but where he himself appointed the members of the Directory and the Legislative Council. In the summer, he dispatched Augereau to protect the triumvirs' coup d'état against Carnot and a royalist restoration.

Immediately afterwards, he settled the conditions of peace with Austria, in the spirit of Leoben, to which he added an unprecedented clause: the suppression of the ancient republic of Venice, conquered in May and given to the Habsburgs in exchange for an enlargement of the new Cisalpine Republic. Austria had to accept the cession of the left bank of the Rhine, less the Cologne region, where there were Prussian possessions. The Treaty of Campo Formio on 17 October 1797 introduced a new element to the Leoben stipulation, borrowed from the arbitrary powers of the kings: the suppression of one of Europe's oldest states, the Most Serene Republic, in the same way that Poland, in 1772 and 1793, had been suppressed by the monarchies of central and eastern Europe.

Campo Formio took place after 18 Fructidor in Paris. That month of October, which had brought back the revolutionary Republic and its exceptional measures at home, also set the seal on the triumph of its arms abroad: the Terror and victory; a paradoxical combination, with a division of the roles, Barras in the first and Bonaparte in the second.

DIFFICULTIES OF THE DIRECTORY

There was indeed a Terror: but this was not the Year II, with its surveillance committees and the revolutionary Tribunal. It was the application of the exceptional laws of 19 and 22 Fructidor (5 and 8 September 1797) against returned émigrés and those suspected of royalist conspiracies on the one hand, and refractory priests on the other: six years after the beginnings of the Legislative Assembly, here again were the two great categories of the guilty who had served as fodder for the revolutionary dynamic.

The royalist danger had reawoken hatred for the nobles. There were 160 death sentences in Paris between autumn 1797 and spring 1799. According to La Révellière's memoirs, Sieyès seems to have proposed to the Directory – where two ex-ministers, Merlin de Douai and François de Neufchâteau, had replaced Carnot and Barthélémy – the banishment of all nobility outside the Republic, which would have actualized the expulsion suggested in a passage of *Qu'est-ce que le Tiers État?* But the idea, defended in the Five Hundred by Boulay de la Meurthe in October, was finally reduced to civic exclusion by deprivation of political rights. As the list of those excepted had yet to be drawn up, the law could not be applied.

After the aristocrats came the refractory priests, also the subject of a very vast repressive legislation since 1792, revived in October 1797. The death penalty was replaced by deportation to Guiana. More than a thousand were arrested, of whom 263 left for the penal colony, while the rest remained dumped in the most appalling conditions on the hulks of Ré and Oléron. As usual, repression varied between the regions, local situations and the state of mind of the administrations. But it revived a climate: censored press, domiciliary visits, preventive arrest, where former scenes were re-enacted and vengeance taken. Also as usual, the arbitrariness of the laws increased disobedience to those laws. The France of Catholic loyalty, chiefly the rural west but also the south-east, slipped outside public authority.

In this bourgeois version of the revolutionary Terror, there reappeared two themes from the great epoch, but in a watered-down administrative form: civil religion and the regeneration of the citizen. There is no period in revolutionary history when the administration took a greater hand in the organization of a new cult, with celebrations every *décadi*, and on the anniversaries of the Revolution's principal dates: 21 September (birth of the Republic), 21 January (death of the tyrant), 9 Thermidor (end of the other tyrant) and 18 Fructidor (unmasking of the last royalist conspiracy).

Re-christened 'temples', the churches were used for three forms of worship: the constitutional Catholic Church, caught in the pincer movement between refractory priests and the administrators of the republican religion, theophilanthropy, and the official ceremony of *décadi*, when the citizens and municipal authorities honoured the laws. Only this last had the government seal of approval, and it was just as well to be seen there if one had something to ask for – or perhaps something one would like forgotten.

Thus the Revolutionary calendar had found full use under the Directory; the new era, opened by the Revolution, had a regulated form of worship, overseen by the administration, to liberate citizens from superstition and the tyranny of priests. The idea of reason, rather than virtue, served as a basis for the republican civics to be inculcated: civil religion was closer to Condorcet than to Robespierre. If the citizens were enlightened, and therefore reasonable, they could not desire other than the public good, which was also their own. That gave rise to great emphasis on education, inherited from the first years of the Revolution; schools became the essential means of regenerating citizens, which was indispensable to the foundation of the Republic. The role Robespierre had assigned to the Terror had devolved into the pedagogy of reason.

The most ambitious projects date back to the Convention which, in 1793, had debated the educational plans of Condorcet, then those of the Montagnard Michel Le Peletier, and had even voted in December 1793 for compulsory primary education at the expense of the state. But the practical measures were not taken until after Thermidor, and were put into effect by the Directory. Under the *ancien régime*, education had been dispensed by the Church and was therefore obscurantist; with the Revolution, it became public and secular. The Montagnards had legislated for all the Republic's children, the Thermidorians were chiefly concerned about the children of *propriétaires*.

The fundamental law had been that of 3 Brumaire (25 October 1795), on the eve of the Convention's dispersal, the same day as the vote on the bill against émigrés' families. The primary school was sacrificed; for the teacher once more became an employee of local communities, as before 1789, and nothing was said about compulsory schooling, which had been emphasized in 1793: in actual fact, it was a return to the old system, and many semi-clandestine little schools were reopened under the leadership of a refractory priest who had reappeared as an instructor, rivalling the public teacher maintained by the administration.

The republican efforts of the Thermidorians had been directed at the secondary and higher levels; these terms are still not quite adequate, for the 'central schools' planned by the law of 24 February 1795 to replace the *ancien régime* schools run by religious orders were midway between the two levels, organized in the chief town of each *département*. They were a

somewhat utopian kind of grammar school, with optional courses made up
in three successive sections: firstly, drawing, natural history, ancient and
modern languages; next, the sciences (mathematics, physics, chemistry)
from fourteen to sixteen years of age; beyond that, what the law calls
'general grammar': great literature, history, legislation, taught according to
the science of sensualist psychology, in which the origin of ideas was to be
found by analysing the sensations of individuals, and thus in a study of
their development by means of their environment. All the disciplines were
remodelled so as to form the reason of young citizens through science, in a
spirit that was incredibly revolutionary on the educational plane, without precedent and also without issue; a good many of the century's
propositions were included: secularism, the promotion of the sciences,
encyclopaedic ambition, the supremacy of French over ancient languages,
and the reign of reason.

Above these central schools was a whole network of higher establish-
ments, also created by the Thermidorian Convention, which would enjoy a
longer life: the Conservatory of Applied Arts and Crafts; the School of
Public Services for the army, the navy and highways, which would become
the present-day Ecole Polytechnique; three Schools of Medicine in Paris,
Lyon and Montpellier; the Ecole Normale Supérieure, with the task
of training teachers; the School of Oriental Languages, the Museum of
French Monuments, the Museum, the Observatory. If the Thermidorians
had surrendered part of the Montagnard ambitions for junior schools –
although they were still fighting on that ground too, even if they were
retreating – they had reconstructed on the ruins of universities abolished
together with the trade guilds (even the Académie Française had not
escaped the common law), higher teaching institutions which were freed
from clerical administration and conceived according to the spirit of the
Enlightenment.

At the very summit, they had devised the Institut, to crown this structure of knowledge, enlighten politics and give a central impetus to the
minds of the public: the system already contained the spirit of a 'republic
of teachers', in which opinion had to be carefully formed and informed by
the most learned men in order eventually, with the help of time, to weld
together a body politic of citizens. The Institut had three classes to crown
the ensemble of disciplines – physical sciences and mathematics, literature
and fine arts, and (a great novelty) political and moral sciences.

This was the spiritual powerhouse of the regime, envisaged in the
constitution, like the councils and the Directory, peopled with the great
notables of science and public life: Monge, Berthollet, Lagrange, Chaptal,
Lamarck, Cuvier, Geoffroy Saint-Hilaire, Daunou, Marie-Joseph Chénier,
La Révellière-Lépeaux. Bonaparte, having returned to Paris after Campio
Formio, had himself elected to it at the end of 1797 in place of the
wretched 'Fructidorized' Carnot. The passage of the hero of Italy to a place
among the thinkers was a good investment. France was still a country
which loved literature and ideas.

Heaven knows, the survivors who were running the country had re-discovered the importance of interests, but they hung on to 1789's fundamental plan to found society on reason, and that characteristic would distinguish their heirs right up to the twentieth century. For the political and intellectual elite of the epoch, that plan had taken the form of what was called 'ideology', which was the reigning doctrine, the last-born of the Enlightenment, and would bring the era to its close. It was an experimental rationalism, which eschewed any metaphysical explanation of knowledge, any input by God, or innate ideas, and wanted to found a science of intellectual formation starting from the senses. From that stemmed an ambition to arrive also at a science of morals and behaviour, and the content of 'moral and political sciences'.

Bonaparte was honoured to be the colleague of Dr Cabanis, Destutt de Tracy and Constantin Volney; at the time, he signed his documents 'Bonaparte, General-in-Chief and Member of the Institut National'. In this post-Revolution learned world lay a completely revitalized eighteenth century, its rediscovered encyclopaedic ambition mocked by the brothers Goncourt: 'Not only German, but also Greek, not only Spanish but also Latin, logic *and* rhetoric, geography *and* history, foreign exchange *and* weights and measures, man *and* the decimal system, philosophy *and* grammar, the reason for God, book-keeping, even French. Paris wants to learn all about everything in between two quadrilles.'[9] Learned societies were being reborn, public education was fashionable, the great new institutions were surrounded by general respect. The Republic may not have been sheltered from arbitrariness, but it was indivisible from science.

Here, once again, was the French Revolution torn between its universalist ambition and the arbitrariness of its laws. It revered the Institut as the beacon of its historic mission, but it had just purged the councils by an illegal intervention of the army. That second characteristic had struck the Revolution's institutions a crippling blow: the councils' authority was broken by this enforced amputation, and that of the Executive, which had provided the means, had gained nothing from it. Public safety was no longer in danger, and the discredit cast on the politicians extended to the Directors. The relationship between Barras and Bonaparte had been inverted. In the face of the old Conventionnel, dimming his authority amid pleasures and intrigues, it was the young Corsican covered in glory who embodied the Republic. But he went off in the spring of 1798 to make war on the British in Egypt, and French opinion was left alone with its politicians.

At least the Directory took advantage of the respite gained in Fructidor to put forward a certain number of reforms which prepared the settlement of the Consulate. The most important was financial. The Minister, Ramel de Nogaret, proposed the great financial law of 9 Vendémiaire (30

[9] Edmond and Jules de Goncourt, *Histoire de la société française pendant le Directoire* (1855), pp. 249–50.

September 1797), seeking to reduce the public debt, which was very
onerous for the Treasury, giving state creditors bonds negotiable against
the possessions of the clergy and émigrés – the inexhaustible capital of the
Revolution; two-thirds of the debts were covered in this way, while the last
third was guaranteed repayable in cash.

But this measure, which was intended to regain the *rentiers'* confidence
after it had been so eroded by the dizzying inflation of the preceding years,
ran into competition with all the other bonds in circulation, which were
also paid by the sale of *biens nationaux*, and this bankruptcy of two-thirds
of the debt did not even ensure the maintenance of a constant value for the
last third, payable in coin of the realm. The resumption of the payment of
annuities in cash did not take place until 1801. Ramel succeeded only in
temporarily reducing the debt. He had also tried to get taxes collected in
an organized manner, but was not able to escape what had been the curse
of the Revolution since 1791: resort to 'extraordinary' measures, selling off
new slices of *biens nationaux*, despoilment of foreign countries, facilities
offered to the speculations of contractors, borrowing.

The return to cash as a means of trading ran up against lack of confidence: money disappeared, and the few banks which reopened served
only a very restricted clientele. The financial situation was as always largely
conditioned by public feeling, which did not believe in the future of the
regime. Why should it? Once acquired, the habit of invalidating annual
elections perpetuated itself like a sort of poisoning of the bloodstream: it
was the surest way to maintain the rule of the old Conventionnels. But in
spring 1798, the royalists, intimidated by the repression that had followed
Fructidor, no longer dared appear at the electoral assemblies.

The electorate in the *départements* had swung towards the Jacobins. For
example, Barère was elected while in hiding in Bordeaux after fleeing from
prison in 1795 in order to avoid the penal colony in Guiana. The Directory
then struck out at the left in the batch of deputies of Year VI: it had the
councils invalidate a number of elections, and confirmed others organized
by irregular assemblies; in short, it operated a sorting-out process among
the elected representatives, without even having the pretext or reason, as it
had in the preceding year, of public safety in the face of a royalist restoration. From its origins, the regime had never been able to respect the results
of a single electoral consultation.

The same thing recurred in the following year, 1799, but in the opposite
direction, on the part of the councils against the Directory: the electors
refused to follow the Executive's recommendations after it had designated
its official candidates, and again the assemblies swung in the neo-Jacobin
direction, neo-Jacobins who were in truth new, looking towards the army
generals rather than the sansculottes of the townships. Even before the
newly elected third sat, the Directory had replaced one of its members:
Reubell, one of the ramparts of the Republic, was destined to be the one to
quit. He was replaced by Sieyès, who had just returned from the Berlin
embassy. Still Sieyès, always Sieyès, this time accepting the post he had

been offered in 1795. There was a new chance – at last – to give the Revolution the good constitution that had eluded it since 1789.

War had resumed, but Bonaparte was in Egypt. It is necessary to make a detour through foreign policy in order to understand all the threads of the revisionist conspiracy of which Sieyès became the centre in spring 1799, before the Corsican general became its beneficiary in the autumn.

After Campo Formio, France had beaten all enemies save Britain. The armies of the Revolution had restored to France's ascendancy in Europe, the secret of which it had lost since the middle of Louis XIV's reign. But at that time, there had been a major difference in the general balance of the states: in the eighteenth century, British ambition had asserted itself, the drive of a formidable maritime, commercial and colonial power, a nation modern and ahead of the others, united around a gigantic city which was becoming the warehouse and economic metropolis of the world. The British had driven the French out of North America and India with the Treaty of Paris (1763), and France had taken a small revenge in the war of American Independence. The war had recommenced at the beginning of 1793 after Louis XVI's execution.

The conflict preserved its former features. The two countries clashed overseas, chiefly in the West Indies, and Britain kept a jealous watch over a European equilibrium which it feared would be destabilized by the French Revolution. French Anglophobia went back a long way, as did English Francophobia: one can easily find a list of examples in a large part of Enlightenment thinking within both countries, to say nothing of public opinion on the subject. But the war that had started in Year I had brought new stakes into play and aggravated hostile feelings. The France of 1789 had pleased quite a few British liberals. In 1793 the radical condemnation made by Burke in 1790 of all the principles of the Revolution had acquired a predictive value; it was shared by almost everyone.

The two greatest national histories in Europe, the two almost immemorial monarchies, built on the same basic elements, were thenceforth separated by two pasts, two traditions, two incompatible regimes. The Revolution destroyed what even the schism between the Anglican Reformation and the Catholic faith had left in common between the two nations. Modern liberty now had two contradictory sources, one British, one French. From the starting-point of the common possession that divided them, the two countries were building the future of the world, but each in its own fashion, and each in its own sphere. Britain invented industry; France, equality.

The two public opinions sensed this mutual strangeness very keenly. At the time of the Constituent Assembly, Britain had become the kingdom where aristocracy reigned through a titled upper chamber and a lower chamber in which seats were acquired by intrigue or money. For the Convention, it was personified by the City of London, homeland of banking and selfish opulence, the exact opposite of Jacobin virtue. The Thermidorians had rediscovered interests, but the Republic's commercial interests, like those of the former monarchy, were precisely the opposite of those of the merchant oligarchy reigning in London. At a time when the French were in Antwerp and Amsterdam, how could Britain think otherwise? Thus the French victories and the peace of Campo Formio had not ended the war: with Britain, they had made it inexpiable. 'Peace with England would seem to me the loss of the Republic', said Reubell at that time.

The British had won the colonial war in the West Indies, that treasure house of French slave trading in the eighteenth century. In 1793, they had taken possession of Martinique, St Lucia, Guadeloupe and Santo Domingo, with the help of colonists hostile to the Revolution. In the last of these isles, the great revolt of black slaves led by Toussaint L'Ouverture drove them out, at first to France's advantage, when the Convention abolished slavery (February 1794), but not for long: the black general finally bought the independence of Haiti by a treaty favourable to British trade (1798). There was one exception: Guadeloupe, where a former merchant marine captain, whose extraordinary adventure has been related by Alejo Carpentier,[10] succeeded in driving out the British and keeping the island in the French domain. In the same years, because Holland had become a French protectorate, Britain had seized the Dutch colonies of Guiana, the Cape and Ceylon.

But how could Britain be vanquished, that island protected by its navy, which was at the heart of European aristocratic intrigue against the Republic? The Directory had on several occasions considered the possibility of invasion. But Hoche's Irish operation at the end of 1796 had failed because of storms, and Bonaparte, assigned the task of examining ways and means a year later on his return from Italy, gave up the idea for want of a good fleet. It was then, in the first few months of 1798, that the idea took shape of going to strike at Britain in Egypt: the strategy was proposed by Talleyrand, and endorsed by the Directory on 5 March. The objectives of the Minister of Foreign Affairs have been the subject of a vast literature, even including his supposed intention to render service to the British by diverting the French ships from the Channel towards the Orient: Talleyrand's reputation was so bad, and his venality so notorious, that even the basest interpretation remained a possibility, though there is no certainty about any of them. The former bishop appears also to have had a plan for carving up the Ottoman empire and for a French colonization of Egypt.

The Directory was wary, since it had little desire, with the Eastern question, to open a conflict not only with the Sultan of Constantinople but also, inevitably, with Russia. It supported only the shorter and limited anti-British version of the project: the aim was to hit the enemy's trade, one of the routes by which its wealth passed between India and London.

Did the Directory also wish to distance Bonaparte, that embarrassing

---

[10] Alejo Carpentier, *Le Siècle des Lumières* (Paris, Gallimard, 1982).

figure on the Parisian scene, who stood waiting for his great moment, draped in classical simplicity? Possibly. At all events, Bonaparte himself backed the idea of the expedition, and wanted to be given the mission: it would be a good investment of his Italian capital, which his brothers Joseph and Lucien were in any case managing for him in Paris. Moreover, Egypt was part of his imaginary world, at the other side of the Mediterranean, the heart of Greek and Roman antiquity, where he would tread in the footsteps of Alexander and Caesar. The idea combined the theatrical dimension of his nature, his imagination as a gambler doubling his stake in the Orient, and the realism of a calculated internal policy.

I will omit the Egyptian expedition from this account, because it forms a special history on its own, independent of French events, but essential to an understanding of the Eastern question in the nineteenth century. Having arrived at Alexandria on 1 July 1798 with his ships, his soldiers and the battalion of scientists who had embarked with him, Bonaparte stayed more than a year amid his conquests, victorious over the Mameluke warriors, also beating the Sultan's troops which were assembled against him, organizing an 'enlightened' and tolerant protectorate as if, in Cairo, he were in a sort of Islamic Milan. But almost from the beginning, the affair came to nothing, for the British Admiral Nelson had finally found and sunk the French fleet at anchor in Aboukir harbour. The French army's Egyptian contingent was trapped in Egypt and its leader could not bring it back to France. A year later, in August 1799, he left in great secrecy, entrusting his soldiers to one of his generals, Kléber.

During his absence from France, between the middle of spring 1798 and the beginning of autumn 1799, war had begun again between the Revolution and Europe. Even before his departure in March 1798, the Directory had transformed the Swiss cantons into a unitarian republic (except Mulhouse and Geneva, which were annexed to France). At the same time, the French army occupied Rome, whence the pope was exiled to Tuscany. The Directory even imposed on vassal states the vicissitudes of French internal politics. Exporting French political quarrels to Holland, Switzerland and the Cisalpine Republic, it arbitrated between moderate elements and local Jacobins, gave its backing now to its generals and now to its civil agents, dictated constitutions and regimes.

Everywhere, it extracted money both by pillage and by very one-sided economic agreements: treasure seized in Berne had been used to fund the Egyptian expedition. All that remained of the original emancipatory messianism, when the French arrived, was the abolition of the tithe and personal feudal rights. But those measures counted for little compared with military occupation, soldiers living off the country and the systematic looting of local wealth. The years 1798–9 witnessed the birth of a phenomenon which would reach great proportions during the period of Napoleonic expansion: the revolt of occupied nations against French oppression.

The best-known and also the most significant revolt took place in the south of Italy, in the kingdom of Naples. Rome's occupation by

France had given King Ferdinand IV the idea of seizing Benevento and Pontecorvo, old papal enclaves within his possessions. He imprudently launched an attack in November, and at first drove out the French garrison from Rome, where Jacobins and Jews were hounded by the people. But the Directory reacted by declaring war on Ferdinand IV and, for good measure, the King of Piedmont-Sardinia, his reputed accomplice. Joubert occupied Piedmont, which was annexed to France at the beginning of 1799; Championnet retook Rome, and proceeded as far as Naples where, with the help of bourgeois and liberal nobles, he proclaimed a Parthenopean Republic, systematically bled by his army.

The French occupation of the great town, which swarmed with numerous followers of the landowning aristocracy, unleashed a popular uprising under the banner of the king and the faith. The Directory repudiated Championnet and the new sister republic, but the damage had been done: the Italian liberal notables had condoned French looting, but the example of Naples and its *lazzaroni* (criminals) was followed by the peasants of Calabria, creating a new Vendée of the Italian south in rebellion against the Republic of French atheism. Like France in 1793, foreign peasants were also discovering their popular counter-revolution.

At the end of the winter of 1798–9, war resumed between the Directory and Europe, and the French army had to evacuate the extreme south of Italy in order to confront more urgent tasks. Britain had succeeded in reconstituting a coalition. It had easily gained the ear of the Tsar of Russia, Paul I, who was worried about French designs against the Ottoman empire; the king of Naples was another ally for the asking. The plan was to make France withdraw within its 1792 frontiers: Britain was the great financial backer of the undertaking, as it would be until 1814.

There remained to be found an agreement with at least one of the central European powers, Prussia or Austria. At peace with Prussia since the Treaty of Basle in 1795, the Directory would have liked to resume a tradition of the *ancien régime* and make the Hohenzollern dynasty an ally of republican France: sent as ambassador to Berlin in 1798, Sieyès had striven hard to achieve this, but without success. The Prussians had no interest in tying themselves to a French policy of annexation in German territory; but they stayed neutral, closely watching their Austrian rival. At Campo Formio, the Austrian emperor had subordinated his retreat from the left bank of the Rhine to the approval of the Imperial Diet. Negotiations had begun in Rastatt.

Meanwhile, France had occupied Switzerland and Rome and had included the Cologne region in its Rhineland acquisitions. Austria wanted at least Italian compensations, and the guaranteed independence of Tuscany and the kingdom of Naples. The situation slid towards war in the winter of 1798–9, and Jourdan crossed the Rhine in March. Public opinion in Paris had rediscovered the martial accents of the great days; it denounced a new crime of the Europe of the kings in the assassination of two French plenipotentiaries leaving Rastatt in April.

The combats started badly for the Republic. The army of the Danube, under Jourdan, was beaten in Germany at Stokach by the Austrians. In Italy, Scherer and then Moreau also retreated, and abandoned Milan at the end of April. The Russian troops of Suvorov, the first great counter-revolutionary European general, had joined up with the Austrians, and drove the French out of Italy and Switzerland between June and August. It was at this point, when the spectre of public safety was being reborn in Paris, that Bonaparte decided to leave Egypt – precisely during the first days of August, upon reading the news from France announcing that the Rhine frontier was threatened and Italy – his Italy – lost.

The instructions he had received on his departure the preceding year had authorized him in advance to leave his army to his successor; but the conditions of his leaving, since there was no French fleet to bring back his soldiers, gave it the air of a desertion, surrounded as it was with the greatest secrecy. He took with him only Berthier, Murat, Marmont, Lannes and Duroc, plus Monge, Berthollet and the painter Vivant Denon, who had already become the illustrator of his glory. However, he left to Kléber, the new head of his army without a future, his fine letter of 22 August, his Egyptian testament, which combined the concern of a soldier with considerations of universal history:

I have already asked on several occasions for a troupe of actors; I will take special care to send you one. This is very important for the army and as a starting-point for changing the customs of the country. The major post which you will occupy as chief will at last enable you to display those talents which nature has given you. There is an immense interest in what will happen here, and the results for both trade and civilization will be inestimable; this will be the epoch from which all great revolutions will date.

He did not reach France, on the Mediterranean coast, until 9 October 1799. Meanwhile, the military situation had been put right without him. But his return drastically changed the political situation.

In the autumn, indeed, Masséna had repulsed the Austrians and Russians in Switzerland; Suvorov withdrew to his winter quarters. To the north, in Holland, an Anglo-Russian offensive failed in October and the British re-embarked their troops. The Republic had profited more from the political divisions of the coalition than from its own military capacity. It was victorious, but increasingly threatened by its internal weakness.

Sieyès had been with the Directory since May, having returned from his Berlin embassy. The feeling in the air was Jacobin; since the Fructidor coup of 1797, royalism had been under close surveillance; in spring and summer 1799 the military situation reawoke memories of the threatened homeland. If police reports are to be believed, however, Jacobinism was peculiar to the political and military classes, in a somewhat lethargic Paris. In June the councils voted a *levée en masse*, mobilizing five classes of conscripts, and in August a compulsory loan from the rich; meanwhile, in

July, there was a fearsome law on hostages, intended to terrorize internal enemies once more.

The country was in a state of chronic disobedience, and the Republic had hardly any authority left in the west, where royalist insurrections were spreading. Royalist uprisings broke out in the Midi in August. The law of 24 Messidor (12 July 1799) allowed authorities, in *départements* designated by the councils as in a state of unrest, at the proposal of the Directory to take hostages among the relatives of émigrés or *chouans*, and to deport four of them for each assassination of a public official, purchaser of *biens nationaux* or constitutional priest. This law was not really applied, for the country had become tired of the Terror; but it revived a rhetoric, the obsessive fears, the passions which always formed the heart of national politics.

Sieyès had certainly not agreed to take a hand in affairs only so that Year II should live again. He knew better than anyone the dangers of that collection of memories. Six years afterwards, he could also judge their futility. Republican strength no longer lay in the Parisian faubourgs or *sections*, but in the Republic's administration and its army. As in 1789, the point at issue was still to give the state a regulated form, a good constitution, which would be respected by citizens as the public embodiment of reason. What had failed in 1791, 1793 and 1795 could be achieved in 1799. Everything was in its favour: the time which had passed, men's experience, and even the lack of popular involvement in contrast with earlier egalitarian activism. The Revolution had come back into the grasp of its inventor. The former Vicar General of Chartres had made himself master of the Executive, with the complicity of the councils' left, the Corsican deputy in the forefront – Lucien Bonaparte, who would never leave him. The deputies had nullified Treilhard's election to the Directory, then forced La Révellière and Merlin de Douai to resign. The chosen replacements were obscure and republican, two qualities necessary for supporters of a constitutional revision: Louis-Jérôme Gohier, former Minister of Justice under the Convention; Roger Ducos, ex-Conventionnel regicide, and a general without any glory – but Jacobin – Jean François Moulin.

In the Directory, Sieyès therefore had only one rival, Barras, who had been there from the outset, and for that very reason was rather worn out, a quintessential symbol of the discredit into which the regime had fallen. He was therefore in a position of supremacy. He gave responsibility for internal affairs to Cambacérès, also a former Conventionnel. He despised the rhetoric of public safety from the neo-Jacobins on the councils, but he found attentive listeners among the old Plaine of the great revolutionary Assembly, and even among ex-terrorists like Fouché. His following included post-Thermidor centrist republicans, the ideologists of the Institut, Daunou, Boulay de la Meurthe, Marie-Joseph Chénier, Pierre-Louis Roederer, not to mention Talleyrand, who had just left Foreign

Affairs and was sniffing the wind. With victory lending its aid, Sieyès easily crushed a neo-Jacobin offensive in June and July. He found himself the leader of the post-revolutionary Parisian political milieu, the focus of extraordinary esteem, credited with having a constitutional plan which would at last provide the Republic with institutions. A civil saviour, since the military one was in Cairo.

Anyone who wants to get a picture of the ideas circulating in this revisionist environment since the coup d'état of Fructidor Year V (1797), must turn once more to Benjamin Constant and Madame de Staël, who were at the heart of political *Tout-Paris*, although neither had any official post. Constant yearned for one, and indulged in many intrigues to try to achieve that end, but he was both young and Swiss. Since 1797 he had been one of the organizers of the Constitutional Club, created to assemble the Republicans who supported the institutions against the Clichyens. Like Madame de Staël, he had upheld the triumvirs' coup d'état against the royalists: an uncomfortable position for those defenders of the constitution and the laws, but rendered inevitable by their fear of a counter-revolution, which would be a far worse evil. At that time, their idea was to modify the institutions of Year III so that they should retain the principles and interests born of the Revolution, at the same time avoiding the annual swerves, now to the left, now to the right, which arose from elections to the councils.

In autumn 1798 Madame de Staël wrote a lengthy study on the matter, but it was not published: the situation in 1799 was doubtless too uncertain, punctuated as it was by the illegal replacement of three Directors and the neo-Jacobin upsurge, for her not to fear making a blunder. Moreover, the marginal notes with which Benjamin Constant peppered her manuscript continually put her on her guard against the risk of being misunderstood, or of doing herself a disservice. However, this book, which appeared only in 1906, still remains the best evidence of the political questions which were passionately argued by the Thermidorian political milieu in the last year of the Directory. The title is a programme in itself: *Des circonstances actuelles qui peuvent terminer la Révolution et des principes qui doivent fonder la République en France* (Of the present circumstances which could terminate the Revolution and the principles on which the Republic in France must be founded.).

Madame de Staël had two personalities. The more obvious is that of a turbulent, rather vain, very snobbish woman, an 'incorrigible intriguer', says Constant in his journal, unable to bear the idea of not being in on the latest secrets or in the confidence of the powerful, but a faithful friend for all that, tiring herself out in efforts to get one or other of her protégés struck off the list of émigrés, or persuading Barras to nominate Talleyrand for the post of Foreign Affairs: the services she was able to render also gave proof of her power. When she was not at Coppet, where she often went to visit her father, the elderly Necker, who was also constantly writing about French affairs, she held her salon in Paris, or at the Château de Saint-Ouen, a family inheritance. She received the world of politicians, army suppliers, intellectuals and generals that the society of that epoch had become, midway between nineteenth-century *Tout-Paris* and the salons of the eighteenth century.

She did not live in an era when women could aspire to the leading political roles; but she wanted to be in the centre of everything, the Egeria of the Republic and republicans. When Bonaparte had returned from Italy in 1797, she had almost turned him into a cult figure, and had tried to pay court to him, but in vain: the Corsican general disliked women who were mixed up in politics; he feared the indiscreet enthusiasm of this particular woman, and preferred the austere discussions of the Institut to her dinner parties.

Necker's daughter, however, was also a great writer. It was largely through her that in the France of that period there was a revival of the culture of the Enlightenment, a knowledge of German literature, intellectual cosmopolitanism – in the best sense of the term. From her father she had acquired a taste for political philosophy, and her writings at the time owed something to the *Histoire de la Révolution française* written in 1795 by Necker. She lived with Benjamin Constant, the leading philosophical intellect in Paris: in the *Circonstances actuelles* it is impossible to unravel which parts come from him and which from her. One thing is certain, and that is that a whole group of liberal Republicans found their best spokesperson in her.

Though Germaine was republican, and diverged from her father on that point, it was not, as one might suspect, from Jacobin loyalty. On the contrary, she reworked all Constant's examination of the catastrophe represented by the first two years of the Terror, the shadow of opprobrium they had left on the republican concept and the heritage of constitutional instability, the continuance of which had been demonstrated by the coup d'état of Fructidor Year V, followed by the invalidation of many of the 1798 elected members. She was an unhappy 'Fructidorienne', reacting to the military salvage of the Republic, followed by exceptional laws, in the same way that she thought of the Revolution itself: on balance it was good, because the principles of 1789 were those of the Enlightenment; but the means it used were detestable.

In exploring that paradox, which by then had become classic, at the heart of the Thermidorian impasse, she again used some of Constant's arguments, passions bequeathed by *ancien régime* inequality, and above all anachronism: if the Republic had been instituted by the Terror, it had arrived too soon, in a country and a public opinion ill prepared to receive it, much less to endow it with a legal form. 'The Republic has forestalled the Enlightenment; we must hasten the work of time by all true means of public education, and restore institutions and enlightenment to the same level.' But her opus gave yet another reason, destined to receive its most systematic form in Constant's later works; namely, 'the false application of the principle of sovereignty of the people in representative government'.[11]

Madame de Staël here took up the idea put forward by Sieyès in his two speeches of Thermidor Year III (1795), at the time of the discussion on the constitution of Year III: the sovereignty of the people had installed itself in the absolute sovereignty of the king, simultaneously rebuilding under another form what it had claimed to abolish. The only way of preserving liberty among modern people was to break away from that unlimited and indivisible conception of sovereignty which, because it could not hand absolute power to thirty million citizens, entrusted it to 750 deputies:

Pure democracy, through its disadvantages, has great delights, but the only democracy is in the public square in Athens . . . In Europe, where all states are equally civilized, small associations of men have no spirit of emulation, no riches, no fine arts, no great men, and never would any Frenchman agree to give up all he gains in glory and pleasures from his large association, in order to obtain in exchange perfect liberty in a small space, far from the eyes of the world and the enjoyments of wealth.[12]

The contrast between the liberty of the democracies of antiquity and that of the big modern states gives rise in the latter to the need for representative government, the principle of which is neither the proportional nature of representatives in relation to the numbers represented, nor the indivisible omnipotence of the representation; it is the political arrangement which duly puts in charge of the nation those who represent its legitimate interests, therefore its will, shared among several authorities, and limited by those very interests. Madame de Staël rediscovered Sieyès's idea of a *procuration* given by the nation to certain of its citizens whose interests coincide with those of the association, and whose capabilities allow them to carry out this mandate: property-owners, who are also the most enlightened men. Education would gradually open political equality to an ever-increasing number of men.

But what about in 1798, in 1799? The author was not worried about the present, she knew her world: 'During the lifetime of the present Revolutionaries, the Republic will be maintained at all costs, and will not perish. The events of their lives bind them to its existence. The vote for the king's death is, by itself, a stronger tie than all the institutions in the world; but this sort of guarantee is completely revolutionary.'[13] Exactly; but how were they to get away from it? By allowing the elections to the Five Hundred to take place normally, legally, instead of invalidating them, but also by organizing other authorities in a different way, so as to ensure the unity of the whole; Madame de Staël's revision did not seek to set up

---

[11] *Des circonstances actuelles qui peuvent terminer la Révolution, et des principes qui doivent fonder la République en France*, p. 33.
[12] Ibid., pp. 159–60.
[13] Ibid., p. 164.

a counterweight, after the style of Montesquieu; she remained faithful to Sieyès's clockwork mechanism idea, according to which constitutional machinery must produce political reason. That is why she envisaged several of them, according to the diversity of their missions: a Directory with the right of suspensive veto over laws and the right to dissolve the Five Hundred; a Council of Ancients, elected for life, richly pensioned, filled with past and present notabilities of the Revolution, conservatory of the Republic; a *jurie constitutionnaire* – again an idea of Sieyès – entrusted with verifying the constitutionality of the laws. Such were the institutional conditions which she deemed necessary for the establishment of the principles of 1789 within the law.

BRUMAIRE

At the same time, or perhaps a little later, in the summer of 1799, what were the thoughts of the great specialist in constitutions, the oracle that had become the principal personage of the executive power? For several months, between May and November, he was what he had never been, even in 1789, and what he would never be again: in power, sharing all Madame de Staël's politico-constitutional concern, which had been made more urgent by the military situation of summer 1799 and the neo-Jacobin agitation in the Five Hundred. He was the supreme embodiment of the men of the Revolution, and he made full use of that political capital; he had run the whole length of the course, 1789 and the regicide, 9 Thermidor and 18 Fructidor.

His closest supporters were the Thermidorians of the Institut, Daunou, Roederer, Chénier, Boulay de la Meurthe. With the Ancients his authority was considerable; he extended his influence to the Five Hundred, through Lucien Bonaparte, one of the orators of the left, and he also wanted to take under his wing the 1789 veterans and the Fructidor exiles, La Fayette and Carnot. In the army, he had against him the more Jacobin generals, Augereau, Jourdan, Bernadotte, but he had also sounded out Joubert and Moreau for a helping hand, should the need arise.

His aim was still to terminate the Revolution; to close this strange theatre of a Republic which could not even obtain the obedience of its own administration, yet which paraded its flags from Amsterdam to Milan. But how? Sieyès never revealed the constitution that he kept secretly locked in his mind. What little is known of it comes from the notes of Boulay de la Meurthe, one of his closest confidants, and from the remnants used by Bonaparte after Brumaire. The conservative aspect of revolutionary personnel and interests showed quite clearly, in the replacement of free electoral procedures with lists of notabilities from whom the public authority would make its choice, and in the creation of a Senate intended to perpetuate the Conventionnel caste. But it also contained some original devices, such as the Grand Elector, Chief of State with nothing more than the power to arbitrate, while the Executive went to two Consuls, one for external and the other for internal affairs. The concept of this public office had fed the accusation against Sieyès that he intended it for a prince; but it was so much a part of his general constitutional ideas that the imputation may be discounted.

In the France of that era, a coup d'état backed by the army had become sufficiently customary for the plan to come almost naturally into the Director's mind. He still had to find 'the sword', as he called it. He had spoken about it to Joubert, a young Republican general appointed to the army of Italy, which was a promise of glory; but Joubert had been beaten and killed at Novi on 15 August. Sieyès was thinking of Moreau, when Bonaparte disembarked at Fréjus.

Bonaparte's return can be depicted in the colours of a marital spat or in those of a triumph. The former is the private aspect. When the news of his arrival reached Paris on the evening of 13 October, Josephine rushed to take a carriage to go and meet him before he could see his family tribe: she had a number of infidelities for which to ask his pardon. But she took the Burgundy road, whereas Napoleon came back by the Bourbonnais, where he first encountered Joseph and Lucien, who went on interminably about his wife's misconduct. He was the first to arrive in Paris, on the 16th, and two days later there was a great scene with Josephine, who had come in tears, with her two children, to knock at the hero's door; but he already had other ideas in mind.

For the other aspect of his return was its triumphal nature. Between Fréjus and Paris, the country had fêted the general: the magic of Italy more than ever surounded this conqueror who was returning from Egypt, minus his army, but bringing back in his own person the glory of the nation – a glory which the men of the Directory had forfeited, as they had forfeited public authority, but which already robed him like a king in public opinion. How distant were the times when the Abbé Sieyès had defined the idea of nation by the exclusion of the privileged, by the constituent power of free and equal individuals!

Ten years later, having gone through war, the Terror, the coups d'état, the French were tired of pursuing that ambition which had so often let them down; they were bound to the Revolution by private interests and no longer by ideas; by the greatness of their country and no longer by the sovereignty of the people. From having been the voice of the nation in the face of the king and aristocracy, Sieyès was now nothing more than the representative of an oligarchy of survivors; the royal role, the only great one in French history, had been reallocated by the history of the Revolution and had been out of use since the people as a body had been driven away from it. By a bizarre fate, it fell to the little Corsican noble who had entered so recently, but with such brilliance, into the annals of the nation.

Bonaparte drew almost unanimous acclamation from an exhausted France. On the evening when Paris learned of his return, the theatres stopped their performances. Along the route, villages were lit up to mark the passing of his coach. There is an observation made just prior to the event, bearing witness to the prevalent mood, in the account of a royalist writer 'Fructidorized' in 1797, Joseph Fiévée, who was then in retirement in Champagne: 'One observation alone reminded me of politics', he wrote; 'every peasant that I met in the fields, the vineyards or the woods approached me to ask if there were any news of General Bonaparte, and why he did not come back to France; never once did anyone enquire about the Directory.'[14]

Sieyès therefore had no choice. For his coup d'état, the scenario of which had been ready since summer, the 'sword' could belong only to Bonaparte. Moreover, the Parisian political milieu itself was caught up in the new situation. The Five Hundred, where Lucien was playing a leading role, enthusiastically greeted the news of the return. Paris flocked around the returned conqueror, scenting the power in the offing. The hero of the day spent the last two weeks of October receiving, listening and distributing kindly words to everyone; he knew that he must not be tied to any party or coterie; that he held the stakes, that he was irreplaceable, whereas Parisian politicians were unpopular. He wanted to remain what he called 'national'. He mistrusted the ambitions of Sieyès, who in turn mistrusted his.

Conversations took place at first through other people, chiefly Lucien, but also Talleyrand, who had to smooth out questions of precedence in the visits of one to the other: for Sieyès was uncompromising about his prerogatives as a Director; nor did he possess a courtier's temperament. Bonaparte also had discussions with Barras, but it was Sieyès who held the political entourage he needed for the success of a coup d'état. Starting from 10 Brumaire (November 1), agreement was reached on the scenario finalized by Sieyès, but Bonaparte had introduced a major modification: the coup d'état would not be intended to substitute the Convention envisaged by Sieyès for that of Year III, but to form a government of three Consuls, charged with drawing up a new Constitution with the help of a parliamentary commission made up from within the councils.

The *coup* was carried out in two days, 18 and 19 Brumaire (9 and 10 November 1799). On the first day, everything went as planned; on the second, everything was nearly ruined.

On 18 Brumaire the Ancients, who had been summoned together in the early hours, voted for the transfer of the councils to Saint-Cloud, on the pretext of an anarchist plot, and entrusted the execution of the decree to Bonaparte. Meeting together at eleven o'clock, the Five Hundred, with Lucien as president, were already very hostile towards Bonaparte, but agreed to adjourn to Saint-Cloud the next day. Meanwhile, Bonaparte had arrived at the Tuileries surrounded by troops and a staff of generals; there Sieyès joined him. The Directory was neutralized: Sieyès and his under-

---

[14] Joseph Fiévée, *Mémoires*, p. 202.

study, Roger Ducos, were in on the plot; Barras had agreed in the morning to sign a letter of resignation which was handed to him, and to retire to his property of Grosbois. The two others, Gohier and Moulin, were put in the Palais du Luxembourg under military guard.

The ministers, the administration, rallied round, the value of stocks rose, Paris was covered with posters prepared by Roederer giving the watchword: Save the Republic! Moreover, in the morning, in a public altercation carefully planned against Barras's secretary in the Tuileries gardens, Bonaparte had set the tone, with the acclamation of the troops:

In what sort of state did I leave France, and in what sort of state do I find it again? I left you peace and I find war! I left you conquests, and the enemy is crossing our frontiers. I left our arsenals full, and I find not a single weapon! I left you the millions of Italy, and I find spoliatory laws and poverty everywhere!

This speech already contained a few too many 'I's' to have pleased Sieyès.

In the preparations for the next day, the former priest had taken a clearer view than the general. He would have liked to imprison a few dozen of the Jacobin members of the Five Hundred in the afternoon, but Bonaparte insisted on remaining as 'legal' as possible: he wanted to obtain a blank cheque from the two councils. But on 19 Brumaire (10 November) things went badly at Saint-Cloud. Lucien could not control his assembly, which decided to proceed with a solemn oath of loyalty to the institutions of Year III by a roll-call vote. Even the Ancients wavered, and began to negotiate with their Jacobin neighbours on the election of new Directors.

After several hours of idle talk came the arrival of Bonaparte, who was rather out of his depth: he delivered a military harangue, which missed its target. Nevertheless, he wanted to start again with the Five Hundred, whom he had just insulted; he was greeted with cries of 'Outlaw!', jostled and rescued from the deputies by his aides-de-camp. It was Sieyès who gave the practical advice: get the soldier out of here. And it was Lucien, President of the Five Hundred, himself threatened with being outlawed, who on horseback declaimed the decisive address before the troops, whom he asked to drive the 'seditious' members from the assembly. The final act was directed by two generals, Leclerc, Napoleon's brother-in-law, and Murat, his brother-in-law to be: at twilight their grenadiers dispersed the people's representatives.

The Ancients became tractable once more and did what Sieyès asked of them, replacing the Directory with an executive commission of three members – himself, Roger Ducos and Bonaparte, after which they went to dinner. After dinner, however, Lucien wanted a vote from the Five Hundred for his communiqué of the next day. Some one hundred deputies, scattered among the cafés of Saint-Cloud, were rounded up, and this difficult day was brought to a close by candle-light, by a successive vote: the Ancients had had to quash their first vote, so that the second, during the night, could be valid. There were therefore three Consuls, assisted by two legislative commissions representing the Councils; and just in order to remain true to tradition, the victors had excluded sixty-two deputies from the Legislative Body.

Before dawn, everyone went home to a Paris that had stayed quite calm.

5

Napoleon Bonaparte: 1799–1814

At the time, 18 Brumaire did not have the meaning for its contemporaries which they attributed to it a little later, and which history has permanently fixed: the institution of a despotic regime founded on the authority of one person alone, inaugurating a new period – the last – in the history of the Revolution. The Republic had known so many illegalities since its birth – from Vendémiaire Year IV to Prairial Year VII, by way of Fructidor Year V – that the two days of Brumaire merely meant one more, at least comparable with Fructidor: intervention by the army, expulsion of deputies, annulment of regularly constituted powers. Even a law of proscription against the Jacobins was not omitted. Furthermore, the Republic continued, armed with three Consuls in place of five Directors, stronger than ever in its two great supports: the army, in the person of Bonaparte, and the political framework born of the revolutionary upheaval, represented by Sieyès.

However, one man had grasped the whole picture on 19 Brumaire, apart from Sieyès, who had been eclipsed the day before by the Corsican general and all his praetorians on horseback. That man was Benjamin Constant, who had been in the Director's circle all the summer, but not important enough to be party to the secret; during the morning of 19 Brumaire he in fact wrote to him:

Citizen Director, After the first wave of joy which news of your deliverance inspired in me, I had some other thoughts on the matter which I beg you to read, even if I am attaching too much importance to them: I believe this is a decisive moment for liberty. There is talk of adjourning the councils, but such a measure would seem disastrous to me at this time, since it would be to destroy the only barrier which could be set up against a man whom you associated with yesterday's events but who is thereby only more of a threat to the Republic. His proclamations, in which he speaks only of himself and says that his return has raised hopes that he will put an end to France's ills, have more than ever convinced me that in everything he does he sees nothing but his own elevation. Nevertheless, he has on his side the generals, the soldiers, the aristocratic populace and everyone who enthusiastically embraces the appearance of strength. The Republic has on her side yourself – and certainly that is a great deal – and representation which, good or bad, will always be capable of erecting a barrier to the designs of an individual.[1]

This advice forms a kind of belated echo of Sieyès's own misgivings since Bonaparte's return. It was futile now, because the die had been cast on 19 Brumaire. Today, the historian is struck by the lucidity of their words, and by their blindness. Constant was the first to realize – whereas Mme de Staël, who had just returned from Coppet, greeted the coup d'état with joy – that the days of Brumaire had sounded the knell of what, for him, constituted the Republic: representative government, assemblies, a collegial executive, liberty. It would not prevent him from paying court to Bonaparte in order to obtain at least a post within the new authorities, at the end of the year. He would not be there for long: the impression he had established on 19 Brumaire fixed his opposition to dictatorship for the next fourteen years.

Yet this very intelligent man reveals a great lack of comprehension of the state of the nation. Heaven knows, however, that he had grasped and commented on the extraordinary collective traumatism created in public opinion by the revolutionary years, and the extreme difficulty of reconstituting, on so many accumulated ruins and antagonistic memories, a body politic freely agreed by the citizens. He had stepped up his flow of writings, before and after Fructidor, to try to convince enlightened opinion to rebuild its unity around a Republic and the principles of 1789. But his was a voice crying in the wilderness.

Among the republicans he was defending, it was the regicides of the Convention who set the tone – those who had relaunched the Terror after Fructidor: an unfortunate way of exorcizing bad memories. As for that France he was speaking of and which he was addressing, it was the France of Parisian society, members of the Institut, deputies to the councils, who shared with him both the philosophy of the Enlightenment and a taste for bourgeois society.

The people with whom he liked best to talk were constitutional royalists, whom he wanted to rally. He knew very little about the depths of the nation. He was a stranger to one of its most powerful passions – national greatness inseparable from glory. When, in his letter of 19 Brumaire to Sieyès, he speaks of the 'aristocratic populace', he is putting his finger on Bonaparte's popularity, but misinterpreting it. For this 'populace', if it is true that it loves the spectacle of strength and arms, is not 'aristocratic', that is to say, counter-revolutionary. It is the arms of the Revolution that it salutes, in the person of the general of Italy and Egypt. Against these, what was the importance of a group of politicians who had clung on to power for so long; and what was the importance of Sieyès, their man?

[1] Letter published in Norman King and Etienne Hofman (eds), 'Les Lettres de Benjamin Constant à Sieyès', *Annales Benjamin Constant*, 3 (1983).

There are two ways of entering that France of 1799, whose state of mind Tocqueville penetrated so brilliantly in the two completed chapters of what would have been his history of the Revolution: firstly, through personal interests, and secondly through national glory. Neither path led to liberty, but both to Bonaparte.

Everyone had suffered from the chaos of events. But, at the end of the road, many people benefited. Peasants and people from the towns had purchased lands and property belonging to the Church and, to a lesser extent, to the émigrés. This was an immense transfer of property, forming the Revolution's bank, with a guarantee that was completely political: it would be nullified by the return of the kings. France today can offer enough abbeys or monastic buildings which at that time were transformed into factories or barns, to give some idea of that huge redistribution of the land and property interests.

The most obvious fortunes in speculation, built up by way of these state sales, were almost hidden by the multiplicity of small deals, or simply of acquired benefits. The inflation which resulted from revolutionary management of public finances had accelerated transfers of ownership. It had also, to a large extent, liberated debtors from their debts and the French from taxes. Lastly, the Revolution had created a very large number of jobs in the public sector, both in the administration and in the army: many posts which, before 1789, had been sold like a formal office, were now open to anyone with ability, and their numbers had increased. The principles of 1789 created a whole democracy of interests, and were therefore now bound to a policy of conserving them.

Was the Republic capable of conserving? Did it know how to? It gave no reassurance on this point to the public. The Thermidorian politicians presented a caricature rather than a picture of beneficiaries of the Revolution. Who would want to be like them? They were too rich, too powerful, too corrupt – in short, too 'bourgeois' – to impart anything but remorse for the immense adventure, whereas the French, on the contrary, wanted to enjoy their new possessions in security, erasing all trace of their recent or questionable origin.

Moreover, the Republican form of the state had allowed the exercise of authority only by the guillotine; since the Terror had ended, the Directory maintained the ascendancy of Robespierre's feeble conquerors, come hell or high water, only by means of a permanent coup d'état. But it had arrived at the end of the road, incapable of truly silencing the two parties threatening the new property-owning France – the Jacobins and the royalists.

It was also incapable of confronting the eternal coalition of European monarchies against the Revolution, as the crisis of summer 1799 had shown. Since 1795, and above all since the Italian victories, France had presented this strange spectacle of a Republic with a weak and divided government, gradually sliding towards internal anarchy, and yet within a few years building a formidable French power outside France: occupying

Belgium, Holland, Italy, Switzerland, the left bank of the Rhine, planting the tricolour flag much farther afield than any king of France had ever done. Public opinion set great store by these victories and conquests, far beyond mere calculation of the gain to be derived from them; much more than because of simple national pride, and on a different plane – the ventures of its armies provided the Revolution with a treasury of good memories to offset the bad ones; they transfigured its image. They had managed to get the Terror excused, and would provide the Republic and its soldiers with a halo.

Military glory – which Constant would soon explain was foreign to modern society, engaged as it was in the productive works of peaceful times – would, on the contrary, in France accompany the birth of democracy. It was gradually transforming its nature. The heroism of the soldier was replacing the civic virtue of the sansculotte. While it opened up swift and unlimited opportunities for advancement on merit, the army at the same time offered a powerful channel for the classical tendencies of the Revolution's passion for equality. In the space of ten years, the ideas of 1789 and hatred of the aristocracy had thus turned into a tremendous national investment. But by looking favourably on this evolution – for want of any other cards to play – the Directorial Republic had also dug its own grave.

As an example which took place a little more than a year before Brumaire there is the festival of 9 Thermidor Year VI (27 July 1798) when the Directory celebrated its birth, as it had each year after 1794. Bonaparte, who had been gone since May, had already gained a foothold in Egypt; yet he alone was the hero of the celebration. In fact, the government had given up the theme of Robespierre's downfall, which smacked too much of civil war; instead, it substituted the triumphal procession of all the looted treasures from Italian churches and palaces.

The comment of Etienne Delécluze, David's young student, in his memoirs was:

This fête which, according to contemporary taste, was given all the appearances of an ancient ceremony, singularly flattered the nation's self-esteem and caused the name of the young Bonaparte – who was just about to make his entry into Cairo – to resound amid still more enthusiasm and gratitude. Scientific and artistic objects, books, manuscripts, antique statues and paintings won by the army of Italy, had been unloaded at Charenton; and during the ten days preceding their entry into Paris, a crowd of the curious had gone along the Seine as far as this village to observe from every angle the packing-cases containing the treasures accumulated by the sword of Bonaparte. Yielding to a generous and peaceable inspiration, the government of the Directory had seized the opportunity to remove from the fête of 9 Thermidor the malevolent political character it had had until then, in order to bring back French hearts, as far as possible, to a spirit of Concord through a common sentiment – national pride.[2]

_____
[2] E. J. Delécluze, *Louis David, son école et son temps*, ch. 7.

There followed an interminable procession of books, minerals, animals and *objets d'art*, divided into four sections so as to give it an encyclopaedic nature, 'an idea which then dominated every speculative intelligence'; each of the four divisions was surrounded by military detachments, members of the Institut and actors from the lyric theatres, who sang hymns of joy to the victorious arms of France. From the Jardin des Plantes to the Champ de Mars, where the Directors stood, there were vast throngs of people: France was simultaneously celebrating her victories and encyclopaedic reason, identifying her conquests with the progress of the human mind, and uniting by her arms temporal order – even territorial order – and spiritual power. The important person missing from this new version of the festival of unity was Bonaparte, since it was his sword which had made it all possible.

Ten years after 1789, the French Revolution had largely become in public opinion that very special something which eluded Constant's analysis: a universalist nationalism, in which the historian can discern its component elements of anti-aristocratic passion and rationalism, transfigured by the idea of the nation's historico-military election. The Directory could no more identify this mixture of sentiments than it could reassure those whose interests were threatened. On both sides there was the implicit demand for a king, but one who was radically different from other kings, since he would be born of the sovereignty of the people and of reason. This was where Napoléon Bonaparte, king of the French Revolution, was born. In 1789, the French had created a Republic, under the name of a monarchy. Ten years later, they created a monarchy, under the name of a Republic.

The matter was not concluded on 19 Brumaire. Bonaparte appeared only in third position on the list of the three Consuls drawn up on that night, coming after Sieyès and Roger Ducos. Unlike the oracle of the revolutionary assemblies, the general did not have his constitution 'in the bag'; he had acted as he would on the battlefield, though less brilliantly, which he would later explain in his phrase: 'One advances and then one has a look round.' That was why the weeks and months which followed were more important than the two days of Brumaire.

Stendhal would write later in his *Vie d'Henri Brulard*, that he had been surprised by news of the coup d'état when in Nemours, on the road leading from his native Grenoble to Paris: 'We learned of it in the evening, and I didn't understand much about it, but I was delighted that young General Bonaparte had made himself king of France.' This snippet says a great deal about the kind of spell this event cast over a large part of French republican tradition in the nineteenth century: it would take the coup d'état of 2 December 1851 to destroy its magic. But Stendhal telescoped several months, between the end of 1799 and the middle of 1800: those during which Bonaparte *was becoming* king of France.

If he lost his head slightly on 19 Brumaire, he played the rest of the game like a great politician, fully aware of the superiority he possessed over his rival, Sieyès. He was not a man to share with others, and he was the only one who could provide a guarantee. Everything took place within the two parliamentary commissions which had survived the Brumaire shipwreck, where he himself, Sieyès and Daunou had the most influence. As days went by, the Parisian political milieu sensed where the strength lay and inclined towards him. Everyone agreed on the need to reinforce the Executive: this was a great innovation, to say the least, in the theory of republican power.

At the head of the Republic, Sieyès would have liked to see a Grand Elector, an arbitrating power charged with the task of designating two Consuls. Did he want the office for himself, finally to become the supreme guardian of the institutions, lavishly maintained by the state, the ultimate incarnation of his doctrine? Had he thought he would swamp his young rival with honours? The first version seems more probable to me. But Bonaparte, helped by Boulay and others, made use of the antagonism between Sieyès and Daunou – each with his own plan – to impose a text which suited him. He kept Sieyès's list of notabilities, which dispensed with true elections, and three assemblies which neutralized one another – Senate, Tribunate, Legislative Body. He put aside the Grand Elector and set up an executive of three Consuls, of whom only the first truly exercised power, with the ability to initiate laws. It was the end of the Republican idea under the name of the Republic.

The electoral system gives a fair indication of the limits of universal suffrage, which the Brumairians had wanted to re-establish in homage to the great principles. In reality, the popular vote was destined only to provide, at all levels in the country, from the commune right up to the Senate, 'lists of notabilities' among which a sorting operation could be effected from above. This procedure had been thought up by Sieyès, in order to avoid the annual hiccups which had dislocated the preceding regime; in fact, it instituted a power which was no longer controlled by the people, even if it continued to call on the spirit of the people: a good definition of enlightened despotism.

At the most, the people would be invited from time to time to ratify an initiative of the authority with a massive 'Yes'. But the doctrine of the new regime, together with the old dream of the Enlightenment, lies in this comment by Cabanis: 'The ignorant classes no longer exercise any influence on either the legislature or the government . . . everything is done for the people and in the name of the people; nothing is done by them, or at their unconsidered dictation.'[3]

One month after Brumaire, before the end of 1799, the constitution of Year VIII thus put Bonaparte into power. Sieyès, who became president of the Senate, received the right to find jobs for his friends. He disappeared under a heap of honours, among the debris of his own ideas, which were

[3] P. J. G. Cabanis, *Quelques considérations sur l'organisation sociale en général, et particulièrement sur la nouvelle constitution*, 25 Frimaire Year VIII (16 December 1799).

used in the triumph of his erstwhile associate. As First Consul, Bonaparte chose two colleagues whose names formed a bridge between the present and the two great national memories: Camabacérès, a man of the Revolution, and Charles-François Lebrun, a servant of the *ancien régime*. The first had been a Conventionnel and regicide (but he had voted for a reprieve); the second was a former secretary of Chancellor Maupeou, the last great defender of royal authority against the parlements. Both had the sceptical maturity born of experience, and preferred honours to power. Through them, the two Frances of yesteryear provided the young hero with his retinue.

But this national reconciliation – one of Bonaparte's great ideas – was not a rehabilitation of the past, or even a search for balance between the *ancien régime* and the Revolution. On the contrary, it assumed an acceptance of what had happened since 1789, and the desire to defend revolutionary attainments, both at home and abroad. The First Consul was more keenly aware than anyone, during that first winter when he needed to keep an eye on everything, that his destiny was being decided outside France, on the battlefields where he was awaited by the European coalition which had been repulsed – but not vanquished – in the autumn. For the fundamental contract between Bonaparte and public opinion was the guarantee of revolutionary conquests, and therefore of a victorious peace. The rest – his power, soon to become his regime, internal order, the reconciliation of the French – was subordinate to this suspensive condition: victory. Should this delay or falter, he would be questioned, condemned and as good as lost.

Several months after the coup d'état, Bonaparte was already impatient of any resistance. But having so recently attained supreme power, he still did not control everything, and political society had not yet got the measure or the habitude of his despotism. As witness the incidents which increased over the first few weeks with Madame de Staël and her friends. Benjamin Constant, who had for so long dreamed of being a representative of the people, had in the end been appointed to the Tribunate, the assembly which was supposed to discuss the laws, while the Legislative Body would vote on them. But he realized his ambition just when it no longer meant anything. On 5 January 1800, during one of the first sessions, he affirmed the assembly's independence and its deliberative authority, without which 'there is nothing but servitude and silence – a silence which the whole of Europe would hear.' The First Consul immediately had a violent press attack unleashed against him and Madame de Staël, organised by Fouché, the Minister of Police. It was the first skirmish.

Deep-rooted opinion in the country, exhausted after so many years of revolutionary talk, no longer took any interest in political liberty. Bonaparte's power was based in France on tired consent to servitude, in exchange for the return of order. Bonaparte had had the law of proscription revoked, in order to show clearly that it had belonged to Sieyès. But he had to conquer outside the country. This was the whole story of Marengo, seven months after Brumaire.

The campaign was just right to seize the imagination: the assembling of
the army in Burgundy, the crossing of the Alps by the St Bernard and
taking the enemy from the rear – the Austrian armies besieging Genoa.
Indeed, the French descent into the rich Milanese countryside reawoke the
happiness of 1796; but at Marengo, near Alessandria, on 14 June, the
decisive clash with the troops of the Austrian General Melas almost turned
to a rout. For Bonaparte, in the impeccable lay-out of a strategic design,
had committed a tactical error by dispersing his troops in order to 'sound
out' his adversary, and with reduced numbers he had encountered the
entire Austrian army. At three in the afternoon the French were losing
ground, outnumbered, when at the end of the day the arrival of Desaix's
corps changed the outcome of the battle.

In Paris news of the defeat had arrived before the final recovery; during
several hours, the First Consul vanished from political calculations. Already,
while he was with the armies, intrigue and speculation had resumed in all
the little Parisian groups, around Daunou, Sieyès and in the salon of
Madame de Staël. Possible successors were talked about – ambitious
or jealous generals like Moreau and Bernadotte; sober symbols of the
Revolution like Carnot; or even those eternal candidates for a constitutional
monarchy, personified since 1789 in the Ducs d'Orléans, father and son.
Even Joseph, Napoleon's elder brother, had thrust himself forward, while
Fouché and Talleyrand, for their part, were working chiefly for themselves.

But lo and behold, rescued by chance – and by Desaix, who lost his life
– Bonaparte came straight back to Paris after throwing together a hasty
armistice with Melas. He returned on 2 July amid popular jubilation and
the nervous silence of the 'politicos'. He had realized that Marengo, far
more than Brumaire, had been the true coronation of his power and his
regime. This was a coronation which no longer came by divine right, since
it was the result of the most one-sided contract that a nation had ever made
with its leader, who was forced into a commitment never to be vanquished.
It is in this sense that, between Marengo and Waterloo, between the arrival
of Desaix and the absence of Grouchy, between fortune and misfortune,
there is a difference which is both minute and tremendous: the regime
itself was dependent on it. In June 1800, therefore, it was founded. The
royalist agent Hyde de Neuville noted at the time that 'Marengo was the
baptism of Napoleon's personal power.'

FIRST CONSUL

Then began the happiest period of his life: his marriage with the French
Revolution. Republican terminology survived the loss of liberty because it
still defined the new France, under the spell of this new sovereign who was
her most brilliant son. All that was royal about Bonaparte derived from his
being the hero of the Republic. A French Washington, very young and
belatedly discovered. The Revolution had exhausted its repertoire, cut off

its provisional leaders in the prime of their life, changed those who lived on
into mere survivors, and its conquerors into bourgeois. Just at the time
when it was closing its theatre it finally found its great man, with his own
particular genius: this thirty-year-old Washington did not love liberty and
would not finish his days as father of his country. But for several years –
until the coronation – he was the master of events and the man who
founded the modern state on the heritage of the Revolution.

In order to understand or define him, one can start from what roots
him so deeply in French history – this Corsican, Italian, foreigner, this
'Buonaparte' of the Restoration dowagers: his election by the French
Revolution, from which he received the strange power not only to embody
the new nation – others had had it, such as Mirabeau or Robespierre – but
also finally to fulfil it. He had been so acutely aware of it that his writings
on St Helena would return almost obsessively to this origin, less in order
deliberately to make it into a weapon of posthumous propaganda – which it
would nevertheless be – than from a need to recollect those parts of his
extraordinary life which might have some explanation.

The 'Citizen Consul', at thirty, was physically at his peak: less sallow
than the general of Italy, not yet podgy like the emperor. He lived amid
the resonance of his glory and the exhilaration of government work – the
two passions of his daily life – even giving up a little of his time to
pleasures and amusements: these were the lovely days of Malmaison,
recounted by Laure Junot, the future Duchesse d'Abrantès. Bonaparte had
not yet acquired a court, and lived surrounded by his aides-de-camp and
generals who were his friends, above them all but not separated from
them. Josephine had finally realized her exceptional luck, and both of
them, by the remarkable nature of their life and love, gave a good representation of the opportunities to be had in the new society; these two
'marginals' of the Revolution, the courtesan from the West Indies and the
little Corsican soldier, had ended up by personifying property-owning
France. Opinion discovered in the leader it had given itself a style and
habits which had all the characteristics of republican simplicity and a civil
government. The First Consul had none of the Bourbons' stupid habits: he
ate quickly, used to wear the same sort of clothing all the time, liked old
hats, and had no wish to waste his time in court ceremony; he hunted
little, if at all; he worked and made decisions.

Those images were for his publicity – which he knew very well how to
manage – but they also match the truth of the period. Napoleon the Consul
mingled the qualities of republican hero and bourgeois king with those
despotic and uncontrollable traits which his personality already possessed.
He had fully understood the objective conditions which had carried him to
power and the civil character of his dictatorship:

I do not govern as a general, but because the nation believes I have the civilian
qualities befitting government; if it did not hold that opinion, the government
would not survive. I was well aware of what I was doing when, as an army general,

I became a member of the Institut; I was sure of being understood even by the least drummer boy. In the present day, one must not argue about centuries of barbarism. We are thirty million men, united by the Enlightenment, property-ownership and trade. Three or four hundred thousand soldiers are as nothing compared with this great mass.[4]

Enlightenment, property, trade: a definition of the nation which could have been supplied by Necker or Sieyès or Benjamin Constant, and which they had already given, having learnt it from the century's *philosophes*, but without being able to master its potential for instability and civil strife. He also wanted to be its heir and its emblem, the country's guarantor – discovered at long last – and there was a strong bourgeois streak in him which accorded well with this role: unassailable rights of ownership, the idea of marriage and the family, the woman in the home, order in the streets, careers open to anyone with ability.

On the one hand, he endowed all that – which was basically the legacy of 1789 in plain words – with the flamboyant character of his own genius; and on the other, he enveloped it in a sort of Corsican exaggeration, mingling a patriarchal spirit in the birth of modern France. In doing so, he doubly satisfied the national desire. Having just emerged from the epic of the Revolution, the French would not easily have accepted a leader with less national éclat; but exhausted with the Revolutionary repertoire and intent upon their acquisitions, they wanted the strengthening of the guarantees offered to property and law and order.

Both revolutionary and conservative, these rural petits-bourgeois found the Bonaparte of the Civil Code. They spontaneously subscribed to the programme defined in November 1800 in the Council of State: 'We have finished the novel of the Revolution: now we must begin its history, looking only at what is real and possible in the application of its principles, and not what is speculative and hypothetical. If today we followed another path, it would be to philosophize and not to govern.'

A dictatorship of opinion intended to assure the Revolution, the Consulate was also, in Bonaparte's mind, the 'beginning' of its history. The 'novel' of the Revolution had been written by intellectuals who had explored its 'speculative' aspect: he was certainly thinking of Robespierre, and the Republic of virtue, but also to some extent about everyone, from the Constituent Assembly to the Institut, and to Sieyès, for example, his temporary ally of Brumaire, the man of the perfect Constitution.

To begin the real history of the Revolution meant using practical reasoning to deal with the problem which they had approached from the metaphysical standpoint; in short, to found the modern state on experience and reality. This was the other adjunct of the Consulate, by which Bonaparte replaced the model of enlightened despotism through the heritage of post-revolutionary society. An idea which, as far back as 1790, Mirabeau had

---

[4] 4 May 1802, in the Council of State, in A. C. Thibaudeau, *Mémoires sur le Consulat, 1799 à 1804*, p. 79.

vainly tried to whisper to poor Louis XVI, in his secret correspondence with the court:[5] Why do you jib, he had written in so many words, in the face of the new state of affairs? Instead of bewailing aristocratic society, nobility, parlements and the privileged groups who endlessly hindered your authority, on the contrary, make the most of their disappearance to entrench the monarchy in the new society, by becoming the leader of the nation.

That was a piece of advice that the *ancien régime* king had not accepted or even understood, but one which the new sovereign was well able to put into practice: by temperament he was a thousand times more authoritarian than the former king, and he was governing more than ever a society composed of equal individuals, who were far more helpless than in the past in confrontation with the state. He had the additional advantage over 1790 of a revolutionary tide which had been on the ebb for some years – which, as it receded, revealed with all its strength intact the idea of absolute power, inherited from the kings of France and put to the use of democracy.

The sovereignty of the people had replaced that of the monarch, but it had in no way abdicated from its unlimited extent or its indivisible nature. The consular monarchy thus drew together, to its own advantage, three elements which made it into a stronger power than any other in history. On the one hand, it reigned over isolated men, denied the right to unite into a body, whose equality was guaranteed; on the other, it received its authority from the people, relieved by those same people of fear of God's watchful eye – which had acted as one of the brakes on the power of kings; lastly, it unconsciously drew part of its strength from absolutist tradition. France was still imbued with the very strong feeling that she had broken her ties with the past, and war, émigrés and the king's brothers were there to remind her of it. But the First Consul had fully understood – he said so several times – that his power also partly came from this past and from national habits.

Such were the foundations on which he established his most lasting achievement: the construction of the modern state in France. For the Civil Code, the entire work of juridical unification and legislation, had been started before him, and could have been achieved without him, in a way which would ultimately have been little different. But the new spirit of the state's administrative structures bore his imprint. He drew largely on tradition: Cartesian rationalism imported into the political sphere, enlightened despotism, the long task of centralization carried out by the absolute monarchy, the jurisprudence born of the endless conflicts between the state and the guilds under the *ancien régime*, the trend of customs and minds. He added his mark, both Corsican and military – the mark of one who placed order and authority above all the needs of man, and was so tolerant of his own chief passion: undivided domination.

The administration was the nerve of the state. It had to function on its

---

[5] Mirabeau, *Correspondance avec le comte de Lamarck (1789–1791)*.

own, like a vast framework of men intended to transmit the wishes of
government from the centre as far as the most outlying places, with the
automatism of a living organism:

I had made all my ministries so easy that I had put them within reach of everyone,
as long as they possessed dedication, zeal, energy and capacity for hard work . . .
The organization of the prefectures, their activities and results were admirable and
prodigious. The same impetus was given at the same moment to more than forty
million men; and, with the help of local centres of action, the movement was as
swift at the farthest points as in the very heart.[6]

Thus centralization, while allowing the actualization of the unity and
ubiquity of rational government, excused its agent from everything except
'work' and 'dedication'. All the prefects were 'little emperors' in their
départements, but that power was independent of their merits or their
personal qualities: it was merely the representation in actuality of the
central power.

In vain did Bonaparte periodically resume the argument of 'public
safety', saying that this state dictatorship over the citizens, which virtually
extinguished local life, was due to the war situation; it was difficult to
believe, for these ideas were so imprinted with the marks of his upbringing
and character. For the strong point of the system was also its weak point:
himself. In masterminding the administration, he brought to bear all the
care and attention of his electrifying yet realistic genius. He was capable of
assimilating very different things very rapidly, loving the variety offered by
circumstances to men who govern, knowing the value of detail and the
application of decisions on the spot, intoxicated with the passion for
knowing everything in order to be in command of everything, as if on the
field of battle. He was 'involved in all things', Chateaubriand would write;
'his intellect never rested; he had a sort of perpetual motion of ideas.
Because of his impetuous nature, he advanced by leaps and bounds,
instead of making straightforward and unbroken progress; he threw himself
on the universe and shook it.'[7]

But this activity in itself contained its principle of corruption, and the
ambition for absolute authority implied that authority's debasement into
tyranny; the corruption and debasement were very quickly noticeable in
the First Consul. Nobody could execute his orders swiftly enough, and
nobody ever obeyed him completely. In a country where paying court was
a national tradition, flattery exerted its damage on a personality which
endlessly sought it, aroused it and was very soon intoxicated by it. Hence,
side by side with the famous charming smile, there came that impatience
with contradiction, that violent and sombre eloquence, those rages, that
coarse vulgarity in insults, which Bonaparte used so frequently. Following

[6] Council of State, 1806, in Napoleon, *Pensées politiques et sociales*, ed. A. Dansette (Paris,
Flammarion, 1969), p. 81.
[7] Chateaubriand, *Mémoires d'outre-tombe*, book XXIV, ch. 6.

a very French dialectic, the same man who had deified the abstract sovereignty of the state had made it more fragile by personifying it as if it resided entirely within him. Napoleon was the Louis XIV of the democratic state.

But his possessive passion had never blinded him to the point where he confused private and public. Quite apart from his temperament, the extraordinary nature of his ascent would suffice to explain his tendency to consider everything he had acquired as an inheritance, including the Republic; nevertheless, he was the heir of the Revolution against the *ancien régime*, because the basis of the administrative state which he set up against local authorities was the universality of the law.

Although he increased arbitrary acts, as time went by, and re-established a nobility endowed by the state, the strength of his hold over the nation derived from the fact that he was the delegate of popular sovereignty to make the law and see that it was respected, since it was identical for every citizen. In this sense, he was the last avatar of the crisis of political representation which characterized the French Revolution. He had resolved this crisis by becoming the unique representative, by making a monarchy out of universal suffrage through the screening of lists of notabilities, and out of legislative power through the dispersal of the assemblies' responsibilities. But he himself – and the administration which was merely the extension of his arm – remained the symbols of a new state, founded on the consent of equal citizens and upholding the general interest of the nation.

Through this collective image, he obtained the nation's agreement, re-established order and even effected the reconciliation of those Frenchmen who had been divided by the Revolution: ex-Constituents, ex-Girondins, ex-terrorists and, of course, Thermidorians filled his administration, and provided State councillors, magistrates, prefects, commissioners to the armies, thousands upon thousands of jobs, from top to bottom of the public officialdom. Even the émigrés returned, and many of them rediscovered – enlarged, democratized, but also adorned with incomparable splendour – the two great careers in which their ancestors had proved so illustrious: state service and the army.

As for the position of courtier, they needed no one to teach them. The First Consul despised them, and in talking about them would use the tone of the 1789 Abbé Sieyès: 'I have offered them officer ranks in my army; they didn't want them; I have offered them posts in the administration, and they refused them; but when I opened my antechambers to them, they rushed to get in.' A terrible statement, in which he presented, as he so frequently did, a concentration of absolutist tradition and revolutionary spirit. The French aristocracy had been subdued by the former before being broken by the latter. In the Tuileries salons, gathered round this false prince from Corsica, it had even lost its identity.

Elsewhere, and almost everywhere, in every area which had played a role – no matter how tiny – in France since 1789, what a mad dash there was for employment! The Consulate was an extraordinary job market where, on a national scale, Bonaparte played one of the great roles of the king of France at court: handing out rewards, honours and jobs. He had more than any king had ever had, since he was founding the modern state; he had to provide not only for 'vanity', but also for the needs of a large administration and an immense army. Even more than any past king, he played on the national passion for 'positions'. This democratic trans-figuration of absolutist practices was the Corsican noble's final secret; it reinstated in the nation, in its own fashion, that court heritage which the Revolution had detested and wanted to abolish. It thus provided the hero of modern politics with a reinforcement from the past.

One last trait brought the soldier from Ajaccio close to national tradition: he had absorbed the Catholic religion in his cradle. Not that he was a believer, or that he had a deep relationship with it, but it was a part of his Italian heritage and his French world. Into the conception which he had of it, he introduced Enlightenment utilitarianism – the basis of the culture he had learnt – and political reason pure and simple, unencumbered by the useless passions of the revolutionary years, which led him to reconcile his regime with the age-old beliefs of religion. When he spoke of matters of faith, he introduced into his reflections a typically French bourgeois wisdom, which derived from Voltaire rather than Machiavelli, and which would feed nineteenth-century conservative policy: 'If you remove faith from the people, you are left with nothing but highway robbers.'[8]

Such was Bonaparte, First Consul, son and king of the Revolution; he was the product of an event which the French feared in retrospect but cherished as an inheritance, and because of this wanted to be finally assured of peaceful enjoyment of their lives and possessions. He was the self-made republican dictator, who had given the crown to equality as well as to himself. About this meeting between a man and a nation – so brief, but so dazzling, and one which would take such a long time to forget, since it would last for almost a century – Chateaubriand wrote the most profound comment:

Everyday experience proves that the French turn instinctively towards power: they have no love at all for liberty; equality alone is their idol. Now, equality and despotism have secret links. From both these aspects, Napoleon drew his strength from the hearts of the French, who were militarily inclined towards power, and democratically in love with the idea of equal status. When he ascended the throne, he brought the people to sit there with him; a proletarian king, he humiliated kings and nobles in his antechambers; he levelled out ranks, not by lowering them, but by raising them: to bring them down would have given further encouragement to plebeian envy, raising them was more flattering to their conceit.[9]

---

[8] Council of State, 29 March 1805; A. Marquiset, *Napoléon sténographié au Conseil d'Etat, 1804–1805* (1913), p. 71.

[9] Chateaubriand, *Mémoires d'outre-tombe*, book XXIV, ch. 6.

Marengo had given his brand-new reign a victorious peace, that contradictory dream of public opinion in France. To end the war was an undertaking of the same order as ending the Revolution: they both needed the crowning touch. Marengo had not been enough to bring Austria to her knees; but Moreau's victory at Hohenlinden in December 1800 brought the Austrian emperor's diplomats to the negotiating table: this was the peace of Lunéville, signed in February 1801, which extended the losses of Campo Formio (Belgium, Luxembourg and the left bank of the Rhine) and confirmed the French protectorate over the Batavian, Swiss and Italian Republics. The second coalition was completely dismantled. After the failure of the Anglo-Russian enterprises in Holland, Tsar Paul had changed sides and approached France, depriving the British government of its last continental troops.

Paris and London were then obliged to talk by force of circumstance, despite all reservations. Bonaparte wanted to keep Egypt, and Britain refused even indirect acceptance of a Franco-Russian alliance. But Egypt was all the more indefensible since Kléber's death in June 1800. In London, Pitt had fallen; in Petersburg, the assassination of Tsar Paul removed some of the British reluctance to negotiate. There remained a weariness with the war on both sides of the Channel, Britain's social and economic difficulties and Bonaparte's wish to be the man of peace: these explain the preliminaries in London in autumn 1801, and the peace of Amiens (March 1802). England would give back Egypt to Turkey, Malta to its Knights, the Cape of Good Hope to Holland; France would evacuate Naples, and the two powers would guarantee the independence of Portugal and the Ionian Islands. This drawn match, accepted very half-heartedly by both sides, was greeted as a lasting return to peace; but at the same time it was felt by French opinion to be the international recognition of revolutionary legitimacy. If London accepted that the 'great nation' extended as far as Flanders and the Rhine, it was because Bonapartist pacification had kept the promises of Year II.

In the same way, the internal power of the First Consul had continued to consolidate its position in deeds and in the law. After Brumaire, the new government, by reassuring opinion, had drawn the political teeth of *chouannerie*; the military insurrection abated all the more quickly because the royalist leaders at first banked on the coup d'état for the pretender's early restoration. When Bonaparte offered them only the option to come over to his side, they had lost their troops, and the *chouannerie* hatched a plot. On 24 December 1800, in the rue Saint-Nicaise, while his carriage was conveying him to the theatre, the First Consul very narrowly escaped the explosion of a bomb: he used this as a pretext to wipe out the remainder of a Jacobin opposition which had hardly been a threat, and shortly afterwards tracked down the real culprits. Two implacable *chouans* were executed, the others went over to England. In the west, a mixture of clemency and severity would do the rest.

THE RECONSTRUCTION OF FRANCE

Besides, Bonaparte had at his disposal against the royalist leaders a political weapon which was much more daunting than repression: this was agreement with the Catholic Church. He had inherited a difficult task, for the constitutional Church, organized by Bishop Grégoire, had not succeeded in winning over the majority of the faithful, and the civil cults founded under the Directory – the *décadaire* and theophilanthropic religions – had remained merely cold ceremonies for the notables. The refractory and Roman Church, therefore, in the name of the past, united the religious feelings of the great mass of the peasantry.

Bonaparte approached the problem like a politician; he dropped the great dream of secularizing consciences in order to rally the country around his authority: he did not for a moment believe in the idea of rebuilding a civil religion around the Revolution. In his eyes, that sort of idea belonged to a notable or intellectual, a plan which typified the revolutionary 'novel' he was trying to bring to a close. Even the constitutional Church, which Grégoire had had such diffculty in keeping alive, and which had been the victim of both terrorist dechristianization and the détente of 1795, was sacrificed by Bonaparte without any regret on the altar of reconciliation. According to his view of affairs, he was negotiating with the pope as one sovereign with another, by acknowledging the other's territory, which the Constituent Assembly had wanted to deny: he could not settle the situation of the Church of France without a negotiated agreement with the pope.

To deliver the Catholic people from the clutches of the refractory priests, and therefore also to free them from royalism, he had to go over their heads and reconcile his regime with Rome:

Fifty émigré bishops, paid by England, today guide the French clergy. Their influence must be destroyed; for that, the pope's authority is necessary. He must dismiss them or make them resign. It is said that, as the Catholic religion is followed by the majority of Frenchmen, its practice must be organized. The First Consul appoints fifty bishops, the pope institutes them. They appoint the *curés*, the state gives them a salary. They take the oath. Priests who do not submit are deported. Those who preach against the government are handed over to their superiors for punishment. The pope confirms the sale of the clergy's possessions: he consecrates the Republic. *Salvam fac rem Gallicam* will be sung. The bull has arrived. There are only a few phrases to be altered. They will say that I am a papist; I am nothing at all; in Egypt I was a Mohammedan; here I will be a Catholic, for the good of the people.[10]

In the rough language of the First Consul, these were the terms of the Concordat. With regard to Rome, Bonaparte had made two demands: the acknowledgement of the sale of the Church's possessions, and his right to appoint all bishops, after eliminating the old ones – both refractory and

[10] June 1801, Thibaudeau, *Mémoires*, pp. 152–53.

constitutional – and wiping the past clean at one vast stroke. In short, a guarantee for property acquired since 1789, and a clergy under his thumb: this was a double coup which made him king of the peasants, with God's blessing. The dialogue had been long and difficult; but he had obtained satisfaction in return for the obligation to maintain the new Church, whose bishops would be 'instituted'. On the Catholic side, the compromise with France's new master meant that the Church was founding the bases of the alliance between what the nineteenth century would call the Throne and the Altar. Those who, following the pope's example, chose to give their support, seized the unexpected opportunity to re-establish Catholicism's moral and spiritual authority in the rediscovered harmony with the temporal power.

The agreement roused the anger of refractory priests and counter-revolutionaries; but this was a period when moderate royalist opinion, which had been so agitated against the Directory, accepted the new master as a good substitute for the old vindictive monarchy of the émigrés. Times had changed. Chateaubriand, returned from exile, had just published the *Génie du Christianisme*. Protest, without being really noisy, was more noticeable in Paris, among Republican bourgeois, the people of the Institut. When, at Easter 1802, some weeks after the signing of the peace of Amiens, the capital celebrated with due solemnity Consular France's reunion with the Church of Rome, there were plenty of moans and groans from high-ranking civil and military personnel in the regime – those who had grown old in the struggle against 'superstition'.

The Tribunate had already been purged in March of any possible elements of even virtual 'opposition', by the removal of about twenty of its members, including Benjamin Constant and those ideologists who were high priests of civil religion: Chénier, Cabanis, Ginguené and Daunou. Madame de Staël also hated the Concordat, but for other reasons. Unlike the men of the Institut, but like her father, she believed the Christian religion to be indispensable to modern society; but she had explained at great length in the *Circonstances actuelles* that the state religion associated with the Republic should be Protestantism, which was essential for the lasting foundation of liberty. Bonaparte replied to her later, from St Helena, in a conversation with Las Cases: 'What would I have gained by proclaiming Protestantism? I would have created two great parties in France, whereas I did not want any at all; I would have brought back the fury of the religious wars, whereas the enlightened men of the century, together with my will, had the sole aim of making them vanish completely.'

One of the essential dates of the first 'end' of the Revolution was this peace with the Church, though it did not entirely bury the conflict which had begun in 1789–90, as what followed would show, but at least calmed it down for a while. Bonaparte had not dealt, and had not wanted to deal, with any of the spiritual and moral questions which lay at the heart of the conflict; he had shackled the Church to his success. The Concordat bore the imprint of his realistic genius: an intelligent use of his strong situation, tempered by a sense of tradition and a bourgeois philosophy of religion. To this Catholic Church which had been despoiled of its possessions, snatched from its past by the Revolution, he had restored not its heritage – which had passed to the new gentlemen in both town and country – but its unity and status, in exchange for a far tighter subordination than in the times of the kings of France.

He was dealing with a Church which was no longer the powerful body it had been under the *ancien régime*, intertwined with aristocratic society by a thousand ties; he could give himself the public benefit of restoring it without returning its former powers, as a kind of buttress to his authority. That was what his old Institut friends had not understood, or perhaps what they had understood only too well: they saw in it the end of the Republican spirit, by the re-creation of religious oppression on individual consciences. As a concession to them, Bonaparte postponed the promulgation of the Concordat, which he accompanied with a unilateral declaration, 'Gallican' in tone; but this mini-rebellion of notables, parliamentarians and generals was a mere nothing compared with public opinion's deep approval of the double guarantee afforded by the Concordat to property and consciences.

In the Bonapartist reorganization, the dispositions of the Consulate rested chiefly on the general feeling that a strong government had become the best instrument for consolidating revolutionary acquisitions. The *rente* (the rate of return on government stock) had risen again, business had picked up, the countryside was breathing once more, and the towns were quiet. It was on the basis of this almost organic calming down that Bonaparte founded the administrative institutions of contemporary France, after ten years of tension and violence. There, as in other areas, the various revolutionary powers had done much of his work for him, without having ever achieved, after 1789, the minimum social consensus necessary for any lasting effectiveness.

Naturally, the organization of executive power received all the First Consul's attention. Beside the government, whose members were appointed by him and responsible to him, there now existed the Council of State, the heir to the king's Council of State which had been so important in the running of the former monarchy. Moreover, its role was similar: to perfect bills before they were submitted to the Tribunate, whose task was to discuss them, and to deal at top level with any administrative litigation. The councillors, to whom junior officials and legal advisers were added later, were chosen most carefully by Bonaparte, who loved this competent and discreet top bureaucracy.

The same principle was applied at local level: Bonaparte retained the *départements*, increasing the numbers in line with his conquests, heading each with a prefect, whom he appointed and could dismiss, as on a lower level the sub-prefect of the *arrondissement*. Alongside them, a general council for the *département* and an *arrondissement* council enjoyed merely illusory powers. The prefect was both the representative and the departmental equivalent of the country's new head: he appointed the mayors of the small communes, while the First Consul directly designated those of the larger ones, so that nothing should be left to chance. Contemporary France was born amid this liquidation of local anarchies which had been inherited from the Revolution, and this posthumous reconciliation of Louis XIV and Robespierre.

The same centralizing and authoritarian spirit presided over the re-organization of other sectors of public life, where Bonaparte proved himself to be both the heir and the liquidator of the Revolution. He retained the hierarchy of courts established by the Constituent Assembly, but suppressed the eligibility of judges and limited the powers of juries to criminal matters. He considerably increased the role and numbers of the police, who under Fouché became one of the essential mechanisms of government.

In matters of finance, the work of the last years of the Directory was consolidated by the care given to the Treasury administration and taxes. The tax system remained based on the Constituent Assembly's three direct taxes, which yielded a fairly low amount, but its typically bourgeois character can be seen in the considerable rise in indirect taxes, which had been very light during the revolutionary decade. In order to combat Britain's economic supremacy, Bonaparte – more of a Colbertist than he thought – also endowed France with financial institutions: the law of 1805 fixed for over a century the gold weight of the 'Germinal franc'; above all, there was the creation of the Banque de France, a private company in the hands of the wealthiest bankers, but responsible for state treasurership.

Education also became a service unified by the state, and received its title in 1808 as the Imperial University. The new regime took no more interest than the Thermidorian Convention or the Directory in primary education, which was left to private initiative, most frequently on the part of the clergy; but it took great care of secondary education – the nursery of the bourgeois elite: the training of future state executives must not be left to chance. The Thermidorian 'central schools', once their pedagogic boldness had been removed, became those mournful secondary schools evoked by Musset in his *Confessions d'un enfant du siècle*, and much akin to the monarchy's Jesuit and Oratory colleges: places where the children were wakened by drumbeats to study the classics. In higher education, the great schools created by the Convention took precedence over the university faculties: this was a specific characteristic of French higher education, dating from the monarchy and persisting right down to the present day.

In short, all those names which are inseparable from national memory – prefects, Banque de France, lycées, *grandes écoles* – which flow from the pens of historians of that epoch, still evoke the France we are living in today, at the end of the twentieth century. The Consulate's weak point was its organization of public authorities, for it depended on the life of one man. The foundation of the modern administrative state was its durable part, since that was the result of a military energy enlightened by under-standing of civil history. It had its monument, crowning the legislative work of the Revolution and regulating relations between citizens of the new society in the Code Napoléon or Civil Code, the most important of the great post-Revolutionary legal Acts, which became the very symbol – both within the country and internationally – of France after 1789.

In the text of its promulgation, in 1804, there is a kind of celebration of a centuries-old ambition which has finally been realized, after so very many efforts: 'Roman laws, decrees, general or particular customs, statutes, regulations cease to have the force of general or special law in matters which are the subject of the said laws composing the present Code.' Thus, for all Frenchmen, there was but one Act governing the civil relations which bound them together, one single law for the nation. Here was an old monarchic enterprise, endlessly worked on by the kings' lawyers, constantly called for by the Estates-General, established as an imprescriptible rule by the rationalism of the Enlightenment, worked and reworked by the assemblies of the French Revolution.

The *ancien régime* had never succeeded in building a rational order out of the 'gothic' edifice of its various customs, one which would offer protection against the arbitrary by the uniformity of its measures, and be equally applicable to every citizen. But on this ground, the differing currents of eighteenth-century thought had been almost unanimous in recommending it, from jurisconsults to *philosophes*, from *Encyclopédistes* to physiocrats: Chancellor d'Aguesseau, Voltaire, Linguet and Turgot, all together. There is probably no other domain in which the causal chain linking the Revolution to Enlightenment philosophy and the spirit of the century can be more clearly seen than in that of civil legislation.

Besides, to a large extent, the old monarchy which had so often served the *philosophes* as a scapegoat, had set an example. But, imprisoned by tradition and the financial mechanisms which had tied it inseparably to particularisms and privileges, it had never been able to get to the bottom of the kingdom's juridical diversity; as de Tocqueville explained, the parts it had destroyed only made more odious the parts it had left or was endlessly trying to reconstruct. By overthrowing the corporate or, if you will, 'aristocratic' structure of old society, the 1789 Revolution had flung open the door to the French passion for laws, in which the rationalist universalism which is one of its dominant characteristics finds its finest expression. The new social world comprised only equal individuals, subject to the same laws which fixed their rights and obligations, and which – in case of litigation – the judge had to apply rather than interpret.

The reconstruction of civil legislation had begun at the time of the Constituent Assembly, when a whole series of important debates were devoted to paternal authority, the nature and limitations of the marriage contract, and the freedom to make one's will: even at that period, the dominance was apparent of the spirit of absolute equality of succession among heirs, without the testator's being able to favour any one of them – for fear that privilege for the eldest son might be reconstituted.

The object, written into the Constitution of 1791, was the establishment of a general code of civil law, which the Legislative Assembly inherited. The latter, as has been seen, was very quickly dragged into the slide towards war and the fall of the monarchy; nevertheless, before breaking up, it voted in September 1792 for the secularization of births, marriages and deaths and the institution of divorce. The hardest part of the work had been effected during the revolutionary years by the Convention's Committee for legislation, under the presidency of Cambacérès, the future Consul after 18 Brumaire.

A first project of the Code had been presented by him to the Convention in August 1793, during one of the most dramatic months in the Revolution's history. It bore the mark of the radical spirit of the time, decreeing for example not only equality of succession, but also the admission of recognized natural offspring to rights of inheritance identical with those of legitimate children; paternal power reduced to protective status; marriage and divorce only at the wish of partners who were of age; community of property to be the only matrimonial regulation.

A second bill, again presented by Cambacérès in September 1794 after the fall of Robespierre, put forward the three great principles of the future Code: liberty, property-ownership and the right of contract. The articles proposed did not go back on those of the preceding year. Under the Directory, in June 1796, Cambacérès advanced yet a third plan of the Code, discussion of which was again interrupted by the vicissitudes of the political situation, as if the Revolution, obsessed by problems of its very existence, could not manage to institute itself in civil legislation: these adjournments imposed by circumstance fairly symbolized its course. There had been nothing more unanimous or more definitive in its progress than the decrees of 4–11 August 1789; and in the ten years that followed property-owning individualism did not manage to write its code of statutes.

When Bonaparte got hold of the file, by order of the Consuls on 24 Thermidor (12 August 1800), many of the elements were ready: property, freedom of contract, secularization of births, marriages and deaths, divorce, etc. The new element introduced by the First Consul, apart from the ardour he put into the undertaking, was the search for a politico-legal compromise between revolutionary novelty and ancient customary laws.

The idea was already apparent among the men in charge of drawing up the Code, who would constitute the main working and editing group. The central figure was Portalis, one of the most distinguished barristers in the Aix-en–Provence parlement before 1789, an *ancien régime* jurist who had kept himself apart from the Revolution, and made his appearance only with the constitution of Year III; having returned to public affairs after Brumaire, he was one of the authorities of the Council of State. With him were Tronchet, who had defended Louis XVI, Bigot-Préameneu and Maleville, who had also learnt and practised the civil law of ancient customs and royal decrees.

At last, they were about to start work on realizing the old idea of unifying and setting customary law down in writing. At the same time, their action caused the re-emergence of the spirit of Montesquieu and a tradition of jurisprudence which had largely disappeared from view. But specialists from the revolutionary assemblies were also involved with the preparatory work on the Code, including former Jacobins like Cambacérès and Treilhard. In this way the homoeopathic synthesis which was one of the First Consul's secrets took effect: moderating the French Revolution with a pinch of *ancien régime*.

He had no need to go against his own nature to work out the correct balance. For, although the ultimate aim of his internal policy was to translate the principles of 1789 into laws, the basis of his temperament and upbringing was Corsican, patriarchal, inflexible over paternal authority, woman's subordination, and the primordial nature of the family and good morals. He was too aware of the new realities to refuse divorce, for that would be to reopen the door to Catholic Church authority over society, but he was sufficiently attached to the central value of marriage within the social order to make its dissolution less simple than by the will of the parties concerned. He frequently participated in discussion on the principles and the text, to which he attached extreme importance: the future Code was one of the great instruments of national reconciliation.

As it was promulgated in 1804, it affirmed the unity of a civil law applicable to the entire nation, and the state as the unique source of this law; but it left magistrates a certain latitude in the application of the general maxims, thus reintroducing the idea of jurisprudence into the Revolution's legicentric passion. Besides, the articles were often the result of digesting customary law, to the advantage of Parisian custom, which even before 1789 was the most widespread.

With regard to ownership of property, the drafters hardly had anything but land in view, and it was chiefly a matter of establishing the liquidation of seigneurial property. In these articles, which have so often been read anachronistically as heralding a capitalist economy, a rural France is confirming its rights; a France both bourgeois and peasant, which had emerged from a very long history, and was now liberated from the humiliating, costly and useless yoke of the seigneurs. There was no longer any distinction between lands and properties, which their possessors could enjoy and make use of 'in the most absolute manner'. Fifteen years after the great burgeoning of ideas in 1789, when the new France made its appearance amid the establishment of its interests, a nation of property-owning peasants fixed for ever their rights over the land. At the same time, it confirmed all that had been acquired between 1789 and 1792: a society of individuals, freedom of consciences, contracts and work, and the secularism of the state.

However, between 1789 and the Consulate, political evolution was reflected in a certain number of the articles drafted, which also illustrated the new civil law's slight shift towards conservatism: notably as regards the family. Divorce was retained, but kept within stricter limits. Paternal authority, called into question by the Convention, was reaffirmed; the *patria potestas* inherited from Roman law was restored, but limited to the age of majority and it was no longer permissible to disinherit a child by way of punishment. A natural child lost its right to be a full heir. Adoption remained possible, but that too was limited: the adopting person had to be childless and past the age of marriage.

Women were the principal victims of the Code's legislators, spurred on by the First Consul, who was very 'Mediterranean' in this respect: in his comments, he continualy insisted on the wife's subordination to her husband, which was essential to social order and was a part of the natural weakness of women. The latter were hit by not being allowed any part in the administration of household possessions, rendered dependent in everything concerning administrative or judicial acts, placed under the guardianship of their husbands, to whom they were inferior in rights in cases of both adultery and divorce. The equality of the sexes, proclaimed if not practised by the Convention, was denied by the Code Napoléon.

In the matter of equality of succession, the First Consul's jurists also reinterpreted the unconditional egalitarianism which had linked 1789 and 1793, in order to take into account the diversity of the old France's customs, and to give the head of the family the possibility of favouring an heir. This was an old peasant practice in written law in the French Midi, intended to maintain the continuity of farming businesses. The freedom given to testatory right, as also the coexistence of the dowry and communal estate systems, allowed a clever reconciliation of diverse and incompatible traditions according to the country's regions.

Such was the famous Code – a compromise between the spirit of enlightened despotism and the legacy of the ideas of 1789. The pride of the regime and of Napoleon, this symbol of the new France in Europe and the world was destined to have many imitators. It adjusted the law to the state of minds and morals, thereby rediscovering Montesquieu, whom it reconciled with the dominant rationalism. Basically the First Consul would always make it the monument of his fundamental treaty with the French, whom he understood so well.

The creation of the *Légion d'Honneur* (1802), intended to reward the good servants of the state, did not reinstate inequality; it simply honoured the best in equal competition. The idea of 'national morality', to which the law must be adapted, was so powerful in Napoleon's mind that it explained, a little later (1808), the way in which he treated French Jews, withdrawing from the principles of the Constituent Assembly. In his eyes, the Mosaic particularism of the Askenazim in Alsace was so contrary to French equality and civil unity that he subjected them to special legislation, chiefly in commercial matters, despite recognition by a solemn Assembly – the Grand Sanhedrin – of civil marriage and religious practices controlled by the state, like those of other beliefs.

Like the structures of the administrative state, the Code Napoléon is the Consulate's lasting legacy to modern France. In the two centuries which separate us from it, and most particularly during the course of the nineteenth century, political regimes would change, monarchies, Republics and even another Empire would come and go, but the country would not change its entire foundation, as it had in 1789; it had received its administrative institutions and the decisive features of its law for a long time to come.

The price paid for this national establishment of the principles of 1789 was the disappearance of a representative government, subject to the free choice of the citizens. Bonaparte had invaded the whole political theatre, and occupied it entirely on his own. The democracy of notables, both great and small, which emerged from the Revolution, had rebuilt a *de facto* monarchy, infinitely more powerful and despotic than the old one, since there was no longer any intermediary body to oppose its domination over equal individuals. In these first few years of the nineteenth century, it is easier than at any other time in our history to understand that equality had been the Revolution's ruling passion; and that Bonaparte reigned over France by embodying that alone.

Prisoners of the unforgettable memory of the popular dictatorship of Year II and of the European war, why would the French fear a strong man, if that man was born of their own history? In this sense, despite appearances, there had never been a less military *coup* than Brumaire; there had never been a more civil power than the consular dictatorship of the General-in-Chief of Italy and Egypt, since it was the profound movement of the whole of society which assured him of the conditions for his success and guaranteed for the future his reform of the state.

This national awareness, just as much as personal interests, explains the revolutionary personnel's general support for the Consulate: although the list of émigrés had been declared at an end some months after Brumaire, and Bonaparte had appointed several returned nobles to his administration or given some bishoprics to former refractory prelates, the framework of consular France was secured by men who had served successively and faithfully, like the First Consul himself, the 1791 regime, the dictatorship of the Committee of Public Safety and Robespierre, and Barras's Republic. Where political moralists denounce successive betrayals, here by contrast a fundamental loyalty to the struggle of revolutionary France is revealed.

Only a handful of liberal intellectuals or democratic Jacobins sulked over the Bonaparte of the Consulate; but the men of 1789 and 1793 filled the Council of State: Cambacérès, Roederer, Regnault de Saint-Jean-d'Angély, Boulay de la Meurthe, Antoine Thibaudeau, Treilhard. Bonaparte's ministers: Talleyrand, Carnot, Chaptal and Fouché came from the Constituent Assembly, the Convention, the Committee of Public Safety and the Terror. Since Year II, the army had been, *par excellence*, the body which enjoyed democratic promotion by ability; even the episcopacy, since the Concordat, had been almost completely renewed, as Bonaparte retained only sixteen pre-Revolution prelates.

What was true of the great state careers was probably even more so among the lesser ones, and more clear-cut the line which led the former militant of the Terror to a police commissariat, a sub-prefecture or a minor military rank. The Consulate's great internal strength lay in the fact that careers had been laid open to those with ability, and that Bonaparte was both its symbol and guarantor: it was the paradox of the little Corsican noble who, by the roundabout path of war, had become king of a property-owning France, proud of its state and its army.

TOWARDS THE EMPIRE

Rather than king, he was the precarious sovereign of a political situation, the new Caesar, without legitimacy and without a foreseeable heir, at the mercy of an assassin. He himself said so to his secretary, revealing that stay-at-home facet so surprising in an adventurous man, on that evening in February 1800 when he was moving to the Tuileries, leaving the Luxembourg of the ex-Directors: 'Bourrienne, getting into the Tuileries is not everything; I have to *stay* there.'

Moreover, the legitimate pretender to the throne had been very swift to demand his dues: from his distant Courland, where he had been forced to take refuge, the Comte de Provence had twice urged him to be his General Monk and to prepare the way for his restoration. Bonaparte had taken his time and replied only after Marengo, in September: 'Sir, I have received your letter, and thank you for the courteous things you say. You should not seek to return to France; you would have to walk over one hundred thousand corpses. Sacrifice your interests for the sake of France's peace and happiness. History will take account of your action.' And at the end he added these two sentences, in which can be seen both the habit he had already acquired of speaking as a sovereign, and the unbridgeable gulf which separated him from royalism: 'I am not insensitive to your family misfortunes. I will contribute with pleasure to the pleasantness and tranquillity of your retirement.' In private, as usual he employed a more military turn of phrase: 'The king is in Mitau – let him stay there!'

Brumaire's fundamental pact would therefore not be betrayed; but the first royalist response only narrowly missed the First Consul: that was the bomb explosion in December. However, excluding a royalist restoration was not enough to define the future of the consular regime, which was raising many queries. Before Marengo, a possible replacement had been sought; since then, questions were being asked about a successor. Each group, each clan, busied itself around the sphinx: who was to come after?

Very soon, the ten years promised to him by the Acts of Year VIII had seemed rather absurdly temporary, for a man who was so young and had so quickly become sovereign. The old idea of hereditary power inevitably reappeared under the new incarnation of the state. But what was the solution? Josephine was unable to give him an heir; she knew only that she must oppose the ambitions of the Bonaparte clan – and Joseph and Lucien, her old enemies, who wanted to take all the credit for themselves and be written in at the top of the will. But Lucien unmasked his guns too soon and had to leave the Ministry of the Interior for the embassy in Madrid. Bonaparte was not in too much of a hurry for talk of his succession: at thirty, without children or any hope of having any, why should he go and tie up his future with some ambitious man, creating his own rival? For one person chosen, how many malcontents would he make?

If he had no taste for contemplating his succession, he at least agreed to consolidate his power: less perhaps *vis-à-vis* the royalists, whose hostility he could not hope to break, than in relation to the rival ambitions of his army colleagues, the Bernadottes and the Moreaus. In that political society where his accession to supreme power had provoked among certain of his peers the inevitable 'Why not me?', the life Consulate accorded to him in August 1802 by the vote of three and a half million Frenchmen was an important grip on the future; he added to it the right to designate his successor.

This time, therefore, he was king of the Revolution – and of a Revolution so completely 'ended' that it abandoned even the shadow of an elective system: what was called the constitution of Year X reserved eligibility to a moneyed oligarchy, since the district assemblies, where everyone voted, would be compelled to choose the members of the *département* assembly from among the six hundred most highly taxed notables. This tightly *censitaire* college, elected for life, still only designated candidates to public or representative office, the choice being finally effected by the Senate or the First Consul himself. Thus, the institutional alterations of 1802, completed by the reduction of a somewhat recalcitrant Tribunate and the raising of a docile Senate, revealed the dual desire to create a stable government, to place it at the summit and to bind that government very closely to a property-owning society which had emerged from the Revolution. At bottom, the system was not so far removed from that imagined by Turgot, with his *municipalités*, or Necker, with his provincial assemblies; but in order to work, it would have needed the elimination of both the aristocracy and the king: notables to replace nobles, and a lifetime monarchy substituted for that of the Reims coronation.

It seemed, therefore, that in this lucky year of 1802 the contradictions of the French equation had finally been resolved by political consolidation of a recent society and a huge delegation of powers to the leader it had chosen. Internally, a real balance had been found. Once again, everything would depend on relations with Europe which brought to a climax the national adventure of France, henceforth dominated by yet another mystery, in the person of Bonaparte. It was not enough to end the Revolution on the inside: it still had to be brought to a close externally, which meant both defining its frontiers and getting them accepted by Europe. Was France able to? Did Napoleon want to? Was Europe ready for it? Would Britain give a lasting pledge? So many important questions, to which facts gave a negative reply, for war resumed in 1803. But they still divide historians: as always, it is easier to untangle the elements of Franco-British and Franco-European strife than to formulate a general interpretation of the conflict or to throw light upon the personality of its principal hero.

These elements are well known: Lunéville had brought back and aggravated the problems arising from Campo Formio, and the peace of Amiens (1802) had been signed, on both sides, only as a compromise without any true settlement. At no time, and on neither side, had there been any temptation to bring about a lasting coexistence between the revolutionary 'great nation' and the rest of Europe. Bonaparte made Britain unhappy by his wish to protect French space by customs barriers, and by resuming a colonial policy in Santo Domingo, Louisiana and even in India; he irritated the whole of Europe by developing the Thermidorian policy of sister republics in Holland, Switzerland and Italy: in 1802, he had himself elected President of the new Italian Republic, and kept tight control over the Batavian Republic and the Swiss Confederation.

The reorganization, to his advantage, of the German states, by the ordinance of 1803, foretold the liquidation of the old Germanic Roman Empire and of Habsburg influence. But the *casus belli* of 1803 was the Mediterranean problem: contrary to its undertakings of the preceding year, Britain refused to evacuate Malta; France retaliated by maintaining its garrisons in Naples and the ports of the Papal States. In short, there was a kind of mutual agreement to a break, which took place on 12 May 1803, when Britain recalled its ambassador in Paris. It was the start of the second Napoleonic venture.

But the first, which had brought him from his victories in Italy right to the Tuileries, came to a close only in 1804, since the war continued to determine French internal policy: it was the resumption of the war that influenced the last metamorphosis of Bonaparte's power, by inevitably reviving worries about his succession. Not only did war reawake the image of a leader vulnerable to the hazards of battle, but it also automatically cast doubt – as in 1792, in Year III and on the eve of Brumaire – on the entire revolutionary experience: it was therefore necessary to consolidate both, leader and Revolution, by pursuing the logic of a life Consulate to its very end, that is to say, by hereditary power.

For their part, the enemies of the French Revolution understood this logic, and put it into practice: the European courts still had an eye on Mitau, where Provence had given up none of his legitimate rights; Britain had gathered up Artois and his *chouan* killers who had escaped the 1801 net. In August 1803, it got Georges Cadoudal and his men to cross the Straits of Dover, with the mission of assassinating Bonaparte: British interests and royalist fanaticism had not had much difficulty in thinking up this thrifty way of putting an end to both the war and the Revolution. General Pichegru, deported as a royalist after 18 Fructidor, having escaped from Guiana and taken refuge in England, was brought into the plot; Moreau, the old rival, refused to commit himself to it when he was informed. His silence nevertheless indicated that Bonaparte's assassination was not, in France, merely a royalist idea, and that several republican

generals were ready to lend an indulgent ear. But an informer revealed the
plot to the police and everyone was put under lock and key in March 1804.
Pichegru committed suicide in prison, Moreau was banished; Cadoudal
and his accomplices were executed.

During the interrogation, one of the plotters revealed that the signal for
the attempt was to have been the presence on French soil of a prince of
Bourbon blood. Bonaparte had the ports watched, looking for the Comte
d'Artois. But in vain. It was then that Fouché informed him of the
presence of the son of the last Condé, the Duc d'Enghien, in the town of
Baden, some kilometres from the Rhine; simply on the assumptions of the
police, which in any case were imaginary, he had him arrested in a foreign
country, brought to Paris, tried and shot forthwith at dawn on 21 March in
the ditches of Vincennes. Bonaparte always claimed full and complete
responsibility for this crime of state, which had been suggested to him by
Fouché and in which others saw the hand of Talleyrand.

Even if he had been afraid, if he had retaliated like a man who has
sensed assassins prowling about him, he explained the Duc d'Enghien's
execution as a public safety measure, 'quite simply because blood-letting is
one of the devices of political medicine'. He never repudiated his comment
of 21 March: 'Those people wanted to sow disorder in France and kill the
Revolution in my person; I had to defend and avenge it. I showed what it
was capable of.' Why should we doubt these reasons of state? They express
the same reasoning as that of the assassins: regicide. Fouché's way of
thinking, certainly, since 1793, but also Bonaparte's – and now he had
his 21 January: he also had shed Bourbon blood, and by resuming on his
own account the collective action of the Convention, he had invested his
authority with the irreversible sacrament of the Revolution. The likelihood
of a compromise between himself and the *ancien régime*, between himself
and the Europe of the kings, was weaker than ever.

In fact, Bonaparte was thinking of taking the step from which even
Cromwell had recoiled: making himself king. In the spring of 1803,
through Talleyrand and the intermediary of Prussia, he had made
approaches with the aim of obtaining from the Comte de Provence the
renunciation of his rights to the throne. And it was just after the failure –
only to be expected – of this exploratory tactic, that he asked the Minister
of the Interior to plan the erection of a statue of Charlemagne in the Place
Vendôme. He was already striding across the fallen dynasty, to the glory of
the one which had preceded it.

The Duc d'Enghien's execution provided the opportunity. Eight days after
the Vincennes shooting, there came the Senate's first indication in favour
of the right of inheritance, and the Tribunate – by now duly brought to
heel – followed suit. The discussion had begun in the Council of State, and
the First Consul had not concealed his designs. On 22 Germinal (12 April
1804), in a conversation with Joseph, he confessed that he had 'always
intended to end the Revolution by the establishment of the right of

inheritance'.[11] This return to the past in order to guarantee the future offered several advantages. For right of inheritance, by fixing the manner of access to supreme authority, did away with a lacuna in the constitution of Year VIII. Although internally it founded a Bonapartist dynasty, this traditional method of transmitting power also weakened the very reasons for external threat, both royalist and terrorist. Yet on the other hand, it abandoned all reference to the Republic and the sovereignty of the people. At the very time when he was farthest from the kings of old Europe, Bonaparte wanted to found his domination on their principle. Therein lay the strangeness of the plan, and of the coronation, by which he distanced himself from the Revolution without drawing any nearer to the kings.

What was more, the problem was not simple from a technical viewpoint. The Consul had no children, or the hope of having any. He was not the eldest son, so there was no sense in instituting a rule of primogeniture; besides, any collateral succession presupposed a common predecessor, who did not exist. Hence arose family warfare with Joseph, his elder brother, to whom Napoleon preferred Louis, one of his three younger brothers, who was married to Josephine's daughter Hortense, through whom the hated Beauharnais yet again appeared among the Bonapartes. In the end, the future sovereign arranged to be given the right to adopt a successor, in default of which Joseph, then Louis, would be able to claim the crown. Lucien had been cast aside because of a marriage disapproved of by Napoleon. The principle of right of inheritance was therefore badly handled from the start, and in the right to choose a successor, Madame de Staël would soon denounce an oriental-style despotism.[12] In the Tribunate, Carnot voted against Curée's motion on the right of inheritance, declaiming against the risk represented by the desire to perpetuate a temporary dictatorship; he recalled the example of Caesar.

To tell the truth, the reactions of political people were mixed. If one takes into account the general climate of flattery which reigned in the Tuileries, they were often unenthusiastic. Miot de Mélito, Councillor of State from 1803 to 1806, whose wife was lady-in-waiting in Joseph's household, gives a melancholy assessment in his memoirs: 'So much blood spilt, so many fortunes destroyed, so many sacrifices . . . will have come to nothing more than giving us a change of master, substituting a family which was unknown ten years ago and was scarcely French at the time when the Revolution began, for a family which had reigned over France for eight centuries!'[13] Even in the heart of the army, feelings were also tormented. Roederer, who had followed the affair very closely, mediating between the First Consul and Joseph, noted in his journal that, among the troops he visited in Metz during June, there were 'feelings of repugnance towards emperorship':

[11] Miot de Mélito, *Mémoires*, vol. 2, p. 176.
[12] Madame de Staël, *Dix années d'exil*, part I, ch. 18.
[13] Miot de Mélito, *Mémoires*, vol. 2, p. 171.

People are humiliated to have gone the full circle of the Revolution just to come back to the same system; or to what is seen as the same system; people are ashamed to disavow what they have done and said against royalty and to forswear the attachment they had professed so strongly and in such good faith under the Republic. Therefore, it is not an aversion to the supreme dignity which torments us; it is the humiliation of admitting the aversion we have shown towards it, of calling it false and hypocritical, or absurd and contemptible, after showing such zest and enthusiasm.[14]

Nevertheless, the matter went forward quickly, since Napoleon wanted it. And on the whole, the Revolution's personnel followed, Roederer at the forefront. The Tribunate had therefore asked at the beginning of May that the title 'Hereditary Emperor of the French' be conferred on him. A new modification of the institutions, proposed by the *senatus consultum* of 18 May 1804, was ratified by an even more massive plebiscite than that of Year VIII, since fewer than ten thousand 'no' votes were counted. This was the last republican homage to what was a fourth dynasty, after the Merovingians, the Carolingians and the Capetians, which belonged to another political world.

THE CORONATION

The proof: the new emperor wanted a coronation. He harboured an idea which is often found even in liberal monarchic literature – Burke or Necker, for example – according to which power must be inseparable from an imposing apparatus of majesty, making a great impression on the people's imagination. The coronation must make a display of this splendour, by which Napoleon abandoned the universe of Washington to try to bring back to life the tradition of the kings: nothing less than to form a link with Charlemagne once more, since the Capetians had been excluded in 1789 from their history with the nation. The emperor himself explained this to Roederer after the stormy meeting of the Brumaire private Council, still in connection with Joseph's rights:

I have raised myself up by my actions, he has stayed at the point where birth placed him. To reign in France, one must be born in grandeur, have been seen from childhood in a palace with guards, or else be a man who is capable of standing out from all the others . . . Right of inheritance, if it is to be successful, must pass to children born in the bosom of greatness.

This gave rise to all that re-establishment of court life which accompanied coronation year, the creation of imperial 'houses', the rebirth of an aristocracy modelled on the old one, with precedences, distinctions

[14] P.-L. Roederer, *Autour de Bonaparte. Journal. Notes intimes et politiques d'un familier des Tuileries* (1909), p. 197.

and a ridiculous determination to rediscover the secrets of the etiquette surrounding kings. As recorded by Pelet de la Lozère:

'An old gentleman, a former page to the King was summoned from the provinces to impart the traditions of Versailles. His arrival in the Tuileries salon was a real event. Except at the theatre, it was a long time since anyone had seen personages from the old court, with their powdered and curled hair, and their frivolous, self-important airs; this gentleman appeared like an oracle who was going to reveal the secrets of past ages and, as they say, rejoin the links with the past. With his help, it was possible to rediscover the laws of ancient etiquette and to compile a volume of them as hefty as that of the Civil Code.'[15]

The coronation ceremony took place in Notre-Dame, on 11 Frimaire Year XIII (2 December 1804). Since the private Council of 3 Floréal (23 April), which had fixed the coronation date for 14 July,[16] and the *senatus consultum* of 28 Floréal (18 May), which fixed the oath to the people during the two years following the emperor's accession, the date and place of the ceremony had changed several times: 14 July, 27 Thermidor (15 August, Napoleon's birthday), 18 Brumaire (9 November); Champ de Mars, church of the Invalides were the dates and places suggested during the six months between the proclamation of the Empire and its celebration. The detailed history of these discussions illustrates very well the meaning which it was desired to attach to the coronation in relation to memories of the Revolution, new democratic legality and the civil authority of the state in the face of the Church of Rome's religious authority. In fact, these discussions intertwined with the diplomatic negotiations which had been opened with the Vatican to persuade the pope to attend the ceremony. At first somewhat reticent, as it wanted guarantees, then favourable, though on very precise conditions, the papal court strewed the negotiations with uncertainties to a point where it unleashed a sort of ultimatum from the French. The result of these laborious discussions would be a very strange, absolutely unique, ceremonial: Napoleon's coronation had no precedent and would have no imitators.

Things went the same way regarding the place. The choice of Notre-Dame was belated. It won the day over the church of Saint-Louis des Invalides, originally proposed by the decree of 21 Messidor (10 July), for practical reasons such as the amount of space available, but also for symbolic reasons, such as its 'more august nature, more suitable for surrounding the ceremony with a sort of divine respect'.[17] But at the start, the idea had been to use the Champ de Mars. Discussed in the Council of State, defended by Regnault de Saint-Jean-d'Angély, this proposal was strongly rejected by the emperor:

---

[15] Pelet de la Lozère, *Opinions de Napoléon sur divers sujets de politique et d'administration, recueillies par un membre de son Conseil d'État*, p. 69.

[16] Miot de Mélito, *Mémoires*, vol. 2, p. 183.

[17] Pelet de la Lozère, *Opinions*, p. 89.

Jacques Louis David The Coronation of Napoleon I *1806–1807, Musée du Louvre, Paris. (Photo: Lauros-Giraudon)*

The Champ de Mars was thought of as a reminder of the Federation, but times have changed: then the people were sovereign, everything had to be done before their eyes: let us be careful not to let them think things are still the same. The people today are represented by legal powers. In any case, I should not like to think that I was seeing the people of Paris, still less the people of France, in twenty or thirty thousand fishwives, or others of that ilk, who would invade the Champ de Mars: they would just be the ignorant and corrupt populace of a large town. The real people, in France, are the presidents of the cantons, and of the electoral colleges; they are the army, in whose ranks are soldiers from every commune in France![18]

As for the setting, planned by the architects Percier and Fontaine, the work inside the cathedral organized space around two centres. On the one hand, the chancel, blocked off by a dais, and on the other, the great imperial throne, at the entry to the nave. This division of the places matched the two parts of the ceremony. The first, essentially religious, which joined the consecration with the crowning according to the pope's wishes, would take place in the cathedral chancel. To the left of the altar, which was reached by eleven steps, the pope's throne was installed. The cardinals took their places on the right. On either side of the chancel were the archbishops, bishops and clergy of Paris. In the middle were the chairs, cushions and prie-dieu for the emperor and his wife, who was playing a leading part in the rite despite the grumbles of the Corsican tribe. The second part of the ceremony, secular and constitutional, would take place at the other end of the church, at the entrance to the great nave. There the grand throne was situated, at the summit of a stairway of twenty-four steps, under a triumphal arch decorated with eagles and hung with red velvet drapery. The Paris cathedral was decked out in the taste of the day, a Greek temple to celebrate the new Alexander.

Apart and opposite to each other, the two spaces were linked, so to speak, by the continuity of the nave, where six thousand invited guests had their places. Starting from the emperor's great throne, on both sides down the steps were ranged ministers, high officials, Councillors of State and presidents of the Legislative Body and the Tribunate. The hierarchy of the Empire in its entirety was seated in descending order of dignity as one approached the altar. Near the great throne, therefore, were senators, legislators, tribunes, members of the Appeal Court, great officers of the Légion d'Honneur, in short, all the constituted authorities, both national and provincial. Raised platforms, to right and left of the throne, were reserved – according to *ancien régime* custom – for high-ranking guests, members of the court and the diplomatic service.

Invited by sealed letter to attend the coronation ('Divine providence and the constitution of the Empire, having placed the imperial dignity in our family . . .'), the arrival of the guests in the cathedral marked the commencement of the solemn function. But the real start of the ceremony

[18] Ibid.

was tied to the arrival of the pope. According to protocol, Pius VII would have to leave the Tuileries where he was staying in the Pavillon de Flore, at nine in the morning. After being welcomed in rather cavalier fashion by the emperor who, while hunting at Fontainebleau, had feigned a chance meeting, Pius VII continued to be the object of a protocol intended to limit his symbolic importance. It had thus been decided that he would arrive at Notre-Dame ahead of Napoleon. But outside the cathedral, on the Seine side, Percier and Fontaine had erected a wooden gallery, decorated with eagles with spread wings, in order to link the archbishop's palace to the church.

Pius VII would first be received by the archbishop of Paris, then in the great hall of the palace he would don his papal vestments. The first diminution of his splendour: using the pretext of the narrowness of the gallery along which he would have to pass to reach the church, French diplomats had persuaded the pope to give up the use of the *sedia gestatoria* borne by twelve grooms in red damask. Thus Pius VII made his entrance under a white canopy, but on foot. He was preceded by the bishops, wearing their mitres, and arranged by order of their canonical institution by the pope, and not according to the order of their consecration following their appointment by the temporal sovereign, as the emperor would have liked.

Napoleon's arrival was planned to be one hour after that of the pope. But on the appointed day, the wait was much longer – which compounded the Vatican's grievances. Accompanied by Josephine, Napoleon was late in getting to the archbishop's palace, where he donned the coronation robes. This costume, established by decree on 29 Messidor (18 July), was composed of a crimson velvet robe, scattered with golden bees; sprays of olive, laurel and oak were embroidered around the letter N. The long mantle, lined with ermine, was to be the sign of the unique power and extraordinary pre-eminence of the emperor over all the other princes in the family and the great dignitaries of the Empire. Indeed, some weeks before the coronation, Napoleon had ordered that no one but he should wear a long cloak.[19]

Heaven knows how full the cathedral of Paris was that day of princes and dignitaries of the new Empire! Their titles commingled the tradition of the old French monarchy and the grandeur of the Holy Roman Empire. There was a Grand Elector, Joseph; an Arch-Chancellor, Cambacérès; an Arch-Treasurer, Lebrun; also a Constable, Louis; a Grand Admiral, Murat; a Grand Equerry, Armand de Caulaincourt; and a Grand Chamberlain, Talleyrand – not to mention all those Marshals of France, who were most devoted to Republican principles but who bore the title Monseigneur in order to ensure that the imperial divinity had the title Majesty, as Napoleon explained it to Roederer. Nevertheless on that day none of them had the right to wear a long cloak.

---

[19] Miot de Mélito, *Mémoires*, vol. 2, p. 234.

The allocation of places and roles had of course been the subject of bitter arguments over precedence, whereby the France of Napoleon I reanimated, with a different public, that of Louis XIV. The most violent disputes had brought the women of the family into opposition, the Bonapartes and the Beauharnais. The sisters, Elisa, Pauline and Caroline, were in a permanent rage about the place given to Josephine. They finally agreed to carry the never-ending train (23 metres!) of the empress's cloak only on condition that they should merely 'hold it up', and that they too should have attendants for their own 'train'.

The emperor's crimson mantle, open on the left side, revealed the sword, supported by a white satin scarf embroidered in gold. Napoleon thus made his entrance already wearing the symbols of power. The golden crown of laurel on his head, the sceptre in his right hand and the hand of justice in his left, indicated that he already possessed full sovereignty. This was a remarkable innovation in comparison with the tradition of the royal coronation – from which many ceremonies had been omitted, such as the 'lever du roi', and the old ritual preceding arrival in the church, when the king had to appear clad in a simple tunic and totally divested of the emblems of power. This ritual simplification revealed the desire to expunge all trace of ecclesiastical investiture from the imperial coronation. It also indicated the amount of liberty taken in regard to the historic tradition of the Capetian monarchy.

The visual symbol of the dual historical reference which the Empire had chosen, Clovis and Charlemagne dominated the triumphal arch in which the wooden gallery ended, and which concealed Notre-Dame's portal on the forecourt side. The arch was overhung with the emperor's arms and the figures of the sixteen cohorts of the Légion d'Honneur: a sign that military synthesis joined the founder of a dynasty with the 'philosopher prince, legislator, patriot and conqueror'.

A legacy of the republican interpretation of Mably, Charlemagne lent himself perfectly to the Empire's political plan, offering it an inaugural link. He allowed the new monarchy to be defined by bestowing on it a past which was not the detested *ancien régime*, but a venerable tradition which eighteenth-century philosophy had elaborated. Napoleon had for some time had an eye on this tradition, because he had intended to erect a statue of Charlemagne on the column in the Place Vendôme; in the months preceding the coronation, he had ordered medieval relics of his great predecessor to be collected, and he had gone to meditate on the tomb at Aix-la-Chapelle.

On the day of the coronation, the protocol planned for great splendour to surround the insignia representing the 'honours of Charlemagne'. There was a golden crown, fashioned in accordance with old designs, and held by Kellermann; a sword, carried by Lefebvre; a sceptre, by Pérignon. Napoleon's 'honours', which were entrusted to Bernadotte, Eugène de Beauharnais (Napoleon's stepson) and Berthier, included an object unprecedented in the coronation of former kings: an imperial globe, to evoke

Ingres' portrait of Napoléon, *Musée de l'Armée, Paris.*
(*Photo: Roger-Viollet*)

the Holy Roman Empire. When the emperor arrived in the cathedral, the Marshals carried the 'honours' to the altar, where they laid them down; then they stood just opposite, where they can still be seen, immortalized in David's painting of the event.

Did the idea of a universal monarchy also enter into this Carolingian kitsch through which Napoleon was showing that he belonged to nobody but himself? At all events, the other dominating feature of the ceremony was the limiting of the role of the Roman pontiff. The emperor had wished him to be present at the coronation, in order to receive the unction at his august hands, but also to have him there at Napoleon's triumph in a subordinate position.

By going to the altar on his own, he did not subject himself to the pope's traditional admonition to the sovereign. In response to the ritual inter-rogation, everything had been cut out of his profession of faith as a Christian sovereign concerning the promise to maintain the Church's possession of goods which it no longer had: this concession was agreed by the Holy Father on condition that he was not obliged to be present at the swearing of the constitutional oath which was to follow the religious ceremony. After the profession of imperial faith ('Profiteor', Napoleon said quite simply) came the prayers, the pope kneeling, his mitre on his head, the emperor and Josephine remaining seated on the small thrones; then the sovereign couple received the triple unction.

At that point the solemn mass began, during which the insignia were blessed – hand of justice, ring and sceptre – and the coronation, properly speaking. Napoleon ascended to the altar, took the crown and placed it on his own head. Then, he took the empress's crown, stood before her and put it on her head; meanwhile the pope recited the prayer used by the archbishop of Reims at the coronation of the kings of France. The suggestion that this was an improvised action (an idea substantiated by Adolphe Thiers and the Comte d'Haussonville in the nineteenth century) is incorrect: Pius VII had agreed to it beforehand on the eve of the ceremony. The Minister of the Interior, Champagny, had impressed upon him that

the emperor also wants to take up the crown in order to avoid any argument between the great dignitaries of the Empire, who would claim to be giving it to him in the name of the people. He thinks that His Holiness blessing the crown and saying a prayer while the emperor places it on his head will be considered an adequate fulfilment of the ancient ceremonial.

Thus crowned, the imperial couple, surrounded by princes, dignitaries, and the grand officers carrying the insignia of the emperor and of Charlemagne, left the chancel for the cathedral entrance, where the great throne was situated. The pope rejoined Napoleon there and enthroned him, using the Reims formula. Then he returned towards the altar, amid *vivats*, and intoned the Te Deum, before the end of the Mass: this was a fundamental detail, and for once a concession from the emperor, for it allowed him to make his departure once the Mass was over and not to be present for the constitutional oath which was to close the ceremony. But beforehand he would have to accept a final infringement of the religious element: the written record of the coronation makes no allusion whatsoever to the communion of the emperor and his wife. In fact, after at first accepting the idea of taking the sacrament, at the last moment Napoleon had insisted on being excused from it: this was an exorbitant demand, which incidentally cancelled the religious value of the unctions, but which Pius VII had had to accept.

The Mass ended, the pope left the cathedral. He removed his vestments in the sacristy, while preparation was made to celebrate the secular part of the inaugural rite. The constitutional oath took place around the great throne. The Grand Almoner brought the gospel to the emperor. The Grand Elector, Prince Joseph, who in the end had yielded to his brother's will, presented to him the president of the Senate (Neufchâteau), the most senior president of the Council of State (Defermon), the president of the Legislative Body (Louis de Fontanes) and the president of the Tribunate (Fabre de l'Aude). They placed the form of oath before the emperor, then lined up to the left of the throne. Napoleon, wearing the crown, his hand raised over the gospel, took the oath while seated. He swore

to maintain the integrity of the Republic's territory, to respect, and cause to be respected, the laws of the Concordat and the freedom of worship, equality of rights, civil and political liberty, the irrevocability of the sales of *biens nationaux*; neither to levy nor to introduce any tax, except in accordance with the law; to maintain the institution of the Légion d'Honneur; to govern with the sole aim of the interests, happiness and glory of the French people.

It was a promise to end the Revolution without betraying its heritage.

Fresh acclamations were followed by an artillery salvo. The clergy came back to the throne with the canopy to conduct the sovereigns to the archbishop's palace once more. Then the emperor's procession, followed by the pope's, went through the streets of Paris. The itinerary led to the Châtelet across the Pont au Change, then to the boulevards and the Place de la Concorde. Michelet, who was six years old, was among the crowd. Fifty years later, in his volumes on *L'Histoire du XIXe siècle*, he recollected having noticed nothing on that day other than a 'mournful and dismal silence'.

THE NEW ORDER

From that point begins a history which cannot be separated from what went before, because the same man fills its entire space; yet it is quite distinct, both at home and abroad. One can understand this watershed, starting from the coronation ceremony, which provides an excellent symbol. Napoleon I was no longer the king for life of the French Republic, as he had been since 1800, but was now hereditary absolute sovereign, surrounded by a court and soon by a new aristocracy. The emperor had a foreign policy which less and less could be defined in terms of revolutionary heritage or even national tradition. In the Carolingian myth lies the mystery of great conquerors and nothing else, so that a large part of that extraordinary life belonged just as much, if not more, to the memory of Europe as to that of France. Everything lasting – or almost everything – that Bonaparte did in national history had been accomplished between 1800 and 1804. Nothing of all his upheaval of frontiers and the country's international situation survived his fall. When he came to grief in 1814, the Bourbons found the same territory belonging to the kingdom that they had left a quarter of a century before.

Let us start the inventory from the inside. Madame de Staël had described the Empire as a despotism which was 'oriental and Carolingian both together', operating a counter-revolution. She meant it firstly in the political sense, to depict the authority's autocratic nature, the generalized police surveillance, the meticulous check kept on opinion and the ever-increasing numbers of 'prisoners of state': after all, liberty was also part of the promises of 1789. But she meant, too, that

Bonaparte conceived the idea of making the counter-revolution work to his own advantage, by preserving nothing new in the state, so to speak, apart from himself. He re-established the throne, the clergy and the nobility: a monarchy, but without legitimacy and without limit; a clergy who preached nothing but despotism; a nobility made up of old and new families, but who had no authority in the state, and served merely as an ornament to the absolute power.[20]

In short, in this return of 'old prejudices', Madame de Staël saw the *ancien régime* being restored by the man who had been the Revolution's most brilliant soldier.

Was she right? No, not entirely. For even amid the Carolingian bric-à-brac of the coronation, the civil ceremony and the swearing of the oath of fidelity to the great conquests of 1789 had survived. The emperor had guaranteed the civil and political liberty of the French; he kept only the first part of the undertaking (in any case, who could have nurtured any illusions about the second?), but , in that part, he abandoned nothing vital. He remained the guarantor of the sold *biens nationaux*, and therefore of the despoilment of clergy and émigrés. He upheld the new civil right of free and equal individuals, recognized and organized minority religions (Protestant and Jewish), codified criminal investigation and criminal law. It is true that he re-established a court and increased pensions, distinctions and emoluments; but since none of these advantages included any legal privileges and were not hereditary, they sanctioned the new meritocracy, which was mostly military, to which they gave the character of public

---

[20] Madame de Staël, *Considérations sur la Révolution française*, part IV, ch. 11.

service. The dialectic of equality and status wove Napoleonic society together more closely than ever.

In fact, Madame de Staël's criticism is better applied to what the emperor became after 1808, the date of the *senatus consultum* which re-established a true nobility: a nobility of office, which he granted for services rendered, but hereditary, bound up with the great fiefs which he granted in his vassal states, or with *majorats*, domains which were trans-missible to the eldest son. His divorce from Josephine and the Habsburg marriage in 1810 accentuated the evolution towards the aristocratic spirit of the *ancien régime*. The court was increasingly filling up with former nobility. It was at this period that the emperor said to Mathieu Molé: 'Those doctrines which are called the principles of 1789 will always be a threatening weapon to be used by malcontents, the ambitious and ideol-ogists at any time.' Nevertheless, even during the years of his Austrian marriage, even after the birth of the King of Rome in 1811, Napoleon would never manage to give his Empire true dynastic legitimacy, guarded by a serving aristocracy. His domination over France retained, as its fundamental bases, the guarantee of the new civil law and military glory. It remained dependent on his victories. By making himself emperor, and even by marrying Marie-Louise, he had not gained entry into the family of the kings.

But had he really wanted to? What typifies Napoleon I's history between 1804 and 1814 is not what he did inside the country: the meeting, then the wedding, of the Corsican general with France had already been celebrated, and had already produced their fruits when the young chief of the consular Republic decided to become emperor. What began then – or rather, what had begun in 1803, when war with Britain had resumed – was his affair with Europe. It was perpetual, victorious war, impossible to halt, right up to the point of defeat. The venture of the great conqueror had definitively supplanted the founder of the modern French state; the authoritarian organizer of a nation of property-owners had given way to the emperor who wanted to redesign the history of the civilized world. The two personalities had always coexisted in Bonaparte, but the Carolingian Napoleon of the coronation revealed a sovereign who had become largely independent of the French Revolution. The Brumaire contract had been fulfilled; the emperor's destiny unfolded outside France, like an adventure without end.

Nevertheless, in this series of events, before speaking about him, the Revolution must still have its share. Napoleon had inherited from it a very large army, recruited by conscription, on the terms of Jourdan's law of 1798; as well-off young men could escape the military obligation by paying a replacement, this national army was largely a peasant army: Napoleon would take more than a million men from the French countryside. The fall in the birthrate, which manifested itself in the last decades of the eighteenth century, had not yet affected the age groups which could be called up. Viewed from this angle, the Empire's wars could appear to be supplementary employment offered to the numerous children of old rural France, and an indirect encouragement to wage rises, since there were fewer workers available. But there is less reason to conclude the demographic or economic 'necessity' since many other factors had simultaneously contributed to the reduction of French overpopulation: the drop in the number of children per family and the increase in peasant ownership through the purchase of *biens nationaux* must have led in this directon.

Still more, the economic revival and relative prosperity which marked the end of the Directory, and chiefly the 1800s: good harvests, return to metal coin, then to confidence, industrial and commercial revival, widening of offers of employment, rise in profits and wages. It would therefore seem difficult to think that post-revolutionary France should find itself in the economic impossibility of demobilizing its army and restoring several hundreds of thousands of soldiers to their civilian activities. Certainly, French ascendancy in Europe would not have been possible without the strong demographic growth of the eighteenth century; but the latter is not enough to explain the former.

In truth, reasons of another kind, but perhaps more decisive, contribute to an understanding of the realities and the dreams on which the France of this era fed its soldiers. The reality was social promotion: Napoleon himself was its symbol *par excellence*, the little Corsican officer who had become emperor and yet still remained the *Petit Caporal*, the imaginary brother of all those men whose wounds and battles mapped out their advancement, the abrupt departure from rural life in quest of adventure, the achievement of rank, sometimes even honours. Glory was also a career. Everything had begun with the volunteers of Year I and the *levée en masse*, and the framework of the army remained ensured by the heroes of the threatened Republic, who ten years afterwards had become young veterans. How could they envisage a future other than the very recent glory of the past. Neither 9 Thermidor nor 18 Brumaire nor even the coronation of 2 December had very deeply stirred this republican army, if it is true that the opposition of a Moreau or a Bernadotte to the Empire stemmed more from individual jealousy than from ideology. The soldiery had intervened in public life only on 18 Fructidor, precisely in order to rescue the threatened Republic. The other great internal ruptures in French political life had not put the army's future in doubt.

That future was not confined to an individual promotion, and this army – which was both the seed-bed and the crowning achievement of abilities – was not a professional army; it was the incarnation of the national dream, the great liberating nation struggling against the tyrants of the people. The transfer of French messianism to the army, which was as old as the revolutionary war itself, had become more pronounced in step with the dwindling of popular passions within France: it has been seen that, after Thermidor, the syndicate of regicides governing the Republic were all the more in favour of war since they had disarmed the Parisian faubourgs; they could not wrest the Terror away from the sansculottes unless they preserved for them at least the war with the Europe of the kings.

After Brumaire, in the vast silence of internal political life, the psychological and ideological attachment to the Republic as liberator of the people was invested in the former General-in-Chief of Italy, and it was not by chance that, in the first years of the Empire, there existed this dual designation of the state, 'French Republic. Emperor Napoleon'. Napoleon had not stopped being the great Republic's authorized representative. The hero of the international war was approved by a vast majority for the same reasons as the man of the civil peace; that powerful authority, that glorious dynasty, which together exorcised both the Terror and the return of the kings were, at the same time, conditions and symbols of the French mission in the world. Internally, France had made peace with the past. But it was still combating the *ancien régime* outside its frontiers.

Nevertheless, there is no doubt that French opinion had greeted Lunéville, then Amiens, with satisfaction; but at the cost of a misunderstanding. Because, for France, it was a matter of a victorious peace, that is to say, implicit recognition by Europe and England of the 'great nation' and its universal mission. Now, it looked as if nothing had changed; in December 1802, less than a year after the signing of the peace of Amiens, at the news that the Comte d'Artois, 'wearing an order of a monarchy which England no longer recognizes', had reviewed a regiment, Bonaparte asked Talleyrand to make representations in London

that it is a matter touching our dignity and, we make bold to say it, the honour of the British government that the princes should be expelled from England, or that, if it is desired to give them hospitality, they should not be allowed to wear any order of a monarchy which England no longer recognizes; that it is a permanent insult offered to the French people: that the time of tranquillity has come in Europe.

This 'tranquillity' was so little in evidence that, hardly had the war resumed, when Britain was paying assassins for the Bourbons against the usurper of Paris. This was what made Bonaparte say, on the morning of the Duc d'Enghien's execution: 'I will never consent to peace with England until it expels the Bourbons, as Louis XIV expelled the Stuarts, because their presence in England will always be dangerous for France.' What the First Consul was expressing in terms of dynasty – at bottom, in the same language as his assassins – was merely the translation of the popular conviction according to which there would never be peace between the liberating Republic and the oppressor kings. For peace continued to mean for everyone the return of the kings, and war meant the Republic's victory. In this sense, the Empire, built on a pyramid of notables, remained a peasant and democratic royalty: that would be very clear in the Hundred Days.

Although this war was democratized by a revolutionary ideology which mixed nationalism and universalism, if its ruthless nature arose from its being a conflict of values, the fact remains that it had other sources, from before and after the Revolution. Harking back, the Anglo-French conflict was age-old, marked by French losses at the Treaties of Utrecht (1713) and Paris (1763); economic and colonial rivalries had often roused public opinions against each other, and the sterile egoism of the London plutocracy was a physiocratic theme before becoming a revolutionary aphorism.

The British industrial revolution, which had taken off in the 1780s, had increased London's economic pressure on foreign markets; the political fears which the Revolution of 1789 had swiftly aroused had been reinforced by French expansion in Europe during the Directory years, and by the protectionist and colonial policy of the Consulate: a French Belgium, a 'Protected' Holland, western and Mediterranean Europe tied to French manufactures, the reconquest of Santo Domingo and the short-lived French aspirations in Louisiana – here were a number of factors which were unacceptable to British trade, even in the short term. If the peace of Amiens was broken on account of Malta, it was also because all that had weighed heavily in the side of the scale tipping towards war. The problem of colonial hegemony would quickly be solved, to Britain's advantage; but the stake of the European market would stay at the centre of the Anglo-French struggle, superimposed on the ideological war: a vast stake on the British side, because of its precocious industrial development and its trade structure, and certainly less on the French side, in that territorial domination of Europe did not appear as a necessity written into the still modest turnover of industrial production and national exports. The emperor's neo-Colbertist policy was more a consequence than a cause of his policy, pure and simple.

His policy: this was the great problem, downstream of the revolutionary torrent which had swept him into power. What did he want, this awesome and accidental heir of an exceptional moment in the nation's history? The interminable war against the *ancien régime*, which had brought him to the imperial throne, had also transformed his republican princedom into a royal dictatorship which hung upon his character and his destiny. It was from the time of the coronation in 1804, when his domination over the Revolution became royalty, that it most perceptibly eluded a definition of ends and means; when he was hereditary king he was most independent of revolutionary France, but also the most subjected to what must be termed his 'star'.

His policy: this was the great problem. Internally, it increasingly revealed, day after day, the corruption effected on his domineering nature by the exercise of absolute power, his mania for controlling and deciding everything, his overestimation of his luck and his strength, the development of a police tyranny of which Louis XIV would not have dared to dream. But the French, prisoners of his glory still more than of his police, had no alternative political future: the Bourbons would bring back the nobles; the Republic, the Terror or disorder. The Empire's destiny was being acted out beyond its frontiers, that is to say, in the mystery about Napoleon's intentions and the luck of his wars.

What *did* he want? What had he wanted? Nothing more than his chimera: 'I am destined to change the face of the world; at least, I believe so. Perhaps some ideas of fatalism are mingled with this thought, but I do not reject them; I even believe in them, and this confidence gives me the means of success.'[21] It is easier to define what he had at his command, which explains the wide margin of superiority he enjoyed in comparison with each of his adversaries, taken in isolation. He was master of a modern state, centralized and efficient, and could mobilize all its resources to the best advantage; he was the head of a society founded on civil equality, in which both the administration and the framework of the army were recruited from all strata of the social body. In short, no technological secrets – it was Britain that had those – but a social secret: an eighteenth-century country and army, which had been freed by the revolutionary explosion and rationalized by enlightened despotism.

However, the most important secret was his genius for action and tireless energy, which he threw into dominating the world: for if the Revolution had never clearly defined the objectives of its war – Danton had had his own, as had Carnot and Sieyès – he was even less able to do so. He had learnt war, he had encountered it, had been born of it and had ceaselessly modelled his life on it; doomed not only not to make peace, but also never to lose a battle, he repeatedly laid out on history's table a stake which also continually grew larger.

In this connection, Bonaparte-Charlemagne remained identical with Bonaparte-Consul, obsessed with the unique adventure of his existence. If his army became increasingly a professional one, if he married a daughter of the Habsburgs, if he dreamed of a universal empire, he nevertheless remained at the mercy of fate. The minute he laid down his arms in 1814, his son and heir disappeared with him from the world's stage. Basically, only his administrative reorganization of France had any solidity, born of necessity; that was the bourgeois part of his life. The remainder was the improvisation of an incomparable artist, who drove deep furrows through the history of Europe but in the end reduced France's frontiers to those of the first years of the Revolution.

The fact remains that all those events from which this improvisation was woven formed the history of Europe and of France within Europe: let us now briefly go over the principal features of that history.

TRIUMPH AND DISASTER

In 1803, at the time of the break-up of the Amiens peace, Bonaparte found himself – exceptionally and for a very short while – facing a sole adversary,

---

[21] Napoléon to Joseph, November 1804, in Miot de Mélito, *Mémoires*.

since he had won a vassal Holland and a weak Spain to his camp. Here, then, was his great plan, which he had already studied in 1798 between Italy and Egypt: to land in England and bring the war to a definitive close in its very heart, in London. During the whole of 1804, at the same time that he was making himself emperor, he continued to press on with preparations for the Boulogne camp, the building of invasion barges, the inventory of necessary equipment. Evidence of his typical style of conducting a war lies in this note to Marshal Soult in April 1805: 'Let me know whether, within a fortnight, horses, provisions, men and everything can be embarked. Do not give me a metaphysical reply to this question, but go and look at the stores and the different warehouses.' But in order to land and get to London quickly without being cut off from the rear, Napoleon needed control of the Channel, at least for several weeks: whence the orders given to French and Spanish squadrons to attract the British fleet – which was superior in numbers and still more in quality – towards the distant Antilles.

The plan overestimated the value of the French fleet, together with that of its crews and its command. Admiral Villeneuve, head of the strongest squadron, refused to confront Nelson in the Caribbean seas and recrossed the Atlantic, only to be ingloriously blockaded at Cadiz. The emperor had never been able to gain the freedom of the Channel. In any case, in the middle of 1805, it was too late: Pitt, having returned to power, had bought a Russian alliance, and Austria, Naples and Sweden joined the Anglo-Russian treaty during the summer, to form a new coalition (the third since 1793) against France. Napoleon, deferring the British plan – which he would never take up again – swung his Boulogne troops towards the Rhine, marching to the aid of Bavaria, his ally: it was the most classic of his campaigns, in which luck – his old partner – completely gave way to his genius.

By means of rapid troop movements, he was able to beat the enemy armies separately – the main one was barring the route to Vienna. Within a month the Grand Army was at the Rhine: it was an admirable instrument of war, the best that Napoleon would ever have, troops with experience and enthusiasm, who were rested and confident; surrounded in Ulm, the Austrian General Mack capitulated on 20 October, and Napoleon was sleeping at Schönbrunn less than a month later. Emperor Francis II had given up the defence of Vienna in order to link up with the Russian army more to the east in Moravia: on 2 December 1805, the anniversary of his coronation, in the presence of the three Emperors, Russians and Austrians were cut to pieces near the village of Austerlitz.

Meanwhile, the triumphs of Ulm and Austerlitz had been offset by Trafalgar (21 October 1805): Villeneuve, lashed by Napoleon's reproaches, had rashly left Cadiz only to be annihilated by Nelson. Temporarily, the imperial publicity services shielded Trafalgar behind Ulm, Vienna and Austerlitz, but the elimination of the French fleet was to be a most important factor of the European conflict: it condemned Napoleon to an inability to attack Britain except in continental Europe. Indeed, an entire reorganization of Europe was already being outlined, with the collapse of Austria: the Treaty of Pressburg, in December 1805, hardened the terms of Campo Formio and Lunéville by doing away with all Austrian influence in Italy; the Habsburgs were similarly ousted from Germany, to the profit of the Electors of Bavaria, Württemberg and Baden.

The end of the Holy Roman Empire gave birth, in July 1806, to a Confederation of the Rhine, of which Napoleon became the 'Protector' and which was entered by the 'vassalized' princes laden with the spoils of Francis II. Thus the Elector of Bavaria took the title of king, and princes were quite simply 'created', like Napoleon's brother-in-law, Murat, who became Grand Duke of Berg. The eldest brother, Joseph, had been 'appointed' to Naples a little earlier, to replace the Bourbons who had been deposed by decree and had taken refuge in Sicily. The family had started acquiring crowns.

Until then, Prussia had not made a move, being content to occupy British Hanover, which had been left to its covetous grasp, while the Tsar had returned home. But the German reorganization upset Berlin all the more because, in the course of unofficial negotiations between France and Britain in the summer of 1806, Napoleon proposed to the British the restitution of Hanover: Frederick William III did a volte-face and turned against France, on the side of the Russians. Since Valmy, France had never confronted this fearsome army, the terror of the eighteenth century, heir of the great Frederick: now, in six days and two battles, Jena and Auerstädt, it had ceased to exist, together with the state whose backbone it had formed; on 27 October 1806 Napoleon entered Berlin.

There remained the Russians, in the strength of their endless plains, who were already posing formidable strategic problems to Napoleon: the emperor was a man for short distances, good roads and lightning concentrations of troops. Now this lover of speed, this Mediterranean man full of nervous energy, dragged out his lines interminably across the great frozen plains of the north. At the end of a terrible campaign, he carried off a dubious and bloody success at Eylau in February 1807, conquered eastern Prussia and freed Poland, and finally beat the Russians at Friedland in June. Neither of the two victories was decisive, even though Napoleon remained in control of the land: but already, on both sides, it had been decided to substitute alliance for war.

Alexander was tired of the British alliance: Britain paid badly and made no attempt to create a diversion in Europe. Napoleon wanted a Russian alliance: he hated this cruel and interminable war which kept him away from the Tuileries for so long, where as usual the great dignitaries of his regime were calculating the opportunities and risks behind his back. He needed the Russians to settle the Prussian dispute which had been left in abeyance, and to put a stop in the east to any possible revenge from Frederick's heirs; but above all, to achieve his great anti-British project and close the whole of Europe to London merchants.

Would he have to venture as far as Moscow to obtain peace? No: in 1807 he succeeded where he would fail five years later; this was the Tilsit meeting, the raft on the Niemen where the two emperors – who were enchanted with each other – made Prussia pay for the new map of Europe, by creating firstly a Grand Duchy of Warsaw, which was given to the loyal king of Saxony, and secondly a kingdom of Westphalia, of which the crown went to Jerome, Napoleon's youngest brother, who became a new member of the Rhine Confederation. Napoleon promised his support against the Sultan, Tsar Alexander his against Britain: the Franco-Russian alliance became the axis and guarantee of the new European equilibrium, which was entirely directed against Britain.

Once more, Britain was the sole adversary: Pitt had died, as had his great rival Fox, but the new authorized representatives of the British oligarchy were more than ever resolved upon a merciless struggle. Since Trafalgar, it was impossible to resume the invasion plan. So Napoleon wanted to change his strategy and turn the weapon of its own industrial and commercial superiority against London.

In the last half of the eighteenth century, the idea was very prevalent that Britain was a giant with feet of clay, because of its credit system and trading structures. In fact, the British economy, whose vast export industries gave a livelihood, through external trade, to a quarter of the population, and depended on massive imports of foodstuffs and raw materials, could be vulnerable to a seriously directed blockade policy: Sieyès had thought about it in 1798, before the setting-up of the expedition to Egypt. But since 1793, thanks to its naval superiority, Britain had been the one to try to ban neutrals from trading with its enemies, and had declared 'blockaded' the ports which it did not control. The aim was not to starve French Europe, the great producer of corn, but to deprive it of the colonial and industrial products necessary to its economy.

In 1803, when war resumed, Napoleon had riposted by banning colonial goods and industrial products of British origin from entering France. In 1806, strengthened by his conquests, he wanted to extend the system of these 'customs posts', as he called them, which were held, for example, by Louis in Holland and Joseph in Naples: this was what lay behind the decrees of Berlin and Milan. The first, signed just after his victory over Prussia (1806), declared 'the British Isles to be in a state of blockade' and forbade all trade with Britain, not only in France, but in all the allied or occupied countries, from Spain to the Vistula. At Tilsit, the following year, Russia gave its backing. It was a matter of asphyxiating British exports and thus of creating industrial overproduction and a generalized crisis in British economy. Britain retaliated by bombarding Copenhagen, opening up the Baltic by cannon fire, and aspiring to control the traffic of neutral countries. The second Napoleonic document, signed in Milan at the end of 1807, held that any neutral vessel 'controlled' by the British should be seized. The Continental System from then on prohibited any neutrality: but the whole of Europe had to be French, peopled with soldiers and customs officers.

Portugal inaugurated the series of 'economic' annexations: in the face of this old British ally's hostility, Napoleon sent Junot to close the port of Lisbon. In a foreseeable sequence of events, the occupation of Portugal brought in its wake that of Spain, arbitration by the emperor over the lamentable quarrels of the reigning family, and finally the appointment of Joseph to the throne of Madrid, while Murat went to Naples. But now Napoleon, accustomed to defeating the mercenary armies of the kings of Europe in open country, found popular guerrilla warfare confronting him: Joseph's throne had to be won back from a people demanding their legitimate kings. Triggered off in May, the insurrection soon gained mastery of the country and, in July at Bailén, forced one demoralized French army to capitulate: this was a thunderbolt for Europe. Shortly afterwards, Junot had to yield Lisbon to the British. What did it matter that Napoleon, who had hastened over at the head of the Grand Army, reinstalled Joseph in December? He left at his heels a Spain that was on its feet, a marvellous parade ground for the invading corps of the future Wellington, who still bore the name Wellesley. In the same year, the logic of the Continental System broadened the emperor's Italian policy: annexation of Tuscany and Parma to the Empire, occupation of Rome, which would be added the following year. Pius VII retaliated with excommunication; he was placed in a guarded residence in Savona, a solitary martyr who was just as dangerous as all the Spanish guerillas.

To these additional costs, to these new adversaries, were added the first tears in the very fabric of Napoleonic Europe: the Franco-Russian alliance and French Germany. Two years afterwards, the spirit of Tilsit no longer reigned in Erfurt; Napoleon, on the point of leading the Grand Army into Spain, would again have liked Alexander's promise. But doubly sensitive to pressure from his boyars and the French failure in Spain, the Tsar resorted to trickery and temporized, secretly encouraged by Talleyrand; he informed Vienna that he would stay neutral should a fresh conflict arise between France and Austria.

In the autumn of 1808, the Viennese court had rebuilt its army and was preparing once again to avenge Campo Formio, Lunéville and the humiliation of the Treaty of Pressburg (1805): as usual, it had received money from London, but this time it could count on the backing of a German population which was weary of French domination. War broke out in the spring of 1809, at the same time as uprisings in the Tyrol and in northern Germany. Napoleon was victorious in three months, after a close shave with defeat; the Archduke Charles had let him enter Vienna by withdrawing his troops towards the east, on the left bank of the Danube; at the end of May, part of the French infantry, which had ventured on to this bank over makeshift bridges, was obliged to beat a hasty retreat before the Austrian counteroffensive. The Grand Army did not manage to cross the river until, a month later, it carried off a decisive victory at Wagram on 6 July. The peace of Vienna, signed in October, took Galicia from Austria and gave it to the Grand Duchy of Warsaw, while all that remained of the Adriatic provinces was directly united to the Empire.

At the end of 1809, Napoleon's construction was at its apogee. Let us take a look at the fantastic and temporary map of French Europe: an Austria excluded from Germany and cut off from the sea, a Prussia almost reduced to its origins, and a French Empire of 131 *départements* stretching from Brest to Hamburg, from Amsterdam to Rome and Trieste – 750,000 square kilometres, plus seventy million inhabitants, of whom thirty million were French. On top of this empire were the satellite states, arranged in a curve: the Rhine Confederation, a 'mediatized' Switzerland, the Italian Republic, with Murat in Naples, Joseph in Madrid. Finally, France's advance guard towards the east, the Grand Duchy of Warsaw, the figure of a Poland being reborn but still frail, trapped by the ambiguities of the Franco-Russian alliance.

This French Europe, built up of bits and pieces during the course of events, corresponded less and less with the aims of its founder and more and more with the hopes of his adversaries. It had been built in order to ruin British trade. In fact, in 1808, the Europe of Tilsit and the beginning of Milan was closed to British products, in the Baltic – despite Sweden – as in the Mediterranean – despite the Maltese entrepôt. At the same time, the retaliatory measures taken by the United States against the attacks of which her vessels had borne the brunt, worsened the deficit in British exports, which went down by more than a quarter; Britain was choked with unsold stocks, and their prices fell dangerously, causing industrial paralysis, unemployment and social unrest.

But after this drop, the curve of exports picked up outstandingly in 1809, reaching a maximum: indeed, British goods were achieving an even better penetration of northern Europe, through the development of Swedish contraband, the self-interested connivance of a certain number of French officials and the reopening of Dutch ports, since Louis had yielded to the pressure of his new subjects; so true was it that the blockade had a boomerang effect, that Napoleon himself had half-opened France's doors to British trade by the granting of special licences. In the same year British trade with the United States slowly picked up, and developed chiefly with Spanish and Portuguese America, facilitated by the exile of the Portuguese dynasty to Brazil and the dislocation of Spanish trade with the South American empire. British prosperity was so dazzling that in 1810 Napoleon tightened the meshes of his net, took Louis's kingdom from him and put under his own direct authority the German shore of the North Sea. But how could he close the American outlet and reservoir?

Paradoxically, the economic crisis which hit Britain in the midst of its prosperity at the end of 1810, did not arise from the Continental System: it represented a cyclical recession, made worse by inflation which financed the costs of war, and the disorganization of the traditional trading structures. It had all begun with the fall of the pound sterling and the catastrophic harvest of 1809, the brutal leap in the price of grain and the threat of famine. At the same time, the tightening of the blockade, saturation of the South American market because its capacity had been overestimated, renewed difficulties and soon war with the United States deeply affected exports: in the long term, the New World countries could pay for British products only with colonial goods – which could not be sold by London except in Europe. The British crisis of 1811–12 was therefore extremely serious, and the people's wretched poverty brought its usual train of workers' riots and savage violence: this was the moment when, as a result of the combination of the economic crisis and the shutting off of the United States, the Napoleonic system struck at the very heart of Britain.

By a piece of good luck for Britain, the Continental System was truly applied for only two years, from the middle of 1810 until Napoleon plunged into the immensity of Russia. Furthermore the great crisis of 1811 spared neither France nor Europe. The trade rupture with Britain aggravated matters in its turn, even though at first it was favourable to the expansion of continental production. If the landowning aristocracy could no longer export its corn or its wood – so be it: it had never liked, and even less upheld, the parvenu soldier of revolutionary France. But now European people and bourgeoisies were rising up in their turn against him, and even in France his rule no longer seemed to be other than a chance venture.

The failure of the Continental System concealed another failure, more long-standing and fundamental: that of a French Europe, rallying to support the ideological and social model born of the Revolution. The imperial and consular conquests had been accompanied by the extension of French social and administrative reforms in the satellite countries: the abolition of serfdom, seigneurial rights and the tithe, civil equality, the Code Napoléon, freedom of worship and conscience, governmental centralization. In Germany, for instance, the states of Baden, Württemberg and Bavaria, which were considerably enlarged, had been profoundly transformed; Napoleonic creations, such as Murat's Grand Duchy of Berg or Jerome's Westphalia, were taken in hand, like model states, by high-quality French personnel who were frequently well received by local society. Thus the young Stendhal, who had himself addressed as 'Monsieur l'Intendant', or even 'Monseigneur', passed delightful youthful years in the small provincial society of Brunswick, which was attached to Westphalia: for French reforms, in Germany, Italy, to say nothing of the Grand Duchy of Warsaw, had won over a good proportion of the elites formed by the eighteenth century. The economic boom had also made its contribution, encouraged by the climate of prosperity, the improvement of roads and the birth of a protected European market.

However, even in these regrouped, rationalized states, liberated from their tiny reactionary oligarchies, the French occupation's fiscal and military inroads formed the basis, in the long run, of general discontent: war nurtured war, and Napoleon's army became ever less French and ever more European, being drawn from the Grand Empire and the satellite states. While the elites were scared by a venture which seemed to have no end in sight, the part of the French Revolution's glorious message which

got through to the people was no longer civil equality or social liberation, but national oppression; thus French revolutionary messianism
would breed throughout Europe a counter-revolutionary and nationalist
messianism, which was an unexpected windfall for the priests, seigneurs
and kings.

In 1807 two significant condemnations of the Napoleonic enterprise
came to light: one from Talleyrand, who believed in a balanced Europe,
and was both a lucid and corrupt interpreter of tradition and of the
future, preparing in advance – at the same time as another career – the
compromise he deemed necessary between French and European elites.
The other came from German millennialists who identified Bonaparte with
the Anti-Christ; they were, so to speak, the foam on the powerful wave
which would sweep European peasants along under the banner of religion
and the kings: a vast and fresh Vendée which rose in Spain to reach as far
as Germany and Italy, and which would have Russian mujiks as its most
redoubtable soldiers.

If this counter-revolutionary crusade was to gain strength, it was
essential that the big European states should get themselves better
organized than in the past. That was exactly what happened. The old
central and eastern European monarchies had preserved their hatred
for the revolutionary ideas which, in their eyes, Napoleon had always
embodied; but, accustomed as they were to measuring an adversary by the
worth of his army, they had inevitably succumbed to the fascination of the
French organization. After Jena (1806), Prussia had relaxed the rigidity
of Frederick's state, integrating peasants and bourgeois in an effort to
resurrect a sense of nation. In Austria, where the aristocracy refused
to surrender anything of its social ascendancy, the army had nevertheless been reorganized, to become an instrument of revenge. The old
eighteenth-century conflicts between aristocracy and monarchic centralization had disappeared, to the advantage of the national priority glorified by
teachers and students, which would unite the masses of the people to the
most traditionalist states in Europe.

This was also the case in Russia, where Alexander and his councillors at
times nursed wild dreams of liberalism without, in the end, doing anything
to modify the traditional balance which would make illiterate peasants into
the most fanatical defenders of orthodox priests and the Tsar. the 'great
nation', turned Empire, saw its own message of liberation turned against
itself and against the values it had claimed to universalize. In short, there
was a terrible anti-Napoleonic reaction, that is to say, national and counter-
revolutionary both together, which gained support from the revival of the
Catholic faith and the philosophies of nationalism and authority.

Around 1810–11, everything contributed to speed up this evolution:
France's increasing fiscal and military pressures in conquered or vassal
countries, the conflict between the emperor and the pope, the Russian
alliance which had been tottering since Erfurt, the deep economic crisis
which was sweeping away business prosperity. Even in France, the imperial

magic was coming undone, conscription had become a very heavy burden, and the war extremely costly. The immense collective passions which go to make great wars had passed over to the adversary.

Napoleon was aware of all that. Once more – and for the last time – on his return from Wagram, he faced the eternal question: how could he make his great venture legitimate, how could he stabilize what had become the Empire? Behind his back, as usual, everyone was talking about a more restful and manageable successor – Joseph, Murat or even Eugène de Beauharnais. He no longer contemplated adoption, since the death of Louis and Hortense's eldest son; after his affair with the Polish Countess Walewska, he knew he was capable of fathering a child; he decided on a divorce and a royal marriage. At the time when Europe was borrowing the Revolution's methods, the soldier of the Revolution went seeking a wife amid the *ancien régime*.

He had in mind a Russian princess, one of the Tsar's sisters, intended to perpetuate the Europe of Tilsit; but Alexander deliberately caused the matter to hang fire, and then sheltered behind her mother's refusal. So then Napoleon leaped at the Habsburg marriage, proposed by the court of Vienna with a view to gaining at least a respite and perhaps a form of insurance; he married Marie-Louise, the daughter of Francis II, at the beginning of April 1810. By taking Europe's first princess into his bed, did he perhaps feel that he had finally gained entry to the select circle of the kings – he who had already been tricked, fifteen years earlier, by Josephine's tales of her 'birth'? By repeating the pattern of Louis XVI's marriage, he believed – just like a Bourbon – that he was ensuring a guarantee for himself with Vienna. But he also thought that he was ensuring for his heir half a true monarchic legitimacy, and that he would reinstate this grandson of the Revolution in the tradition of the kings of France. It was his way of expressing his mother's famous 'Let's hope it lasts!'

The King of Rome, born the following year, was therefore the last and most moving of Napoleon's insurances against the future. But he was also the most illusory: it was vain for the emperor of the French to try to bring the *ancien régime* to life again in forms and customs, to appoint more and more aristocrats to his councils and to increase examples of his absolute power, since for Europe he had never stopped being the crowned incarnation of the Revolution. Could he even have been taken in by words? Though he would write to Francis II 'My dear brother and father-in-law', he knew perfectly well that he was still a usurper. Scarcely more than a year after the birth of his son, the monarch who had everything would once more be the 'Little Corporal'.

To the question, how could Napoleon gamble everything and lose everything at the point when he seemed to dominate everything, there is no other answer than the extraordinary precariousness of his territorial ascendancy in 1811. Napoleon tended to attribute this precariousness – of which he was more than ever aware – to the break-up of what he had always looked on as the axis of his European system: the Franco-Russian agreement. This gave rise to the war of 1812, which was perhaps intended less to break an adversary than to re-establish a partnership.

Relations between Napoleon and Alexander had constantly deteriorated since Erfurt; the growing disagreement concealed both real grievances and assumptions of intent. In their overwhelming numbers, the Russian boyars continued to detest everything connected with the French Revolution, whether from near or far; traditional exporters of corn and wood from their domains to Britain, they were damaged by the Continental System. Sensitive to pressure from them, Alexander's attention to the application of Napoleonic decrees steadily diminished; he had vacillated during the 1809 campaign, used trickery again in the marriage affair before refusing. He feared French expansion towards the east, to which the plan of the Continental System was leading: after Holland, which had been taken from Louis, the Hanseatic towns were 'united' with the Empire, then the Grand Duchy of Oldenburg, on the other side of the Danish peninsula, was seized from a brother-in-law of the Tsar.

In the face of this endless spreading of the French Empire, what was the worth of Russian acquisitions since Tilsit – Galicia, Finland or Bessarabia? Who could say whether Napoleon, in spite of his promises, would not reconstruct a true Poland, a child of France right in the middle of the Slavonic world? For all these reasons, Alexander was ready for the split at the beginning of 1812; he had the secret support of the new regent and crown prince of Sweden, Bernadotte, who had espoused his subjects' hostility to the Napoleonic blockade, and the no less secret assurance of Austrian and Prussian non-intervention.

On his side, Napoleon felt strengthened by the official alliance with Vienna and Berlin. Once more, it was a matter of placing the final stone on his European edifice by a final war, that is to say, of re-establishing the spirit of Tilsit, the condition of the application of the Continental System and victory over Britain: therefore a short war, a great battle, a new raft on the Niemen. This is what he wrote to Alexander, on 1 July, at the time he entered Russia: 'War is therefore declared between us. God himself cannot undo what has been done. But I will always lend an open ear to peace negotiations.' All the drama of 1812 lies in this illusion, in which he was reliving 1807: Napoleon had not realized that the very conditions of the European war had changed.

He himself crossed the Niemen at the head of a cosmopolitan army, nearly half foreign, which had been raised from the Empire and its dependencies; notably 200,000 German soldiers out of 700,000 men. Ahead of them lay the desert, the Russian army which vanished into its retreat, the mujiks burning their crops; and the invasion was already proving difficult: the Russians had altered the rules of the game. In order to attempt to break the national alliance of the Tsar and his people, Napoleon had one weapon at his disposal, and had thought of using it: to re-enact the revolutionary war of his youth and proclaim the emancipation of the mujiks. But, now he was a cousin of kings, and haunted by the imminent agreement with Alexander, as he supposed, he decided not to use it.

Delayed by provisioning difficulties, already depleted by desertions, the immense army entered Smolensk only in the middle of August, and did not reach the Moskva until the beginning of September. The Russian troops, taken in hand by old Marshal Kutuzov, finally gave battle at Borodino, but it was a bloody and uncertain fight: Napoleon entered Moscow on 14 September, at the very end of the summer, with weakened troops and without having seriously worn down those of the enemy. He at least hoped that the capture of the huge exotic city, at the other end of Europe, would provide a pledge of peace: master of the dead metropolis, which had been devastated by fires, he waited in the Kremlin for Alexander's emissaries.

In mid-October, when it had finally dawned upon him that there was to be no new Tilsit, he decided to return home; he had never liked to be absent for long from the Tuileries. But it was already too late. Kutuzov barred a return via the south, so he had to retrace the interminable route to Smolensk, which had already been laid waste by the pillage of the outward journey. Pursued by the enemy, harassed by the Cossacks, decimated by the prematurely cold weather, which swiftly dropped to minus twenty degrees, the Grand Army fell apart into a vast, wretched, frozen column of men who could barely get across the Beresina: at the beginning of December, Napoleon led a mere 100,000 survivors back towards the Niemen. The great Empire was without an army.

It was the signal for the entire system to go into a state of general crisis. The European states saw the arrival of their long-awaited moment of revenge: Prussia turned to Russia and declared war on France in the spring of 1813, while Austria prepared a mediation loaded with menaces. Britain, emerging from the crisis and seeing its trade start to flourish again with the French retreat, had just brought in a government intent on putting an end to the matter. Everywhere public opinion revived the movement which had started to stir in 1809: in Spain, where popular guerrilla activity had resulted in assemblies and a liberal programme, Anglo-Spanish troops drove Joseph from Madrid and soon advanced as far as the Pyrenees. Revolts swept through Italy, their flames fanned by the exile of Pius VII, and Murat quickly left the remains of the Grand Army to look after his own interests in Naples. Popular uprisings broke out on all sides in German territory occupied by the French, while the princes bided their time, one eye on Vienna and the other on Paris.

Immediately on his return, Napoleon had spent the winter raising more soldiers and preparing for war in the spring; but the internal climate was very ominous, and defeat had reawoken a weariness with the endless conflict, together with a growing rejection of the despotism of one man alone. Liberal royalism, which was spreading among the country's notables, showed how far distant were the times of consular unanimity; the whole of affluent France was ready to put an end to the venture, even to take back its former kings, in return for a firm insurance contract on its possessions.

It was clear that in spring 1813 there was no longer any imaginable compromise between Napoleon and Europe: Napoleon could not continue to reign, even in France, unless he had a new victory; outside France, the Europe of both the kings and the people had not risen up for a little territorial readjustment. That is why the Austrian mediation, which proposed a return to Lunéville, had no chance of success on either side: after the French victories over the Russo-Prussians at Lützen and Bautzen in May, the short negotiation which got under way was little more than a general stay of execution. Napoleon insisted on the frontiers of 1812. In August, Austria and Sweden joined the coalition, adding more than a million soldiers. *In extremis*, Napoleon could negotiate only with his prisoners, Pius VII or the Bourbons of Madrid: but what did it matter, since it was all a gamble on the field of battle?

Whether through lack of cavalry, or the youth of his troops, or the fatigue of their leader, Napoleon allowed the junction of three enemy armies, under Bernadotte, Blücher and Schwarzenberg, and the decisive battle was engaged at Leipzig, with two against one, 320,000 members of the coalition army against 160,000 French and allied soldiers; the law of numbers, plus the defection of allied German contingents on the third day of the battle, explain a defeat which quickly became a rout. Napoleon found himself on the Rhine with the debris of his army, and France threatened on its oldest frontiers.

But this time, it was a weary France, broken by despotism and hazardous undertakings, a country of discontented notables, tired marshals and revolutionaries grown old. Napoleon might well be able to get his new conscripts, the 'Marie-Louise', to perform a few strategic feats, but he could no longer mobilize any national force to counterbalance, either in number or will to win, the formidable enemy coalition. His only recourse was the relative moderation of Metternich, who feared Russo-Prussian ambitions; but the iron fist of Britain, handing out grants and orders, was there to impose a war to the finish, and to the French frontiers of 1792. At that time Napoleon's brilliant French campaign, in which he once again displayed against three enemy armies the liveliness and rapidity of the Bonaparte of Italy, could only delay the day of reckoning: Paris, left to the notables by Marie-Louise and Joseph, capitulated on 30 March, and Napoleon resigned himself to abdicating on 6 April, before going to the tiny island of Elba which had been assigned to him by his conquerors.

Deposed by the Senate, abandoned by his Marshals, he had tried to save the throne for his son. But his house, his monarchy, disappeared with him like sandcastles, bringing the Bourbons and the France of the Revolution face to face, after a quarter of a century.

He had realized this beforehand. He had said in 1813, after Leipzig, at the beginning of the shipwreck: 'After me, the Revolution – or, rather, the ideas which formed it – will resume their course. It will be like a book from which the marker is removed, and one starts to read again at the page where one left off.'[22]

[22] Mathieu Molé's speech on receiving Tocqueville into the Académie Française on 21 April 1842, reported in the Marquis de Noailles' *Le Comte Molé*, vol. I.

Appendix 1: Chronological Table

1770

The Dauphin marries the Archduchess Marie-Antoinette.

June–December Conflict of the government with the parlement regarding the Duc d'Aiguillon.

December Disgrace of Choiseul.

1771

20 January One hundred and thirty magistrates of the parlement of Paris are exiled.

23 February Chancellor Maupeou reorganizes the legal system: magistrates are appointed by the government and the Paris parlement split up.

1774

10 May Death of Louis XV.

24 August Maupeou and Terray leave the government which Maurepas, Vergennes and Turgot had joined shortly before; the latter becomes Controller-General of Finance.

13 September Turgot establishes free trade in grain.

12 November Louis XVI recalls the parlements.

1775

Coronation of Louis XVI.

Malesherbes and the Comte de Saint-Germain join the government.

Edict of the Comte de Saint-Germain.

Du Pont de Nemours writes up for Turgot his *Mémoire sur les municipalités à établir en France.*

April–May The Flour War.

1776

January–February Turgot abolishes the guilds and replaces the *corvée* with a money tax.

12 May Disgrace of Turgot.

4 July American Declaration of Independence.

1777

June   Necker becomes Director General of Finance.

1778

Birth of Madame Royale.
Death of Voltaire and Rousseau.
6 February   Treaty of alliance between France and the United States of America.
12 July   Creation of a provincial assembly in the Berry.

1779

Abolition of serfdom in the royal domains.

1781

Birth of the Dauphin.
Ségur's edict.
February   Necker publishes his *Compte rendu au roi.*
May   Dismissal of Necker.

1783

3 September   Peace treaty with Britain.
10 November   Calonne becomes Controller-General of Finance.

1785

Birth of the future 'Louis XVII'.
Affair of the Diamond Necklace.

1786

Franco-British trade treaty lowering customs duties in both countries.
20 August   Calonne proposes his plan for reform.
29 December   Louis XVI announces the impending convocation of an Assembly of
   Notables.

1787

22 February   Meeting of the Assembly of Notables.
8 April   Dismissal of Calonne; ministry of Loménie de Brienne.
25 May   Dissolution of Assembly of Notables.
June–August   The parlement of Paris refuses to register Loménie de Brienne's
   edicts and calls for an Estates-General; the *parlementaires* are exiled.
September   Negotiation between Loménie de Brienne and the parlement of Paris.
17 September   The American Constitution is adopted by the Congress.
November   Edict of toleration.
19 November   Royal session of the Paris parlement; Louis XVI orders the registration of the financial edicts and exiles Philippe d'Orléans to Villers-Cotterêts.

1788

3 May   The Paris parlement publishes a *Déclaration des lois fondamentales du
   royaume.*

5 May Arrest of parlement counsellors Duval d'Eprémesnil and Goislard de Monsabert.

8 May Lamoignon's judicial reform reducing the powers of parlements.

May Resistance of provincial parlements.

7 June 'Day of the tiles' in Grenoble.

5 July The King's Council orders research to be made into earlier Estates-General.

21 July Vizille assembly.

8 August The Estates-General are convened for 1 May 1789.

24–6 August Dismissal of Loménie de Brienne and recall of Necker.

September Re-establishment of parlements; the Paris parlement demands that the Estates-General be convened in the 1614 form.

5 October Convocation of a second Assembly of Notables.

6 November Meeting of the Assembly of Notables.

November Sieyès publishes the *Essai sur les privilèges*.

27 December The King's Council declares itself in favour of doubling the Third Estate's representation.

1789

January Sieyès publishes *Qu'est-ce que le Tiers Etat?*

24 January Electoral regulation for the Estates-General.

March Beginning of elections to the Estates General.

26–8 April 'Réveillon' riot in Paris.

4 May Procession for the opening of the Estates-General at Versailles.

5 May Opening of the Estates-General.

6 May The deputies of the Third Estate demand common verification of the powers of the three orders.

4 June Death of the Dauphin.

10 June The Third Estate decides to commence the verification of powers on its own.

13 June Three Poitevin *curés* leave the Chamber of the Clergy to join the Third Estate.

17 June The Third Estate constitutes itself a National Assembly.

19 June The clergy decide to join the Third Estate after a close ballot.

20 June The Tennis Court Oath.

23 June Royal session when Louis XVI sets out his programme and commands the orders to hold separate sittings; when the session is over, the Third Estate's deputies and part of the clergy refuse to leave the hall, contrary to the king's orders.

25 June Forty-seven deputies from the nobles join the Third Estate.

27 June The king enjoins the clergy and nobility to meet with the Third Estate.

End of June–beginning of July Movement of troops towards Paris and Versailles.

11 July Dismissal of Necker.

14 July Taking of the Bastille; its governor, de Launay, and the *prévôt des marchands*, Flesselles, are assassinated.

16 July Recall of Necker.

17 July Louis XVI wears the cockade at the Paris Hôtel de Ville, where he is received by Bailly, the new mayor.

End of July–August Peasant revolts and the Great Fear in the provinces.

22 July Murders of Foulon de Doué and Bertier de Sauvigny in Paris.

4 August Destruction of the feudal regime formulated between 5 and 11 August.

26 August Declaration of the Rights of Man and of the Citizen.

10 September The Assembly rejects the institution of a second chamber.

11 September The king is accorded a suspensive veto (the right to refuse the promulgation of laws during two legislatures).

5 October Women of Paris march on Versailles.

6 October The king is brought back to Paris; the Assembly installs itself in Paris shortly afterwards.

29 October Decree of the 'silver mark'.

2 November The clergy's possessions are put at the nation's disposal.

7 November The Assembly decides that ministers may not be chosen from its ranks.

December New territorial organization: *départements* and *municipalités*.

19 December Creation of assignats.

1790

13 February Abolition of monastic vows.

13 April The Assembly refuses to declare the Catholic religion to be the state religion.

17 April Assignats become legal currency.

April–June Confrontations between Catholics and Protestants in southern France.

12 July Vote on the Civil Constitution of the Clergy.

14 July Festival of the Federation in Paris.

31 August Mutiny of the Swiss garrison at Nancy put down by Bouillé.

4 September Necker's resignation.

November Publication of Burke's *Reflections on the French Revolution*.

27 November Ecclesiastical public officials have to take the oath of the constitution.

1791

2 March Allarde's law: suppression of the guilds.

10 March and 13 April Papal briefs condemning the Civil Constitution of the Clergy.

2 April Death of Mirabeau; on 4 April his body is placed in the church of Sainte-Geneviève, transformed into the Panthéon on 3 April.

18 April Louis XVI forbidden to leave Paris to celebrate Easter at Saint-Cloud.

16 May Vote on the ineligibility of Constituents to the next Legislative Assembly.

14 June Le Chapelier's law banning workers' coalitions.

20 June Louis XVI and Marie-Antoinette flee from Paris.

21 June Arrest of the royal family at Varennes.

25 June The king is brought back to Paris.

17 July The National Guard puts down a demonstration at the Champ de Mars.

August–September Revision of the constitution.

27 August Suppression of the 'silver mark' for eligibility to the Assembly, but increase in electoral property qualification.

14 September Louis XVI takes the oath to the constitution; Avignon and the Comtat Venaissin are united with France.

30 September   Last session of the Constituent Assembly.

1 October   First sitting of the Legislative Assembly.

29 November   Ecclesiastics refusing to take the oath are declared suspect.

1792

9 February   Decree confiscating émigrés' possessions.

3 March   Rising at Etampes during which the mayor, Simoneau, who opposed the fixing of grain prices, is killed.

20 April   War is declared on the 'king of Bohemia and Hungary'.

27 May   Decree on the deportation of refractory priests.

8 June   Decree on the formation of a camp of *fédérés* in Paris.

11 June   Louis XVI places his veto on the decrees of 27 May and 8 June.

12 June   Dismissal of the ministers, Roland, Clavière and Servan, by Louis XVI; the Assembly renews its confidence in them.

20 June   The mob invades the Tuileries to compel the king to lift his veto; Louis XVI refuses to yield but has to don the red bonnet.

11 July   The Assembly declares 'the country in danger'.

3 August   Publication of Brunswick's manifesto.

10 August   The Tuileries stormed; Louis XVI, taking refuge within the Assembly, is suspended.

11 August   Constitution of an Executive Council in which Danton is Minister of Justice, Roland Minister of the Interior, Clavière Minister of Finance and Servan Minister of War.

13 August   The royal family is incarcerated in the Temple under the supervision of the Paris Commune.

19 August   La Fayette, unable to persuade his army to march on Paris, joins the Austrians, who intern him.

23 August   Fall of Longwy.

30 August   Capture of Verdun.

2–5 September   Massacre of prisoners in the Paris prisons.

20 September   Victory at Valmy; last sitting of the Legislative Assembly: it decrees divorce and the secularization of births, marriages and deaths.

21 September   The Convention meets and abolishes royalty.

27 September   The Convention renews the incompatibility of the offices of minister and deputy; Roland chooses to be a minister and Danton a deputy.

9 October   Returned émigrés are liable to the death penalty within twenty-four hours.

6 November   Dumouriez beats the Austrians at Jemappes.

7 November   Mailhe's report concluding that the king should be tried by the Convention.

13 November   Saint-Just declares that the king should be fought rather than tried.

14 November   French troops enter Brussels.

20 November   Discovery of the 'iron cupboard' containing the royal family's papers in the Tuileries.

27 November   Savoy is united with France.

3 December   Robespierre demands the death of the king.

11 December   First appearance of Louis XVI before the Convention.

26 December   Louis XVI's second appearance.

27 December   Salle moves an appeal to the people regarding the king's sentence.

1793

4 January Barère rejects the proposal of appeal to the people, which Buzot and Vergniaud supported in the case of Louis XVI's trial.

16–18 January The Convention votes for the death of the king.

21 January Execution of Louis XVI.

22 January Roland resigns from the Ministry of the Interior.

1 February Declaration of war on Britain and Holland.

24 February The Convention decrees the levy of 300,000 men.

Beginning of March Austrian counteroffensive in Belgium while Dumouriez pursues his plans in Holland.

7 March Declaration of war on Spain.

9 March The Convention decrees the dispatch of representatives on mission to the *départements*.

10 March Creation of the extraordinary criminal Tribunal (the revolutionary Tribunal).

10–11 March Machecoul massacres (start of the Vendée insurrection).

18 March Defeat of Dumouriez at Neerwinden.

19 March A republican army is defeated by the Vendéens at Pont-Charrault.

21 March Institution of local revolutionary watch committees.

4 April Dumouriez goes over to the Austrians, taking with him the Duc de Chartres (the future Louis-Philippe).

6 April First Committee of Public Safety, whose most important members are Danton and Barère.

24 April Marat, decreed under indictment by the Convention on 13 April, is acquitted by the revolutionary Tribunal and taken in triumph to the Convention.

4 May The Convention decrees the Maximum for grain prices.

10 May The Convention leaves the Salle du Manège to sit in the Tuileries.

18 May Creation of the Commission of Twelve, whose members are Girondins, given the task of inquiring into the Paris Commune.

24 May The Commission of Twelve has Hébert, deputy prosecutor of the Paris Commune, and Varlet, one of the leaders of the *Enragés*, arrested.

25 May Isnard threatens the representatives of the Commune who have come to demand the release of Hébert.

29 May In Lyon, the municipality is in the hands of Girondins and royalists.

31 May The Paris *sections* invade the Convention.

2 June Bid for power by the Paris *sections* against the Convention: fall of the Girondins.

June Fewer than sixty departmental administrations protest against the Parisian bid for power.

9 June Capture of Saumur by the Vendéens.

18 June Capture of Angers by the Vendéens.

24 June The Convention votes for a constitution (which does not come into force).

25 June Jacques Roux presents a petition to the Convention on behalf of the Cordeliers (the *Enragés*' manifesto).

29 June Nantes repulses the Vendéens.

July Publication of the *Contributions destinées à rectifier le jugement du public sur la Révolution française* by Fichte.

10 July Renewal of the Committee of Public Safety; at this date it comprises Barère, Couthon, Gasparin, Hérault de Séchelles, R. Lindet, Prieur de la Marne, Jean Bon Saint-André, Saint-Just and Thuriot.

13 July Assassination of Marat.

17 July Execution of Chalier in Lyon.

23 July Capitulation of Mainz; the French garrison assigned to the west.

27 July Robespierre enters the Committee of Public Safety (replacing Gasparin).

28 July Capitulation of Valenciennes.

1 August The Convention decides on the destruction of the Vendée.

14 August Entry of Carnot and Prieur de la Côte-d'Or to the Committee of Public Safety.

23 August The Convention decrees a *levée en masse*.

24 August Creation of the Great Ledger of the public debt.

27 August Toulon gives itself up to the British.

5 September The Terror is put on the agenda by the Convention, invaded by sansculottes; arrest of Jacques Roux.

6 September Entry of Collot d'Herbois and Billaud-Varenne to the Committee of Public Safety.

8 September Victory of Houchard at Hondschoote.

9 September Organization of the revolutionary army.

11 September The Maximum for grain and fodder is decreed.

17 September Vote on the law on suspects.

19 September Kléber and the Mainz army are beaten by the Vendéens at Torfou.

29 September Vote on the general Maximum.

9 October Capture of Lyon by the Convention's army.

10 October The Convention proclaims revolutionary government until the advent of peace.

16 October Jourdan beats the Austrians at Wattignies; Marie-Antoinette is executed.

17 October The Vendéens are beaten at Cholet by Kléber and Marceau; following this defeat they cross the Loire.

31 October Execution of the Girondins.

7 November Convention sitting regarding dechristianization.

8 November Execution of Mme Roland.

10 November Festival of Reason at Notre-Dame de Paris.

11 November Execution of Bailly.

14 November The Vendéens fail to take Granville.

17 November Arrest of Basire, Chabot and Delaunay, compromised in the Indies Company scandal.

21–2 November Robespierre and Danton tackle the antireligious masquerades.

24 November Adoption of the republican calendar.

29 November (9 Frimaire Year II) Execution of Barnave.

4 December (14 Frimaire) Organization of the revolutionary government.

5 December (15 Frimaire) Appearance of the first number of Camille Desmoulins's *Vieux Cordelier*.

12 December (22 Frimaire) The republican army crushes the Vendéens at Le Mans.

19 December (29 Frimaire) Recapture of Toulon.

23 December (3 Nivôse) Republican victory at Savenay over the Vendéens; the war in the west peters out in guerrilla warfare.

1794

12 January (23 Nivôse) In the night of 12–13 January, arrest of Fabre d'Eglantine, compromised in the Indies Company affair.

26 February–3 March (8–13 Ventôse) Vote on the sequestration of suspects' goods and their distribution to the needy.

4 March (14 Ventôse) The Cordeliers call for an insurrection.

13 March (23 Ventôse) In the night of 13–14 March, arrest of the Hébertists.

24 March (4 Germinal) Execution of the Hébertists.

28 March (8 Germinal) Suicide of Condorcet.

30 March (10 Germinal) In the night of 30–1 March, arrest of Danton and Camille Desmoulins.

6 April (16 Germinal) Execution of the Dantonists.

7 May (18 Floréal) The Convention recognizes the existence of the Supreme Being.

8 June (20 Prairial) Festival of the Supreme Being in Paris.

10 June (22 Prairial) Law on the revolutionary Tribunal which inaugurates the Great Terror.

26 June (8 Messidor) Victory of Jourdan at Fleurus.

27 July (9 Thermidor) Fall of Robespierre.

31 July (13 Thermidor) Renewal of the Committees.

1 August (14 Thermidor) Repeal of the law of 22 Prairial.

18 September (2nd complementary day) The Republic pays no salary to any religious cult.

11 October (20 Vendémiaire Year III) Transfer of Rousseau's remains to the Panthéon.

23 October (2 Brumaire) Capture of Koblenz; meeting of the armies of the Sambre et Meuse and the Rhin et Moselle.

1 November (11 Brumaire) Hoche is appointed Commander-in-Chief of the western army.

12 November (22 Brumaire) Closure of the Jacobin Club in Paris.

8 December (18 Frimaire) Reintegration of the '73' (Girondins excluded from the Convention).

24 December (4 Nivôse) Abolition of the Maximum.

1795

21 January (2 Pluviôse) Celebration of Louis XVI's execution.

3 February (15 Pluviôse) Formation of the Batavian Republic.

8 February (20 Pluviôse) Marat 'depantheonized'.

15 February (27 Pluviôse) La Jaunaye agreements: pacification of the west.

21 February (3 Ventôse) Decree proclaiming the freedom of worship.

2 March (12 Ventôse) Arrest of Barère, Collot d'Herbois and Billaud-Varenne.

1 April (12 Germinal) The Convention is invaded by a sansculotte demonstration.

5 April (16 Germinal) Treaty of Basle; Prussia recognizes the French Republic.

April–May Development of the White Terror in the Rhône valley and the Midi.

7 May (18 Floréal) Execution of Fouquier-Tinville.

20 May (1 Prairial) The Convention is invaded by demonstrators demanding 'bread and the 1793 constitution'; they kill the deputy Féraud.

24 May (5 Prairial) Disarmament of the Parisian *sections*.

30 May (11 Prairial) Unsold churches are restored to the faithful.

8 June (20 Prairial)   Death of Louis XVII.

17 June (29 Prairial)   Death sentence on six Montagnard deputies, who commit suicide.

23 June (5 Messidor)   Boissy d'Anglas's report on the constitution.

24 June (6 Messidor)   Proclamation of Louis XVIII in Verona.

21 July (3 Thermidor)   At Quiberon, Hoche crushes the émigré landing.

27 July (9 Thermidor)   Celebration of the fall of Robespierre.

18 August (1 Fructidor)   Decree on the 'two-thirds'.

22 August (5 Fructidor)   The Convention adopts the new constitution.

1 October (9 Vendémiaire Year IV)   Annexation of Belgium.

5 October (13 Vendémiaire)   Barras and Bonaparte crush a royalist rising in Paris.

12–21 October (20–9 Vendémiaire)   Elections.

25 October (3 Brumaire)   Reapplication of terrorist legislation against priests.

26 October (4 Brumaire)   Separation of the Convention.

3 November (12 Brumaire)   Entry into office of the Directory, composed of Barras, Reubell, La Révellière-Lépeaux, Letourneur and Carnot (who replaces Sieyès, who had refused though elected).

1796

19 February (30 Pluviôse)   The issue of assignats is halted.

2 March (12 Ventôse)   Bonaparte is appointed General-in-Chief of the Italian army.

9 March (19 Ventôse)   Bonaparte marries Joséphine Beauharnais.

14 March (24 Ventôse)   Pichegru, suspected of royalism, is replaced by Moreau at the head of the Rhin et Moselle army.

27 March (7 Germinal)   Bonaparte joins his headquarters in Nice.

12 April (23 Germinal)   Victory of Bonaparte over the Austrians at Montenotte.

13 April (24 Germinal)   Victory over the Piedmontese at Millesimo.

15 April (26 Germinal)   Victory over the Austrians at Dego.

21 April (2 Floréal)   Bonaparte's victory over the Piedmontese at Mondovi.

27 April (8 Floréal)   Benjamin Constant publishes *De la force du gouvernement actuel de la France et de la nécessité de s'y rallier*.

28 April (9 Floréal)   Armistice of Cherasco between Bonaparte and the king of Piedmont-Sardinia.

10 May (21 Floréal)   Bonaparte's victory over the Austrians at Lodi; the Directory arrests the leaders of the Conspiracy of the Equals.

15 May (26 Floréal)   Bonaparte enters Milan.

20 May (1 Prairial)   Resumption of the Rhine campaign.

3 June (15 Prairial)   Withdrawal of the Austrians to the Tyrol, but they leave a garrison in Mantua.

12 June (24 Prairial)   The French army penetrates into papal territories.

23 June (5 Messidor)   Armistice of Bologna between Bonaparte and Pius VI.

16 July (28 Messidor)   Capture of Frankfurt by Jourdan.

5 August (18 Thermidor)   Bonaparte beats the Austrians at Castiglione.

24 August (7 Fructidor)   Jourdan is beaten at Amberg; the French armies of the Rhine have to retreat.

4 September (18 Fructidor)   Bonaparte beats the Austrians at Roverdo.

8 September (22 Fructidor)   Bonaparte beats the Austrians at Bassano.

9 September (23 Fructidor)   Failure of the 'camp de Grenelle' conspiracy in Paris.

16 October (25 Vendémiaire Year V)   Proclamation of the Cispadane Republic.

15–17 November (25–7 Brumaire)   Victory of Bonaparte at Arcola.
December   Failure of Hoche's expedition against England (the Irish expedition).

1797

14 January (25 Nivôse)   Bonaparte beats the Austrians at Rivoli.
2 February (14 Pluviôse)   Surrender of the Austrian garrison in Mantua.
19 February (1 Ventôse)   Peace treaty of Tolentino between the pope and France: Pius VI recognizes the annexation of Avignon and the Comtat Venaissin and has to pay a heavy indemnity.
March–April   Legislative elections; royalist success.
18 April (29 Germinal)   Signature of peace preliminaries between Bonaparte and Austria at Leoben.
22 April (3 Floréal)   Hoche and Moreau learn of the Leoben preliminaries and suspend their offensive manoeuvres in Germany.
26 May (7 Floréal)   Babeuf sentenced to death; Barthélémy is elected Director in place of Letourneur.
June   Barras, Reubell and La Révellière-Lépeaux, having learnt of Pichegru's negotiations with Louis XVIII, decide to appeal to Hoche and his troops.
9 July (21 Messidor)   Proclamation in Milan of the Cisalpine Republic.
8 August (21 Thermidor)   Augereau, sent by Bonaparte to support the republican Directors, is appointed local commandant in Paris.
15 August (28 Thermidor)   Opening in Paris of the first national council of the constitutional Church.
4 September (18 Fructidor)   Coup d'état.
8 September (22 Fructidor)   Merlin de Douai and François de Neufchâteau are elected Directors.
19 September (3rd complementary day)   Death of Hoche.
17 October (26 Vendémiaire Year VI)   Peace of Campo Formio between Bonaparte and Austria; ratified by the Directory, 26 October.
28 November (8 Frimaire)   Opening of the Congress of Rastatt.
25 December (5 Nivôse)   Bonaparte is elected a member of the Institut.

1798

January   French intervention in Switzerland.
11 February (23 Pluviôse)   French troops enter Rome.
11 May (22 Floréal)   Numerous Jacobins and royalists elected in April are removed from office.
15 May (26 Floréal)   Treilhard is elected Director to replace François de Neufchâteau.
19 May (30 Floréal)   Departure of the expedition to Egypt.
11 June (23 Prairial)   Capture of Malta by Bonaparte.
1 July (13 Messidor)   Bonaparte disembarks at Alexandria.
21 July (3 Thermidor)   Bonaparte wins the battle of the Pyramids.
1 August (14 Thermidor)   Nelson destroys the French fleet at Aboukir.
5 September (19 Fructidor)   Vote on Jourdan's law instituting compulsory military service.
November (Brumaire Year VII)   Mme de Staël works on *Des circonstances actuelles qui peuvent terminer la Révolution.*

December Championnet beats the Neapolitan army which had driven him out of Rome.

29 December (9 Nivôse) Treaty of alliance between Russia, Britain and Naples.

1799

26 January (7 Pluviôse) Proclamation of the Parthenopean (Neapolitan) Republic.

February Uprising of the Calabrian peasants against the French and their partisans; Bonaparte marches towards Syria.

2 March (12 Ventôse) Jourdan and Bernadotte resume their offensive on the Rhine.

12 March (22 Ventôse) France declares war on Austria.

25 March (5 Germinal) Jourdan, beaten, retreats to the Rhine.

March Defeats of the Italian army commanded by Scherer.

28 March (8 Germinal) Pius VI is arrested by French troops.

April Legislative elections favourable to the Jacobins.

27 April (8 Floréal) Defeat of Moreau at Cassano; the French evacuate Milan.

28 April (9 Floréal) Assassination attempt on the French plenipotentiaries at the Congress of Rastatt.

16 May (27 Floréal) Sieyès is elected Director to replace Reubell.

17 May (28 Floréal) Bonaparte lifts the siege of Saint-Jean d'Acre and retreats towards Egypt.

4 June (16 Prairial) Masséna resists the Austrian offensive in Switzerland.

17 June (29 Prairial) Treilhard, removed from office, is replaced by Gohier on the Directory.

18 June (30 Prairial) Merlin de Douai and La Révellière-Lépeaux are forced by the Councils to resign; Moulin replaces the second on the 20th.

12 July (24 Messidor) Law on hostages.

14 July (26 Messidor) Pius VI is interned at Valence.

13 August (26 Thermidor) Sieyès has the Jacobin Club closed after it had opened at the beginning of July.

15 August (28 Thermidor) Joubert, commander of the Italian army, is killed at the battle of Novi.

23 August (6 Fructidor) Bonaparte embarks for France.

29 August (12 Fructidor) Death of Pius VI.

19 September (3rd complementary day) Victory of Brune at Bergen.

25–6 September (3–4 Vendémiaire Year VIII) Victory of Masséna at Zurich against the Russians and Austrians, who evacuate Switzerland.

6 October (14 Vendémiaire) Victory of Brune at Castricum against the British and the Russians.

9 October (17 Vendémiaire) Bonaparte disembarks in France.

17 October (25 Vendémiaire) Bonaparte is received by the Directory.

1 November (10 Brumaire) Interview between Sieyès and Bonaparte.

9–10 November (18–19 Brumaire) Coup d'état.

15 December (24 Frimaire Year VIII) Proclamation of the constitution.

25 December (4 Nivôse) Establishment of the Council of State.

27 December (6 Nivôse) Establishment of the Senate.

28 December (7 Nivôse) Reopening of churches on Sundays.

1800

1 January (11 Nivôse) Establishment of the Tribunate and the Legislative Body.
13 February (24 Pluviôse) Creation of the Bank of France.
17 February (28 Pluviôse) Law on the administrative organization of France.
19 February (30 Pluviôse) Bonaparte installed in the Tuileries.
3 March (12 Ventôse) Closure of the list of émigrés.
14 March (23 Ventôse) Election of Pius VII.
18 March (27 Ventôse) Law on judicial organization.
May–June Recapture of Italy.
14 June (23 Prairial) Battle of Marengo; assassination of Kléber in Egypt.
18 June (27 Prairial) Bonaparte attends a *Te Deum* in Milan cathedral.
2 July (13 Messidor) Bonaparte returns to Paris.
12 August (24 Thermidor) Appointment of the preparatory commission for the Civil Code.
3 September (16 Fructidor) The British retake Malta.
7 September (20 Fructidor) Bonaparte replies in the negative to approaches from Louis XVIII.
20 October (28 Vendémiaire Year IX) Striking off from the list of émigrés of 48,000 émigrés.
5 November (14 Brumaire) Beginning of Concordat negotiations.
3 December (12 Frimaire) Victory of Moreau over the Austrians at Hohenlinden.
24 December (3 Nivôse) Attempt on Bonaparte's life in the rue Saint-Nicaise.

1801

5 January (15 Nivôse) *Senatus consultum* orders the deportation of 130 Jacobins as a consequence of the attempted coup of 24 December.
7 February (18 Pluviôse) Law on the special courts.
9 February (20 Pluviôse) Peace of Lunéville: the main points of the Treaty of Campo Formio are confirmed and France obtains the left bank of the Rhine.
29 June (10 Messidor) Opening of a national council organized by the constitutional clergy in Paris.
June–August The British gain control of Egypt.
15 July (26 Messidor) Signing of the Concordat.
23 July (4 Thermidor) Beginning of the discussion on the Civil Code in the Council of State.

1802

26 January (6 Pluviôse Year X) Bonaparte becomes president of the Italian Republic.
6 February (17 Pluviôse) Leclerc, sent to quell Toussaint-L'Ouverture's revolt, lands in Santo Domingo.
18 March (27 Ventôse) Purge of the Tribunate and the Legislative Body.
25 March (4 Germinal) Peace of Amiens.
3 April (13 Germinal) *Articles organiques* concerning the Catholic and Protestant religions.
14 April (24 Germinal) Chateaubriand publishes *Le Génie du Christianisme*.
18 April (28 Germinal) Promulgation of the Concordat.
26 April (6 Floréal) Amnesty for émigrés still figuring on the list of émigrés (if

they return and swear loyalty to the regime), with the exception of about a thousand.

1 May (11 Floréal) Law on public education: creation of the *lycées*.
19 May (29 Floréal) Creation of the Légion d'Honneur.
2 August (14 Thermidor) Consulate for life granted to Napoleon.
4 August (16 Thermidor) Constitution of Year X.
11 September (24 Fructidor) Piedmont joined to France.

1803

23 January (3 Pluviôse Year XI) Reorganization of the Institut.
24 March (3 Germinal) Empire ordinance adopting the French plan of 23 February for the reorganization of Germany.
28 March (7 Germinal) The value of the franc is fixed at 5 g of silver.
9 April (19 Germinal) Creation of junior officials of the Council of State.
14 April (24 Germinal) The Bank of France receives the privilege of issuing notes.
3 May (13 Floréal) Sale of Louisiana to the United States.
12 May (22 Floréal) Breaking of the peace of Amiens.
20 June (1 Messidor) Bonaparte prohibits goods of British origin.
1 December (9 Frimaire Year XII) Institution of the worker's identity card.
2 December (10 Frimaire) The army of the Boulogne camp takes the title of the army of England.

1804

February–March Arrest of Cadoudal and his accomplices: compromised, Pichegru commits suicide and Moreau is banished.
21 March (30 Ventôse) Execution of the Duc d'Enghien at Vincennes; promulgation of the Civil Code.
18 May (28 Floréal) Bonaparte becomes hereditary emperor of the French.
June Execution of Cadoudal and his accomplices.
2 December (11 Frimaire Year XIII) Coronation of Napoleon.

1805

9 March (18 Ventôse) Creation of a Press Bureau to supervise publications.
26 May (6 Prairial) Napoleon is crowned king of Italy in Milan.
26 August (8 Fructidor) Napoleon abandons the conquest of England and plans the Austrian campaign.
September–October Bavarian campaign.
20 October (28 Vendémiaire Year XIV) Mack's Austrian army surrenders at Ulm.
21 October (29 Vendémiaire) Nelson crushes Villeneuve's fleet at Trafalgar.
14 November (23 Brumaire) Napoleon enters Vienna.
2 December (11 Frimaire) Napoleon beats the Russians and the Austrians at Austerlitz.
26 December (5 Nivôse) Treaty of Pressburg.
31 December End of the republican calendar.

1806

18 March Creation of industrial tribunals.
30 March Joseph Bonaparte becomes king of Naples.

4 April   Publication of the imperial catechism by Bernier and d'Astros.
10 May   Foundation of the University.
5 June   Louis Bonaparte becomes king of Holland.
12 July   Creation of the Confederation of the Rhine.
6 August   Dissolution of the Holy Roman Empire.
14 August   Creation of the *majorats* (hereditary fiefs of the Empire).
October   Prussian campaign.
14 October   Battles of Jena and Auerstädt.
27 October   Napoleon enters Berlin.
21 November   Continental System: prohibition of all trade, even for neutral countries, with Britain.

1807

January–June   Prussian campaign.
7–8 February   Battle of Eylau against the Prussians and the Russians.
14 June   Napoleon beats the Russians at Friedland.
8 July   Peace of Tilsit; Franco-Russian alliance.
9 August   Talleyrand leaves the Ministry of Foreign Affairs.
16 August   Jerome Bonaparte becomes king of Westphalia.
19 August   Suppression of the Tribunate.
11 September   Commercial Code.
16 September   Creation of the Revenue Court.
November–December   French intervention in Spain and Portugal.
17 December   Worsening of the Continental System: neutral ships permitting British boarding parties will be treated as hostile.

1808

2 February   Occupation of Rome.
1 March   Organization of the imperial nobility.
23 March   Murat enters Madrid.
May   Beginning of the Spanish rebellion.
15 July   Murat becomes king of Naples.
20 July   Joseph, appointed king of Spain, enters Madrid.
22 July   Capitulation of General Dupont at Bailén in Spain.
August   British landing in Portugal.
30 August   Capitulation of Junot at Cintra in Portugal.
17 September   Monopoly of teaching granted to the University.
27 September   Interview at Erfurt between Napoleon and Tsar Alexander: France evacuates Prussia.

1809

10 April   Austrian offensive.
12–13 May   Capture of Vienna.
17 May   Annexation of Papal States.
22 May   The Austrians halt the French at Aspern-Essling.
5–6 July   Battle of Wagram; arrest of Pius VII.
14 October   Peace of Vienna.
15 December   Divorce of Napoleon.

1810

6 January   Franco-Swedish alliance.
17 February   The city of Rome is united with France.
2 April   Marriage of Napoleon with Marie-Louise, daughter of Francis II, emperor of Austria.
6 June   Creation of the Council for trade and manufacture.
9 July   Annexation of Holland to the Empire.
21 August   Election of Bernadotte as heir to the throne of Sweden.
31 December   Breaking of the Franco-Russian alliance.

1811

20 March   Birth of the King of Rome.
17 June–20 October   National synod in Paris.

1812

23 February   Breaking of the Concordat.
5 March   Franco-Prussian alliance.
9 April   Russo-Swedish alliance.
8 May   Fixing of grain prices.
June   Beginning of the Russian campaign.
19 June   Pius VII is brought to Fontainebleau.
5–7 September   Battle of the Moskva.
14 September   Napoleon enters Moscow.
19 October   The French army abandons Moscow.
26–8 November   Crossing of the Beresina.
5 December   Napoleon leaves the Grand Army.
18 December   Napoleon arrives in Paris.

1813

25 January   Concordat of Fontainebleau.
January–February   Prussia breaks its alliance with France and joins Russia.
March   Uprising of northern Germany; Bernadotte reinforces the coalition.
30 March   Organization of a Regency Council.
14 April   Austria breaks the French alliance but remains neutral.
May   The French evacuate Madrid.
May–June   French offensive in Germany.
12 August   Austria joins the coalition.
September–October   German campaign.
16–19 October   Battle of Leipzig.
November   Murat turns to the allies.
29 December   The Legislative Body declares itself against pursuing the war.

1814

January–April   French campaign.
24 January   Joseph is appointed Lieutenant-General of the Empire.
25 January   Fall of Lerida, last French post in Spain.
12 March   The Duc d'Angoulême is enthusiastically welcomed in Bordeaux.
30 March   Capitulation of Paris.

1 April   Formation of a provisional government presided over by Talleyrand.

2 April   Senate declares deposition of Napoleon.

6 April   Abdication of Napoleon at Fontainebleau; vote on the senatorial constitution.

24 April   Louis XVIII lands at Calais.

2 May   Royal Declaration of Saint-Ouen.

30 May   First Treaty of Paris: France is reduced to its 1792 frontiers.

4 June   Proclamation of the Charter.

27 November   Publication of Chateaubriand's *Réflexions politiques*.

November 1814–June 1815   Congress of Vienna where Talleyrand represents France.

Appendix 2: The Republican Calendar for Year II (1793–1794)

Vendémaire, An II. Sept.–Oct. 1793		Brumaire Oct.–Nov.		Frimaire Nov.–Dec.		Nivôse Dec. 1793–Jan. 1794		Pluviôse Jan.–Feb.		Ventôse Feb.–March		Germinal March–April		Floréal April–May		Prairial May–June		Messidor June–July		Thermidor July–Aug.		Fructidor Aug.–Sept.	
1	22	1	22	1	21	1	21	1	20	1	19	1	21	1	20	1	20	1	19	1	19	1	18
2	23	2	23	2	22	2	22	2	21	2	20	2	22	2	21	2	21	2	20	2	20	2	19
3	24	3	24	3	23	3	23	3	22	3	21	3	23	3	22	3	22	3	21	3	21	3	20
4	25	4	25	4	24	4	24	4	23	4	22	4	24	4	23	4	23	4	22	4	22	4	21
5	26	5	26	5	25	5	25	5	24	5	23	5	25	5	24	5	24	5	23	5	23	5	22
6	27	6	27	6	26	6	26	6	25	6	24	6	26	6	25	6	25	6	24	6	24	6	23
7	28	7	28	7	27	7	27	7	26	7	25	7	27	7	26	7	26	7	25	7	25	7	24
8	29	8	29	8	28	8	28	8	27	8	26	8	28	8	27	8	27	8	26	8	26	8	25
9	30	9	30	9	29	9	29	9	28	9	27	9	29	9	28	9	28	9	27	9	27	9	26
10	1	10	31	10	30	10	30	10	29	10	28	10	30	10	29	10	29	10	28	10	28	10	27
11	2	11	1	11	1	11	31	11	30	11	1	11	31	11	30	11	30	11	29	11	29	11	28
12	3	12	2	12	2	12	1	12	31	12	2	12	1	12	1	12	31	12	30	12	30	12	29
13	4	13	3	13	3	13	2	13	1	13	3	13	2	13	2	13	1	13	1	13	31	13	30
14	5	14	4	14	4	14	3	14	2	14	4	14	3	14	3	14	2	14	2	14	1	14	31
15	6	15	5	15	5	15	4	15	3	15	5	15	4	15	4	15	3	15	3	15	2	15	1
16	7	16	6	16	6	16	5	16	4	16	6	16	5	16	5	16	4	16	4	16	3	16	2
17	8	17	7	17	7	17	6	17	5	17	7	17	6	17	6	17	5	17	5	17	4	17	3
18	9	18	8	18	8	18	7	18	6	18	8	18	7	18	7	18	6	18	6	18	5	18	4
19	10	19	9	19	9	19	8	19	7	19	9	19	8	19	8	19	7	19	7	19	6	19	5
20	11	20	10	20	10	20	9	20	8	20	10	20	9	20	9	20	8	20	8	20	7	20	6
21	12	21	11	21	11	21	10	21	9	21	11	21	10	21	10	21	9	21	9	21	8	21	7
22	13	22	12	22	12	22	11	22	10	22	12	22	11	22	11	22	10	22	10	22	9	22	8
23	14	23	13	23	13	23	12	23	11	23	13	23	12	23	12	23	11	23	11	23	10	23	9
24	15	24	14	24	14	24	13	24	12	24	14	24	13	24	13	24	12	24	12	24	11	24	10
25	16	25	15	25	15	25	14	25	13	25	15	25	14	25	14	25	13	25	13	25	12	25	11
26	17	26	16	26	16	26	15	26	14	26	16	26	15	26	15	26	14	26	14	26	13	26	12
27	18	27	17	27	17	27	16	27	15	27	17	27	16	27	16	27	15	27	15	27	14	27	13
28	19	28	18	28	18	28	17	28	16	28	18	28	17	28	17	28	16	28	16	28	15	28	14
29	20	29	19	29	19	29	18	29	17	29	19	29	18	29	18	29	17	29	17	29	16	29	15
30	21	30	20	30	20	30	19	30	18	30	20	30	19	30	19	30	18	30	18	30	17	30	16

Note: Five 'complementary days' (equivalent to 17–21 September) were set aside for republican festivals. As a result of leap years, correspondence with the Gregorian calendar varies in some years after 1793–4.

Bibliography

The following pages are not intended to be an exhaustive bibliography of the French Revolution – an undertaking which in any case becomes increasingly problematical as the years pass. Nevertheless I wished to provide the reader with a carefully thought-out list of articles and books which have furthered my own work, chapter by chapter, and I hope that this acknowledgement of my debt of gratitude may also serve as a guide to students.

I   THE ANCIEN RÉGIME

This chapter is an introduction to the revolutionary crisis. Rather than attempting to provide a complete description of old French society and the old monarchy, I have sought to explain the factors in their radical negation by the *tabula rasa* of 1789.

On the concept of the *ancien régime*, as developed by the Revolution to designate a past that it totally rejected:

VENTURINO, Diego, 'La Naissance de l'Ancien Régime', in *The French Revolution and the Creation of Modern Political Culture*, vol. 2: *The Political Culture of the French Revolution*, ed. Colin Lucas, Oxford, Pergamon Press, 1988.

FURET, François, 'L'Ancien Régime' in *Dictionnaire critique de la Révolution française*, Paris, Flammarion, 1988 (English translation, François Furet and Mona Ozouf (eds), *Critical Dictionary of the French Revolution*, Cambridge, Mass., Harvard University Press, 1990).

On the *ancien régime*, and the relationship of continuity-discontinuity that links it to the French Revolution, the decisive work, to which this book owes much of its intellectual structure, remains that of:

TOCQUEVILLE, Alexis de, *L'Ancien Régime et la Révolution française* (1856), in *Oeuvres complètes* (18 vols, part II, vols 1 and 2 (for de Tocqueville's fragments and unpublished notes on the Revolution), Paris, Gallimard, 1952, 1953 (reissued in coll. 'Folio Histoire', 1987) (English translation, *Old Régime and the French Revolution*, Doubleday, 1955).

See also:

TAINE, Hippolyte, *Les Origines de la France contemporaine* (1876–96), reissued Paris, Robert Laffont, coll. 'Bouquins' (part I: *L'Ancien Régime–La Révolution*;

part II: *La Révolution–Le Régime moderne*) (English translation, *The Origins of Contemporary France*, University of Chicago Press, 1978.

GOUBERT, Pierre, *L'Ancien Régime*, 2 vols (vol. 1, *La Société*; vol. 2, *Les Pouvoirs*. The second volume is more particularly concerned with the cohesion between society and the state), Paris, Armand Colin, coll. 'U', 1969–73.

FURET, François, *Penser la Révolution française*, Paris, Gallimard, coll. 'Folio Histoire', 1978 (English transl. *Interpreting the French Revolution*, Cambridge University Press, 1981).

On the spirit that presided over the formation of the absolute monarchy, the two most important philosophical works seem to me to be:

BODIN, Jean, *Les Six Livres de la République (1576)*, 6 vols, Paris, Fayard (Corpus des oeuvres de philosophie en langue française), 1986.

BOSSUET, Jacques-Bénigne, *Politique tirée des propres paroles de l'Ecriture Sainte (1709)*; reissued Geneva, Droz, 1967.

On institutions:

LEMAIRE, André, *Les Lois fondamentales de la monarchie française d'après les théoriciens de l'Ancien Régime*, Paris, 1907; reissued Geneva, Slatkine, 1975.

MOUSNIER, Roland, *Les Institutions de la France sous la monarchie absolue, 1598–1689*, Paris, PUF, 1974–80.

ANTOINE, Michel, 'La Monarchie absolue', in *The French Revolution and the Creation of Modern Political Culture*, vol. 1, *The Political Culture of the Old Regime*, ed. Keith Michael Baker, Oxford, Pergamon Press, 1987.

On the functioning of those institutions in the eighteenth century:

ANTOINE, Michel, *Le Conseil du Roi sous le règne de Louis XV*, Paris and Geneva, Librairie Droz, 1970.

On the constant reworking of aristocratic society by the absolute monarchy's sale of offices and titles, the best author is an American historian, David Bien: 'Offices, Corps and a System of State Credit: The Uses of Privilege under the Ancien Régime', in *The French Revolution and the Creation of the Old Regime*. This article is essential for an understanding of *ancien régime* society. See also 'La Réaction aristocratique avant 1789: l'exemple de l'armée', *Annales ESC* (1974). See also:

BOSSENGA, Gail, 'From "Corps" to Citizenship: the "Bureaux des Finances" before the French Revolution', *Journal of Modern History* (September 1986).

On the nobility and its relations with the rest of society:

MEYER, Jean, *La Noblesse bretonne au XVIIIe siècle*, 2 vols, Paris, 1966; reissued Flammarion, 1972.

FORSTER, Robert, *The Nobility of Toulouse in the Eighteenth Century*, Baltimore, 1960.

TAYLOR, George, 'Non-Capitalist Wealth and the Origins of the French Revolution', *American Historical Review*, (1967).

COBBAN, Alfred, *The Social Interpretation of the French Revolution*, Cambridge University Press, 1968.

LUCAS, Colin, 'Nobles, Bourgeois and the Origins of the French Revolution', *Past and Present*, 60 (1973).

CHAUSSINAND-NOGARET, Guy, *La Noblesse française au XVIIIe siècle, de la Féodalité aux Lumières*, Paris, Hachette, 1976; reissued Brussels, Ed. Complexe, 1984.

On the parlements and their conflicts with the monarchy in the eighteenth century, see:

FLAMMERMONT, Jules, *Remontrances du Parlement de Paris au XVIIIe siècle*, 3 vols, Paris, Imprimerie Nationale, 1888–9; reissued in facsimile, Geneva, Megariotis, 1974.

On institutions:
DOYLE, William, *The Parlement of Bordeaux and the End of the Old Regime, 1771–1790*, New York, St Martin's Press, 1974.
BLUCHE, François, *Les Magistrats du Parlement de Paris, 1715–1771*, Paris, Economica, 1986.

On the conflict:
EGRET, Jean, *Louis XV et l'opposition parlementaire*, Paris, Armand Colin, 1970.
DOYLE, William, 'The Parlements of France and the Breakdown of the Old Regime, 1771–1788', *French Historical Studies* (1970).

On the ideas for which the conflict served as a vehicle, the principal work, absurdly unrecognized today, is:
CARCASSONNE, Elie, *Montesquieu et le problème de la Constitution française au XVIIIe siècle*, Paris, 1927; reissued in facsimile, Geneva, Slatkine, 1970.

See also:
BICKART, R., *Les Parlements et la notion de souveraineté nationale au XVIIIe siècle*, Paris, F. Alcan, 1934.
RICHET, Denis 'Autour des origines idéologiques lointaines de la Révolution française: élites et despotisme', *Annales ESC* (1969).
VAN KLEY, Dale, *The Jansenists and the Expulsion of the Jesuits from France, 1757–1785*, New Haven and London, Yale University Press, 1975.

On the financial crisis of the French monarchy in the eighteenth century, the best introduction is still Necker's *L'Administration des finances de la France*, which came out in 1784 vols 4 and 5 of the *Oeuvres Complètes*, 15 vols, Darmstadt, Scientia Verlag Aalen, 1970 reprinted from the Paris edn, 1820).

Two recent important articles:
MORINEAU, Michel, 'Budgets de l'Etat et gestion des finances royales au XVIIIe siècle', *Revue Historique* (1980).
GUERY, Alain, 'Le Roi dépensier: le don, la contrainte, et l'origine du système financier de la monarchie française d'Ancien Régime', *Annales ESC* (1984).

Lastly, an excellent book:
BOSHER, John Francis, *French Finances, 1770–1795, from Business to Bureaucracy*, Cambridge University Press, 1970.

On the philosophy of the Enlightenment and its influence on the mores and minds of the French in the eighteenth century, there can be no substitute for turning to the authors themselves, both major and minor, in every genre: treatises, essays, history, economics, novels and correspondence. I will not even attempt here to broach the vast literature engendered by the movement of ideas and the great authors over the last two centuries, but I would like to mention that the best synthesis remains:
CASSIRER Ernst, *The Philosophy of the Enlightenment*, Princeton University Press, 1951 (published in 1932 in Tübingen as *Die Philosophie der Aufklärung*).

For half a century, historians have paid particular attention to the circulation of ideas in society. See, for example:

MORNET, Daniel, *Les Origines intellectuelles de la Révolution française, 1715–1789*, Paris, Armand Colin, 1933, 6th edn 1967.

GROETHUYSEN, Bernard, *Les Origines de l'esprit bourgeois en France*, Paris, Gallimard, coll. 'Tel', 1977.

ROCHE, Daniel, *Le Siècle des Lumières en province, académies et académiciens provinciaux, 1680–1789*, 2 vols, Paris and The Hague, Mouton, and École des Hautes Etudes en Sciences Sociales, *Civilisation et Sociétés*, 62 (1978).

TUCOO-CHALA, Suzanne, *Charles-Joseph Panckoucke et la librairie française, 1736–1798*, Paris, Pau Marrimpouey Jeune, 1977.

DARNTON, Robert, *The Business of Enlightenment, A Publishing History of the Encyclopedie, 1775–1800*, Cambridge, Mass., Harvard University Press, 1979.

DARNTON, Robert, *The Literary Underground of the Old Regime Enlightenment*, Cambridge, Mass., Harvard University Press 1982.

For a grasp of the general elements of the relationship between the ideas of the Enlightenment and the French Revolution, two very old works, almost contemporaneous with the event, remain useful:

MOUNIER, Jean-Joseph, *De l'influence attribuée aux philosophes, aux francs-maçons et aux illuminés sur la Révolution de France*; Tübingen, J. G. Cotta, 1801.

PORTALIS, Jean-Étienne Marie, *De l'usage et de l'abus de l'esprit philosophique durant le XVIIIe siècle*, 2 vols, Paris, A. Egron, 1820. The second edition contains also an *Essai sur l'origine, l'histoire et le progrès de la littérature française et de la philosophie* (Paris, Moutardier, 1827, 3rd edn 1834). (Tocqueville, in dealing with this problem, borrows part of his analysis from Portalis.)

A recent collection of articles from the last ten years focuses on the penetration of the Enlightenment's ideas into the political culture of the Ancien Régime:

BAKER, Keith, *Inventing the French Revolution. Essays on French Political Culture in the Eighteenth Century*, Cambridge University Press, 1990.

A more recent study can be found in Furet and Ozouf, *Critical Dictionary*. See the articles 'Montesquieu' and 'Rousseau' (by Bernard Manin), 'Voltaire' (by Mona Ozouf), 'Physiocrats' (by Pierre Rosanvallon), 'Enlightenment' (by Bronislaw Baczko).

Below are some of the most useful works on the different political episodes discussed in this chapter.

On Maupeou's reform, see:
ANTOINE, Michel, *Louis XV*, Paris, Fayard, 1989.

On Turgot's ministry:
FAURE, Edgar, *La Disgrâce de Turgot, 12 mai 1776*, Paris, Gallimard, coll. 'Trente journées qui ont fait la France', 1961.

On Necker:
EGRET, Jean, *Necker, ministre de Louis XV (1776–1790)*, Paris, Champion, 1975.

Lastly, on Louis XVI and Marie-Antoinette:
GIRAULT DE COURSAC, Pierrette, *L'Education d'un roi: Louis XVI*, Paris, Gallimard, 1972.

BLUCHE, François, *La Vie quotidienne au temps de Louis XVI*, Paris, Hachette, 1980.

MADAME DE CAMPAN, Jeanne Louise Henriette, *Mémoires sur la vie de Marie-*

Antoinette, Paris, Firmin-Didot, 1879.
Madame de Campan: première femme de chambre de Marie-Antoinette, Paris, Mercure de France, coll. 'Le Temps retrouvé', 1988.
THOMAS, Chantal, 'L'Héroïne du crime: Marie-Antoinette dans les pamphlets', in Jean-Claude Bonnet, *La Carmagnole des muses. L'homme de lettres et l'artiste dans la Révolution*, Paris, Armand Colin, 1988.

2 THE REVOLUTION OF 1789

General histories of the Revolution

MICHELET, Jules, *Histoire de la Révolution*, 7 vols, Paris, Chamerot, 1847–53; ed. Gérard Walter, 2 vols, Paris, Gallimard, La Pléiade, 1976–7. (This work remains the cornerstone of all revolutionary historiography and is also a literary monument.) Also available in Éditions Robert Laffont, coll. 'Bouquins', vol. 1, books I–VII; vol. 2, books VIII–XXI, 1979 (English translation, *History of the French Relovution*, University of Chicago Press, 1967).
TAINE, Hippolyte, *Les Origines de la France contemporaine*. (This is the greatest counter-revolutionary historical work. English translation, *The Origins of Contempory France*, University of Chicago Press, 1978).
JAURÈS, Jean, *Histoire socialiste de la Révolution française*, (1901–4); ed. J. Rouff, 10 vols, Paris, n.d.; ed. A. Mathiez, 8 vols, Paris, Librairie de l'Humanité, 1922–4; ed. A. Soboul and E. Labrousse, 7 vols, Paris, Messidor/Ed. Sociales, 1968–73. (A classic social history of the Revolution, combined with an assiduous political and parliamentary history.)
LEFEBVRE, Georges, *La Révolution française*, Paris, PUF, coll. 'Peuples et Civilisations', 1951, reissued 1980. (A historian of Jacobin inspiration, Georges Lefebvre, is the great twentieth-century specialist in the history of the French Revolution, and the man with the most complete and reliable information on the subject. English translation, *The French Revolution*, New York, Columbia University Press, 1970).
PALMER, Robert R., *The Age of the Democratic Revolution. A Political History of Europe and America, 1760–1800*, 2 vols, Princeton University Press, 1959–64. (An excellent setting of the French Revolution in an international perspective, intelligent and informed.)

Apart from these general works, the reader who is interested in more recent debate on the interpretation of the French Revolution may like to consult:
COBBAN, Alfred, *The Social Interpretation of the French Revolution*.
FURET, François, *Penser la Révolution française*, Paris, Gallimard, coll. 'Folio Histoire', 1978 (English translation, *Interpreting the French Revolution*, Cambridge University Press, 1981).

On the pre-Revolutionary years 1787–9, sometimes called the 'pre-Revolution', the best available synthesis is that of
DOYLE, William, *Origins of the French Revolution*, Oxford University Press, 1980.

See also:
COCHIN, Augustin, *Les Sociétés de pensée et la Révolution en Bretagne (1788–1789)*, 2 vols, Paris, Plon, 1928.

EGRET, Jean, *La Pré-Révolution française, 1787–1789*, Paris, PUF, 1969; reissued Geneva, Slatkine reprints, 1978.

EGRET, J. *La Révolution des notables. Mounier et les Monarchiens 1789*, Paris, Armand Colin, 1950.

GRUDER, Vivian, *Class and Politics in the Revolution: the Assembly of French Notables of 1787*, in Ernst Hinrichs, Eberhard Schmitt and Rudolf Vierhaus, *Vom Ancien Regime zur Französischen Revolution Forschungen und Perspektiven*, Vandenhoeck and Ruprecht, 1978.

On the convocation and meeting of the Estates General, the fundamental documentary work is by

BRETTE, Armand, *Recueil de documents relatifs à la Convocation des Etats généraux de 1789*, 4 vols, Paris, Imprimerie nationale, 1894–1915.

See also:

COCHIN, Augustin, *La Campagne électorale de 1789 en Bourgogne*, Paris, Champion, 1904.

HALÉVI, Ran, 'Etats généraux' in Furet and Ozouf, *Critical Dictionary*.

FURET François, 'La monarchie et le règlement électoral de 1789', and Ran Halévi, 'La Monarchie et les élections: position des problèmes', in *The French Revolution and the Creation of Modern Political Culture*, vol. 2, *The Political Culture of the Old Regime*, ed. K. M. Baker; and Furet and Ozouf, *Critical Dictionary*.

The great events of the year 1789 may be approached by way of a vast contempory literature, in which there are two categories of works. The first is composed of accounts by witnesses and participants of what took place at Versailles and in Paris. Among the most interesting are:

YOUNG, Arthur, *Travels during the Years 1787, 1788 and 1789*, New York, AMS Press (reprint of 1794 edn).

MORRIS, Gouverneur, *Diary and Letters of Gouverneur Morris*, Jersey City, Da Capo (reprint of 1888 edn, American Public Figures Series).

LAMETH, Alexandre, Comte de, *Histoire de l'Assemblée Constituante*, 2 vols, Paris, Moutardier, 1828–9.

DUQUESNOY, Adrien-Cyprien, *Journal d'Adrien Dusquesnoy, député du Tiers-Etat de Bar-le-Duc, sur l'Assemblée Constituante, 3 mai 1789–3 avril 1790*, ed. Robert de Crèvecoeur, 2 vols, Paris, Picard et fils, 1894.

FERRIÈRES, Charles Elie, Marquis de, *Mémoires du marquis de Ferrières, avec une notice sur sa vie*, 3 vols, Paris, Baudouin fils, 1821.

BAILLY, Jean Sylvain, *Mémoires*, 3 vols, Paris, Baudouin fils, 1821–2.

Lastly, particular mention must be made of the memoirs of the Swiss

DUMONT, Etienne, *Souvenirs sur Mirabeau et sur les deux premières assemblées législatives*, a posthumous work, ed. J. L. Duval, Paris, C. Gosselin, 1832. (This is a fundamental work for knowledge of the debates in the Constituent Assembly.)

The second category contains works which are more directly linked with the debates and new political matters at stake: newspapers, pamphlets, speeches. The various political writings of Emmanuel-Joseph Sieyès have recently been edited, unfortunately without critical apparatus, by Dorigny Marcel (EDHIS): the reader will find there Sieyès's three fundamental pamphlets of autumn–winter 1788–9: the 'Essay on privilege', 'Views on the means of action available to the representatives of France in 1789', and the famous 'What is the Third Estate?' (the last is also published by Droz, 1970, and PUF, coll. 'Quadrige', 1982). There is no better introduction to the events of 1789 than these three pieces of writing.

On Sieyès:
BASTIDE, Pierre, *Sieyès et sa pensée*, Paris, Hachette, 1970; Geneva, Slatkine, 1978.
BREDIN, Jean-Denis, *Sieyès, la clef de la Révolution française*, Paris, Ed. de Fallois, 1988.

Two articles specifically devoted to Sieyès's political thinking:
CLAVREUIL, Colette, 'Qu'est-ce que le Tiers-Etat?', in François Chatelet, Olivier Duhamel and Evelyne Pisier, *Dictionnaire des Oeuvres politiques*, Paris, PUF, 1986.
BAKER, Keith, 'Sieyès', in Furet and Ozouf, *Critical Dictionary*.

An anthology of speeches and supporting memoirs of the other great leaders of opinion in 1789:
FURET, François, and Ran Halévi, *Orateurs de la Révolution française*, vol. 1, *Les Constituants*, Paris, Gallimard, La Pléiade, 1989. (My recommendation would be to give priority to reading Mounier and Lally-Tollendal for the *Monarchiens*, Mirabeau and Sieyès for the Patriots.)

Lastly, as essential reading, two great witnesses of the era on the year 1789: the celebrated *Reflections on the Revolution in France* by Edmund Burke, published at the end of 1790 (available in Penguin Classics), and a *Histoire de la Révolution française*, written in 1795 by Jacques Necker during his Coppet exile, in *Oeuvres complètes* repr. from the Paris edn of 1820 (Darmstadt, Scientia Verlag Aalen, 1970; *De la Révolution française*, vols 9 and 10). The first is the great source from which all criticisms of the great French event drew sustenance. The second offers a detailed account and a profound analysis of the chain of circumstances which wove together the year 1789, by one of the principal actors in the drama.

On the main stages in the development of the Revolution, in 1789, the following books and articles are important.

On the composition of the Constituent Assembly:
LEMAY, Edna-Hindie, 'La composition de l'Assemblée Nationale Constituante: les hommes de la continuité?', *Revue d'histoire moderne et contemporaine*, 16 (July–September 1977).

On 14 July 1789:
GODECHOT, Jacques, *La Prise de la Bastille: 14 juillet 1789*, Paris, Gallimard, coll. 'Trente journées qui ont fait la France', 1965.

On the rural uprising:
LEFEBVRE Georges, *La Grande Peur de 1789*, Paris, Armand Colin, 1932; reissued (with *Les Foules révolutionnaires*) 1988 (English translation, *The Great Fear of 1789*, New York, Schocken, 1989).

On the night of 4 August, the best analysis is to be found in:
JAURÈS, Jean, *Histoire socialiste de la Révolution française*, vol. 1, ch. 3, 'Journées révolutionnaires', pp. 393ff. in the Messidor/Ed. Sociales edition, 1968–73.

Also read
FURET, François, 'The Night of 4 August', in Furet and Ozouf, *Critical Dictionary*.

The Declaration of the Rights of Man: the subject has recently been freshly dealt with by

GAUCHET, Marcel, *La Révolution des Droits de l'homme*, Paris, Gallimard, 1989.

On the decisive constitutional debates of August–September 1789, the two great Chambers and the right of veto, see the following articles:

'Sieyès', 'Constitution', 'Sovereignty' by Keith Baker. 'Monarchiens' by Ran Halévi and 'Mirabeau' by François Furet, in Furet and Ozouf, *Critical Dictionary*.

On the colonial question:

JAURÈS, Jean, *Histoire socialiste de la Révolution française*, vol. 2, ch. 4, 'Le mouvement économique et social en 1792 – la question coloniale'.

The central political question which dominated the entire history of the Constituent Assembly was that of the monarchy, the keystone of the *ancien régime*, destroyed and yet preserved as a power subordinate to the new Assembly. The *Monarchiens* were unable, in August–September 1789, to win a more active role for it, and the *journées* in October 1789 confirm *de facto* the purely theoretical nature of the suspensive right of veto granted to the king in September. Mirabeau afterwards vainly devoted his efforts to the reinstatement of the principle of monarchic authority within the Revolution. The most interesting work on this period is Mirabeau's secret correspondence with the Comte de la Marck:

MIRABEAU, *Correspondance entre le Comte de Mirabeau et le Comte de la Marck*, ed. A. de Bacourt, 3 vols, Paris, Librairie Vve Le Normant, 1831; ed. Chaussinand-Nogaret, *Mirabeau entre le roi et la Révolution: notes à la Cour et discours*, Paris, Hachette, coll. 'Pluriel', 1986.

On religious matters and the Civil Constitution of the Clergy, one may begin with a study of how Church possessions and property were placed at the nation's disposal, with the articles 'Biens nationaux' by Louis Bergeron and 'Assignats' by Michel Bruguière, in Furet and Ozouf, *Critical Dictionary*.

On the religious question: the book which best enables one to understand to what extent it formed the philosophical and political heart of the revolutionary enigma, is that of

QUINET, Edgar, *Le Christianisme et la Révolution française* (1846), reissued Paris, Fayard, 1984.

See also:

MATHIEZ, Albert, *Rome et le clergé français sous la Constituante*, Paris, Armand Colin, 1911.

LA GORCE, Pierre de, *Histoire religieuse de la Révolution française*, 2 vols, Paris, Hachette, 1946–50.

TACKETT, Timothy, *Religion, Revolution and Regional Culture in Eighteenth-Century France: The Ecclesiastical Wrath of 1791*, Princeton University Press, 1985.

VAN KLEY, Dale, 'The Jansenist. Constitutional Legacy in the French Pre-Revolution', *Historical Reflections*, 13 (1986).

Varennes and the revision of the constitution: a good introduction to the period of the Constituent Assembly is given by the speeches and posthumously collected writings of Barnave, who was both its politician and philosopher. For Barnave the politician, see Furet and Halévi, *Orateurs de la Révolution française*. For Barnave the philosopher, see Barnave, *Oeuvres*, ed. Bérenger de la Drôme, 4 vols (1843), chiefly the first two sections. See the reissue, arranged and annotated by Patrice

Gueniffey, entitled *La Révolution et de la Constituante* (Presses Universitaires de Grenoble, 1983). Another work essential to an understanding of this period:
MICHON, Georges, *Essai sur l'histoire du parti feuillant, Adrien Duport*, Paris, Payot, 1924.

On Barnave and Duport, see Furet and Ozouf, *Critical Dictionary*, the articles 'Barnave' by François Furet and 'Feuillants' by Ran Halévi.

On the activities of the Constituent Assembly in general and the Constitution of 1791, the most important work for an understanding of the constitutional thinking of the Constituent and the absolute sovereignty of the law, the principle established by the representatives of the people, is that of the great lawyer:
CARRÉ DE MALBERG, Raymond, *Contribution à la théorie générale de l'Etat*, 2 vols, Paris, Sirey, 1920–2; reissued Paris, CNRS, 1962.
CARRÉ DE MALBERG, Raymond, *La Loi, expression de la volonté générale*, Paris, Sirey, 1931; reissued Economica, 1984.

Another legal contribution to the study of the same matter, from a different angle, belongs to:
DUCLOS, Pierre, *La Notion de Constitution dans l'oeuvre de l'Assemblée Constituante de 1789*, Paris, Dalloz, 1934.

See also:
TROPER, Michel, *La Séparation des pouviors et l'histoire constitutionnelle française*, Paris, LGDJ, Bibliothèque Constitutionnelle et de Science Politique, 1973, reissued 1980.

Among all the Constituent Assembly's measures which might be called indivisibly social, economic and financial, the sale of the Church's possessions, followed by the creation of the assignat and its rapid transformation into paper money, had the most far-reaching consequences.

Michelet is the most constant commentator on the transfer of property which was effected to the benefit of the bourgeois and peasant through the alienation of the Church's estates. He continually underlines its primary role in the marriage between the Revolution and the new landowners (books III–X of *Histoire de la Révolution française*).

On the financial policies in which the Constituent Assembly became engulfed in 1790, the conscious choice of inflation as a means of financing public expenditure and the social and political consequences it brought about, there is a good general clarification in a recent book:
AFTALION, Florin, *L'Economie de la Révolution française*, Paris, Hachette, coll. 'Pluriel', 1987.

On the management of public finances in general during the Revolution there is very little, but recently an excellent work has appeared by:
BRUGUIÈRE, Michel, *Gestionnaires et profiteurs de la Révolution. L'administration des finances françaises de Louis XVI à Bonaparte*, Paris, Olivier Orban, 1986.

3   THE JACOBIN REPUBLIC

Perhaps the best way to approach this 'heroic' period of the Revolution, which has fed so many passions and debates, is through works that evoke the atmosphere of the times either directly, through contemporaneous writings and speeches, or indirectly through memoirs published later, chiefly under the Restoration, by active participants. In the first category, I would recommend above all the speeches of Brissot and Vergniaud on the war in autumn and winter 1791–2, those concerning the trial of the king between November 1792 and January 1793, the presentation by Condorcet of his democratic constitution (February 1793), and of course Robespierre's great interventions in the Convention, mainly in autumn and winter 1793–4. References are given below. As for the second group of sources, the authenticity of which must always be verified instance by instance (certain so-called 'memoirs' having been largely rewritten), I would give priority to the following authors:

THIBAUDEAU, Antoine Claire, Comte de, *Mémoires, 1799–1815*, Paris, Plon, Nourrit, 1913.

MADAME ROLAND, *Mémoires de Madame Roland*, Paris, Mercure de France, coll. 'Le Temps retrouvé', 1966 (English translation, *The Private Memoirs of Madame Roland*, New York, AMS Press, repr. of 1901 edn, Women of Letters Series). A shortened version appeared in 1795 under the title *Appel à l'impartiale portérité*; ed. Champagneux in 1800 under the title *Oeuvres de M. J. Ph. Roland*; ed. Berville and Barrière in 1820 in the *Collection des mémoires relatifs à la Révolution française*. Madame Roland's manuscripts were properly studied in 1864 for the edition by Dauban and Faugère. In 1905 Claude Perrous published the *Mémoires de Madame Roland* in a critical edition.

BUZOT, François, *Mémoires sur la Révolution*, Paris, Béchet aîné, 1923; reissued Pichon and Didier, 1928.

PÉTION, Jérôme, François BUZOT and Charles-Dauban BARBAROUX, *Mémoires inédits de Pétion*, followed by memoirs of Buzot and Barbaroux and previously unpublished notes by Buzot, Paris, Plon, 1866.

LA RÉVELLIÈRE-LÉPEAUX, Louis-Marie, *Mémoires*, 3 vols, Paris, Plon, Nourrit, 1895.

NODIER, Charles, *Souvenirs, épisodes et portraits pour servir à l'histoire de la Révolution française et de l'Empire*, Paris, A. Levassour, 1831; reissued as *Souvenirs de la Révolution et de l'Empire*, 2 vols, Paris, Charpentier, 1850; reissued as *Souvenirs et portraits de la Révolution et de l'Empire*, 2 vols, Paris, Tallandier, coll. 'Intexte', 1988. (These volumes by Nodier are perhaps the most valuable item in the immense literature of French Revolution memoirs.)

Of all the revolutionary Assemblies, the Legislative is the poor relation. It sat for one short year, driven out by the popular rising which brought down the throne and took away both its *raison d'être* and its authority. Wedged between the two formidable bodies of the Constituent Assembly and the Convention, it had no chance of competing with either its predecessor or its successor. Nevertheless, it played a major role in the march towards war and the radicalization of the Revolution. To understand that one need only compare the last two months of the Constitutent Assembly, which were marked by Feuillant stabilization, and the first two of the Legislative (October and November 1791), when the spirit of revolutionary excess, flourished by Brissot and his friends, broke out again in full force. I tried to make sense of that contrast in a talk given to a Symposium on the Girondins held at Saint-Emilion (April 1990). The secret lies broadly in the elections of summer 1791: on this subject see the major contribution made by Patrick Gueniffey's thesis devoted to the 1791 and 1792 elections, and defended in 1989 at the Ecole des Hautes Etudes en Sciences Sociales (to appear in 1991).

On the war which began in April 1792 between the Revolution and the Habsburgs, to be extended to much of Europe in the following year, there is the admirable work of

SOREL, Albert, *L'Europe et la Révolution française*, 9 vols, Paris, Plon, Nourrit, 1903–6 (which highlights the continuity of the Revolution's foreign policy and that of the Bourbons).

An old book by the German historian Henri von Sybel should also be consulted (4 vols, Düsseldorf, 1853–1870; French translation, *Histoire de l'Europe pendant la Révolution française*, 3 vols, Paris, Germer Baillière, 1869–1875). This work is more quoted than read by French historians, but remains a monument of erudition and intelligence comparable to Sorel's, but more sensitive to the novelty of the revolutionary phenomenon.

On the declaration of war of 20 April 1792, and the Girondins' political responsibilities in it, the best analysis is that of Jaurès, in vol. 2 of *Histoire socialiste de la Révolution française*, ch. 2, 'La Guerre ou la paix'. The socialist historian explains how the war, for Brissot and his friends, was a manoeuvre of internal politics, intended to bring them to power against the Feuillants, taking the risk that the throne might fall.

On 10 August 1792, the temporary dictatorship of the Paris Commune, the first Terror and the threats of September, the meeting of the Convention, the most detailed account of the circumstances of 10 August remains

MATHIEZ, Albert, *Le 10 Août, 1792*, Paris, 1931; reissued Montreuil, Ed. de la Passion, 1989.

A work may be added with a general bearing on the sociology of the great Parisian *journées* during the Revolution:

RUDÉ, Georges, *The Crowd in the French Revolution*, Oxford University Press, 1959.

On the Paris commune, a very old book still speaks with authority:

BRAESCH, Frédéric, *La Commune du 10 Août 1792. Étude sur l'histoire de Paris du 20 juin au 2 décembre 1792*, Paris 1911; reissued Geneva, Mégariotis Reprints, 1978.

On the massacres of September 1792 in the Paris prisons, the classic work is:

CARON, Pierre, *Les Massacres de Septembre*, Paris, Maison du Livre Français, 1935.

As a complement, in the evaluation of responsibility and complicity:

Bluche, Frédéric, *Septembre 1792: les logiques d'un massacre*, Paris, Robert Laffont, 1986.

The Convention elected in August met in September 1792. There is a *Dictionnaire des Conventionnels* by Auguste Kuscinski (Paris, Rieder, 1916), a work posthumously published under the aegis of Aulard (reissued Breuil-en-Vexin, Éd. du Vexin Français, 1973).

On the political composition of the new assembly, the best work available is that of

PATRICK, Alison, *The Men of the French First Republic: Political Alignments in the National Convention of 1792*, Baltimore, Johns Hopkins University Press, 1972.

In fact, the Convention immediately became the arena of conflict between the Girondins and Montagnards: the main body of the Assembly, its centre, which was known as the Plaine, was the arbiter between the two groups.

Nineteenth-century historiography, which was still linked to events by oral history, never really closely examined the social and political reality of the Girondin/Montagnard dichotomy. Twentieth-century historiography, when written under the influence of Marxism as in France, desperately tried to trace a line of class, or sub-class, between the two groups, but was never convincing; there is testimony to these vain efforts is the 1975 Symposium, *Girondins and Montagnards*, the Proceedings of which were edited by Albert Soboul (Paris, Société des Etudes Robespierristes, 1980).

For its part, English-language historiography has for a quarter of a century been questioning the validity of the very idea of 'Girondin' and 'Montagnard' groups. Doubt was cast by Michael J. Sydenham, *The Girondins*, (1961; reissued, London, Greenwood, 1973). Alison Patrick, in the book cited above, measured the growing coherence of the group from the six roll-calls which took place in the Convention between the king's trial and the re-establishment of the Commission of the Twelve: she concluded that there was an evident distinction between a fairly amorphous 'Plaine' and a 'Girondin' minority.

A recent article, the work of three American historians, slightly modifies Alison Patrick's conclusions, showing that a true coherence of Girondin votes cannot be spoken of before spring 1793, that is to say, on the eve of defeat: 'Was There a Girondist Faction in the National Convention (1792–1793)?', *French Historical Studies*, 15 (Spring 1988), no. 3, by Michael S. Lewis, Anne Hildreth and Alan B. Spitzer.

As for the problems and positions which separated Girondins and Montagnards, the best synthesis is provided by two articles by Mona Ozouf, in Furet and Ozouf, *Critical Dictionary*.

On the king's trial, the central event of the Revolution but little studied by twentieth-century historians, the two essential authors who explore the implications of the head-on confrontation between the monarchy and the Convention are:

MICHELET, Jules, *Histoire de la Révolution française*, book X.

JAURÈS, Jean, *Histoire socialiste de la Révolution française*, vol. 5, *La Mort du roi et la chute de la Gironde*, ch. 2, 'Le Procès du roi'.

On the progress of the trial itself and the difficulty in counting the different votes at the moment of judgement, see:

JORDAN, David, *The King's Trial: Louis XVI vs the French Revolution*, Berkeley, University of California Press, 1979.

PATRICK, Alison, *Men of the First Republic*.

WALZER, Michael, *Regicide and Revolution: Speeches at the Trial of Louis XVI*, Cambridge, 1974 (French translation by J. Debouzy, under the title *Régicide et Révolution: le procès de Louis XVI*, followed by *Discours au procès de Louis XVI*, translated by A. Kupiec, Paris, Payot, 1989).

This work contains the main speeches given in the Convention concerning the king's trial, preceded by a long introduction. In the French edition, the book's epilogue is a discussion between M. Walzer and F. Feher; the American political scientist defends the idea that the trial was conducted with the maximum legality compatible with the political situation, whereas the Hungarian philosopher who took refuge in the US sees in it a precursor of the Terror.

On the crisis of summer 1793, the best overall picture can be found in Georges Lefebvre's course on 'Le Gouvernement revolutionnaire', duplicated copies from

Centre de Documentation Universitaire, Paris, 1947.

There is only one scholarly work devoted to the *journées* of 31 May and 2 June 1793:

SLAVIN, Morris, *The Making of an Insurrection. Parisian Sections and the Gironde*, Cambridge, Mass. Harvard University Press, 1986.

But it is in Michelet (*Histoire de la Révolution française*, book X) and Jaurès (*Histoire socialiste de la Révolution française*, vol. 5, ch. 10, 'La Révolution de 31 mai et 2 juin 1793') that the most detailed account and the most profound analysis of the purge of the Convention are to be found.

On the origins of the war in the Vendée a vast literature exists, both old and recent, caught up for many years in the long survival of memories of the civil war into the nineteenth and twentieth centuries. The reader may begin with one of the latest books on the matter, by Jean Clément Martin, *La Vendée et la France* (Paris, Le Seuil, coll. 'L'Univers historique', 1987), and also the synthesis which I have tried to make of the question in the article 'Vendée' in Furet and Ozouf, *Critical Dictionary*. The 'white' and 'blue' historiographies of the Vendée have long been as divided as the two sides whose incompatible glories they celebrated. Now, at the end of the twentieth century, such confrontations have lost a little of their intensity and the ideas which fed them have altered; Jean Clément Martin's work is one of the signs of this, as is Alain Gerard's *Pourquoi la Vendée* (Paris, Armand Colin, 1990).

On the counter-revolutionary episode in Lyon beginning in May 1793, see the excellent book by

HERRIOT, Edouard, *Lyon n'est plus*, 4 vols, Paris, Hachette, 1937–8.

On what has been called the 'federalist' crisis following the expulsion of the Girondins, the Montagnard dictatorship and the revolutionary government, much study has been devoted to the schism between Girondins and Montagnards from the angle of social conditions: the temporary alliance between Montagnards and sansculottes was sealed by the exclusion of the Girondins. The Montagne was not without an ulterior motive in forming this alliance with the militants of the Parisian sections.

Since the Second World War this has been one of the most exhaustively researched subjects, with a profusion of works and articles. I will limit myself to three principal authors who are all, each in his own way, very significant:

GUÉRIN, Daniel, *La Lutte des classes sous la Première République: bourgeois et bras nus (1793–1797)*, Paris, Gallimard, 1946; reissued, 2 vols, 1968; abridged version under the title *Bourgeois et bras nus (1793–1797)*, Gallimard, coll. 'Idées', 1973. Left-wing interpretation of the French Revolution, with Robespierre as a 'bourgeois' centrist.

SOBOUL, Albert, *Les sans-culottes parisiens en l'an II: mouvement populaire et gouvernement révolutionnaire, 2 juin 1793–9 thermidor an II*, Paris, Clavreuil, 1958 (English translation, *The Parisian Sans-Culottes and the French Revolution*, London, Greenwood, 1979, repr. of 1964 edn). Social and political interpretation of the alliance between Montagnard bourgeoisie and Parisian lower classes, under Robespierre's leadership.

COBB, Richard, The *Police and the People: French Popular Protest 1789–1820*, Oxford University Press, 1970. This work contains a critism of the concept of a sansculotte 'movement' in favour of a more individualistic conception of social marginality.

We must not forget the work that made the above ones possible by raising the question of the relationship between economic regulation and popular movement: MATHIEZ, Albert, *La Vie chère et le mouvement social sous la Terreur*, 2 vols, Paris, Payot, 1927, reissued 1973.

The institution of the revolutionary government: the substitution of a *de facto* government for the Montagnard constitution hastily assembled by Hérault de Séchelles in June was effected in two major stages (March–April, and July/ September 1793), from the creation of the Committee of Public Safety to putting the Terror on the agenda.
PALMER, Robert R., *Twelve who Ruled: The Committee of Public Safety During the Terror*, Princeton University Press, 1941, a work which gives a good account of the largely improvised nature of the revolutionary government.

For the chronology of the process, see Georges Lefebvre's duplicated course, quoted above, and my article 'Gouvernement révolutionnaire', in Furet and Ozouf, *Critical Dictionary*. Finally read Robespierre's great speech to the Convention on 25 December 1793; it is the philosophic manifesto of the revolutionary government. The speech is reproduced notably in
ROBESPIERRE, Maximilien de, *Discours*, Paris, UGE, 10/18, reissued 1988.

Jacobinism and the Terror: the dictatorial nature of the revolutionary government was not merely or exclusively the product of a defensive reaction in the face of danger, but also the manifestation of a potentiality of the French Revolution's political culture. Not that the Terror was a necessity built into the principles of 1789; but the undeniably exceptional circumstances of 1793 inflamed ideas and passions that were not compatible with the establishment of political liberty. For a general discussion of this interpretation, the reader may refer to my articles 'Jacobinism' and 'Terror', in Furet and Ozouf, *Critical Dictionary*.
   The first line of analysis consists of looking behind the revolutionary dictatorship to the authority of orthodoxy wielded on a national scale by the Jacobin Club. On this point, the two major authors are:
MICHELET, Jules, *Histoire de la Révolution française*, book X.
COCHIN, Augustin, *Les Sociétés de pensée et la démocratie*, Études d'histoire révolutionnaire, Paris, Plon, 1931.

One may add:
BRINTON, Crane, *The Jacobins: An Essay in the New History*, New York, Macmillan, 1930.
JAUME, Lucien, *Le Discours jacobin et la démocratie*, Paris, Fayard, 1989.

On the Terror properly speaking, there is a lack of case studies, for instance on the revolutionary Tribunal in Paris, or the punitive action of particular representatives on mission, or the massive executions without trial, as in Lyon or the Vendée. We must also distinguish between the period before and the period after the centralization of the Terror in Paris, from April 1794. One of the best analyses of the revolutionary Terror is to be found in
QUINET, Edgar, *La Révolution*, Paris, 1865 (books XVI and XVII); reissued Paris, Belin, 1987.

In modern scholarship, a classic work:
COBB, Richard, *Les Armées révolutionnaires, instrument de Terreur dans les départements: avril 1793–floréal an II*, 2 vols, Paris, EHESS, and Mouton de

Gruyter, 1961 (English translation, *The People's Armies*, New Haven, Yale University Press, 1987).

A good recent monograph:

LUCAS, Colin, *The Structure of the Terror: The Example of Javogues and the Loire*, London, Oxford University Press, 1973.

A study, also recent, of the mass repression in the Vendée between January and May 1794:

SECHER, Reynald, *Le Génocide franco-français: La Vendée-vengé*, Paris, PUF, 1986.

A statistical study of those sentenced to death under the Terror:

GREER, Donald, *The Incidence of the Terror During the French Revolution: A Statistical Interpretation*, Cambridge, Mass., Harvard University Press, 1935.

Robespierre's dictatorship: in order to understand Robespierre's domination over the course of the Revolution which, between April and July 1794, he exercised alone, it is essential to read his great speeches.

Robespierre's works have been the subject of several editions: Laponneraye (3 vols, 1840), Vellay (1910) and, after the departure of Vellay, the edition continued by the Société des Etudes Robespierristes.

Robespierre's great speeches may be found either in vol. 10 of his *Oeuvres complètes*, (ed. Bouloiseau and Soboul, 1967), containing the speeches from 27 July 1793 to 27 July 1794; or, more easily, in the three volumes of *Textes choisis*, (ed. Jean Poperen, Paris, Éditions Sociales, coll. 'Les Classiques du peuple', 1974).

French biographies of Robespierre are spoilt by hagiography, such as *Robespierre* by Ernest Hamel (Ledrappier, 1987); *Robespierre* by Jean Massin (Paris, Livre Club Diderot, 1956; reissued Aix-en-Provence, Alinéa, 1988); and *Robespierre* by Gérard Walter, 2 vols (1936–40; reissued Paris, Gallimard, 1961).

I would suggest:

THOMPSON, J. M., *Robespierre*, 2 vols, Oxford, Basil Blackwell, 1935.

JORDAN, David P., *The Revolutionary Career of Maximilien Robespierre*, New York, Free Press, 1985.

See also the article 'Robespierre' by Patrice Gueniffey, in Furet and Ozouf, *Critical Dictionary*.

On the battle of the factions, the elimination of the Hébertists and the Dantonists by Robespierre, there is a vast scholarly twentieth-century century literature, frequently polemical, since the subject revives the old Aulard–Mathiez debate between Dantonists and Robespierrists. Georges Lefebvre acted as arbiter, in his courses and his work on *La Révolution française*, (PUF, coll. 'Peuples et Civilisations', 1951, reissued 1980). There is no doubt that Danton was not the model of patriotic virtue described by Aulard, but his execution, quite unconnected with the passion for morality in Robespierre celebrated by Mathiez, was motivated by Robespierre's hunger for power.

On the problems of the dechristianization advocated by the sansculottes in autumn 1793, the sharp check given by Robespierre and the revolutionary cults that were to replace Catholicism, the reader may begin with Michelet *Histoire de la Révolution française*, book V (*La Religion*) and book XVI (*La Religion sous la Terreur*), which blame the Revolution for its timidity in the affair. See also Aulard and Mathiez:

AULARD, Alphonse, *Le Culte de la Raison et de l'Etre suprême, 1793–1794*, Paris, F. Alcan, 1892.

MATHIEZ, Albert, *La Révolution et l'Eglise*, Paris, Colin, 1910.
MATHIEZ, A., *Origines des cultes révolutionnaires: 1789–1792*, Paris, Société Nouvelle de Librairie et d'Edition, 1904.

One of the mysteries of this period is the worsening of the Terror by the law of 22 prairial (10 June), two days after the Festival of the Supreme Being. There is no convincing work or article on this mystery. The epoch of the Great Terror has not yet found its historian.

On 9 Thermidor, and the growing isolation of Robespierre since the last fortnight in June, there is an evocative book:

Ollivier, Albert, *Le Dix-huit Brumaire, 9 novembre 1799*, Paris, Gallimard, 1959.

4   THE THERMIDORIAN REPUBLIC

With the downfall of Robespierre began the period when the despotic and egalitarian Revolution stopped its rush forward, and the movements of civil society became visible again. The ideas of 1789 spawned a simultaneous system of private interests and a fund of contradictory memories and passions: all this was almost impossible to manage, and was supplemented by the logic of war and conquest, personified from 1796 in the glory of a young general.

It was in this era that the most profound commentators and the best observers of the French Revolution made their appearance.

In the first group, I would pick out two intellectual families: firstly that of the inaugurators of the liberals' great debate on the mixed nature of revolutionary events, the contrast between the principles of 1789 and the terrorist drift of 1793: foremost, Benjamin Constant and Madame de Staël, whose detailed works written between 1795 and 1799 are still fundamental.

CONSTANT DE REBECQUE, Benjamin de, *Lettres à un député de la Convention*, published in *Nouvelles politiques, nationales et étrangères, juin 1795 (Messidor an III)*, collected in *Recueil d'articles 1795–1817*, Geneva, Droz, 1972, 1978, 1980.
CONSTANT, B., *De la force du gouvernement actuel de la France et de la nécessité de s'y rallier*, no place, 1796.
CONSTANT, B., *Des réactions politiques*, n.p., Year V (1797); 2nd edn with *L'Examen des effets de la Terreur* added, n.p., Year V.

Certain of Benjamin Constant's writings under the Directory were first published by Olivier Pozzo di Borgo under the title *Ecrits et discours politiques*, (2 vols, Paris, Pauvert, 1964) (English translation, *Political Writings*, Cambridge University Press, 1988).

Recently reissued writings: *De la force du gouvernement actuel de la France with Des réactions politiques*, and *Des effets de la Terreur*, (Paris, Flammarion, coll. 'Champs', 1988), preface and notes by Philippe Raynaud.

STAËL, Germaine de, *Réflexions sur la paix adressées à M. Pitt et aux Français*, no place or publisher, 1795.
STAËL, G. de, *Réflexions sur la paix intérieure*, published anonymously.
STAËL, G. de, *De l'influence des passions sur le bonheur des individus et des nations*, Lausanne, Mourer, Hignon, 1796; 2nd edn, Paris, Dufart, 1797, Desenne, 1797.
STAËL, G. de, *Des circonstances actuelles qui peuvent terminer la Révolution et des principes qui doivent fonder la République en France* (written in 1798 but

unpublished at the time), Paris, Fishbacher, 1906; reissued Geneva and Paris, Droz, 1979.

Roederer (notably his contributions to the *Journal d'Économie Publique*) and Lezay-Marnesia, may also be added:

ROEDERER, Pierre-Louis, *De l'usage à faire de l'autorité publique dans les circonstances présentes*, with a *Traité de l'émigration*, Paris, Desenne, Year V.

ROEDERER, P.-L. DE *Mémoires sur quelques points d'économie publique*, read at the Lycée in 1800 and 1801, Paris, Firmin-Didot, 1840. See also his *Oeuvres*, 8 vols, Paris, Firmin-Didot, 1853–9.

LEZAY-MARNESIA, Adrien, *Des Causes de la Révolution et de ses résultats*, Paris, Desenne, 1797.

LEZAY-MARNESIA, A., *De la faiblesse d'un gouvernement qui commence, et de la nécessité où il est de se rallier à la majorité nationale*, Paris, B. Mathey, Year VI.

There is a German book on Adrien Lezay-Marnesia:

WESTERHOLT, Egon Graf von, *Lezay-Marnesia, Sohn der Aufklärung und Präfekt Napoléons (1769–1814)*, Meisenheim am Glan, Hain, 1958.

Lastly, on all the debates between liberals under the Directory, the reader may refer to the articles 'Constant' and 'Staël' by Marcel Gauchet in Furet and Ozouf, *Critical Dictionary*.

The second intellectual family embraces the first great French counter-revolutionary authors:

MALLET DU PAN, Jacques, *Considérations sur la nature de la Révolution française et sur les causes qui en prolongent la durée*, Brussels, Plon, 1793.

MALLET DU PAN, J., *Correspondance inédite de Mallet du Pan avec la cour de Vienne (1794–1798)*, 2 vols, Paris, Plon, Nourrit, 1884.

MALLET DU PAN, J., *Correspondance politique pour servir à l'histoire du républicanisme française*, Hamburg, P. F. Fauche, 1796.

MALLET DU PAN, J., *Mémoires et Correspondance pour servir à l'histoire de la Révolution française*, 2 vols, Paris, Amyot and Cherbuliez, 1851.

MALLET DU PAN, J., *Mémoires* (extracts), Paris, M. Gautier, 1894.

MAISTRE, Joseph de, *Considérations sur la France*, Neuchâtel, 1796, and London, Fauche-Borel, 1797. See *Oeuvres complètes*, 7 vols (14 parts), part I, Geneva, Slatkine Reprints, 1979, repr. from the edn of Vitte and Perrussel, Lyon, Librairie Générale Catholique et Classique, 1884–6. *Considérations sur la France*, followed by *Essai sur le principe générateur des constitutions politiques*, reissued Brussels, Ed. Complexe, 1988.

BONALD, Louis de, *Théorie du pouvoir politique et religieux dans la société civile, démontrée par le raisonnement et par l'histoire, par M. de B.*, gentilhomme français, published anonymously, 3 vols, Konstanz, 1796. See vols 12–15 of *Oeuvres complètes*, 15 vols-in-9, Geneva, Slatkine, 1982, repr. from the Paris edn, Librairie d'Adrien Le Clerc 1817–43.

BONALD, Louis de, *Essai analytique sur la loi naturelle de l'ordre social*, published in 1797; reissued 1801 under the title *Essai analytique sur la loi naturelle ou Du pouvoir, du ministre et du sujet*. See *Oeuvres complètes*, vols 1 and 2.

Lastly, a look at memoirs of the period is essential, especially

MOLÉ, Comte, *Souvenirs d'un témoin de la Révolution et de l'Empire: Mathieu, comte Molé 1791–1803*, ed. Marquise de Noailles, Geneva, Ed. Milieu du monde,

1943; see also Marquis de Noailles, *Le Comte Molé, 1781–1855, sa vie, ses mémoires*, 6 vols, Paris, Champion, 1922–30.

PASQUIER, Etienne-Denis, Chancellor, *Histoire de mon temps. Mémoires du chancelier Pasquier*, ed. Duc d'Audiffret Pasquier, 6 vols, Paris, Plon, 1893–5. (Vols 1–3 are concerned with the Revolution, the Consulate and the Empire, vols 4–6 with the Restoration.)

BARRAS, Paul, *Mémoires de Barras, membre du Directoire*, ed. G. Duruy, 4 vols, Paris, Hachette, 1895–6.

CHASTENAY, Comtesse Victorine de (or Madame de), *Mémoires 1771–1815*, ed. A. Roserot, 2 vols, Paris, Plon, Nourrit, 1896.

LA TOUR DU PIN, Henriette-Lucie, Marquise de, *Journal d'une femme de cinquante ans (1778–1815)*, edited by her great-grandson, Colonel Comte Aymar de Liederkerke-Beaufort, 4 vols, Paris, Imprimerie de R Chapelot, 1907–11.

LA RÉVELLIÉRE-LÉPEAUX, Louis-Marie, *Mémoires*.

DELÉCLUZE, Étienne-Jean, *Louis David et son temps*, Paris, Didier, 1855; reissued Macula, 1983.

SAND, George, *Histoire de ma vie*, 20 vols, Paris, V. Lecou, 1854–5 (English translation, *Story of My Life: The Autobiography of George Sand*, State University of New York Press, 1991, Woman Writers in Translation Series); reissued Michel-Lévy frères, 1856; recent reissues: Paris Stock, 1985; and Gallimard, La Pléiade, 1970–1: *Oeuvres autobiographiques*, 2 vols (vol. 1, *Histoire d'une famille, de Fontenoy à Marengo – Mes premières années, 1800–1819 – De l'enfance à la jeunesse, 1810–1819*; vol. 2, *Du mysticisme à l'indépendance, 1810–1822 – Vie littéraire et intime, 1832–1850*).

Memoirs by émigrés:

FRENILLY, Auguste-Francois, *Mémoires: 1768–1848. Souvenirs d'un ultra-royaliste*, reissued Paris, Librairie Académique Perrin, 1987.

MONTLOSIER, Comte de, *Souvenirs d'un émigré, 1791–1798*, ed. Comte de Montlosier-Larouzière and Ernest d'Hauterive, Paris, Hachette, 1951.

ESPINCHAL, Comte d', *Journal d'Emigration*, ed. Ernest d'Hauterive, Paris, Perrin, 1912.

FABBRY, Abbé de, *Mémoires de mon émigration*, Paris, Champion, 1933.

BLONDIN DE SAINT-HILAIRE, *Onze Ans d'émigration. Mémoires du chevalier Blondin d'Abaucourt, adjutant major des gardes-suisses*, Paris, 1897.

General Histories of the period:

LEFEBVRE, Georges, *Les Thermidoriens*, Paris, Armand Colin, 1937.

LEFEBVRE, Georges, *Le Directoire*, Paris, Armand Colin, 1946.

SCIOUT, Ludovic, *Le Directoire*, 4 vols, Paris, Firmin-Didot, 1895–7.

MATHIEZ, Albert, *Le Directoire du II Brumaire an IV au 18 Fructidor an V*, Paris, Armand Colin, 1934.

FURET, François and Denis Richet, *La Révolution française*, vol. 2, Paris, Hachette, 1966; reissued Fayard, 1973, Hachette-Pluriel, 1986.

One may read more specifically on the crises that punctuated the entire political history of the period:

MEYNIER, Albert, *Les coups d'État du Directoire*, 3 vols, Paris, Presses Universitaires de France, 1927–8 (vol. 1, *Le Dix-huit Fructidor an V*; vol. 2, *Le Vingt-deux Floréal an VI (11 mai 1798) et le Trente Prairial an VII (18 juin 1799)*; vol. 3, *Le Dix-huit Brumaire an VIII (9 novembre 1799) et la fin de la République*).

SURATTEAU, Jean-René, 'Les Opérations de l'assemblée électorale de France (4 Brumaire an IV–octobre 1795)', *AHRF* (*Annales historiques de la Révolution française*) (1955).
SURATTEAU, J.-R., 'Les elections de l'an V aux Conseils du Directoire', *AHRF* (1955).

On 13 Vendémiaire Year IV:
ZIVY, H., *Le 13 Vendemiaire an IV*, Paris, 1898, fasc. 6 de la Bibliothèque de la Facultédes Lettres de l'Université de Paris.

On Babeuf and Babvouvism, there is an immense communist-inspired literature, very repetitive and already very dated. It is preferable to refer to the book that founded the Babouvist tradition:
BUONARROTI, Philippe, *Conspiration de l'Égalité dite de Babeuf*, followed by the trial to which it gave rise and its written evidence, etc., 2 vols, Paris, 1828; reissued Paris, Editions Sociales, 1957.

There is also a recent interesting article by an American historian on the Parisian sociology of Babouvism:
ANDREWS, Richard M., 'Réflexions sur la conjuration des Egaux', *Annales ESC* (1974).

On 18 Fructidor, Year V:
BALLOT, Charles, *Le coup d'État du 18 Fructidor: rapports de police et documents divers*, Paris, Société de l'Histoire de la Révolution Française, 1900.
MATHIEZ, Albert. 'Saint-Simon, Lauraguais, Barras, Benjamin Constant et la réforme de la constitution de l'an III après le coup d'État du 18 Fructidor an V', *AHRF* (1929).

On the coups d'état of 22 Floréal Year VI and 30 Prairial Year VII, see:
MEYNIER, Albert, *Les Coups d'Etat*, vol. 2.
On 18 Brumaire Year VIII:

VANDAL, Albert, *L'Avènement de Bonaparte*, vol. 1, *La Genèse du Consulat. Brumaire. La Constitution de l'an VIII*, Paris, Plon, Nourrit, 1902.
BAINVILLE, Jacques, *Le 18 Brumaire*, Paris, Hachette, 1925.

I would also advise a reading of several recent works on the political culture of the era, notably on the tyranny exercised over men's minds by memories of the Convention and the Terror:
OZOUF, Mona, 'Thermidor ou le travail de l'oubli', in *L'Ecole de la France, essais sur la Révolution, l'utopie et l'enseignement*, Paris, Gallimard, coll. 'Bibliothèque des distoires', 1984.
BACZKO, Bronislaw, *Comment sortir de la Terreur: Thermidor et la Rèvolution*, Paris, Gallimard, coll. 'Essais', 1989.
WOLLOCK, Isser, *Jacobin Legacy, The Democratic Movement under the Directory*, Princeton University Press, 1970.

An old but important book on the emigration:
DAUDET, Ernest, *Histoire de l'émigration pendant la Révolution française*, vol. 3, *Les Emigrés et la seconde coalition, 1797–1800*, Paris, Librairie Illustrée, 1886–90.

A collection of documents necessary for a feel for the state of public opinion:
AULARD, Alphonse, *Paris pendant la réaction thermidorienne et sous le Directoire*, 5 vols, Paris, Le Cerf, 1898–1902.

On the Italian campaign:

GUYOT, Raymond, *Le Directoire et la paix de l'Europe des traités de Bâle à la deuxième coalition (1795–1799)*, Paris, F. Alcan, 1911.

FERRERO, Guglielmo, *Aventure, Bonaparte en Italie (1796–1797)*, Paris, Plon, 1936.

REINHARD, Marcel, *Avec Bonaparte en Italie, d'après les lettres inédites de son aide de camp, Joseph Sulkowski*, Paris, Hachette, 1946.

GODECHOT, Jacques, *Les Commissaires aux armées sous le Directoire. Contribution à l'étude des rapports entre les pouvoirs civils et militaires*, 2 vols, Paris, Fustier, 1938.

BONAPARTE, Napoléon, *Lettres à Joséphine, pendant la première campagne d'Italie, le Consulat et l'Empire*, Paris, Firmin-Didot, 1833.

BONAPARTE, Napoléon, *Lettres de Napoléon à Joséphine et lettres de Joséphine à Napoléon*, Paris, Le Livre Club du Libraire, 1959.

BONAPARTE, Napoléon, *Napoléon et Joséphine, leur roman*, complete edn. Numerous unpublished letters from Napoleon to Josephine, collected by Jean Savant, Paris, Fayard, 1960.

BONAPARTE, Napoléon, *Lettres de Napoléon à Joséphine et de Joséphine à Napoléon*, complete edn, ed. J. Haumont, Paris, J. de Bonnot, 1968.

5   NAPOLEON BONAPARTE

The best approach to this period of history, dominated and even personified by one man alone, is to begin by reading Napoleon's own writings which portray him far better than any commentary. These are mostly military or government papers, or things recorded by his close associates; for example, they may be found in:

Vie de Napoléon par lui-même, d'après les textes, lettres, proclamations, écrits, Paris, Gallimard, 1930.

NAPOLÉON BONAPARTE, *Proclamations, ordres du jour, bulletins de la Grande Armée*, Paris, UGE, 10/18, 1964. Also consult Napoleon's *Correspondance*, published at the instigation of Napoleon III, 32 vols, Paris, Imprimerie Impériale 1858–69.

The second category of sources is formed by contemporary witnesses, quite numerous, as it happens. I would cite:

ABRANTÈS, Joséphine Amet, Duchesse d', *Mémoires ou souvenirs historiques sur Napoléon*, 18 vols, Paris, Ladvocat, 1831–5; reissued, 10 vols, Garnier frères, 1893.

BARANTE, Amable, Baron de, *Souvenirs*, 8 vols, Paris, 1890–1901 (see vols 1 and 2).

BOURRIENNE, Louis Antoine Fauvelet de, *Mémoires sur Napoléon, le Directoire, le Consulat et la Restauration*, 10 vols, Paris, 1829–31; reissued, 4 vols, Garnier frères, 1899.

BEUGNOT, Jacques Claude, Comte de, *Mémoires du comte Beugnot, ancien ministre (1783–1815)*, 2 vols, Paris, E. Dentu, 1866.

CHASTENAY, Comtesse Victorine de (or Madame de), *Mémoires, 1771–1815*, ed. A. Roserot, 2 vols, Paris, Plon, Nourrit, 1896.

HYDE DE NEUVILLE, Jean Guillaume, Baron, *Mémoires et souvenirs*, ed. Madame de Sardonnet, 3 vols, Paris, 1888–92.

MIOT DE MELITO, André François, Comte de, *Mémoires du Comte Miot de Melito, ancien ministre, ambassadeur, conseiller d'Etat et membre de l'Institut (1788–1815)*, 3 vols, Paris, Michel-Lévy frères, 1858.

PASQUIER, Etienne-Denis, Chancelier, *Histoire de mon temps. Mémoires du chancelier Pasquier*, ed. Duc d'Audiffret-Pasquier, 6 vols, Paris, Plon, 1893–5.

PELET DE LA LOZÈRE, Comte Privat Joseph, *Opinions de Napoléon sur divers sujets de politique et d'administration, recueillies par un membre de son conseil d'État*, Paris, Firmin-Didot frères, 1833.

SAVARY, René, Duc de Rovigo, *Mémoires pour servir a l'histoire de Napoléon*, 8 vols, Paris, A. Bossangre, 1828; reissued 4 vols, Garnier frères, 1900.

TALLEYRAND-PÈRIGORD, Charles-Maurice, Duc de, *Mémoires du prince de Talleyrand*, ed. Duc de Broglie, 5 vols, Paris, Calmann-Lévy, 1891–2; ed. Paul-Louis Couchoud, 2 vols, Paris, Plon, 1957 (English translation, *Memoirs of the Prince de Tallyrand*, New York, AMS Press, repr. of 1892 edn).

SÈGUR, Philippe, Comte de, *Histoire et mémoires*, 7 vols, Paris Firmin-Didot, 1873.

The third category of written documents to which priority should be given is the vast literature of portraits of Napoleon. Here is one very selective list in chronological order:

STAËL, Madame de, *Mémoires de Mme de Stael, Dix années d'exil*, ed. Duc de Broglie and Baron de Staël, Paris, 1818; reissued Charpentier, 1861; Plon, Nourrit, 1904.

STENDHAL (Henri Beyle), *Vie de Napoléon*, Paris, Calmann-Lévy, 1876; reissued Payot, 'Petite Bibliothèque Payot', 1969 (English translation, *Napoleon*, ed. Ernest Abravanel and Victor Del Litto, 2 vols, New York, French and European, 1970).

CHATEAUBRIAND, François-René, Vicomte de, *Mémoires d'outre-tombe*, La Presse (Paris), 1848–50; 12 vols, Paris, Penaud frères, 1849; reissued, 6 vols, Paris, Dufour, Mulat and Boulanger, 1860; Paris, Garnier frères, 1895; ed. Edmond Bire, 1899–1900; ed. Levaillant in the Flammarion centenary edn. Recent editions include: Gallimard, La Pléiade, 1947, 1951 (vol. 1, books I–XXIV; vol. 2, books XXV–XLIV). Also in paperback, 3 vols, Livre de poche.

TAINE, Hippolyte, *Les Origines de la France contemporaine (1876–1896)*, reissued Paris, Robert Laffont, coll. 'Bouquins' 2 vols (vol. 1, *L'Ancien Régime–La Révolution*; vol. 2, *La Révolution–Le Régime moderne*. See *Le Régime moderne*, ch. 1 devoted to Napoléon Bonaparte.)

FAURE, Elie, *Napoléon*, Paris, CRES, 1921.

Finally, though of lower literary quality, there is the fundamental work:

MASSON, Frédéric, *Napoléon et sa famille*, 13 vols, Paris, Ollendorf, 1897–1919.

General works:

BAINVILLE, Jacques, *Napoléon*, Paris, Fayard, 1931.

This is still the most brilliant synthesis on the man and his deeds.

LEFEBVRE, Georges, *Napoléon*, Paris, PUF., coll. 'Peuples et Civilisations', 1935; reissued 1947, 1965 (English translation Napoleon, 2 vols, New York, Columbia University Press, 1990).

MARKHAM, Felix, *Napoleon*, London, Weidenfeld and Nicolson, 1963.

TULARD, Jean, *Napoléon ou le mythe de sauveur*, Paris, Fayard, 1977; reissued Hachette, 'Pluriel', 1988.

TULARD, J., *Napoléon à Sainte-Hélène*, Paris, R. Laffont, coll. 'Bouquins', 1981.

TULARD, J., *Napoléon et la noblesse d'Empire*, with a list of members of the imperial nobility (1808–15), Paris, Tallendier, 1986.

MISTLER, Jean, *Napoléon et l'Empire*, 2 vols, Paris, Hachette, 1968.

Imperial France. On the ideas used as a basis for the legitimacy of the regime, the most significant author is:

FIÉVÉE, Joseph, *Correspondance et relations de J. Fiévée avec Bonaparte (1802 à 1813)*, 3 vols, Paris, A. Desrez, 1836.

On the civil legislation:

FENET, P. Antoine, *Recueil complet des travaux préparatoires du Code civil*, 15 vols, Paris, 1827; reissued Paris, Videcoq. 1836.

SAGNAC, Philippe, *La Législation civile de la Révolution française (1784–1840), essai d'histoire sociale*, Paris, Hachette, 1898.

GOY, J., 'Code civil', in Furet and Ozouf, *Critical Dictionary*, which may be used as an introduction to these studies.

On the government and administration:

PONTEIL, Félix, *Napoléon Ier et l'organisation autoritaire de la France*, Paris, Armand Colin, 1956.

DURAND, Charles, *L'exercice de la fonction législative de 1800 à 1814, Annales de la Faculté de Droit d'Aix-en-Provence* (1958).

THUILLIER, G., 'L'administration vue par un préfet de l'Empire', *La Revue administrative* (1955).

TULARD, Jean, *Paris et son administration (1800–1830)*, Paris, Ville de Paris, Commission des Travaux Historiques, 1976.

On the coronation, an excellent work:

CABANIS, José, *Le Sacre de Napoléon (2 décembre 1804)*, Paris, Gallimard, 1970.

On the Concordat and the temporary settling of relations between the Catholic Church and post-revolutionary society:

DANSETTE, Adrien, *Histoire religieuse de la France contemporaine*, Paris, Flammarion, 1948, vol. 1.

LEFLON, Jean, *E. A. Bernier, évêque d'Orléans, et l'application du Concordat*, 2 vols, Paris, Plon, 1938.

DELACROIX, Simon, *La réorganisation de l'Église de France après le Concordat (1801–1809)*, Paris, Ed. du Vitrail, 1962.

GODEL, Jean, *Histoire religieuse du départment de l'Isère. La reconstruction concordataire dans le diocèse de Grenoble après la Révolution (1802–1809)*, La Tronche, the author, 1968.

LANGLOIS, Claude, *Le diocèse de Vannes (1800–1830)*, Rennes Université, Klincksieck, 1974.

On the social foundations of the imperial regime:

BERGERON, Louis and Guy CHAUSSINAND-NOGARET, *Les Collèges électoraux du Premier Empire*, Paris, CNRS, 1978.

TULARD, Jean, 'Les composantes d'une fortune: le cas de la noblesse d'Empire', *Revue historique* (1975).

VALYNSEELE, Joseph, *Les maréchaux du Premier Empire, leur famille et leur descendance*, Paris, the author, 1957.

VALYNSEELE, J., *Les Princes et ducs du Premier Empire, non-maréchaux, leur famille et leur descendance*, Paris, the author, 1959.

France's foreign policy and dominance in Europe: because I wished to concentrate on France's domestic policy, I have left this major aspect of Napoleonic history aside. The pages devoted to it draw their principal inspiration from the following works:

SOREL, Albert, *L'Europe et la Révolution française*, vols 5–8.
LEFEBVRE, Georges, *La Révolution française*.

The reader will find a systematic bibliography in
GODECHOT, Jacques, *L'Europe et l'Amérique à l'époque napoléonienne*, Paris, PUF.,
coll. 'Nouvelle Clio', 1967.

Glossary

Commune The revolutionary government of Paris formed in 1789; taken over by an insurrectionary committee in August 1792. The name was revived in March 1871 when a left-wing municipality defied the French (Versailles) government.

Constituent Assembly The body formed by representatives of the Third Estate and their allies in the Estates-General. It drafted France's monarchical constitution and acted as a provisional legislature from 1789 to 1791.

Convention The revolutionary single-chamber parliament, 1792–5.

Cordeliers Paris revolutionary club on the left bank of the Seine with a large working-class membership.

Corvée Unpaid feudal work on land or roads.

Cour des Aides The court of law supervising taxation.

Dévots Catholics emphasizing state support for the Church as their main policy.

Estates-General The consultative assembly summoned by Louis XVI in 1789 to consider taxation and expenditure.

Farmers General Officially appointed syndicate contracting to collect taxes.

Feuillants Constitutional monarchists who broke away from the Jacobins in protest at moves to depose Louis XVI.

Gallicanism The doctrine of the French Church's national independence (and freedom from papal control).

Generalité Tax district under the supervision of an *intendant*.

Girondins Revolutionary members of the Legislative Assembly and Convention (their nucleus was a group from the Gironde in south-western France), largely eliminated by the Jacobins in 1793.

Jacobins Paris revolutionary club of 'Friends of the Constitution' meeting in a former Jacobin (Dominican) monastery; the main centre of revolutionary, and increasingly left-wing, discussion, influential nationally through a network of Jacobin Clubs in the provinces.

Jansenists Sect believing in predestination, influential in the seventeenth century but persecuted by Louis XIV to make its members submit to state and Church authority.

Legislative Assembly The single-chamber parliament elected under the constitutional monarchy, 1791–2.

Lit de Justice Royal session of the Paris parlement at which the king presided and enforced registration (i.e. acceptance) of his edicts.

Marais See *Plaine*.

Mercantilists Advocates of protection of industry, state regulation of trade, and intervention to ensure food supplies and control prices.

Montagnards Jacobin members of the Convention occupying the highest seats (the *Montagne*), and generally supporting extreme revolutionary policies.

National Guard Civil militia formed in 1789 to maintain order and guard against counter-revolution.

Parlement High court of law in charge of regional justice, and with the right of remonstrance at royal legislation.

Perpetuels Members of the Convention automatically appointed to serve in the new assembly (1795) under the Law of the Two-Thirds.

Philosophes The rationalist and sceptical writers of the eighteenth century (e.g. Voltaire, Montesquieu, d'Alembert, Diderot) who called for the use of reason (as opposed to custom, tradition, faith or superstition) in the organization of society and the state.

Physiocrats Advocates of a free economy based primarily on agriculture, with a minimum of state regulation and internal restriction.

Plaine (or Marais) The middle group of members of the Convention, uncommitted either to the Girondins or the *Montagne*.

Provincial Estates Local assemblies of the three orders (clergy, nobility and commons).

Sansculottes Revolutionaries who made a virtue of plain dress (*culottes*, breeches, being regarded as a mark of privilege).

Sections The forty-eight areas into which Paris was divided by the Commune, each run by a revolutionary watch committee and able to organize armed *sectionnaires* to intimidate the government.

Thermidorians The politicians who took power after the fall of Robespierre on 9 Thermidor (27 July 1794).

Third Estate The commons (i.e. not clergy or nobility) in the Estates-General.

Index of Names

Index of Subjects